Kingdoms of the Blind

STUDIES IN STATESMANSHIP
of the
WINSTON S. CHURCHILL ASSOCIATION

Harry V. Jaffa, General Editor

Harold W. Rood, *Kingdoms of the Blind: How the Great Democracies Have Resumed the Follies that so Nearly Cost Them Their Life*

Jeffrey D. Wallin, *By Ships Alone: Churchill and the Dardanelles*

Harry V. Jaffa, ed., *Statesmanship: Essays in Honor of Sir Winston Spencer Churchill*

Forthcoming

Kirk Emmert, *Churchill and Empire*

Angelo M. Codevilla, *The Limits of Grandeur: The Statesmanship of Charles de Gaulle*

Steven Maaranen, *The Illusion of Peace and the Coming of War: The Foreign Policy Debates in the House of Commons, 1932-1939*

Kingdoms of the Blind

HOW THE GREAT DEMOCRACIES HAVE
RESUMED THE FOLLIES THAT SO
NEARLY COST THEM THEIR LIFE

by

Harold W. Rood

DURHAM, NORTH CAROLINA

CAROLINA ACADEMIC PRESS

LCC card no. 79-54442
ISBN 0-089089-121-4
Printed in the United States of America

Carolina Academic Press
P.O. Box 8795, Forest Hills Station
Durham, North Carolina 27707

To the Memory of

James Grant Ferguson, Stanford University, Class of '08, Second Lieutenant, 8th Battalion, the Royal Highland Regiment—the Black Watch, killed in action 19 July 1916, Longueval, France.

Contents

Foreword

IT IS A PLEASURE AND AN HONOR to have Professor Rood's *Kingdoms of the Blind* inaugurate the Studies in Statesmanship of the Winston S. Churchill Association.

Churchill once wrote that a man must nail his life, to the Cross either of Thought or of Action. Churchill himself was certainly a man of action. Yet he was surely among the most thoughtful of such men; and he told the tale and pointed the moral of his own life in an incomparable manner. In the end, his thoughts about his actions form a legacy that transcends even those actions. Churchill's greatest action—his resistance to Hitler—ended, by his own account, not in triumph but in tragedy. But Churchill did not intend us thereby to despair. We must remember the importance to Churchill of Shakespeare. In Shakespearian tragedy, the pity and the terror are more than a catharsis—they are the ground of political wisdom. Hamlet begs Horatio to absent himself from felicity awhile, to tell his story. Hamlet, although confident that he is to enter Paradise, yet cares that his story be known. For he cares for Denmark no less than for his immortal soul.

Churchill once compared strategy—the art of the general—to the art of the painter. Although Churchill himself was a greater strategist than painter, he considered the art of the painter to be a greater art than that of the general. To hold in harmonious relationship all the elements of light and shade, of color and form, of foreground and background was, he thought, a greater test of the powers of the soul, than the simultaneous grasp upon all the changing forces of a battlefield, or of a theater of war. Professor Rood is something of a painter of the strategic scene. The combination of what at first appears to be insignificant details, the discovery of a harmonious relationship among seemingly discrete events, is accomplished by him in a manner that would have delighted Churchill the painter no less than Churchill the strategist. The absence of camouflage from the Soviet missiles during the crisis of October, 1962—like the dog that was silent in the night—illuminates a thousand other Soviet actions, not only in Cuba, but around the world, then and since. Here we have, by a painstaking reconstruction, out of the most authentic materials, the most comprehensive account until now, of the strategic intention and strategic design of our Soviet adversaries. Here we have that design and intention illuminated—as of old, step by step—in a manner no one would have appreciated better than Sir Winston. Let us hope that it may yet aid us to avert what surely would be another "unnecessary war."

HARRY V. JAFFA, President

Winston S. Churchill Association
Claremont, California

Preface

> For four years every effort toward preparedness had been resisted to the utmost by the President and his advisers . . . nothing was done to prepare the youth of America for the supreme test to which they were so soon to be subjected. The other many millions, under the spell of a fatuous pacifism, passed by with smiling unconcern the warnings brought them by each issue of the daily press in ever-rising chorus. . . . Our sons, once more, have paid with their determined valor and their lives for the dreams of those placed temporarily at the head of our affairs. . . . If those costly errors are referred to here it is with the hope that we may, by peace-time preparation, avoid them when another emergency comes upon us. In the light of our history that hope is but a faint one, yet the lives of our sons may come to be valued more highly than impractical sentiment or even than elections.
>
> Robert Alexander, *Memories of the World War: 1917–1918.*

THIS WORK IS A REMINDER OF THE DANGEROUS INCLINATION DEMOCRATIC PEOPLES HAVE OF DISCOUNTING THE LIKELIHOOD OF WAR. It is an inclination that causes carelessness in strategic matters and promotes vagueness about defense. The passage from Robert Alexander's book cited at the head of this page was written about a war upon whose battlefields in France the United States entered only months after the phrase, "he kept us out of war" helped win re-election for President Wilson. The echoes of the motto "We want no war nor will there be any war," had barely subsided when the United States was in the war. With borrowed artillery and borrowed aircraft, American soldiers learned the craft of war in the midst of the fighting because there had been no time to learn it before. What pious pledges there were after that war about how America would never *again* be caught unprepared. Yet the words quoted above could easily have been written about those disastrous days of 1941 and 1942 when, for a second time within twenty-five years, the United States entered a war for which it was ill-prepared.

If the United States was less than well-prepared to fight a world war in 1941, the state of preparedness of Britain and the other countries that would suffer the attentions of the Axis powers was hardly better.

Those circumstances leading to Nazi domination of Western Europe in 1940 have lessons to teach us in a time when the Soviet Union seems bent on playing now the role played by Germany in the past. To remind oneself that experiences from the past can help one better to see the present is not to suggest that history repeats itself; however those who live on the cusp of portentous events may not always find the line between the two ideas to be so nicely drawn.

To those soldiers of the British Expeditionary Force in France in 1940, who, like Viscount Gort, their commander, found themselves fighting to defend locales over which they had fought a score and some years before, it might have seemed that history indeed had repeated itself. The only difference seemed to be that Britain, having failed to learn from the past, would pay a penalty this time: in those very fields where Allied arms had prevailed in the earlier war, Britain and France would this time be defeated.

In this same way those veterans of the Royal Navy and Royal Naval Reserve who found themselves once more battling U-boats in the North Atlantic, as they had done 20-odd years before, could be forgiven for wondering at the repetition of history. Especially so when those veterans found Britain no better prepared to fight German submarines in 1940 than it had been between 1914 and 1917. At least the first time around there was the excuse that it took time to learn the nature and extent of the threat submarines could pose to the survival of Britain. Who in the thirties, save those of extreme ill-nature and unbridled suspicion, would imagine that the same threat would arise again with consequences even more costly than the first time.

A kind of conspiracy pursued in the name of everlasting peace fostered in Britain a neglect of strategy and a blindness to the German danger. Even after the Nazis came to power and demonstrated the depths of their cruelty and the keenness of their ambition, reluctance to think war possible permitted German advances while paralyzing Allied military policies.

The savings accrued by the peoples of the Western Democracies after 1918, through neglect of defense, were squandered a hundred times over in both blood and treasure when Germany, in defiance of appeasement, conciliation and accommodation, went to war. The peoples of Austria, Czechoslovakia, Poland, Denmark, Norway, the Netherlands, Belgium, Luxembourg, France, Greece and Yugoslavia suffered totalitarian occupation because there was no one prepared to prevent it. Britain alone escaped that fate and fought on until the United States, itself but half-ready, was forced into war by a surprise attack from a country whose ambitions and warlike intentions had been evident for a decade or more.

History does not repeat itself. It is only the behavior of democracies that seems repetitious. When for a short while, the United States was the preeminent military power in the world, how often one heard of America's warlike intentions. "Prepare for war, make war," was the article of fashion amongst those who feared the worst from the United States. Now that the Soviet Union is the preeminent military power in the world, one is assured that Soviet arms are a stabilizing influence whether deployed in Indo-China, Africa or the Western Hemisphere; but in any case they carry no threat of war.

The Soviet Union has not been at pains to conceal that which in any other country would be considered preparations for war. The Soviet Union has not pretended, save to those who so wished to believe, that its revolutionary ambitions for a Communist world have been abandoned. Evidence of Soviet ambitions is presented almost daily in the Western press; and it is as often excused, discounted or rationalized. Yet, the preparations for war and the unbridled ambitions are as much a part of one another as were the re-armament of Germany and Hitler's ambition to seize Europe. Is is really possible still to believe that Soviet air, naval and ground forces in Cuba are not a part of Soviet strategy, but merely an expression of hearty good fellowship of one Socialist nation toward another?

The leader of the Western Democracies—this time it is the United States—casts a blind eye on the terrible preparations going forth in a totalitarian land. Once again the democracies seek sanctuary in the hopes of peace; once again the dictatorships arm. In 1935, Great Britain conceded to Germany the right to parity in submarine tonnage in a gesture of appeasement, in an appeal to Hitler's "good side." In 1972, the United States conceded to the Soviet Union the right to numerical superiority over the United States in ICBMs and submarine-launched ballistic missiles. This, it was said, would foster detente and ensure strategic stability. Hitler had no good side and the German submarine force was used as a strategic arm with which to cripple Britain. The Soviet Union sees detente as one more part of strategy while viewing strategic stability as that which will exist when Russia has secured a monopoly of military power. Britain paid for its lapse of strategic wisdom in merchant seamen and ships lost. The United States will pay in even dearer coin for conceding strategic superiority to the Soviet Union. The scale of payment for such folly is quite different now from what it was in the Second World War. The British could at least fight the German submarines at sea; Soviet ICBMs and submarine-launched ballistic missiles are targeted on the territory of the United States; and the United States lacks that which would protect its people against attack by Soviet rockets.

In 1962, the withdrawal of missiles and medium bombers from Cuba was considered a triumph of moderate statesmanship and political wisdom. Yet the concession that brought about that withdrawal was the granting of an asset to the Soviet Union. The implications of that decision can be seen in Africa, the Middle East, Latin America, and Western Europe.

Recapitulation of past follies ought to remind us of where such follies can lead in a world where democratic good intentions are no match for totalitarian ambitions. There is little in this work about the world of today that any citizen of the United States could not know were he merely to have followed the story in Western newspapers and other commonly-read periodicals. Soviet preparations for war have been reported fully; Soviet gambits in Cuba and elsewhere have been reported at length. However much one may wish to rationalize Soviet behavior as something harmless or even irrelevant to the defense of Western democracy, the hard evidence of Soviet actions can scarcely be misconstrued.

Military policy cannot be based on sentiments for peace however lofty those sentiments may seem. Military policy must fit the requirements for successful strategy and successful strategy does not derive from the notion that war is impossible. Nuclear weapons have not made war impossible, they have only changed the conditions under which wars will be fought. They have in no manner reduced the importance of strategy nor the inherent advantage of military superiority over military weakness.

Concessions made to gain Soviet agreement on limiting strategic arms are only a part of the strategic equation that would decide the outcome of a new world war. Increments of strategic advantage garnered so patiently here and there by the Soviet Union and its allies have reduced the West's capability to resist Soviet ambitions. The modernization and expansion of the armed forces of the Soviet Union and its allies are not socialist eccentricities; they are preparations for war.

This book is intended to call attention to such matters: their neglect will surely mean the end of Western Democracy.

H. W. R.

Menlo Park, October 1979

Acknowledgements

I owe thanks to the Winston S. Churchill Association for its assistance in the publication of this work.

Harry V. Jaffa gave unflagging confidence and enthusiasm to encourage initiation and completion of it. Mrs. Marjorie B. Jaffa typed manuscript endlessly, it seemed, with a generosity of time and effort that cannot be repaid save with the warmest gratitude.

Mr. Steve Maaranen, an authority on British defense policy between the wars and on contemporary U.S. defense policy, read the manuscript offering just and helpful criticism to reduce the number of errors of judgment and fact in it.

Mr. Richard T. Simpson of the Carolina Academic Press edited the manuscript with zest and patience without treading on the fragile confidence of an untried author.

Perhaps best of all was the help I have received from all those with whom, at work, I share common endeavors: my friends and associates whose discussions with me have helped form ideas that otherwise might have remained formless and unexpressed.

Any errors I must claim as my own.

H. W. R.

It is because I am sure that our fortunes are still in our own hands and that we hold the power to save the future, that I feel the duty to speak out. . . . I do not believe that Soviet Russia desires war. What they desire is the fruits of war and the indefinite expansion of their power and doctrine. . . .

From what I have seen of our Russian friends and Allies during the war, I am convinced that there is nothing they admire so much as strength and there is nothing for which they have less respect than for weakness, especially military weakness. For that reason, the old doctrine of a balance of power is unsound. We cannot afford, if we can help it, to work on narrow margins, offering temptations to a trial of strength.

Winston S. Churchill, "The Sinews of Peace,"
Westminster College, Fulton, Missouri, 5 March 1946.

Kingdoms of the Blind

I. To Provide for the Common Defense . . .

It may well be that the United States ought to be preparing for war. It is not a matter that ought to be lightly dismissed nor a subject for partisan division. Defeat in war is seldom kinder to those who refuse to believe in war's coming than it is to those who recognize and warn of the peril. It is difficult to believe war will come unless one has some notion of its consequences. It is not a defect to pray for peace and to hope there will be no war. But those who predict war have statistics on their side; those who predict peace everlasting are always wrong. Nations who are comfortable in the *status quo* prefer peace, those that would overset the *status quo* to establish a new order in the world will resort to force if it is within their capability to do so. Violence and force are intrinsic to revolution, even as they are to good order.

Democracies and Tyrannies

Politics is the organization and application of power to accomplish some purpose. Power includes the capacity to inflict pain, to injure, and to destroy. The weak and the helpless do not exercise power, but have power exercised over them. Regimes that are constitutional and democratic are dedicated to the protection of the weak and the helpless from the unwarranted exercise of power by the state or by elements outside the apparatus of the state who would molest or exploit the helpless. Such precepts of constitutional government and democracy do not ordinarily operate within the international community. Totalitarian regimes, convinced of the ubiquity of politics and the irrefutable nature of the truths they purvey, see no reason to exercise restraint in compelling the powerless to conform to those truths. Those who have the power to threaten the existence of the totalitarian regime must be rendered powerless, coopted or destroyed. Any who express skepticism or doubt about the totalitarian regime's monopoly of truth threaten the regime's existence. Democratic regimes, because they are founded on skepticism and suspicion of authority, are the born enemies of totalitarianism. Liberal democrats who believe that there are private activities that should remain beyond the reach of politics and the interference of the state are inimical to the totalitarian regime. Totalitarian regimes can and do distinguish between those who will perpetuate the regime and those who will not; they distinguish between friends and foes, without ambivalence or ambiguity.

The survival of democratic regimes does not lie alone in the elegance of their principles but in their capability to apply power to those who would destroy them. Liberal democratic regimes are a minority in the international community. The greater part of the world's population suffers under totalitarian regimes. There are perhaps sixteen nations in the world that can be accurately characterized as constitutional democracies. These are countries where the authority of the government may be legally questioned in court or on the street, where office-holders defeated in an election or removed from office for wrong-doing can be expected to surrender to their democratically chosen successors, where the rights of the citizens are not merely guaranteed by law but upheld and protected as an obligation of government. Of these countries, Italy, only recently become democratic, is beset from both extreme right and extreme left and may not survive as a democracy. Great Britain is in the throes of crises that threaten dissolution of the United Kingdom. Canada is threatened by the separation of its French province, Quebec. Of the other countries in the world, India has only just emerged from a dictatorship and there is little evidence that the constitutional crises that led to dictatorship will not continue. Spain has just thrown off an authoritarian regime and adopted a constitution whose fate may be the same as those that preceded the Franco dictatorship. Petty tyrannies abound in Asia, Latin America, Africa, and the Middle East. Finland, one of the world's notable democracies remains so at the pleasure and convenience of the Soviet Union. Israel, the one emergent democracy in the Middle East, is unlikely to survive another war with its Arab neighbors. The continued independence of the Western European democracies depends on the will and capability of the United States to defend them and on their own resistance to the blandishments of the Eurocommunists who would create in Western Europe the same kind of democracy enjoyed in Poland, Hungary, Czechoslovakia, Bulgaria, Romania, Albania, and Yugoslavia. We have reached a point where liberal democrats can consider the new premier of the People's Republic of China to be a "moderate," although he was head of the Secret Police before he became premier.

The two principal dictatorships in the world, the Soviet Union and the People's Republic of China, are totalitarian in the extreme. For the moment they remain sworn enemies of one another as well as of liberal democracy. Their conjunction as allies in the fashion of the Hitler-Stalin Pact, would—as in 1939—shift the balance of power almost irretrievably against the democracies and make war a virtual certainty rather than merely a strong probability.

It is therefore of much more than casual concern that the Soviet Union might be preparing for war: not a "cold war" such as that waged by the Soviet

Union when it was yet an inferior military power; not wars of "national liberation" that have so successfully isolated and divided the democracies, but your standard war, like that outlawed in the General Treaty for the Renunciation of War of 1927.

Those who warn of war and the need to prepare for it are not welcome prophets in a democratic society. They will be dismissed today as "cold warriors," as minions of a "military-industrial complex" and considered beyond the pale of decent folk, even as in the past they have been accused of "jingoism" or worse. Edward Luttwak has, with a fine irony, compared the reception of Winston Churchill's warnings with those warnings given by persons in our own time.[1] It was suggested that Churchill was merely trying to rebuild his shattered political career when he spoke of German "bloodlust" and of the "German Threat," while others of kinder visage were attempting to build a new Anglo-German understanding based "on mutual respect and reciprocity." For Churchill to have had the temerity to question the Air Ministry's estimates of German air strength was like William T. Lee illuminating the unwarranted optimism of fifteen years of Central Intelligence estimates of Soviet Defense expenditures or "Team B" suggesting that the Soviet Union might be preparing for war. Indeed in those days before appeasement had run its course, the editor of the *London Times* would suppress the report of its Parliamentary correspondent on the speech of Duff Cooper when he resigned in outrage over Munich. The editor of the *Times,* who had hopes of "a genuine friendship with the Nazi regime," then substituted a report of his own as though it had been written by the Parliamentary correspondent.[2] And the British Prime Minister would urge Hitler to help provide some support in forming public opinion in Britain. In a speech given in the Berlin *Sportpalast,* Hitler readily complied with an attack on Chamberlain's critics in England, including Winston Churchill.[3] These events took place while the *Times* edited the reports of its own diplomatic correspondent to take out those "rather over-categorical forecasts of German intentions," made by the British foreign office.

But there are no statesmen of the stature of Winston Churchill to warn us today of our impending fate. There are only those minor figures whose cries of alarm are drowned out by the fashionable phrases and the "preferred" truths of that powerful establishment whose stock in trade is optimistic inaction, adroit rhetoric, and strategic carelessness. If there is no Churchill to

1. Edward N. Luttwak, "Churchill and Us," *Commentary,* June 1977, p. 49.

2. A. L. Rowse, *Appeasement: A Study in Political Decline, 1933-39* (New York: The Norton Library, 1963), p. 84.

3. Roger Parkinson, *Peace in Our Time: Munich to Dunkirk* (New York: David MacKay Company, 1971), p. 71.

warn of our fate, neither is there a British Empire to hold the fort alone while those who are half asleep get half ready.[4]

If the threat of war is real and not merely the imagination of disordered minds deaf to the optimistic promises of detente, peaceful co-existence, and nuclear deterrence, then this country and its allies can no longer afford the luxury of violating strategic principles in order to stem the flow of harsh criticism from the Kremlin.

On page two of the *Los Angeles Times* for 28 April 1977, in a section called "News in Brief," where a terse account is given of incidents not reported elsewhere in the edition, the following statement appeared: "The United States does not possess 'a detailed air defense system' and certain planes can penetrate it![5] It is common knowledge our ground-based conventional radars have only line-of-sight capability and cannot detect low-flying aircraft."[6] That statement emerged as a consequence of the report that a Soviet TU-95, bomber aircraft, based in Cuba had flown over a U.S. Navy task force operating seventy miles off the East Coast of the United States. The state of air defense for Continental United States, Alaska and Hawaii, is not a revelation. It has been regularly reported in the *Annual Defense Department Report,* in the *Report of the Chairman of the Joint Chiefs of Staff* and elsewhere. In fact, there are some fifty fewer regular Air Force interceptors dedicated to the air defense of the entire United States today than there were fighters available for the defense of Pearl Harbor on 7 December 1941.[7]

There now are, in addition to the interceptor squadrons, perhaps four battalions of surface-to-air missiles, three in Florida and one in Alaska. Together, these forces are considered to provide the capability "to preclude an aggressor from having *unchallenged* access to the air space over the United States for his bombers and airborne reconnaissance aircraft." Dedicated strategic interceptors are insufficient in number to prevent violation of U.S. air space in peacetime.[8]

4. Rowse, *Appeasement,* p. 85.

5. See "Brezhnev Notes 'Positive' Signs in Carter Statements," *Los Angeles Times,* 17 August 1977, p. 1: "Commenting on Brezhnev's speech Tuesday, one source said, 'I don't want . . . to cast too rosy a glow on this.'" He was referring to: "That Western diplomatic sources interpreted his [Brezhnev's] comments as confirmation of what had already appeared to be a softening in the tone of official rhetoric since Carter's conciliatory speech on Soviet-American relations in Charleston, S.C. last month." The real kindness in all of this was that the Soviet government stopped criticizing the President of the United States and merely criticized the United States.

6. "Soviet Planes in U.S. Defense Zone," *San Francisco Chronicle,* 20 December 1977, p. 9.

7. There are in addition 10 Air National Guard interceptor squadrons: three F-101 squadrons, six F-106 squadrons, and one F-4 squadron dedicated to CONUS (Continental United States) air defense on a part-time basis also some F-4 aircraft of Tactical Air Force squadrons are assigned an air defense role in combination with their tactical role to augment CONUS air defense in an emergency. That is on the assumption that in an emergency the Tactical Air Force squadrons would not be required elsewhere in their tactical role. See *Annual Defense Department Report FY 1978,* p. 138 and *United States Military Posture for FY 1978* by Chairman of the Joint Chiefs of Staff (20 January 1977), p. 25.

8. *Ibid.*, p. 25. Cuba, for example, has 195 first-line aircraft and deploys 24 SAM battalions with

Whatever one may wish to believe about the meaning of phrases like "rough parity" and "strategic sufficiency" it is a solemn fact that on any working day, the Soviet Union may call on 2,600 fighter-interceptor aircraft and 12,000 ground-to-air missiles to defend the air above the 9 million square miles of the Soviet Union and the other members of the Warsaw Pact, without calling up reserves or employing Soviet Air National Guard units, if Air National Guard they have. The United States may, on the other hand, on any working day expect to have not more than 144 fighter-interceptors on instant call, plus an additional 190 aircraft as soon as the personnel of the Air National Guard squadrons can get from their civilian jobs to their aircraft; and, a total of 144 ground-to-air missiles as soon as they can be manned by National Guard personnel. These defenses are meant to protect the air above the 7½ million square miles of territory of Canada and the United States. The Soviet Union's *PVO-Strany,* dedicated to the air defense of the country, comprises 550,000 people, a number equivalent to the number of male personnel in the entire U.S. Air Force.[9]

It is equally solemn a fact that while the Soviet Union deploys, as part of its strategic defense sixty-four *Galosh* anti-ballistic missiles in four sites around Moscow, the one U.S. *Safeguard* anti-ballistic missile site has been de-activated. Further, the United States deploys no defense against the 312 Soviet cruise missiles deployed on 45 nuclear and 21 diesel submarines. It does not appear to be known whether the Soviet Union has a defense against submarine-launched cruise missiles, although it is known that the United States does not now have any submarine-launched cruise missiles or submarines equipped to launch them.[10] Further, while the United States has no defense against inter-continental or submarine-launched missiles, the Soviet Union is continuing to improve its early-warning, battle-management and engagement radars associated with its anti-ballistic missile defense.[11]

---

144 surface-to-air missiles against 144 USAF interceptors for all of CONUS and four battalions (3 in Florida and 1 in Alaska) of surface-to-air missiles.

9. Soviet figures do not include those interceptors and ground-to-air missiles deployed by the other six members of the Warsaw Pact; U.S. figures do not include the 48 Canadian CF-104D aircraft that might be assigned to air defense of North America; Canada has no surface-to-air missiles assigned to North American Air Defense. Figures are given in the *Military Balance, 1976-77* and in *United States Military Posture for FY 1978.* See also, "Canada Will Dismantle 2 Missile Bases," *Los Angeles Times,* 17 October 1971, p. 14.

10. "U.S. Radar Could Miss Russ Attack, General Testifies: Officer Says Sea-Launched Missiles Could Elude System, Defends New Construction at Beale Base," *Los Angeles Times,* 11 August 1977, p. 33. This suggests shortcomings in the system of radar, early-warning of attack by submarine-launched missiles. The article fails to mention that whether radar gives early-warning or not, there are no gun or surface-to-air-missiles employed in CONUS against this threat. Even if there were early-warning of a sea-launched cruise missile, there are no weapons deployed for interception of the missiles. See also, "Cuts in Radar Let Cuban MIG Land: Two or Three Picket Planes Were Grounded Two Days Before," *New York Times,* 6 October 1969, p. 5.

11. "Senate Unit Warned of Soviet ABM Effort," *Aviation Week and Space Technology,* Vol. 107, No. 5, p. 17.

All of the foregoing neither implies nor suggests that the air defense requirements of the United States and of the Soviet Union are the same. But the excellent air defense furnished by the Soviet Union to the North Vietnamese exacted an extremely heavy toll of U.S. aircraft during the war in Indo-China. It is also clear that the air defenses furnished to Egypt by the U.S.S.R., after the 1967 Arab-Israeli War, destroyed many Israeli aircraft and enabled the Egyptian Army to effect and maintain the crossings of the Suez Canal in the 1973 war. The success of those crossings left Egypt in possession of the Suez Canal and of the Western Sinai despite the setbacks inflicted on the Egyptian Army by Israel in the last few days of the war.[12] One cannot therefore suggest that the leaders of the Soviet Union lack the experience upon which to design an air defense for operations in war.

It seems clear that those who have the constitutional responsibility for the safety of the United States and its citizens consider that only a nominal air defense is required to ensure that safety. It is equally clear that Soviet air defense has been designed to protect the Soviet Union and its citizens if there is a war. United States military policy is based on the expectation of continuing peace among the important powers of the world. Soviet military policy seems based on the expectation that there will be a war. The U.S. air defense is designed for *peace;* the Soviet air defense is designed for *war.* That is the crucial distinction and one which raises the decisive question, is there to be a war?

The status of Soviet air defense, civil defense, strategic nuclear forces and general purpose forces reflects the capability to wage war. The People's Republic of China, since 1968, has repeatedly warned that the Soviet Union was preparing for war.[13] Apparently citing Soviet sources, *Peking Review* charged that Brezhnev has bragged that "on the whole front of global confrontation" they are "historically on the offensive" and that they will "launch an extensive and really general offensive" backed by military might and that the Soviet armed forces should be ready "for a war using any weapons," and

12. The elaborate nature of the Soviet-furnished Egyptian air defenses is described in successive issues of *Aviation Week and Space Technology,* "Both Sides of the Suez: Airpower in the Mid East," a special publication (*Aviation Week and Space Technology,* 1974); and, in the *International Defense Review* (Geneva) for the period, *Soldat und Technic* (Munchen), as well as *Strategic Survey, 1973* (London: International Institute of Strategic Studies, 1974). In particular, see "SAM Changes Force New Strategy on Israelis," *Aviation Week and Space Technology,* Vol. 93, No. 20 (May 1971), pp. 16-21 and "Egyptian-Soviet Trick Reported in Placing Sams Along Suez," *Los Angeles Times,* 10 July 1970, p. 1.

13. See for example, "Chinese Foresee U.S.-Soviet War," Washington Post, 27 May 1974, p. A3; "Under Cover of 'Detente' and 'Disarmament' New Tsars' Feverish Arms Expansion and War Preparations," *Peking Review,* No. 48, 28 November 1975; "Kremlin's New Tsars Follow in the Old Tsar's Footsteps," *Peking Review,* No. 35, 30 August 1974, pp. 10f; "Russ Seen as Worst Enemy," *Palo Alto Times,* 12 July 1977, p. 12; "Soviet Social-Imperialism—Most Dangerous Source of World War," *Peking Review,* No. 29, 15 July 1977, pp. 4-10; "Yomiuri Correspondents' Interview with LIAO Cheng-chih," *Yomiuri* (Toyko), 12 March 1973, p. 1; and, "We Must Prepare for the Possibility of an Attack by the Soviet Union," *Le Monde,* 12 September 1973, p. 21 in *FBIs,* 19 September 1973, (P.R.C)., p. B1.

for "launching a tactical offensive with or without nuclear weapons."[14] Asserting that "Moscow has caught up with and is surpassing Washington in Military Might," the Chinese charge that the Soviet Union is using "détente" and "disarmament" to cover hegemonic ambitions.[15] While one may dismiss such statements as mere ritual or flim-flam, the elaborate civil defense measures, including extensive air raid shelters in major cities throughout China, seem to imply some anxiety about the possibility of war.[16]

A correspondent for Hsinhua reported, with evident satisfaction, that Switzerland had provided its people with underground civil defense shelters adequate for two-thirds of the population. These measures were a consequence of the heightened danger of war and because Soviet conventional forces in Eastern Europe "now outnumbered those of NATO."[17]

Peking's warnings to the West have called attention to the Soviet military build-up in the Mediterranean, Northern Europe, and on the NATO Central Front, and to Soviet intervention in Africa, the Middle East, and the Indian Ocean. While they may all be mere Communist bombast, they may also have the same validity as the repeated warnings by Great Britain and the United States to the Soviet Union of the impending German attack in 1941.[18]

The Soviet Union has been equally outspoken about the threat of war. Noting that the people of the "Third World" were rejecting the false line of Chinese dogma because Peking was attempting to promote its own superpower ends,[19] the Soviet Union warns of the threat of global war posed by the People's Republic of China.[20]

Does one accept such statements from the two Communist powers at their face value as one accepts their protestations of peaceful intentions, or is one set of statements true and the other false? If it is the latter, then which are true and which intentionally misleading? The Chinese have quite frankly

14. *Peking Review,* No. 48, 28 November 1975, p. 10.

15. *Peking Review,* No. 29, 15 July 1977, p. 4ff.

16. While the stories of underground streets in Peking and elsewhere may be overdrawn, they seem, nonetheless, to have considerable currency both inside and outside China: "China Not Seeking Hegemony; Underground Air-Raid Shelters in Peking are Second Streets . . .," *Mainichi,* 6 February 1975, p. 2; "Underground Road System Anchors Peking's Defenses," *Washington Post,* 29 June 1975, p. A 17; and, "Tunnel Network Protects China," *The Christian Science Monitor,* 18 June 1974, p. 36.

17. "Report from Geneva: Small Nations Should Also be Prepared," *Peking Review,* No. 15, 9 April 1976, pp. 19 and 24.

18. Barton Whaley, *Codeword BARBAROSSA* (Cambridge: M.I.T. Press, 1973).

19. "Destrukcyjne akcje Pekinu," *Zolnercz Wolnosci* (Warsaw), 4 September 1973.

20. "China Said to Prepare for World War: Peking: A Course Aimed at Disrupting International Detente Under Cover of Anti-Sovietism," *Pravda,* 14 May 1977, pp. 4-5, in *The Current Digest of the Soviet Press,* Vol. XXIX, No. 19, 8 June 1977, pp. 1-4; and see also, "Warning by Russia on Aid to China," *The Times,* 16 May 1977, p. 5; "Peking May Start World War—Pravda," *The South China Morning Post,* 15 May 1977, p. 3; and "Brezhnev Calls China Threat to Detente and World Peace," *International Herald Tribune* (Paris), 1 June 1977, p. 5.

stated that they will "liberate" Formosa by force if necessary.[21] And General Secretary Brezhnev, more recently President Brezhnev, said in Prague in 1968:

> If we want to win we cannot achieve our goals without strong military forces. Did we ever say that we would not use force if it was necessary to support progressive movements in, for example, France, Britain or Sweden? . . . This is the sacred duty of our forces—to protect and support progressive movements.[22]

Those Czechs unfortunate enough to have entertained hopes of living under a less draconian regime would doubtless, if still around, bear witness to Brezhnev's veracity in the matter of force.

Democratic Naivete and War

Is war a likely outcome of the present circumstances in the international community? If it is, should the United States begin to take those measures that are within its power to protect its own citizens and to defend its allies? If the prophets of war are wrong, then whatever the United States may do to prepare for war will be wasteful and pointless. Yet if war should come and the United States is unready, as it has always been in the past, then what will be the penalties for such neglect? What suffering and sacrifice will the American people have to undergo if their government is wrong and the prophets of war correct? Can the United States expect to be set back on its feet after defeat in war, as Germany, Japan, and Italy were, following their defeat in World War II? Are there lessons to be learned from history about the penalties of being unprepared or has the advent of nuclear weapons so altered international politics toward peaceful accommodation that the danger of war amongst the great powers is no longer a consideration worthy of attention?

Joel Markowitz, a psychiatrist and psycho-historian, has suggested that democracies have a blind spot[23] when it comes to their own defense: democracies find it remarkably difficult to begin to prepare for war. They will wait, he says, until further delay is suicidal. The immense casualties and the lost battles, suffered by the democracies in two world wars were a direct result of this shortcoming.

General George C. Marshall summarized the kind of peril the democracies faced in World War II:

> This Nation is just emerging from one of its gravest crises. This generation of Americans can still remember the black days of 1942. . . . In

21. "China Refuses to Rule Out Use of Force Over Taiwan," *Los Angeles Times*, 6 July 1977, p. 9.
22. "Moscow's Brutal Reality," *The Times*, 28 July 1975, p. 12.
23. "Defense: The Blind Spot of Democracies," *New York Times*, 10 April 1977.

> those hours Germany and Japan came so close to complete domination of the world that we do not yet realize how thin the thread of Allied survival had been stretched.
>
> In good conscience this Nation can take little credit for its part in staving off disaster in those critical days. It is certain that the refusal of the British and Russian peoples to accept what appeared to be inevitable defeat was the great factor in the salvage of our civilization.[24]

General Marshall's statement was issued amidst general rejoicing at the end of the war in Europe and Asia, amidst pious pledges from newspaper editors and other worthies that we shall never again be caught unprepared.

The Pacific

The United States Congress was embarked on an investigation of the attack on Pearl Harbor to find out where they could lay the responsibility for that disaster. It turned out the Japanese had done it, but the real fault lay, of course, they said, with American intelligence that had failed, somehow, to anticipate war with Japan.[25] That same august body, the U.S. Congress, had in March 1939, refused to fund the fortification of the island of Guam despite the recommendations of the Hepburn Board, established at the behest of Congress to determine the stategic requirements for the defense of the United States and its outlying territories. The Board had concluded that the development of Guam as an advance fleet base would provide: "*Practical immunity* of the Philippines against hostile attack in force." Congress concluded otherwise and Guam was not provided with defense. In the event, a company of U.S. Marines and of Guamanian constabulary were the only forces to oppose a Japanese Landing Force of naval infantry supported by cruisers, aircraft, and destroyers which took the island in about 20 minutes.[26]

It was not as though no one had ever suggested that the U.S. possessions in the Pacific might be in danger from Japan. *Time* magazine mentioned in passing the statement by Vice-Admiral Kenkichi Takahashi, Commander-in-Chief of the Imperial Combined Fleets, that the "Emperor's future commercial expansion must be directed to Southern Seas . . ." and that Formosa or the Mandated Islands must become bases for the advance of the Imperial

24. *Biennial Report of the Chief of Staff of the United States Army, July 1, 1943 to June 30, 1945* (London: H.M.S.O., 1945), p. 1.

25. "Pearl Harbor Hearings End," *The Stars and Stripes* (Germany, ed.) 22 February 1946, p. 1.

26. See "President Clears Snag Over Guam," *New York Times,* 17 March 1939, p. 12; for the Hepburn Report see, *Report on need of additional naval bases to defend the coasts of the United States Territories and Possessions,* in *House Documents* (Misc.), Vol. I, Dec., No. 65 (27 December 1938), 76th Congress, 1st Session (Washington: U.S.G.P.O., 1939); for the fate of Guam and its tiny garrison, see *Annual Report of the Secretary of the Navy* for the fiscal year ending June 30, 1942.

Fleets, and that their radius must be extended to reach New Guinea, Borneo and the Celebes.[27]

There had been countless warnings of the probability of war with Japan since 1898, although apparently none by anyone sufficiently prominent or influential to catch the ear of Congress or country. Admiral George Dewey warned, at Manila Bay:

> I look forward some 40 or 50 years and foresee a Japanese naval squadron entering this harbor, as I have just done, and demanding surrender of Manila and the Philippines with the plan of making these islands a part of the great Pacific Japanese empire of the future.
>
> I will not live to witness what you will see if you live your ordinary life. That will be the conquest of China by Japan, and when that is done, conquest of all island possessions from north to south off the Pacific Coast of the Far East.[28]

But as everyone knew, the Japanese were not "ten feet tall," to borrow a phrase from an ex-diplomat writing about the Soviets forty years later.[29] In fact they were rather diminutive people and not up to a war with a modern power like Britain or the United States. In fact one professor even pointed out the crucial Japanese shortcomings in aviation:

> The Japanese are excellent imitators, but they are not creative. They assemble parts copied from foreign models. When they have finished the machine takes the air and a little later lies smashed on the ground. . . . 'One has to be a hero to trust one's life to a Japanese aeroplane, even as a tourist, unless one wishes to commit suicide.' The Japanese seem to lack something physical as pilots. I have heard it said that their hearing fails in the air.[30]

That article of faith, along with its fellows—everyone knew about the Japanese battleship that had turned turtle upon launching, and the one whose armor had fallen off—quite drowned out the grimmer facts about Japanese determination and military and naval skill.

Warnings there were galore that Japan and the United States would one day be at war. Homer Lea and Jack London quite early thought such a war likely. Hector C. Bywater wrote of the coming struggle in the Pacific in the

27. *Time,* Vol. XXVII, No. 5, 3 February 1936, p. 23.

28. Remarked by John Barrett, a former U.S. Minister to Siam, on U.S.S. *Olympia,* at the battle of Manila Bay, as cited in James K. Eyre, Jr., "Early Japanese Imperialism and the Philippines," *U.S. Naval Institute Proceedings,* Vol. 75, No. 11, Nov. 1949, p. 1269.

29. Charles W. Yost, "The Really Clear and Present Danger," *Los Angeles Times,* 4 March 1977, p. 5, pt. II. And see, coincidentally, Fred Warner Neal, "Making the Russians Seem Ten Feet Tall," *The Washington Star,* 4 September 1977, p. F-4.

30. Professor E. Guyot, in *Vu,* 25 November 1936, p. 1432, as cited in Max Werner (pseudonym), *Military Strength of the Powers* (New York: Modern Age Books, Inc., 1939), p. 286.

early twenties and in 1925 published *The Great Pacific War*, a description of how the war would probably be fought.[31]

In *Struggle for the Pacific* (1937), Gregory Bienstock would predict that Japan, having conquered China, would undoubtedly make herself mistress of the Western Pacific.[32] In 1922, Graser Schornstheimer would warn in *Current History* that in the event of a war in the Pacific, Japan would be able to advance on Guam and the Philippines without fear of interference from an inferior U.S. Pacific Fleet.[33] Sutherland Deniger and Charles B. Gary predicted the Japanese seizure of Guam, Wake and the Philippines in their *War in the Pacific: A Study of Navies, Peoples and Battle Problems*, published in 1938. This book echoed the warnings given in 1928 that the United States would lose its island outposts in the Pacific in an air war with Japan.[34] A Japanese writer in 1933 described how the Japanese would conduct a war in the Pacific.[35]

As early as 1907, the War Department warned the Commanding General of the Philippine Division of the measures to be taken in the event of war with Japan. Warnings flowed almost unendingly from the Philippine Department of the United States Army. These warnings bespoke the inadequacy of Philippine defenses to respond to a serious threat from Japan.[36]

Admiral Alfred Thayer Mahan wrote in June 1914 to then Assistant Secretary of the Navy, Franklin Roosevelt, to speak of the pressing danger to the United States in the Pacific. The Assistant Secretary agreed with this point in his reply to Admiral Mahan.[37]

From at least 1913 onward, work was afoot in the Army Navy Joint Board's Planning Committee, in the War Plans Division of the Office of Chief of Naval Operations, and in the War Plans Division of the U.S. Army to consider how best to defend the Philippines against an attack from Japan.

31. Hector C. Bywater, *Sea Power in the Pacific: A Study of the American-Japanese Naval Problem* (Boston: Houghton, Mifflin Company, 1921) and *The Great Pacific War: A History of the American-Japanese Campaign of 1931-1933* (Boston: Houghton, Mifflin Company, 1925).

32. Gregory Bienstock, *The Struggle for the Pacific* (London: Kennikat Press, 1970) a reprint of the 1937 work, p. 10.

33. Graser Schornstheimer, "Japan's Naval Mastery in Asia," *Current History Magazine*, August 1922, pp. 744-52.

34. P. T. Etherton and H. Hessell Tiltman, *The Pacific: A Forecast* (Boston, 1928).

35. Shinsaku Hira ta, *How We Shall Make War* (in Japanese) published in Tokyo in 1933 abstracted in *Japnija* (Leningrad, 1934) and in *Kai-zo*, quoted in the *Revue du Pacifique*, No. 3, 1934.

36. The warning is in Letter, War Department to Commanding General of the Philippine Division, 6 July 1907 serial 1260092, The National Archives, Record Group No. 93; on inadequacy of Philippine Defenses see, for example, Letter, Office of the Governor General of the Philippine Islands to Secretary of War, 5 February 1923, National Archives, Record Group No. 225; Joint Letter, The Commander in Chief, Asiatic Fleet and The Commanding General Philippine Department to the Chief of Naval Operations and the Chief of Staff of the Army, dated from U.S.S. *Augusta* (Flagship), 1 March 1934, National Archives, Record Group No. 225.

37. Cited in William L. Neuman, "Franklin Roosevelt: A Disciple of Admiral Mahan," *U.S. Naval Institute Proceedings*, Vol. 78, No. 7 (July 1952), pp. 713-19.

In 1914, in maneuvers held by the Army in the Philippines, the fall-back to a defense of the Bataan Peninsula was tested as the only tenable means of defending Manila and Manila Bay. The defense of these two objectives would come to be the Joint mission of the Philippines Garrison and the Asiatic Fleet under Joint Army Navy Basic War Plan *Orange,* and after the Munich agreement in October 1938, of Joint Army Navy Basic War Plan *Rainbow Five.*[38]

It is not correct to say that the anxiety about the safety of the Philippines and belief in a Pacific War was merely *pro forma* in the Army and Navy or that the development of war plans, mobilization tables and movement schedules were mere exercises to train the general staff. The war plans reflected and were reflected in the development of the doctrine and techniques of amphibious warfare. Despite a lack of equipment and proper landing craft for landings-in-force from the sea, the U.S. Marine Corps, between 1920 and 1934, developed the fundamentals of amphibious operations, rehearsed them in Fleet Exercises and, from 1937, began the training of Regular Army units in amphibious warfare.[39]

It is true to say that Congress did not provide the money for the equipment and landing craft to conduct amphibious operations until the country was on the threshold of war. While it was, and is, the responsibility of Congress to see that the country has the material means and manpower to wage war, they did not exercise that reponsibility until Hitler had conquered most of Europe and the peril from Europe was even greater than that in the Pacific. But then, General Douglas MacArthur, exercising that flair for prophecy for which he would become notable in the Korean War, publicly

38. Examples of the *Orange* Plan with its frequent modifications can be seen in Letter, The Joint Army Navy Planning Committee to the Joint Board, Subj. The Defense of the Philippine Islands, 13 April 1922, National Archives, Record Group No. 225; Letter, Joint Planning Committee to The Joint Board, Subj.: Joint Army and Navy Basic War Plan-*Orange* received at Joint Board, 12 March 1924, located in same place as above; Letter, The War Department to the Joint Board, Subj. Military (including Naval Position in the Far East), 18 December 1935, with endorsements to Secretary of State and War, *loc. cit.;* and Letter, The Joint Planning Committee to the Joint Board, Subj.: Independence of the Philippine Islands; Effect of the Withdrawal of Military Forces, 28 February 1934, *loc. cit.* The testing of the fall-back on Bataan is reported in Brigadier General Clifford Bluemel, "Bataan," *Logistics,* Vol. 2, No. 3 (April 1947), pp. 5-6. See also, Louis Morton, "American and Allied Strategy in the Far East," *Military Review,* Vol. XXIX, No. 9 (December 1949), pp. 23-39 and his, *The Fall of the Philippines,* sub-series: *The War in the Pacific* in series: *U.S. Army in World War II* (Washington: Dept. of the Army, OCMH, 1953).

39. See for example, the handbook of amphibious operations laid out in *Joint Overseas Expeditions,* prepared by the Joint Board, 12 January 1933, J. B. No. 350 (Serial No. 504). Confidential, Typescript in Documents Library, Univ. of California, Berkeley; *Tentative Landing Operations Manual,* 25 May 1935, and cited in *Report of Fleet Landing Exericse No. 2, To the Commandant of the Command and General Staff School,* 15 March 1936, by A. Franklin Kibler, Major, Field Artillery, in Command and Generals Staff College Library, Fort Leavenworth, Kansas; and, "Report of Lt. Col. Thomas E. Watson, U.S.M.C. to Commanding General Fleet Marine Force: Assistance rendered by Marine Corps Instructors in training Army Units in preparation for participation in Fleet Landing Exercise," No. 3, 4 March 1937, 1975-80/11, 4cjh; and Lt. General Holland M. Smith, U.S.M.C., "Amphibious Tactics," *Marine Corps Gazette* (June 1946 through October 1946).

stated in the Fall of 1939, that in his opinion, it was erroneous to suppose that Japan coveted the Philippine Islands. "Proponents of such a theory," he said, "fail fully to credit the logic of the Japanese mind. . . . No national reason exists why Japan or any other country should covet the sovereignty of this country [the Philippines]."[40]

Such comforting words had the ring of a "preferred" truth in 1939, a year in which the Regular Army had a strength of 189,839 officers and men, 109,000 fewer than that number set by Congress as the essential minimum in the National Defense Act of 1920.[41] That same year the First U.S. Army, located in the New York area, was authorized to carry out its once-every-six-year maneuvers. National Guard and army reserve soldiers were called up in order to fill out the skeletonized regular army units, and they had to "kick-back" half their pay to reimburse the Nation for the cost of food, blank ammunition, and equipment used on maneuvers. A private soldier received 21 dollars a month for his services.[42] The end of that same summer of 1939 marked the outbreak of war in Europe, and the invasion of Poland by Nazi Germany and Communist Russia.

Forty years of warnings that war would come in the Pacific were ignored. While it may appear unfair to dwell on now obscure campaigns in a seemingly ancient war, the lesson is nonetheless there. The failure to recognize the direction of Japanese intentions imposed a heavy cost upon the United States, the Asiatic Fleet, the Far Eastern Air Force, the U.S. Army garrison in the Philippines and the Philippine Constabulary and Army. Inadequate equipment—anti-aircraft shells, for example, had to have their modern, mechanical fuses smuggled in by submarine—and a want of sufficient manpower cost the lives of many American and Philippine citizens. They conducted a gallant but futile defense that ended in the death march on Bataan, and the exposure to the brutality of an occupying force of a population for whose safety the United States was responsible. Beyond that it cost the lives of still more Americans and Filipinos to re-conquer the islands. These losses were so severely borne because war seemed too incredible for belief and too undemanding for preparation by those who were responsible for such concerns.

Europe

The belief in the impossibility of war coupled with the failure to contemplate the consequences of defeat explain the weakness that democracies

40. *MacArthur on War: His Military Writings,* edited by Frank C. Lathrop (London: John Lane, The Bodley Head, 1943), p. 310.

41. Army strengths in table Series Y 904,916, "Military Personnel on Active Duty . . .," *Historical Statistics of the United States: Colonial Times to 1970,* Part 2 (Washington: U.S. Dept. of Commerce, 1975), p. 1141. Text of National Defense Act of 1920 in *R.O.T.C. Manual: Infantry, 1st Year Basic,* Vol. I (Harrisburg, Pa.: Military Service Publishing Co., 1937), pp. 38-41.

42. "Two Weeks at Plattsburg," *Fortune,* Vol. XX, No. 5 (Nov. 1939), pp. 66-67, 108-114.

display in providing for their own defense. Optimism about the future of the human condition is the strength and beauty of the democratic regime, but it is its principal weakness when it comes to defense and the conduct of war. Because the exercise of power and the application of force have been diffused and confined by constitutional restraints and the rule of law inside the democratic regime, it is the dominant assumption that similar restraints will always be exercised within the international community. A strong sense of guilt manifests itself within democratic regimes when force has to be applied in the interest of preserving the regime and protecting its citizenry. Recently in the Netherlands, when a group of terrorists seized a passenger train and a school full of children to enforce demands over which the Dutch government could have absolutely no control, the prime minister of the country expressed a sense of defeat and guilt that he could not resolve the issue without force of arms.[43]

There had been no compunction on the part of the South Moluccan terrorists to seize innocent citizens in order to levy demands on the Dutch government that only the government of Indonesia could satisfy. Yet the decent men responsible for peace within the realm of the Netherlands could feel guilt, not anger, not outrage, but guilt because they had been called upon to act in the interest of the citizens held hostage and that that action had shed the blood of some of the terrorists. The Minister of Justice of the Netherlands said, after the affray was ended and the hostages rescued, "*I beseech* you to believe there was no other way. . . . We tried everything, every path of dialogue. . . . We found them all closed." The Prime Minister said, in a radio broadcast to the country: "That violence proved necessary to put an end to hostage seizure is something that we see as a defeat." The hostages had been held, by force, for twenty days.[44]

Neville Chamberlain summarized well the humanitarian aproach to those who threaten violence, war, and death when he outlined his government's foreign policy in respect to Nazi Germany. Some good, he said, must be found in Hitler, and appeals to that good would bring peace; every man has his human side. Fortunately, Hitler did have his human side, he could be killed; unfortunately, not until 12 million inoffensive Europeans had been

43. See, "Molukkers, Wat Nu?" *De Telegraaf* (Amsterdam), 13 June 1977, p. 1; "Regering Na Jongste Acties: Aanpak Wapenbezie en'ordediensten'," *Het Parool* (Rokin), 13 June 1977, p. 1 and elsewhere in both newspapers.

44. Details of the liberation of the hostages are in, "Tension Rises as Dutch Storm Seiged Train: 8 Die," *Sunday Telegraph* (London), 12 June 1977, p. 1; "Why the Pokerplaying Had to Stop," *The Observer* (London), 12 June 1977, p. 11 and elsewhere in that edition; government statement appears therein (Premier: "No Other Way," *Ibid.*, p. 1); and in "Dutch Quelling of Seizures Leaves Racial Tension: Resort to Attack on Train, School is Seen as 'Defeat' by Premier," *International Herald Tribune*, 13 June 1977, p. 1.

methodically exterminated because of their race and religion, other millions killed in battle and half of Europe laid in ruins.[45]

One can perhaps understand why Americans would prefer to ignore the warnings of coming war after World War I and fail to prepare for the occasion. That preference, however, resulted in the unnecessary sacrifice of American citizens, who would have to buy time with their lives while the country prepared for war. This country had always been so distant from the tyrannies of Europe and Asia. And the article of faith about the American involvement in the war against the Kaiser was that it was all just European power politics and that we had been deceived into the war by astute British and French propaganda.[46]

Yet it was disbelief in the probability of war and an unwillingness to prepare that dominated the European democracies before World War II and helped give Hitler the easy victories that would cost so much blood to redress. How could peoples who had lived next door to tyranny since time immemorial have failed to take the measures necessary for their own defense? How could peoples so jealous of their own independence be conquered so easily? The fact is that these countries could not come to grips with the possibility of war and defeat even when the war was upon them. However gallant the resistance fighters were in their efforts to inflict damage on their Nazi conquerors, the very fact that they could only hit and run and then hide, was a measure of the defeat their countries had sustained.

The Danish underground acted with great courage and tenacity. They rescued the greater part of the Jewish population and saw them safely out of the country at great personal cost. Yet in September 1939, Denmark called up five classes of reservists on the outbreak of war to demonstrate the Danish will to defend Denmark's neutrality. But despite the ruthless ferocity of the German campaign in Poland when that country was extinguished in six weeks with the help of the Soviet Army, the Danish reservists were sent home. On 9 April 1940, when German troops invaded Denmark, there were only 20,000 Danes under arms. The concentration of German troops on the border and the reports of an impending German attack did nothing to put Denmark into a state of emergency. Within a few hours after the beginning of the German invasion, all the Danish ports and airfields had been seized and Denmark had become a German possession. There was some delay: the German troops assigned to seize the Citadel in Copenhagen had to ask directions to get to their objective![47]

45. Chamberlain's view of Hitler's human characteristics are in Roger Parkinson, *Peace for Our Time* (New York: David McKay Co., 1971), p. 9.

46. See for example a fine study of the "disillusionment" of the scholarly community in the United States, after the first World War: Selig Adler, "The War-guilt Question and American Disillusionment, 1918-1928," *The Journal of Modern History,* Vol. XXIII, No. 1 (March 1951), pp. 1-28.

47. Only in South Jutland was any resistance even attempted and that ended with the Danish

Norwegian preparations for war were hardly better. Norwegians did not believe in war either. Norway mobilized for war within forty-eight hours *after* the first German troops had effected a landing at Oslo and elsewhere. Yet there had been more than sufficient warning of an impending German attack. The Norwegian General staff had, in the days before invasion, urged the Government to take some measures of defense, but "optimistic inaction" won the day. Where mobilization of army units had taken place, after the first German landings, it had been on the authority of some local commander and not at the behest of the government in Oslo. For Norway held to the teachings of Fridtjof Nansen: "Small nations have a peculiar mission to seek out and find the new paths that humanity must tread in order to abolish war altogether."[48]

The total number of men under arms in Norway on 9 April 1940 was 13,000, fewer than even Denmark had when it was invaded the same day. The Royal Norwegian Air Force had six fighter aircraft, obsolete of course, scattered on five airfields. The Navy was in no better shape. There were no tanks, no anti-tank guns and transport was horse-drawn. The Coast defense fortresses were only partially manned and none had infantry units assigned to provide defense against local attack. Infantry battalions had ceased training as units in 1923. A country that justifiably prided itself on the most up-to-date social services for its citizens, failed in the ultimate social service: the defense of the realm from foreign invasion.[49]

It is told of how at Narvik, General Eduard Dietl, commanding the German 3rd Mountain Division landed with his men from a destroyer, to be met on the quay by a Norwegian officer to whom he said: "I greet the Royal Norwegian Army. The German Army has come to protect Norway and her neutrality." The Norwegian officer convoyed the German general along with the German consul to a conference with the Norwegian commander in the town. While the parley was under way, German troops set up machine guns to enfilade the Norwegian defenses. In the parley, the Norwegian commander agreed to call army headquarters at Harstad to find out whether, as the German said, the rest of Norway had accepted German occupation. The orders from Harstad, of course, were to throw the Germans out. So the town commander told the Germans his troops would open fire in a half hour. But General Dietl pointed out that the town was already invested and the de-

---

government's capitulation. See Per Hyhup, *An Outline of the German Occupation of Denmark*, (Copenhagen: Danish Nations Museum, 1968), p. 1; and, Earl F. Ziemke, *The German Northern Theater of Operations, 1940-1945*, Department of the Army Pamphlet No. 20-271 (Washington, D.C.: U.S.G.P.O., 1959).

48. Cited in J. L. Moulton, *The Norwegian Campaign of 1940: A Study of Warfare in Three Dimensions* (London: Eyre and Spottiswoode, 1966), p. 123.

49. Strength and condition of Norway's defenses are given in T. K. Derry, *The Campaign in Norway* in United Kingdom Military Series, *History of the Second World War* (London: H.M.S.O., 1952), pp. 4-7.

fenses compromised. The town commander thereupon surrendered. It was not that the Germans had sneaked into the town: their destroyers had already opened fire on and sunk Norwegian naval vessels in the harbor. It was not that the Norwegian commander had lacked orders about what to do if the Germans came: he was supposed to defend the town. It was supposed that the Norwegian commander was a Quisling and that that was why he had failed to do what was expected of him. Naturally, when all else fails, one must suspect treachery. But a post-war court martial cleared the unfortunate officer of treason. For he, like so many others, was the victim of both his own and his country's inability to grasp the reality of war soon enough to render an effective defense. Similar incidents occurred elsewhere, yet withal the Norwegian Army fought a gallant defense, for weeks, until forced by want of supplies and equipment to capitulate to a detemined, well-equipped, and competent enemy force.[50] Norwegian armed forces, regular and territorial, fought better, after so many years of irresponsible neglect, than the people of Norway had a right to expect. During those years it was thought that an army, navy, and air force were mere luxuries and of little consequence, save to guard against intrusion upon Norwegian neutrality.

It is difficult to condemn either Norway or Denmark for the neglect of their own defenses. Denmark had not suffered invasion since the war with Prussia, and Norway had not been close to war since the separation from Sweden in 1905. Indeed, Norway held out against the Germans for two months, a week longer than France held out against the German invasion of that country.

If Norway, Denmark, and the Netherlands were unready for war, assuming somehow that the niceties of neutrality would protect them as it had done in the Kaiser's War, how could France and Great Britain have permitted themselves to be unready? How could this happen after the Occupation of the Rhineland, the *Anschluss* and the extortion of the Sudetenland from Czechoslovakia? How could this happen after the seizure of what remained of Czechoslovakia, despite Hitler's solemn pledge to Neville Chamberlain that Germany would respect Czech independence? How could France, after having spent 7 billion francs to build the superb fortifications of the Maginot Line, fail to be ready for war? It had been France that had dragged its feet over the peace settlement for fear of a resurgent Germany. It had been Marshal Foch who had warned of a twenty-year truce. It had been Georges Clemenceau who, on his deathbed, had uttered the warning: "If you make concessions [to Germany] you will have war in twenty years. If you refuse to

50. The incident at Narvik is described in T. K. Derry, *The Campaign in Norway,* p. 41; Earle F. Ziemke, *The German Northern Theater of Operations, 1944-1945*, p. 46; and in J. L. Moulton, *The Norwegian Campaign of 1940,* pp. 82-84. The latter account draws on the Norwegian official history of the war, *Norge Sjokrig,* 1940-1945, Vol. IV (Oslo, 1958), pp. 56-98.

make any, you will have war in forty years."[51] Clemenceau died in 1929 and even he was too optimistic by ten years.

And what of Great Britain, that keeper of the balance of power, always called upon to redress the scales when some tyrant rose to dominate Europe? Did they in Britain not know that Germany was preparing for war?

51. Rene de Chambrun, *I Saw France Fall: Will She Rise Again?* (New York: William Morrow & Company, 1940), p. 15.

II. Tyranny Rearming—Democracy Disarming: The Inter-War Period

THE TALE OF BRITISH APPEASEMENT OF THE DICTATORS IS AN OFTEN TOLD ONE; it seemed at the time that the British Government would betray any ally, friend, or helpless victim, to purchase "peace with honor." In a less innocent and more cynical age, like our own, doubtless Neville Chamberlain would have received a Nobel Peace Prize for his work at Bad Godesberg and Munich, and according to today's standards in such matters, Herr Hitler would likely have been nominated to share the award. What could be more noble and pacific than presiding at the demise of a small country struggling futilely to resist tyranny. Yet Chamberlain and others who supported appeasement until the bitter end were decent men and women however short their sight about Britain's safety. Desperately they sought for some indication of Hitler's good side, that they might appeal to it. Even Lloyd George tried. He who, as Prime Minister during the Kaiser's War, pursued German defeat with a ferocity that held Britain together in the face of the terrible toll exacted by Germany on the Somme, the Aisne, at Arras, Vimy Ridge, Loos, Messines, Ypres, Lens, and the rest, even he spoke of Hitler as the greatest German of the age.[1]

F. T. A. Ashton-Gwatkin at the Foreign Office would argue that British democracy could not be destroyed by what happened elsewhere and would urge economic and political agreements with Germany, Japan and Italy (but with adequate rearmament and *defensive* alliances with France and Belgium); economic recovery in Europe would lessen the danger of war.[2]

Disarmament agreements were pursued with such vigor as to neglect the realities both of strategic position and tactical arithmetic. These agreements came from a British Government that heard its Air Staff repeat in 1937, the warnings of Sir Edward Grey in 1912, on the occasion of an attempt to achieve a naval agreement with Imperial Germany:

1. See "Notes of a Conversation between Lloyd George and Hitler at Berchtesgaden, 4 September 1936," as Appendix in Martin Gilbert, *The Roots of Appeasement* (New York: New American Library, 1966), pp. 197-211.

2. *Ibid.*, Appendix 4, pp. 215-19.

> In the first place you must not rely upon your foreign policy to protect the United Kingdom. That is to say, if you let your margin of naval strength fall below that which may be brought to bear against you rapidly, you are setting foreign policy a task which you ought not to set it. The risk of an attack on the United Kingdom stronger in force than we could meet with the ships we keep in Home waters is not one to be settled by diplomacy.[3]

Although 1937 was already late for such warnings, they were heeded hardly more than earlier ones. It is now clear that German rearmament did not begin with the coming to power of Hitler and the National Socialist German Workers Party. "Secret" rearmament began almost before the Armistice ended the first World War on 11 November 1918. The Nazis merely threw off all pretense and furnished the capstone for a foundation and structure erected in the decade and a half of the Weimar Republic. How could such an enterprise have been kept so well-hidden from democratic governments that they would only respond when it was too late to save Europe?

Germany Prepares for War

Even before the First World War had ended, steps were reported being put in hand by Germany to disperse its war industry beyond the reach of the Allied Powers. In December 1917, *The Scientific American* reported that Krupp's at Essen had opened a branch factory in Lucerne, Switzerland, capitalized at $7,500,000, and as required by Swiss law, had published its intentions: "the fabrication of arms, cannon and munitions of war; the acquisition of factories, mines and metals, also their sale."[4]

Grand Admiral Alfred von Tirpitz closed the first volume of his memoirs, published in 1919, with the remark that "England's day of judgement will have its birth in this very success [victory over the Central Powers]."[5] The words of a bitter old man who had seen the pride of the German High Seas Fleet interned at Scapa Flow? Perhaps.

The *Army and Navy Gazette* in London, cited in February 1920, a letter quoted in the *Times* of 17 January 1920, written by Mathias Erzberger, president of the German Armistice Commission:

3. Cited in Ian Colvin, *The Chamberlain Cabinet* (New York: Taplinger Publishing Company, 1971), pp. 69-70. For a further elucidation of Grey's view of the relations between military (in this case naval) power, and foreign policy, see *Hansard,* 5th Sr. xl 1933-2040 as cited in E. L. Woodward, *Great Britain and the German Navy* (Oxford: Oxford University Press, 1935), pp. 377-78.

4. "New Krupp Plant in Switzerland," abstract of *Scientific American* article, 29 December 1917, in "Professional Notes," *U.S. Naval Institute Proceedings,* Vol. 44, No. 2 (Whole no. 180), February 1918, p. 375. It may be that Oerlikon, established after the war, was the outcome of a similar process.

5. Grand Admiral von Tirpitz, *My Memoirs*, Vol. I (New York: Dodd Mead & Co., 1919), p. 377.

> Another war, he said, between Germany and the Anglo-Saxons is inevitable. France is 'their strongest outpost on the continent; but she has been so thoroughly weakened she will never be able to recover.' If Germany can undertake the restoration of Russia 'she will be ready in ten or fifteen years to bring France, without difficulty, into her power. The March to Paris will be easier than that in 1914.'[6]

In a lengthy article in the *Naval and Military Record* for 8 June 1921, it was reported that "hatred of England is the cement that keeps the German Empire together and saves it from total disruption . . . nine Germans in ten live for the day of reckoning with Great Britain which they believe to be foreordained." Commenting on French reports that Germany was building submarines in defiance of the Treaty of Versailles, the writer found this to be improbable because of the *presumably alert* allied intelligence service. However, the article described a surprise visit by French and British officers of the Naval Control Commission to one plant where they discovered equipment being manufactured for submarines "ostensibly to Dutch order." "Not until," the article said, "the Allied control officers have been withdrawn from Germany shall we have real cause for apprehension in regard to the secret manufacture of submarines, aircraft and other war material. . . . We have not done with Germany yet."[7]

John Maynard Keynes, the English economist, would argue in a book published in 1919, *The Economic Consequences of the Peace,* that the Treaty of Versailles transferred "intolerable financial burdens from the victor's shoulders to those of the vanquished," and his view would prevail. The French writer, Raphael-Georges-Levy, author of the book *La Juste Paix* which was written as a polite refutation of Keynes' view that France had really suffered little damage at the hands of the Germans, would remain obscure. He would remain obscure despite the fact that other experts found German industry to be thriving, and in particular the firm of Krupp to be operating near capacity. German coal and steel exports were exceeding pre-war figures, benefiting apparently from strikes in Britain, and from the reduced capacity of French industry crippled by the war.[8] How, it was asked, could there be men who would assert that Germany should be treated kindly at the expense of the Allies?

6. Cited as "The Disarming of Germany," *The Army and Navy Gazette* (London), 14 February 1920, text in "Professional Notes," *U.S. Naval Institute Proceedings,* Vol. 46, No. 4 (Whole no. 206), April 1920, p. 647.

7. "The German Maritime Revival," in "Professional Notes," *U.S. Naval Institute Proceedings,* Vol. 17, No. 8 (Whole No. 222), August 1921, pp. 1282-84.

8. "Industrial and Economic Situation in Germany," *Engineering* (London), 4 February 1921 in *ibid.,* Vol. 47, No. 4 (Whole No. 218) April 1921, pp. 579-83; the revival of Krupp's is described in an American journal as well. See "Recent Developments in the Krupp Works at Essen," *The Engineer,* 9 December 1921, pp. 611-13.

The *Scientific American,* a journal that still maintains a commitment to disarmament, would report, in its February 1922 issue, that Germany was disarmed and that the provisions of the Treaty of Versailles were being carried out. The last thing it said that the German people were thinking about was another war.[9]

The Treaty of Rapallo

While Article 198 of the Treaty of Versailles prohibited Germany from possessing any aeronautical force whatever, *Le Temps* (Paris) published a review in early 1922, of the "Instruction on the Employment of Aviation to be used for maneuvers, regimental exercises, drills in Tactics," issued by the German Minister of War. The instructions declared that: "In the distribution and employment of the aviation formations we have taken as a basis a modernly equipped army for use in giving decisive combats."[10]

Reports in the *Revue Universelle,* in July 1922, that Germany was shipping diesel engines along with a naval mission to the Russian port of Kronstadt seemed to imply not only German assistance to Russia in restoring the Baltic Fleet but the possible secret construction of German submarines in Russian yards. But "well-informed quarters in London" seemed to know nothing of the shipment of diesels, the naval mission to Kronstadt or anything else untoward with respect to German naval activity, although it was considered possible that the recently concluded Treaty of Rapallo between Russia and Germany had some military understanding, "if not definite agreement," in its text.[11]

Yet John W. Wheeler-Bennett, in his biography of Field Marshall von Hindenburg (1936), would take note of General von Seeckt's proposal of February 1920—General Hans von Seeckt was the genius behind the rebuilding of the German army—of a German-Soviet alliance against the West. This would enable Germany to seize Poland with the help of the Red Army. Wheeler-Bennett would note further, that:

> The Treaty of Rapallo, signed with the Soviet Union during the Genoa Conference of 1922 set the official seal upon the unofficial relations which had already existed between the two general staffs. The Treaty was complemented by a secret military agreement which enabled Seeckt to send each year to Russia a certain number of officers to act as instructors for the Red Army, and a further number to gain all the experience

9. "Germany is Disarmed," *Scientific American,* February 1922, cited in "Professional Notes," *U.S. Naval Institute Proceedings,* Vol. 48, No. 3 (Whole No. 229, March 1922), pp. 458-59.

10. "German Aviation," *Aerial Age Weekly* (London), 3 April 1922; cited in *ibid.,* Vol. 48, No. 6 (Whole No. 232, June 1922), pp. 1015-16.

11. *Naval and Military Record,* 12 July 1922, *ibid.,* Vol. 48, No. 9 (Whole No. 235), September 1922, pp. 1581-82.

they could in the handling of heavy artillery, tanks, armored cars and other weapons forbidden to Germany.[12]

It is difficult to suppose that allied governments could not have known something about the secret aspects of the Treaty of Rapallo, if a prominent student of history and expert on disarmament could know about them in time to write a book published in 1936. Yet as late as 1972, the distinguished journal, *Le Monde Diplomatique,* would speak of the Treaty of Rapallo as "an example of positive cooperation" and based on "good will and a spirit of peaceful cooperation."[13]

Hector C. Bywater, the prophet of the coming war in the Pacific, admitted that there might be some plausibility to the reports of a secret protocol, to the Treaty of Rapallo, providing for military and naval cooperation between Germany and Russia. Bywater, however, discounted entirely any secret development of submarines in Germany and any possibility of Germany using Russian shipyards to rebuild its own fleet.[14]

While the reports of secret protocols to the Treaty of Rapallo surfaced at the time of the treaty's conclusion, its significance then and even later seems to have escaped the attention of the democracies. Even the distinguished historian of international affairs, G. M. Gathorne-Hardy, whose work, *A Short History of International Affairs, 1920-1939,* published under the auspices of the Royal Institute of International Affairs in London, and which went through four editions and 12 impressions between 1934 and 1952, neglects to mention the secret protocols or their importance to Germany's secret rearmament. *Survey of American Foreign Relations 1928*, published in the United States under the auspices of the authoritative Council on Foreign Relations, supposed the Treaty of Rapallo to be nothing more than an effort to open German markets to the east and to avoid the isolation imposed by the Treaty of Versailles. Frederick L. Schuman, the American scholar of international politics who foresaw the coming of war in Europe, considered the treaty a mere effort to obtain mutually advantageous commercial relations.[15]

Whatever indications there may have been to the contrary, it was concluded by the Allied governments that Germany's air arm had been completely dismantled by 5 February 1922 and the Aeronautical Commission of

12. John W. Wheeler-Bennett, *Wooden Titan: Hindenburg in Twenty Years of German History, 1914-1934* (New York: William Morrow & Co., 1936).

13. Andre Stepanov, "Le traite de Rapallow: un example de cooperation postive," *Le Monde Diplomatique,* No. 219 (June 1972), p. 12. It may be significant, however, that the article originated with Novosti and therefore presented a preferred interpretation of Rapallo, to exclude the Soviet role in German rearmament.

14. Hector C. Bywater, "No Signs of German Naval Revival," *Naval and Military Record,* 16 August 1922, *ibid.,* Vol. 48, No. 10 (Whole No. 236), pp. 1792-93.

15. Frederick L. Schuman, *International Politics: An Introduction to the Western State System,* Second Edition, Third Impression (New York: McGraw Hill Book Company, 1937), p. 459.

Control of the Inter-Allied Commission of Control was withdrawn from Germany.[16]

Even in far away America, observers now reported the failure of Germany to comply with the provisions of the Treaty of Versailles and inferred continued preparations for war on the part of the German government:

> Germany has not at any time accepted the treaty in any of its parts but has gone forward with plans to resume war whenever the advantage should swing to her side. The niggardly and false coal returns to the Allies; the secreting of huge quantities of war materials, including guns and airplanes; the maintenance of hundreds of thousands of men under arms at constant drill; the steady output of propaganda designed to gain world sympathy for the "downtrodden and starving Germans"—these and a dozen other major facts prove overwhelmingly that the Versailles treaty is to Germany a detested bargain made only to be broken . . . the work of preparation for revenge upon France and her Allies for the crime of defeating Germany goes on apace. . . . The only thing that restrains her is the fact that she is not ready yet.[17]

It seemed obvious, in some quarters, at least, that Germany was circumventing the treaty. Equally obvious, it was proceeding with all due haste to the task of rebuilding another army.[18]

One American traveller to Germany reported that: "The Germans have used every artifice known to mankind—and several known to the devil—they have inflated their currency until it is next to worthless, they have put their gold in the banks of Denmark, Switzerland, and Holland and in foreign securities, all to avoid payment of reparations, and now they yell poverty and starvation."[19]

The Repudiation of the Treaty of Versailles

By the mid-20s, it was accepted that the German Army was being restored and American soldiers wrote their observations with readily discernible envy: "The German Army is enabled to conduct maneuvers on a large scale. Our own Army has received no such training since the war." The maneuvers held from 13-21 September 1926, for example, were conducted at four division strength (close to 50,000 men). They were realistic with the troops required to dig in whenever halted from the march; there was much

16. "Report on Disarmament," *Army, Navy and Air Force Gazette,* 29 July 1922, cited in "Professional Notes," *U.S. Naval Institute Proceedings,* Vol. 48, No. 10 (Whole No. 236), October 1922, pp. 1793-94.

17. "German Preparations," *Infantry Journal,* Vol. XVII, No. 3 (Sept. 1920), p. 293.

18. George Nester Trioche, "The Menace of the German Army," *Infantry Journal,* Vol. XXII, No. 4 (April 1922), p. 421.

19. Captain Tharratt G. Best, CRC, "Europe Today," *Infantry Journal,* Vol. XXII, No. 6 (June 1923), pp. 639-49.

motorization; and, wireless was widely used.[20] In a report on the Reichswehr in 1928, an observer pointed out how the 12-year term of enlistment required by the Treaty of Versailles made it possible to train private soldiers to be commissioned and non-commisioned officers; that the Reichswehr's policy of early release short of the 12-year term meant three times as many men could be well-trained as that anticipated by the Treaty. Nowhere in the German Army, the observer noted, were there soldiers doing fatigue duty—whitewashing stones or cutting grass. Training time was too precious to waste soldiers on such tasks. All around Germany, he reported, there surfaced strong expressions of nostalgia for the lost German provinces of Alsace and Lorraine. It seemed to him that there would be another war with Germany.[21]

An American cavalry officer reported in 1929 on the use in German maneuvers of wooden tanks; on the designation within German units of the guns to be employed in anti-tank warfare—20 mm. automatic cannon, 37 mm. and 57 mm. anti-tank guns; and horse-drawn and motorized 77 mm. guns. He reported further:

> German technical experts have assisted in the persuasion and presumably in the operation of Russian machines. . . . Dummy tanks are used for training purposes at home; but abroad German engineers are perfecting designs and gaining experience in methods of construction. There can be little doubt that certain German factories now have blueprints and tools for making modern tanks that have been thoroughly tested. When circumstances change, Germany will be well prepared to apply her highly developed industries, if need be, to the rapid production of war machines.

He also observed that details of an experimental American light tank (Ti E 1 model, 1927), including scale drawings, speed, crew-size, armament, armor and vulnerabilities were generally circulated within the German Army, although such details were not yet available generally in the U.S. Army.[22]

It could not be expected that governments of democracies would pay much heed to such obscure reports as these—knowing as we all do of the vested interest that soldiers have in preparedness. Soldiers and sailors always fear the worst when called upon to face an enemy better equipped than themselves. But if American army officers could know of German war prep-

20. "The German Army Maneuvers," *Infantry Journal,* Vol. XXX, No. 1 (Jan. 1927), pp. 60-62.

21. Lt. Leonard H. Nason, "The Reichswehr," *ibid.*, Vol. XXXI, No. 1 (July 1928), pp. 17-19.

22. Major C. C. Benson, "Mechanization in Europe," *ibid.*, Vol. XXIV, No. 6 (June 1929), pp. 565-72. Heinz Guderian recorded his immense satisfaction during the 1932 maneuvers at Grafenwehr and Juterbog when the first armored reconnaissance vehicles, built of steel armor plate, were used. He mentions as well, the existence, from 1926, of a testing station abroad, where German tank performance could be evaluated. See General Heinz Guderian, *Panzer Leader* (New York: E. P. Dutton and Co., Inc., 1952), pp. 26, 28-29.

arations almost from the beginning, it is difficult to know how the British government could have failed to be aware of such preparations.

In 1924, the *Quarterly Review* in England published a report by J. H. Morgan who was not a professional soldier but a lawyer who had served as Home Office Commissioner at G.H.Q. of the British Expeditionary Force in France and after the war on the Inter-Allied Commission of Control in Germany—the body reponsible for seeing to the disarmament of Germany according to the requirements laid down in the Treaty of Versailles. Expert in the German language from attendance at the University of Berlin, before the war, he had been the vice-chairman of the British Government's Committee of Enquiry into War Crimes, and as a Brigadier General, was the British Military Representative at Versailles on the Prisoners of War Commission. In his article written after resignation from the Inter-Allied Commission of Control, he told of how in 1920, he and another British officer sat in mufti in a German nightclub where a comedian regaled an audience of Germans with a song called "Nur Papier." The comedian told his audience of having received a legacy from a dead relative to find that it was "only paper"; and, had bought a pair of ready-made trousers to discover at an indelicate moment that they too were "only paper." The final verse of the song that called forth enthusiastic applause told of how the Entente would one day awake to face a strong and unified Germany and discover that the Treaty of Versailles was "only paper." But beyond that Morgan charged that Germany could, in 1924, place in service, on short notice, an army of 500,000 well-trained soldiers.[23] His experience afforded much support to the view that the German government and the German Army had done everything possible to evade the treaty restrictions that limited the German Army to 100,000, 12-year volunteers. The Treaty had required Germany to be disarmed to the levels set in the disarmament clauses within six months of the ratification of the Treaty. Yet five years after the treaty had been ratified, Germany was still not disarmed. From the beginning the German government had challenged the right of the Inter-Allied Commission of Control to fix the level of production of arms within Germany. They argued that such was purely a domestic matter, in which the Commission had no right to interfere. The German government further demanded that an enormous number of armament factories be authorized in order to promote healthy competition *(einem gesunden Wettbewerb herbeizufuhren)* in arms production. The writer, citing chapter and verse in German Army documents, strength-returns uncovered by the Effectives Commission of the Commission of Control and other evidence demonstrated massive evasion of the letter and the spirit of the Treaty of Versailles.

23. J. H. Morgan, "The Disarmament of Germany and After," *Quarterly Review* (October 1924), pp. 415-57.

This despite the fact that the House of Commons was being assured that the German Army had been reduced to 100,000 men. Examination of the German Army estimates, passed by the Reichstag, showed appropriation for 35,644 non-commissioned officers and 20,000 corporals and only 20,000 privates, although by the time of this revelation (19 April 1924) not a single private had yet been enlisted under the 12-year engagement prescribed by the Treaty of Versailles. The writer, on the basis of evidence collected by members of the Control Commission, stated that German industry, the German government and the Reichswehr conspired to hide German rearmament. *The Daily Mail* (London) reported in its 27 February 1925 issue that "no great newspaper in Germany dared to publish" the matter "for fear of proceedings for treason." These issues arose at a time when the German government was assuring the Reichstag and foreign journalists that the disarmament of Germany was complete. General Morgan then began a book to expose more fully the nature of German preparations for the next war and of the measures undertaken by the German government to frustate the work of the Inter-Allied Commission of Control. Meanwhile, the German government, as the price of its adherence to the Pact of Locarno, obtained the withdrawal of the Commission of Control from German soil and official silence on the part of the Allied governments concerning the violations of the Treaty of Versailles. In the words of the author:

> It became 'bad form' for anyone to question whether Germany was or was not, in a state of grace in the matter of disarmament. To have proceeded, under such circumstances with the publication of a history of the attempt to disarm her under the Treaty of Versailles would have involved such a revelation of the bad faith of Germany . . . as to amount to an 'unfriendly act' particularly in view of her spectacular entry into the comity of the League of Nations.

The consequences were that Morgan did not publish his book until 1945, after the war with Germany was over.[24]

The Times published a letter from General Morgan on 4 November 1933:

> No one who served in Germany on the Control Commission can fail to know that Germany never did fulfill the Disarmament provisions of the Treaty and that she never has been disarmed, materially or morally. The plain facts are that Germany has never acknowledged her responsibilities, has never accepted defeat, is determined to re-arm in any event, and is merely biding her time.[25]

24. J. H. Morgan, *Assize of Arms: The Disarmament of Germany and her Rearmament (1919-1939)* (New York: Oxford University Press, 1946), p. xiii.

25. Cited in Morgan, *ibid.*, p. xviii.

The counter-point to such deadly concern was apparently far more effective than was the tocsin. In 1929, a Member of Parliament, and former Under-Secretary of State for Foreign Affairs in the Ramsey MacDonald government wrote an exposé of British and French propaganda and dirty tricks undertaken to win the war against the Kaiser. In his book, *Falsehood in Wartime,* he set out to demonstrate that the sinking of the *Lusitania* had been thoroughly justified by the fact that she carried arms and munitions of war; that there had been no German atrocities in Belgium; that Germany was in no way contemplating a general war in 1914 but a localized war between Austria and Serbia; that German submarine commanders never indulged in acts of cruelty against the crews of ships that were victims of their torpedoes. All of these things had been mere figments of French and British propaganda and Germany in no way deserved to be fixed with guilt for the war.[26]

Probably there was no particular reason anyone in the English-speaking world would read the diatribes and boasts of an obscure Austrian leader of one of many minor political parties in Germany, when he wrote:

> When at last . . . the will to live of the German nation—instead of continuing to be wasted away in purely passive defense—can be summoned together for a final active showdown with France, and thrown into this in one last decisive battle with the very highest objectives for Germany; then, and only then, will it be possible to bring to a close the perpetual and so fruitless struggle between ourselves and France.[27]

Given only such rumors and reports of secret German rearmament, it is possible to conclude that Germany was so immensely clever in concealing its preparations for war that Allied politicians simply could not have been

26. Arthur Ponsoby, *Falsehood in War-time* (London: 1928); see a stirring review of this book in *Mailing List,* The Command and General Staff School, Vol. VIII, No. 9 (May 1929), p. 113. For a thorough and meticulously documented account of the sinking of the *Lusitania* in reply to a recent revival of the myths about the *Lusitania,* see, Thomas A. Bailey and Paul B. Ryan, *The Lusitania Disaster: An Episode in Modern Warfare and Diplomacy* (New York: Free Press/Macmillan, 1975). On the atrocities in Belgium (and Northern France) inflicted by the German Army, see Arnold J. Toynbee, *The German Terror in Belgium* (New York: George H. Doran, 1917); Arnold J. Toynbee, *The German Terror in France* (London: Hodder and Stoughton, 1917); and, J. H. Morgan, "Outrages Upon the Honour of Women," in *German Atrocities and Official Investigation* (New York: Dutton, 1916). It is inferred that the atrocities were official German policy aimed at demoralizing the Belgian (and French) Army in order to destroy resistance to the German Army's invasion of Belgium and France. For a revival of the German propaganda story in our own day see Robert Kirsch's review of the Bailey-Ryan book seen as an answer to the book of allegations by Colin Simpson in "Torpedoing the Lusitania Myths," *Los Angeles Times,* 24 November 1975, p. 8, pt. IV.

27. Adolf Hitler, *Mein Kampf* (1925) as cited in Alistair Horne, *To Lose A Battle: France 1940* (Boston: Little, Brown and Co., 1969), p. viii. Some there, who took the measure of Hitler quite early, were impressed by his ability to compel the attention of a crowd and by the fanatical nature of the party of which he was the head: Captain Truman Smith, Assistant Military Attaché at the U.S. Embassy in Berlin, interviewed the man and submitted a report to the American Ambassador in November 1922. See William L. Shirer, *The Rise and Fall of the Third Reich: A History of Nazi Germany* (New York: Simon and Schuster, 1960), p. 46n.

expected to detect them. But that is a case extremely difficult to make, if one examines what the German government did even before the National Socialists came finally to power. The actions taken and the efforts made cannot have escaped the view of British naval, military, and foreign office intelligence, however much the leaders of the British Government may have concealed the information from themselves.

Secret Arms Production

There was, for example, the matter of secret production of arms. It was not merely the case of a few stands of rifles and some machine guns squirrelled away by some private enthusiast, but outright production of arms in violation of the Treaty of Versailles. The *Times* would report the discovery of 589 field artillery pieces in one factory in Saxony, all of which had been manufactured in 1919. That cache alone equaled more than double the number of artillery pieces permitted the German Army by the Treaty. So vast was the arms producing capacity of German factories, retained in defiance of the Treaty, that it was estimated that Germany could reach its 1918 level of arms production within a year of the withdrawal of the Allied Commission of Control.[28] In 1920, Zeiss naval rangefinders, manufactured in Jena, were sent to the Zeiss factory in Venloo, Netherlands, for storage beyond the jurisdiction of the Allied Commission of Control.[29]

The German Navy would boast of its blatant evasions of the Treaty of Peace. Arms and equipment were sent to the Danish firm, Daugs & Co. in Copenhagen, for sale to Finland, Estonia, Sweden and China. Sixty percent of the proceeds were returned to the German Navy to finance other clandestine activities, while forty percent went to the firms that manufactured and handled the arms.[30]

Such violations of the Treaty of Peace did not entirely escape the eyes of the Allied Naval Commission of Control, so long as that body remained in Germany—it was withdrawn with its task "completed," in September 1924, at the behest of the Allied Ambassadors' Conference. Shortages of personnel imposed by measures of stringent economy impeded discovery or prevention of many violations. If the British Government took note of the violations they took few measures to suppress them, as they had the right to do under the provisions of the Treaty. In fact, it was almost as though the government found them unbelievable.

28. J. H. Morgan, "The Disarmament of Germany and After," *Quarterly Review* (October 1924), pp. 415-45.

29. Stephen Roskill, *Naval Policy Between the Wars:* Volume I, *The Period of Anglo-American Antagonism* (New York: Walker and Company, 1968), pp. 96-97.

30. Kapitan zur See Schlussler, *Der Kampf der Marine gegen Versailles, 1919-1935,* Dienschrift Nr. 15 (Berlin: Oberkommando der Kriegsmarine, 1937), seen in *International Military Tribunal,* as Document 156-C.

The U.S. Naval Attaché to China informed His Majesty's Consul General at Canton that German firms were importing munitions of war and aeroplane parts via Manila. This was clearly contrary to British attempts to embargo the shipment of arms to the factions involved at that time in the civil war in China. The British Foreign Secretary's view of the matter was that:

> . . . the export of arms from that country [Germany] is, of course, prohibited by article 170 of the Peace Treaty. In so far as German nationals in China are concerned, Germany has lost her extra-territorial rights, and is therefore, even if she were willing, no longer in a position to prevent them from importing arms from *other sources* into China. (Italics added)[31]

The clear implications of the Foreign Secretary's dispatch was that Germany could not be exporting arms to China because it would be a violation of the Treaty of Peace and therefore the arms must be coming from elsewhere to be handled by agents who happened to be German. But the German Navy's records show that the arms were German in origin and indeed were a source of revenue for secret German rearmament.[32]

It must have become obvious by the early thirties that Germany was supplying arms to China. Newsreels showed Chinese troops in German coal scuttle helmets, carrying Mauser rifles. The presence of German military advisers and the pursuit of certain arsenal projects for the Nanking Government must have been something of a commonplace.[33]

The German Armed Forces Rebuild

The case of the resurrection of the German Air Force is equally interesting: that process also began shortly after the dissolution of that body by the Allies at the close of the World War. While the Treaty of Peace forbade Germany a military air arm, Germany was permitted a national police force. In 1919, that police force was equipped with seven air squadrons. In 1920, the Allies forced disbandment of the air elements and imposed a prohibition on any paramilitary flying in Germany. While a freeze was imposed on aeroplane construction in Germany, the development of civil aviation was

31. See Sir B. Alston (Peking) to the Marquess Curzon of Kedleston, No. 398, Telegraphic (F3933/2/10), Peking, October 25, 1921, 12.20 P.M.; and, The Marquess Curzon of Kedleston to Sir A Geddes (Washington), No. 1454 (F3933/2/10), Foreign Office, Nov. 4, 1921. All in *Documents on British Foreign Policy, 1919-1939, First Series,* Vol. XIV (London: H.M.S.O., 1966), pp. 453 and 459.

32. Kapitan zur See Schlussler, *op. cit.*

33. See for example, *Memorandum by an Official of Department IV,* 9078/E63466-68, Berlin, November 27, 1933, zu IV Chi. 2567 II in *Documents on German Foreign Policy, 1918-1945: Series C (1933-1937), The Third Reich: First Phase,* Vol. II: October 14, 1933-June 13, 1934 (Washington, D.C.: U.S.G.P.O., 1959), pp. 154-55. German military advisers were withdrawn from China after the signature of the Anti-Comintern Pact between Japan and Germany in 1936. See John W. Wheeler-Bennett, *The Nemesis of Power: The German Army in Politics, 1918-1945* (London: MacMillan & Co., 1954), pp. 486-87.

not forbidden. Within a few years after the war, some 38 commercial airlines operated starting with Deutsches Luftreederei and Lloyd Ostflug, the latter founded by Professor Hugo Junkers, and a former German naval airman. Eventually, the numerous airlines dwindled to only two, Junkers and Aero Lloyd, which joined to become Deutsches Lufthansa. While it was forbidden to manufacture even commercial aircraft in Germany until 1922, the airlines employed aircraft built in Germany right up until the freeze was lifted in 1922. German airlines even operated air routes into Russia while the German government subsidized the establishment of a secret Junkers factory at Fili outside Moscow. This was one more aspect of the German-Soviet rapprochement begun as early as 1920 and continued, with its ups and downs, through the partition of Poland in 1939, the Soviet attack on Finland, the Fall of France, and until the German attack on the Soviet Union in 1941.[34]

While the Allies recognized, initially, the possible symbiotic relationships between commercial aviation and the development of military aviation by placing a limit on the design of commercial aircraft built in Germany, it appears that the relationship grew to be largely ignored as time passed. For example, in the 1932 Gold Medal Essay of the Royal United Service Institution, a Royal Air Force Wing Commander wrote of the "Importance to Military Aviation of Fostering the Growth of Civil Aviation," and suggested, "Ways in which the latter could in its natural progress take account of the requirements of Military Aviation." The value of the civil aircraft industry, the growth of private flying for recreation, the development of air routes, air transportation of passengers and goods, the organization of private flying clubs, and the increasing popularity of gliding all were seen to contribute to the development of military aviation. But the lesson was deduced only for Great Britain with no implications derived for the preparations for war by Germany.[35]

It is clear that the German government from the very start, recognized the importance of civil aviation as a means of developing an aircraft industry capable of supporting a future German military expansion. But even the military aspects of aviation were not neglected in Germany despite the Treaty of Versailles and the presence of the Allied Commission of Control.

In 1923, the Marinewaffenabteilung of the German Defense Ministry ordered ten aircraft from Ernst Heinkel at Warnemunde. These were naval

34. Early development of civil aviation in Germany after the Treaty of Versailles is reviewed in David Irving, *The Rise and Fall of the Luftwaffe: The Life of Field Marshall Erhard Milch* (Boston: Little, Brown and Company, 1973), pp. 114-24 and in Hanfried Schlephake, *The Birth of the Luftwaffe* (London: Ian Allen, 1971), pp. 12-13. The Junkers enterprise at Fili and related matters are detailed in John W. Wheeler-Bennett, *ibid.*, p. 128f.

35. Wing Commander J. O. Andrews, D.S.O., M.C.,. R.A.F., "Gold Medal Essay (Air) 1932," *The Journal of the Royal United Service Institution*, Vol. LXXVIII, No. 510 (May 1933), pp. 295-316.

aircraft Type HS-1, Hansa-Brandenburg-Type, the payment for which was made through a variety of channels by the German government.[36] They were constructed at Warnemunde, assembled and tested in Sweden where they were equipped with English Rolls-Royce engines and stored in a German warehouse in the freeport at Stockholm. Branches of German aircraft companies in foreign countries undertook development of aircraft for the future Luftwaffe: Dornier in Pisa, Italy; Rohrback in Copenhagen; and Junkers in Malmo, Sweden.

It was at the Junkers works in Limnham, Sweden, for example, that the lineal ancestor of the *Stuka (Sturzkampfflugzeug),* Junkers 87, dive-bomber was built. Starting with the Junkers K 47, presented as a civilian sports plane in 1927, military versions of the aircraft were built in Sweden and tested as dive-bombers at the secret German aviation school at Lipezk, in the Soviet Union. The immediate predecessor of the Ju-87, the Ju 8771, equipped with a Rolls-Royce Kestrel V engine, was tested in the summer of 1935. The design work on the final version of the Ju-87 was begun in 1933, under the second-phase of the German government's *Sofort Programm* (Immediate Programme) for development of dive bombers. The *Stuka* became operational in German air squadrons in 1937, and some of the aircraft were assigned to the Condor Legion in Spain to work out the proper tactics for dive-bombing under combat conditions.[37]

When Winston Churchill challenged from the floor of the House of Commons the accuracy of the British Government's estimate of German air strength in November 1934 and March 1935, he said:

> I am certain that Germany's preparations are infinitely more far-reaching than our own. So that you have not only equality at the moment, but the great output which I have described, and behind that this enormous power to turn over, on the outbreak of war, the whole force of German industry . . . .[38]

A Labour Member of Parliament replied that it was "a scaremongering speech of the Right Honourable Member for Epping who endeavoured to make our flesh creep." Yet Churchill was speaking, as we now know, of preparations for war that had not really ceased since the ending of the Great War. German civil aviation and the aircraft factories that supported it pro-

36. K. zur S. Schlussler, *op. cit.*, p. 51.

37. Peter C. Smith, *The Stuka at War* (New York: Arco Publishing Company, 1971), pp. 1-2; William Green, *Bombers and Reconnaissance Aircraft,* Vol. X (Garden City, N.Y.: Doubleday & Company, Inc., 1968), pp. 52-60. The Development of the JU-87 and other German combat aircraft to be used in the war, are described also in Hanfried Schlephake, *op. cit.,* while the establishment of the training and test facility at Lipetz, Russia is in John W. Wheeler-Bennett, *op. cit.*

38. Martin Gilbert, *Winston S. Churchill: The Prophet of Truth, 1922-1939* (Boston: Houghton Mifflin Company, 1977), pp. 627-28.

vided training of pilots and technicians and the development of designs for combat aviation. Sports flying and gliding kept interest in air matters alive amongst the German population and provided other facilities for training pilots and aircrews. Branches of German aircraft companies abroad permitted the development and testing of new aircraft designs. Soviet cooperation permitted the testing of prototype aircraft and the development of combat tactics hidden from enquiring eyes. All of these before the Nazis ever came to power, and in deliberate violation of the Treaty of Versailles. The German Air Force would come into being well before Adolph Hitler would bestow upon it the title of Reichsluftwaffe in March 1935. Civilian flying schools that concealed military training facilities existed before that event and the first fighter squadron came out of those so-called publicity squadrons *(Reklamestaffein)* used first to advertise aviation and then, under the same designation, as army cooperation squadrons. No. 132 fighter squadron was established at Dubertiz outside Berlin in April 1934. Seventeen squadrons and two auxiliary bomber groups had been established by the end of April 1934. Between March 1935 and August 1935, the German Air Force grew from sixteen air force and naval squadrons to a total of forty-eight squadrons: an establishment organized to absorb some 4,000 aircraft to be supplied by the German aircraft industry.[39]

The development of the German Army during the Weimar period should have been no less alarming. Crucial to this development was the cooperation between Germany and the Soviet Union. Aside from the German air force facility at Lipezk, was the operation of the secret tank training school at Kazan and the poison gas school at Saratov on the Volga. The first German officers to undergo training in Russia, arrived there in 1922. Russian officers came to Germany for training in general staff work while German aircraft took part in the maneuvers of Russian troops to develop the tactics of air-ground cooperation. German officers were attached to Russian units in the field and high-ranking German army officers took part in Russian army maneuvers. At home in Germany, the foundation of the World War II German Army was laid on the basis of the 12-year volunteers, insisted upon by the authors of the Treaty of Versailles. Evasions of the Treaty limits on manpower and the manufacture of weapons and the development of new weapons in German firms abroad, provided the framework for expansion and the industrial capacity with which the Nazis forged a great Army.[40] While

39. Hanfried Schlephake, *op. cit.*, pp. 32-34.

40. Particularly useful in respect to Soviet-German cooperation in the rebuilding of the German Army is F. L. Carsten, "The Reichswehr and the Red Army, 1920-1933," *The Journal of the Royal United Service Institution* (London), Vol. CVIII, No. 631 (August 1963), pp. 248-55. The work of Bernice A. Carroll, "Germany Disarmed and Rearming, 1925-1935," reported on at the annual convention of the American Historical Association, in San Francisco, December 1965, later published in a periodical

much has been made of the great inflation in Germany from 1923 to 1925, following the French occupation of the Ruhr, in promoting the rise of National Socialism,[41] it was in that period that Krupps acquired a controlling interest in Bofors, the great Swedish armaments firm. By December 1925, Krupps held six million out of the 19 million shares of the firm, an investment of considerable hard cash, derived in part from a sizeable government grant to Rheinmetall-Borsig, a firm associated with Krupps.[42] It is presumed that some of the design and development of heavy artillery, antiaircraft guns and tanks was done by Krupps' specialists working in Bofors in Sweden.[43]

The German Navy's defiance of the Allies did not wait upon the conclusion of the Treaties ending the Great War. The Treaty of Versailles was signed by Germany on 28 June 1919. Seven days before that event the officers and men of the German High Seas Fleet, carrying out orders from the Internment Force Commander, Vice-Admiral Ludwig von Reuter, scuttled or drove aground in Scapa Flow the ships of the High Seas Fleet that had been interned in that anchorage. One officer and eight ratings died in the enterprise, preparations for which had been laid on by the order to scuttle *(Der Versenkungsbefehl)* issued in 17 June 1919.[44] Eleven battleships, five battle cruisers, eight light cruisers, and scores of torpedo boats were thereby left to the salvers, the wreckers and the sea off the Isle of Hoy.

Under the Naval provisions of the Treaty of Versailles, Germany was permitted to keep no more than ten battleships. These were all to be of the pre-*Dreadnought* class built before 1908 and not to be replaced before they were twenty years old. Their replacements could not exceed 10,000 metric tons in displacement. Germany could retain only six light cruisers which could not be replaced until they were twenty years old, and replacements could not exceed 6,000 metric tons in displacement. Destroyers were limited to twelve in number and their replacements might not exceed 800 metric tons displacement.[45]

---

concerned with research on peace, contains some very useful documentary references on German weapons production and army matters for the period covered.

41. See for example, Louis L. Snyder, *Basic History of Modern Germany* (Princeton, N.J.: D. Van Nostrand Company, Inc., 1957), pp. 82-83; Dr. Kurt Zentner, *Illustrierte Geschichte Des Dritten Reiches* (Munchen: Sudwest Verlag, 1965), pp. 84-85; and, S. William Halperin, *Germany Tried Democracy* (New York: Thomas Y. Crowell Company, 1946), pp. 252-60.

42. John W. Wheeler-Bennett, *op. cit.*, p. 146.

43. The 8.8 cm. Flak (Fliegabwehrkanon) was produced for troop service in 1934, having gone through the design and development stage, obviously, before its serial production. It appears to have been a Krupps design. See Rudolph Lusar, *Die deutschen Waffen und Geheimwaffen des 2. Weltkrieges* (Munchen: J. F. Lehmanns Verlag, 1962), pp. 178-79; and, *Handbook on German Military Forces* TM-E 30-451, U.S. War Department, 15 March 1945, pp. VII-42-3.

44. Friederich Ruge, *Scapa Flow 1919; Das Ende der deutschen Flotte* (Oldenburg und Hamburg: Gerhard Stalling Verlag, 1969). An English edition appears as Friederich Ruge, *Scapa Flow 1919* (London: Ian Allen, 1973). Both contain copies of documents related to the decision to scuttle.

45. A review of the condition of the German Fleet in 1919 is given along with Treaty Limitations

Suspicion that the German government might be evading the naval provisions of the Treaty were expressed openly at various times. For example, it was considered that the cost of its six *Mowe*-class destroyers, of 800 tons each (1926), was "extraordinarily high, working out at 215 pounds sterling per ton."[46]

In February 1929, Winston Churchill brought before the British Cabinet an "emergency" matter concerning revelations about German construction of a new 10,000 ton vessel of advanced design that would make the then projected, British 8-inch gun cruisers obsolete before they were even constructed.[47] There was no naval response made by Britain to what was to be the *Deutschland*-class of "pocket battleships" and British merchant shipping would pay the price accordingly in the course of the war that was to come.[48]

The one pointed prohibition of the naval articles of the Treaty of Versailles was that against submarines: the German Navy was permitted none. It is an irony that while the German Navy did not violate that provision of the Treaty, it was in respect to submarines that the most interesting clandestine development went forward, a development that would enable Hitler, when he came to power, the capability for the rapid revival of the German submarine force.

Eight German submarines, including two mine-laying boats, were transferred to the Imperial Japanese Navy, as war booty, under the terms of the Armistice. They were to be used only for experiments and were not to enter on commission.[49] A number of classes of Japanese submarines that saw service in World War II were either based on the design of the German boats or were developments of them.[50] Through an arrangement with the Germania and the Vulkan shipyards in Germany, and the Kawasaki shipyards in Japan, the Japanese navy had constructed a cruiser U-boat under the supervision of

---

on the Fleet, in *Jane's Fighting Ships, 1919* (London: Sampson, Low and Marston, 1919), pp. 515f, and in *Taschenbuch der Kriegsflotten, 1922* (Munchen: J. F. Lehmanns Verlag, 1922), pp. 6f. German ships retained in commission are listed in the latter work.

46. *Jane's Fighting Ships, 1931* (London: Sampson, Low and Marston, 1931), p. 233.

47. Martin Gilbert, *Winston S. Churchill: The Prophet of Truth, 1922-1939,* p. 312.

48. *Graf Spee* (Hans Langstraff, commanding) sank or captured 9 British merchant ships (before finally brought to heel by *Exeter, Achilles* and *Ajax,* an eight-inch gun cruiser and two six-inch gun cruisers, in the Battle of the River Plate, December 13, 1939): a total of 50,089 tons of shipping plus cargoes. See Geoffrey Bennett, *Battle of the River Plate* (Shepperton, Surrey: Ian Allen Ltd., 1972). Commodore Harwood's force (flag in Ajax) was outgunned and out-ranged by *Graf Spee: Graf Spee's* eleven-inch guns delivered a broadside weighing 4,164 lbs. to a range of 46,500 yards; *Exeter's* eight-inch guns could reach 29,200 yards while the six-inch guns of *Ajax* and *Achilles* reach 25,000 yards. Total weight of main armament broadside of Commodore Harwood's force was 3,130 lbs. *Graf Spee* had 4-inch armored belt and 5-inch armor on turrets; *Exeter* (the 8-inch gun cruiser) had 2-inch armor and 1 1/2 to two inch on her turrets. *Achilles* had 2-4 inch belt armor and 1-inch on turrets.

49. *Jane's Fighting Ships, 1919,* p. 274; and *Taschenbuch der Kriegsflotten, 1922,* pp. 98-99. The latter work suggests only seven boats were transferred to Japan and that they were used for research and for propaganda work.

50. Anthony J. Watts, *Japanese Warships of World War II* (Garden City, N.Y.: Doubleday & Co., 1973), pp. 161f.

German submarine builders. This and subsequent Japanese submarines built to German design, furnished the opportunity for the German navy to develop and test German submarine designs.[51] Admiral Behnke, set up through the Germania, Weser and Vulkan shipyards (Hamburg-Stettin), a German submarine construction office as a Dutch firm, Ingeieurskantoor voor Sheepsbouw (I.v.S.) in the Hague, Holland. This Dutch firm was under the direction of a German naval captain and employed some 30 submarine technicians. The purpose of the firm was to undertake the development of submarines and to maintain the technical expertise of German submarine builders: to lay the foundation for a future German submarine service. The first two boats were laid down for Turkey in 1925 at the Fijenoord Shipyards in Rotterdam. Other enterprises and projects of a similar nature were undertaken in Finland, Sweden and Spain, and for the same purpose, with the participation of German managers and technicians. U-boats built for the Finnish navy in the Vulkan yards at Turku, Abo, became the prototype for the German boats U-1 through U-24. Boats built for foreign governments in yards outside Germany became not only the means for continuing development of German submarines but also lent the opportunity for the training of German submarine crews. Finally, between 1933 and 1935, the German firm Igewit constructed, at its work in Kiel, a warehouse where were collected the parts of twelve submarines for later fabrication, and a building way for construction of six submarines at a time.

Britain Faces German Rearmament

On 16 March 1935, military conscription was resumed in Germany. On 18 June 1935, the Anglo-German Naval Treaty was signed. The Treaty granted Germany parity in submarine tonnage with Great Britain. The German government agreed, however, to limit its submarine tonnage to 45 percent of British submarine tonnage, unless, in the opinion of the *German* government, a higher tonnage seemed necessary.[52]

Three and one-half months after the German government's resumption of conscription, which was part of the renunciation of the military limitations of the Treaty of Versailles, and ten days after the signing of the Anglo-German Naval Treaty, the first post-war German submarine was commissioned. By 1 October 1935, twelve submarines were in commission, fully

51. Schlussler, *Der Kampf der Marine gegen Versailles, 1919-1935*, p. 38. See also, *Notes by Admiral Assmann, 1943 or later: Extent of and Reason for German U-boat Construction . . .*, Document 854-D in *International Military Tribunal*, Vol. 35 (Washington, D.C., U.S.G.P.O., 1949), p. 554f.

52. Cmd 4593, Treaty Series No. 22 (H.M.S.O., 1935) in *State Papers*, Vol. XXIV, as cited in Captain S. W. Roskill, D.S.C., Royal Navy, *The War at Sea*, Vol. I: *The Defense* in *History of the Second World War United Kingdom Military Series* (London: H.M.S.O., 1954), p. 52.

manned and operational, entering service at the rate of one every eight days. By 7 March 1936, when the German Army marched into the Rhineland, eighteen submarines were in service. Seventeen of these were available for deployment along the French coast as far as the Gironde.[53]

Within less than a year, Germany had acquired only twelve fewer submarines than Britain had commissioned from 1920 until 1935.[54] Britain had of course embraced the Root Resolution at the Washington Naval Disarmament Conference which limited submarine attacks to those made on enemy warships. The British submarine arm was further hamstrung in the London Naval Treaty of 1930: it was the British Government's view that submarines ought not—and therefore would not—be used against merchant shipping.[55]

It is hardly remarkable that Germany should have chafed under the military restrictions imposed by the Treaty of Versailles. It is even less remarkable that successive pre-Nazi German governments should have evaded those restrictions wherever possible. It was even within the realm of reasonable statesmanship for England to have turned a blind eye toward German violations of the Treaty in the interest of bringing Germany back into the family of nations. Neither reasonable nor statesmanlike, however, was the view that clandestine German rearmament and Soviet-German cooperation in military affairs did not impinge on British defense policies.

German rearmament, starting almost as soon as the guns had fallen silent on the Western Front, did not begin to alarm Britain until the Nazis had been in power for three years. Only then did it begin to dawn on them that perhaps, what Germany had been doing from the very start was not merely rearming, but preparing for war. Who could really believe, after the fearful carnage of the Kaiser's war, that any European nation would willingly set its feet on the path to another war? Here is Germany, defeated, dismembered, almost a tributary to the Allies, spending money to prepare for a war to come! Here is Great Britain, victorious, justifiably imperious, mistress of its own destiny, parsimonious on the one thing without which the Empire would surely fail: the capability to wage a successful continental war. And it was all terribly rational.

The Economy of Defense Expenditure: The "Ten-Year Rule"

Clearly it could not be expected that the Royal Navy, Royal Air Force and the Army could justifiably be maintained at war strength when there was

53. Schlussler, *op. cit.*, p. 38. German U-Boat construction is reviewed in Erich Groner, *Die Schiffe der Deutschen Kriegsmarine und Luftwaffe, 1936-45* (Munchen: J.F. Lehmanns Verlag, 1954).

54. One may see the extent of British submarine construction in *Jane's Fighting Ships, 1939*, pp. 73-78.

55. Alistair Mars, *British Submarines at War, 1939-1945* (London: William Kimber, 1971), pp. 19-20.

no war. On 11 August 1919, the Cabinet Committee on Finance of the British Government decided that the Armed Services should proceed (in preparing their annual estimates) on the assumption that "no great war is to be anticipated for ten years." This "Ten-Year Rule" was apparently adopted by the War Cabinet on 15 August 1919. It was never intended that the "rule" would apply year by year without much serious examination. It was, however, a convenient and optimistic statement by which to guide defense expenditures at a time when economy in government appeared the certain route to general prosperity. Indeed, the Air Expansion for Home Defense program, first put forth in 1923, was postponed year after year. As late as 1929, under the assumption that there would be no major war for ten years, this program was further put off until 1938. As it turned out, it would be some months after war broke out that Fighter Command would have available 50 squadrons for Home Defence.[56]

The Royal Navy, which had 57 modern line-of-battle-ships at the close of the World War, gave up all but fifteen such ships as a consequence of the Washington Naval Conference. It was with those ships that Britain would enter the Second World War.[57] One of those fifteen, battle cruiser *Hood* would pay the penalty for its age and uncorrected defects: south of the Denmark Strait, in May 1941, it blew up under the fifth salvo from *Bismarck. Repulse,* a second battle cruiser and one of the fifteen, would pay a similar penalty off Kuantan, Malaya, 10 December 1941.[58]

The "ten-year rule" was not supposed to be an iron-clad principle against which all defense expenditures were to be judged. It was supposed to be an assumption re-examined annually in the light of the world situation prelimiary to setting British defense estimates. The "ten-year rule" became for British military and strategic policy what appeasement was for British foreign policy: the means to avoid the disruption of "business as usual." The consequences were the deterioration of Britain's strategic position abroad and of

56. The origin and fate of the "Ten-Year Rule" are discussed in Martin Gilbert, *Winston S. Churchill: The Prophet of Truth, 1922-1939*, pp. 68-69, 289-92; see also Stephen Roskill, *Hankey: Man of Secrets,* Vol. II: *1919-1931* (London: Collins, 1972), pp. 107f. For a useful short piece see Stephen Roskill "The Ten Year Rule—The Historical Facts," *RUSI, Journal of the Royal United Services Institute for Defense Studies,* Vol. 117, No. 1 (March 1972), pp. 69-71.

57. Comparative strengths of the various fleets at the outbreak of war are given in "Strength of the Fleets of the Rival Powers: Comparative Naval Strengths of the Two Great Warring Alliances," *New York Times,* 6 August 1914, p. 7; see also, *The Naval Annual, 1913* (Portsmouth: J. Griffin and Co., 1913); post-war strengths are in *Jane's Fighting Ships, 1919* (London: Sampson, Low and Marston, 1919); and, comparisons of pre-war, post-war, and post-Washington Naval Treaty strengths are given in *Weyers Taschenbuch der Kriegsflotten XX, Jahrgang 1922* (Munchen: J. F. Lehmanns Verlag, 1922).

58. Plans had been drawn for a major re-fit of *Hood* to follow that of *Renown's* in 1939. It was intended to increase greatly the deck armor, a measure that might have prevented the disaster that took place when *Bismarck's* shells penetrated the lightly armored deck and detonated in 4-inch magazine. See, *Warships in Profile,* Vol. II (Garden City, N.Y.: Doubleday and Company, 1973), pp. 145f. It was, of course, impossible in 1939, to lay-up *Hood* for its planned re-fit.

the armed services and those industries upon which they depended at home. Government decisions that should have, in all prudence, been based on strategic imperatives and military realities, were based instead on financial and political arguments of only transient merit.[59]

The Royal Air Force, those few to whom so many would owe so much in 1940, barely survived the immediate post-war defense policy. Only astute arguments by such champions of air power as Air Chief Marshall Sir Hugh Trenchard preserved the establishment at all. In November 1918, the Royal Air Force had 293,532 officers and men with 22,000 aircraft and 675 airfields and stations. By 1919 there were only 31,500 officers and men, with 371 aircraft in twelve squadrons, a mere skeleton of the 387 operational and training squadrons in existence at the close of the war.[60]

The arguments for the continued existence of the Royal Air Force turned less on the strategic value of the Air Force to Britain's defense, than upon the economies that could be effected by employing aircraft for policing the empire in place of masses of infantry and cavalry.[61] And indeed, from Waziristan to Mesopotamia, from Somaliland to Cyprus, and Palestine to the Gulf, the Royal Air Force proved to be a cheap substitute for forces on the ground.[62]

The very economy that air operations permitted over ground operations in imperial policing, and which justified to a large extent the continued viability of the Royal Air Force between the two wars, would raise a fatal flaw for the defense of Singapore. That flaw was reinforced by the early disbelief in a war with Japan. Even Winston Churchill would urge on the Prime Minister, Stanley Baldwin, in 1924, that: "The only way it would be worth our while to fight with Japan would be to prevent an invasion of Australia, and that, I am certain will never happen in any period, even the most remote, which we or our children need foresee." That opinion stood in bold contrast to Churchill's reasoned judgment of Germany as a country whose "soul smoulders with dreams of a war of liberation or revenge."[63]

59. Brian Bond, "Business as Usual . . .?" cites Professor N. H. Gibbs, *Grand Strategy, Volume I* (London: H.M.S.O., 1976) to the effect that, "The thread of appeasement runs throughout British policy in the inter-war years . . .:" in *RUSI, Journal of the Royal United Services Institute for Defense Studies,* Vol. 122, No. 1 (March 1977), pp. 64-65.

60. War strength and post-war strength returns are in Derek Wood and Derek Dempster, *The Narrow Margin: The Battle of Britain and the Rise of Air Power, 1930-40* (London: Hutchinson, 1961), p. 65. But see also, H. A. Jones, "The Birth of the Royal Air Force," *The Journal of the Royal United Services Institution,* Vol. LXXXIII, No. 529 (Feb. 1930), pp. 1-10.

61. See Andrew Boyle, *Trenchard: Man of Vision* (London: Collins, 1962) for the vicissitude of the R.A.F. in the immediate post-war years. For a description of the Royal Air Force's role in imperial policing, see Air Commodore, C. F. A. Portal, "Air Force Co-Operation in Policing the Empire," *The Journal of the Royal United Services Institution,* Coronation Number, Vol. LXXXII, No. 526 (May 1939), pp. 343-58.

62. See for example, Group-Captain A. G. R. Garrod, R.A.F., "Recent Operations in Kurdistan," *The Journal of the Royal United Service Institution,* Vol. LXXVIII, No. 510 (May 1933), pp. 231-53.

63. Martin Gilbert, *Winston S. Churchill: The Prophet of Truth, 1922-1939,* pp. 76 and 51.

Singapore's fate was sealed by the infelicitous conclusion that aeroplanes and landing fields were cheaper to erect than fortifications and less costly to maintain than ground forces. Singapore would not be held because Malaya could not be defended. Malaya could not be defended because the economy dictated that the landing fields be located close to the coast where they could not be protected from amphibious attack. No one save, perhaps, the Japanese, would, until very late, suppose that Japan might have access to airfields in southern Indo-China. And as it turned out, when the attack on Malaya came the aeroplanes that were so cheap were more urgently required elsewhere. Both the Admiralty and the War Office had maintained that "Japan would be unlikely to give any warning of attack and might well strike when Britain was engaged elsewhere."[64] They were right.

Who in 1924 could imagine a France so helpless after a German invasion that she could not deny the Japanese the use of an airfield at Saigon within easy bombing range of the air bases in Malaya and Singapore? If one could not credit the revival of German military power—the preparations for war—then surely one could not imagine a defeated France. Only the British Army and the Royal Air Force and the Royal Navy, apparently, could visualize a day when all those aeroplanes around which the defense of Singapore was organized would be so urgently required elsewhere.

British Preparation: The Imponderability of Continental War

Fortunately for both England and the United States, the Royal Air Force could sustain itself in the inter-war years chiefly on its merit as a cheap instrument of military power. The British Army had no such good fortune. In 1919, the War Cabinet had decided that "no expeditionary force will be required." Organization, equipment and training for any European war were simply ruled out. Mr. Duff Cooper, Financial Secretary to the War Office in 1933, said: "The British Army is not designed for Continental wars. The purpose of the British Army is to maintain order in the British Empire only." And, later: "The Army is not likely to be used for a big war in Europe for many years to come." The following year, Mr. Duff Cooper became Secretary of State for War.[65]

Initially the Army was to have sufficient infantry battalions for five divisions. The Army Council concluded that there should be a Tank Corps of four battalions, of which, following demobilization in 1919, two had yet to be raised.[66]

64. Major-General S. Woodburn Kirby, *The War Against Japan,* Vol. I: *The Loss of Singapore* (London: H.M.S.O., 1967), pp. 1-13.

65. *The Ironside Diaries, 1937-1940* (London: Constable, 1962), pp. 20-21.

66. Captain B. H. Liddell Hart, *The Tanks: The History of the Royal Tank Regiment and Its Predecessors—Heavy Machine Gun Corps, Tank Corps and Royal Tank Corps, 1914-1945,* Vol. I: *1914-1939* (London: Cassell, 1959), pp. 201-3.

Some would argue quite early, as did the *Army and Navy Gazette* in March 1920, that:

> The new army is to be precisely what the Expeditionary Force was, a symbol, if a splendid one, that this country will not prepare for war on land. The theory, which is held by us, was one of the contributing causes of the Great War, is put together again. That theory was that England could maintain her neutrality by means of her Fleet, and if she could not, her fleet would form a rampart strong enough for her to organize armies behind it. But dangerous to security as the theory was before 1914, it is more so now. In the first place Germany in the past had no motive for breaking the peace but greed. In the future to greed will be added revenge and an overmastering desire to restore her lost prestige. In the second place for the relatively stable Europe and stagnant middle east of the past there is the devastated, revolutionary, and chaotic Europe and middle east of the present, with the possibility of tremendous upheavals looming up on the far horizons. Apparently the Government assumes that the garrisons on the Rhine, in Constantinople, Egypt, northwest Persia are temporary and that the garrisons in Palestine and Mesopotamia can be "enormously reduced" if those territories "are not to be anything but a burden to the British treasury." Such optimism is on all fours with our misplaced optimism before the war.[67]

An oft-spoken criticism of the British Army, after Dunkirk and Narvik, was that it had prepared for the last war: not the one they were called on to fight in 1939. That was sheer hyperbole. Within the narrow constraints of the British Treasury, constraints laid down by successive British Governments, the Army in France in 1940 actually did far more than could reasonably have been expected. The problem was that the Army could hardly apply the lessons of the Great War without the British Government's having done so *first*. And the one lesson of the Great War beyond all others was that Britain had not been prepared. Neither the scale nor magnitude of the demands that would be made on the British Army in 1914 and after had been anticipated. Between the British declaration of war on 4 August 1914 and 20 August, four divisions, organized into I and II Corps plus the Cavalry Division, and four squadrons of the Royal Flying Corps were moved to France. They were deployed where they would engage German forces moving unexpectedly around the flank of the French Fifth Army of General Lanrezac, in the battles of Mons and Le Cateau. Altogether, the British Expeditionary Force was able to bring to bear 110,000 men within 19 days after the outbreak of war.[68] Measured against the deployed strength of the five French

67. Cited in "Professional Notes," *U.S. Naval Institute Proceedings*, Vol. 46, No. 5 (Whole No. 207), May 1920, p. 785.

68. The movement of the B.E.F. to France and its engagement at Mons and Le Cateau is described

Armies the British contribution was nominal and would be treated as such by the French. The consequence of this was that the overall direction of strategy for the war in France would be dominated by French views.[69] The same problem would almost immediately assert itself in 1939 with the movement to France of the British Expeditionary Force: "The relegation of the B.E.F. to the role of a unit in a French formation was a disastrous step. . . . Their [the French] claim to the direction of the war on land was indeed overwhelming. Their army was infinitely larger than ours and it was in France that our forces were to be based."[70]

In 1917, tying the British Army to French strategic policy—despite the strong objection of British General Headquarters to that policy—tied Britain to the disastrous Nivelle offensive. Repeating the error in 1939 led to another catastrophe which could be traced directly to the British Government's policy of unpreparedness for a continental war. The decision made by the War Cabinet in 1919 "that no expeditionary force will be required" was not rescinded until March 1939. At that time—four months before the outbreak of war—it was decided that on the outbreak of war two divisions would be sent to France. Not eleven months before that decision, the General Officer Commanding the Eastern Command in England, wrote: "We are in no state to go to war. . . . I can see the Field Army reaching more and more into the far distance. There are no men and there is no money for equipment and there is no will amongst the Cabinet Ministers to want an Army." This view was voiced four days after the Czech Army began its mobilization and one day after Hitler ordered that an attack be prepared on Czechoslovakia.[71] War was then fifteen months away.

The Unlearned Lesson of the Great War

If the Great War had taught any lesson it was the level of exertion that Britain and France had been forced to make just to hold the German Army in

---

in Sir James E. Edmonds, *Military Operations: France and Belgium, 1914* in *History of the Great War* (London: Macmillan and Company, 1933), pp. 29f. Composition of the B.E.F. is in Major-General Sir Edward Spears, *Liaison 1914* (New York: Stein and Day, 1968), Appendix II.

69. Edmonds, *op. cit.*, p. 30:

> . . . it was settled that the Expeditionary Force should proceed to the zone selected in peacetime by the French Staff . . .; during the conference prior to the Nivelle Offensive, held in London in January 1917, and at the later Calais Conference just before the British attack on Arras, the French insisted on what amounted to full operational control of the B.E.F. The War Cabinet in London held to the belief that the French ought to be deferred to in such matters because 'We were fighting in France,' and 'Because the French Army was the largest force.'

Major-General Sir Edward Spears, *Prelude to Victory* (London: Jonathan Cape, 1939) describes the Allied meetings prior to the Nivelle Offensive. He was present as a liaison officer during the meetings.

70. Major-General Sir Edward Spears, *Assignment to Catastrophe*, Vol. I: *Prelude to Dunkirk, July 1939-May 1940* (New York: A. A. Wyn, Inc., 1954), p. 34.

71. 24 May 1938, extract from diary in *The Ironside Diaries, 1937-1940*, p. 57.

check—to prevent the conquest of France. On 11 November 1919, the British Army had 4.5 million men in uniform of which just under 2 million were in the line in France. There were five British Armies in France. They comprised 61 infantry divisions and 3 cavalry divisions. Amongst those were five Australian, four Canadian and one New Zealand divisions.[72] These armies did not include the nearly one million troops fighting in Mesopotamia, Salonika and Italy, or the garrisons in Egypt and India.

The cost in killed, wounded, and missing in action had been 2,706,154 on the Western Front alone of which nearly a million had been killed.[73] From whence sprang the illusion that somehow another war would be different; would be less exacting for Britain, when the fullest exertions of France and Britain had barely sufficed to attain a stalemate on the Western Front? This stalemate was broken only by the intercession of an American Expeditionary Force of almost 2 million men. As the commander of the 3rd British Division of the new B.E.F. in 1939 would reflect in his memoirs: "How any politician could imagine that, in a world war, Britain could avoid sending her Army to fight alongside the French passes all understanding."[74]

But indeed that was the view that prevailed: to leave the British Expeditionary Force unprepared for war in 1939. The author of the "Gold Medal Essay (Military), 1936," for the *Journal of the Royal United Service Institution,* argued that any future Field Force "must be a small one, not only in peace but also in war. . . . In war *we could not afford again* to be the mainstay of an alliance at sea, in the air, and in the economic sphere, while at the same time maintaining huge armies in the field." He proposed a Field Force of one light division, two medium tank divisions, and two infantry divisions.[75] Even an expeditionary force of that size was beyond the capability of the British Army. In March 1938, the British Army could only put into the field two divisions. And they were short of modern artillery, lacking 2-inch mortars and divisional anti-tank weapons, with no Bren-gun carriers, and desperately short of armored fighting vehicles. There were no armored divisions available, nor would one be ready to go to France until May 1940. Parcels of the 1st Armoured Division arrived in Calais, after German armor had broken through to the Coast at Abbéville, on May 20, and after German Panzer

72. John Terraine, *Ordeal of Victory* (Philadelphia: J. B. Lippincott Company, 1963), p. xvii.

73. British casualties are in Winston S. Churchill, *The World Crisis* (New York: Charles Scribner's Sons, 1931), Appendix, Table I. And, in Arthur Banks, *A Military Atlas of the First World War* (London: Heinemann Educational Books, 1975), rear cover.

74. *The Memoirs of Field-Marshall the Viscount Montgomery of Alamein* (Cleveland, Ohio: The World Publishing Company, 1958), p. 46.

75. Wing Commander J. C. Slessor, Royal Air Force, "Gold Medal Essay (Military), 1936," *The Journal of the Royal United Service Institution,* Vol. LXXXII, No. 527 (August, 1937), pp. 463-84. It is notable that the author as Marshall of the Royal Air Force, and Vice President of the Institute for Strategic Studies (London) would be one of the principal English thinkers on Strategic Nuclear Deterrence. See his *Command and Control of Allied Nuclear Forces: A British View,* Adelphi Paper No. 22, August 1965.

divisions had begun the envelopment of the B.E.F. and the French Group of Armies of the North, from positions on the Somme.

It was not until after the final conquest of Czechoslovakia on 15 March 1939 that it was decided to send four divisions to France instead of only two.[76]

The minority view about the size of the expeditionary force for France asserted that France had to be defended at all costs: France was now the outpost zone of the western democracies, and should she be defeated then Britain would have to become that outpost.

> *If it is our interest to be allied to France in a war against Germany, it is our necessity to support her sufficiently to ensure victory.* That support may or may not involve the use of all our strength on land, sea, or in the air, but if the employment of our whole military strength on the continent is needed to win—it was last time—then that liability must be accepted and implemented. First things must come first and the first thing is to win and not quibble as to whether our action harmonizes or not with 'an historic theory.'[77]

The proponents of the optimistic view of a continental war prevailed. Their view was the foster-child of those who believed war unlikely, and those who thought war either too terrible for contemplation or too expensive for preparation. Thus in 1933, the Chief of the Imperial General Staff, Field Marshall Sir Archibald Montgomery-Massingbird said: "There are certain critics in the press who say we should organize the Army again for a War in Europe, but I will venture to say that the Army is not likely to be used for a big war in Europe for many years to come."[78] In July 1937, remarking on the deficiencies in the British armed forces, Sir Thomas Inskip, Minister for Coordination of Defense, 1936-1939, said that the deficiences could not be made up before 1940, but that would do because the "Germans would have to scrap an enormous number of their tanks which offer no protection against armour-piercing bullets. . . . Thus although in quantity we are far behind our quality is second to none."[79]

That oft-repeated view was echoed before Parliament by the Secretary of State (Hore-Belisha) in October 1939, when he said that the Army sent to

76. Details of the state of equipment of the Field Force are given in *The Ironside Diaries*, pp. 53-54; the decision to provide four instead of two division for France is reported in Major L. F. Ellis, *The War in France and Flanders, 1939-1940* in *History of the Second World War United Kingdom Military Series* (London: H.M.S.O., 1953), pp. 1-14. Deployment of elements of the 1st Armoured Division to France is described on page 153 and following.

77. Colonel R. H. Beadon, "Defense and Defeat," *The Journal of the Royal United Service Institution*, Vol. LXXXIII, No. 529 (February 1938), pp. 58-68.

78. Captain B. H. Liddell Hart, *The Tanks*, pp. 321-22.

79. Nigel Nicolson (ed.), *Harold Nicolson: Diaries and Letters, 1930-39* (London: Collins, 1966), p. 303. Field Marshall Montgomery reports in his *Memoirs* (p. 47) that his division, the 3rd, was furnished with some one-pounder anti-tank guns, "hurriedly bought" from the French and mounted on little hand carts, with a few distributed to each infantry battalion. That was in October 1939.

France, was equipped "in the finest possible manner which could not be excelled. Our Army is as well if not better equipped than any similar army."[80]

But then the Chancellor of the Exchequer, Sir John Simon, not ten months before, within a month of Munich, had argued against a British Army for France, because, "Germany was extremely unlikely to violate the neutrality of Belgium," and because the Maginot Line "was the strongest system of fortifications that had ever been constructed."[81] Such optimism came from a man who had been in the British Government when the Germans had violated Belgian neutrality in 1914. Why the Germans should behave differently in a new war was not made clear. Was there something in the Nazi manner or style that lent credence to the belief that Germany under its new order would behave less ruthlessly than it had under a far less barbarous regime? The nature of the Nazi regime had not been concealed from anyone who had access to a metropolitan or even lesser newspaper of the day.

The Nazi Regime: Consolidation of Intent

Hitler was named Chancellor on 30 January 1933. On the 3rd of February, the new Chancellor, in a secret address to commanders of the Reichswehr, spoke of his plans for restoring German military power and gaining living room for Germany in the East.[82] New elections were called for 5 March 1933; the election campaign concluded with the burning of the Reichstag building which in turn led to suspension of the constitutional guarantees of free speech and freedom of the press. The election gave the National Socialist German Workers Party a plurality in the Reichstag and on 23 March 1933, the Reichstag and Reichsrat passed the Enabling Act *(Ermachtigungsgesetz)* which permitted the prohibition or dissolution of all political parties save the National Socialist.

On the 13th of April, in the frontier province of Grenzemark, a statue was unveiled near the town of Scheidermuehl. The statue bore the inscription: "Never forget, Germans of what blind hatred had robbed you. Bide the hour which will expiate the shame of this bleeding frontier." There followed a list of the nearby towns in Polish territory which awaited liberation. Included thereon was the name of the Free City of Danzig. The Provincial Governor, in his dedication address spoke of a national awakening "in the form of an eruption in the spirit of the German people toward the German East." He continued:

80. Field Marshall Montgomery, *Memoirs,* p. 47.
81. Martin Gilbert, *Winston S. Churchill: The Prophet of Truth,* p. 1014.
82. "Zeittafel," in Dr. Kurt Zentner, *Illustrierte Geschichte des Dritten Reiches,* "Zeittafel," pp. 14-15.

"But, to restore Germans to German soil and to the lap of Mother Germany the whole German nation is needed."[83]

Not a fortnight before, on the 1st of April, the new government declared an economic boycott against all Jewish businesses in Germany. The "Cold Pogrom" as it was called, clearly signalled to German Jews the process of extermination which "will not be by an outbreak of mob violence . . . but by cold Prussian discipline and precision." The pogrom was seen to affect over 3 million people who were all or part Jewish.[84] During the last week of March, all Jews in public offices had been removed from their posts and on 13 April 1933, a law was promulgated barring all Jewish persons from holding office at the national, local, and municipal level. In England, on the 5th of April, Sir Horace Rumbold, the British Ambassador to Berlin, reported to the Foreign Secretary, Sir John Simon, that: "Large concentration camps are being established in various parts of the country, one near Munich being sufficiently large to hold 5,000 prisoners."[85]

The following week, in the House of Commons, a number of members spoke out to protest the German government's actions against the Jewish community in Germany. Amongst those strong in their condemnation were Austen Chamberlain and Winston Churchill. The German government protested formally to the British government on what was considered an intrusion in German affairs. But the Nazi Party newspaper, *Die Volkische Beobachter,* took a much calmer view of the matter: there was nothing surprising in Sir Austen Chamberlain's "invective and those of other Francophiles and friends of the Jews," it was expected however that Prime Minister MacDonald will pursue "the English policy" and that the British Government "will not allow itself to be deflected from its policy of peace by those recrudescences of the past."[86]

There was certainly nothing that occurred in subsequent months that would have indicated to a foreign observer any moderation in the Nazi regime. The following year, between the 30th of June and the 3rd of July, when Hitler constituted himself the "Supreme Court of the Reich" and had executed the leadership of the SA *(Sturm Abteilung)* or storm troops, he was still only Chancellor of Germany. It was not until the 2nd of August following the death of President Paul von Hindenburg that he declared himself to be Reichpräsident as well as Chancellor. At least 70,000 Jews had fled Germany and tens of thousands of others were attempting to leave. Hereditary health courts had been established to determine which residents

83. "Monument Near Polish Border Bids Germans 'Bide Hour That Will Expiate' Lost Provinces," *The New York Times,* 16 April 1933, p. 21.

84. "3,000,000 in Reich Feel 'Cold Pogrom': Economic Ruination of Jews Hits 4 Times as Many Part Jewish or Linked by Marriage," *New York Times,* 16 April 1933, p. 21.

85. Martin Gilbert, *Winston S. Churchill, The Prophet of Truth,* p. 485.

86. "Reich Protests British Speeches," *New York Times,* 16 April 1933, p. 1.

in Germany ought to be sterilized in order to "banish from the German people all dangers of hereditary disease."[87] Other acts of equal enormity were reported regularly by the English, American, and French press, to the extent that they became commonplace. The enactment of the Nürnberg Decree in September 1935 could leave little doubt about the Nazi regime's concerted policy of anti-semitism.

Rationalizing the Nazi Regime

Withal, there was a certain optimism that furnished a counter-point to the horrors reported from Germany. A reviewer of Ernst Henri's book, *Hitler over Europe,* "declined to become excited over" what he dismissed as rhetoric condemning the new regime in Germany. "The case of Germany is rather more psychopathic than political," said the reviewer of what was described as a "panicky volume."[88] Germany's economic circumstances and accompanying food shortages were taken to place the Nazis in an untenable position.[89]

Dr. Nicholas Murray Butler, Chairman of the Carnegie Endowment for International Peace—returning to New York on a North German Lloyd liner, the *Bremen*—worried much about a new arms race but little about Nazism:

> The vast membership of the Catholic and Lutheran Churches [in Germany] will certainly not permit themselves to be permanently suppressed or oppressed by any government. The intellectual leaders who are the successors of those who made Germany great . . . cannot and will not be permanently persecuted or oppressed. Moreover, there is a large body of convinced liberal opinion which . . . cannot be permanently neglected or overridden. What may probably be looked for is an early collapse of Hitlerism. . . . Historic Germany is finding ways to come to consciousness and to reassert itself underneath and against the amazing anti-German Nazi regime.

He went on to say that "despite what one reads in the press from time to time, I do not recall having heard the word 'war' or the possibility of war mentioned by any responsible person. . . . There is not a man in Germany, west of the river Elbe who would go to war."[90]

On 25 July 1934, Austrian Nazis seized the Vienna radio station and took the Austrian Cabinet prisoner in the Chancellor's Office. The Chan-

87. "Sterilization Law Covers Reich Aliens: Berlin Court Rules Foreigners, Resident or Transient, Are Subject to Act," *New York Times,* 25 July 1934, p. 7.

88. "A Violent Vision of Hitlerism Spreading Over Europe," *The New York Times Book Review,* 22 July 1934.

89. "Hitler is Menaced by Food Shortage; Curbs Profiteers," *New York Times,* 16 July 1934, p. 1; "Drought Confronts Hitler With A Perilous Choice," *ibid.,* 22 July 1934, p. 1.

90. "Dr. Butler Warns of New Arms Race: Found Great Aversion to War in Europe. However, He says on return from Peace Session: Predicts Nazi Collapse," *New York Times,* 17 July 1934, p. 1.

cellor, Engelbert Dollfuss, was assassinated. There seemed little doubt at the time, and even less later, that the Nazi Party in Germany was deeply implicated in the attempted *coup d'état.* On the night of the Chancellor's murder, the German News Service issued a report of the overthrow of the Austrian government. This report was made before it was known that the attempt had failed. Asserting that "Germans in Austria have risen against their tormentors. . . . Long ago National Socialism and Germanism became one in Austria. . . . The new government . . . must provide in German Austria once again a home for pan-German ideas." The news report went on to condemn those who would blame Germany for the unrest in Austria.[91]

Hitler was kept informed of the progress of events in Austria, both through the Nazi Party organization and the German Foreign Ministry. The failure of the *coup d'état,* the anxiety of Italy, and the concern expressed by the other European powers, led Berlin to pronounce the affair to be a "purely internal matter and no concern of the Reich."[92]

The crisis passed. Hitler had sought, prematurely as it turned out, to overset the balance of power in Europe and to act in defiance of the Peace Settlement of 1919 which had expressly forbidden German *anschluss* with Austria. He had then been in power eighteen months. The British government took the line that Austria was once again in control of its own affairs and that the Austrian Nazis had been effectively suppressed. Europe, which had held its breath in fear of war, now closed its eyes to what the Nazis were. In Germany, the newspapers declared that Hitler was the "Defender of Europe's Peace." And there was more truth to that then than might have been thought. What would become more and more apparent was that if war came, it would be to suit the Nazis and their leader. War would not come because the European democracies were outraged at the internal frightfulness of the Nazi regime. War would not come because the European democracies were repulsed by the brutal ruthlessness of Nazi foreign policy.[93] Those

91. "Coup Bulletin Put Suspicion on Reich: German Agency's Report Told of 'Overthrow' in Vienna on Night of Uprising: Failure Was Not Known: Habicht Appears to have Been Author—'People's' Revolt was Eulogized," *New York Times,* 31 July 1934, p. 2.

92. "Austria Nervous, Hangs Terrorist," *New York Times,* 25 July 1934, p. 1; "Austrian Nazis Kill Dollfuss, Revolt Fails; 147 Plotters Held; Italian Army, Navy, Planes Ready to Act," *ibid.,* 26 July 1934, p. 1; "Austrian Nazis Routed in Provinces; Vienna Quiet, but Heavily Guarded; Italy Ready, Does Not Expect to Act," *ibid.,* 28 July 1934, p. 1, "Savage Fighting in South Austria . . .," *ibid.,* 27 July 1934, p. 1. For German diplomatic documents demonstrating Hitler's knowledge of events in Austria prior to Dollfuss' assassination, see "Austria," in *Documents of German Foreign Policy, op, cit.,* and in particular, *Memorandum by the Minister to Austria,* Berlin, 10 February 1934, 6114/E454206-11. For post–*coup d'état* Berlin position see "Berlin Declares Hands Off Policy; Asserts Austrian Revolt is a Purely Internal Affair and no Concern of the Reich," *New York Times,* 26 July 1934, p. 1.

93. See "European Capitals Feel Crisis Is Past as Vienna Government Resumes Control"; "Uneasiness Wanes Among the British; War Believed Unlikely; *Evening Standard* Says Reich is the 'Dillinger' Among the States of Europe"; "French See Nazis Injured by Odium But Fear the Death of Dolfuss Removes Last Bar to Gradual Absorption of Austria"; and, "Papen Selection Hailed in Berlin . . . Hitler is Acclaimed 'Defender of Europe's Peace' by Press of Reich," all in *New York Times,* 28 July 1934, p. 1.

things they preferred not to see: to see them and to acknowledge the threat they posed to Europe was to accept the possibility of impending war—and war was unthinkable.

From 1918 to 1933, Germany had laid the foundations for a new war machine. These foundations were laid under the very eyes of those powers who had paid such an enormous price to disarm her. In 1933, Hitler came to power, leading a revolutionary, totalitarian party that carried into law the terror and ruthlessness that had helped it gain power. There was nothing in the actions of the new regime, even before the death of President Hindenburg, that could in any way indicate that Germany, once rearmed, would not attempt to accomplish what the more moderate regime of the Kaiser had not. In effect, British policy toward Germany was shaped not to prevent Hitler from redrawing the map of Europe according to the precepts of the "New Order." Rather, it sought to appease Hitler so that he would not go to war in the process.

The Anglo-German Naval Agreement and Submarine Parity

On 16 March 1935, nine months after the failure of the German attempt on Austria, Hitler denounced the disarmament clauses of the Treaty of Versailles and began openly to do what previous German governments had been doing for sixteen years in decent secrecy. Three months later, 18 June 1935, the Anglo-German Naval Agreement was signed limiting German naval tonnage to 35 percent of that of the British while granting Germany the right to parity in tonnage of submarines. The agreement was consistent with Britain's policy of appeasement. It could reasonably be argued on the basis that it recognized Germany's restoration to the family of nations with the hope that such recognition would moderate Germany's behavior in foreign policy. Yet the agreement illustrates, *par excellence,* the reluctance of Britain to recognize the nature of the threat from Germany and the pursuant likelihood of war. That reluctance reflected itself in Britain's approach to rearmament until the very eve of war: the consequences would be disastrous.

The one thing that had brought Britain closest to defeat in the Great War had been German submarine operations against British and Allied shipping. On 22 September 1914, three cruisers of the British Seventh Squadron, *Hogue, Cressy* and *Aboukir,* patrolling the Broad Fourteens off Holland, were sunk within 90 minutes of one another by a single German U-Boat, U-9 (Lieutenant Weddigen, commanding), with a loss of 1,459 British seamen. Almost from that moment onward, the German submarine threat to the Grand Fleet and to allied merchant shipping grew in magnitude and effect, forcing the diversion of more and more material and men to the protection of the maritime traffic of the Allies. The British had considered the submarine a minor adjunct to other naval forces, but the Germans saw the submarine as a major strategic weapon whose operations could affect the outcome of the war.

On 29 October 1916, Admiral Jellicoe, Commander-in-Chief, The Grand Fleet, addressed the Admiralty on the menace of the German submarine campaign against Allied Shipping:

> The very serious and ever-increasing menace of the enemy's submarine attack on trade is by far the most pressing question at the present time. There appears to be a serious danger that our losses in merchant ships may, by the early summer of 1917, have such effect on the import of food and other necessaries into the allied countries as to force us into accepting peace terms which the military position on the Continent would not justify, and which would fall far short of our desires.[94]

During 1915, British monthly shipping losses to German submarine attack had averaged 71,000 tons. From August 1916 to the end of December, the allies lost over 1,250,000 tons of shipping, 85% of which fell victim to German submarines. The situation had become so serious for allied shipping by the end of 1916, that French munitions factories were shutting down for want of English coal; London was down to two days' reserve wheat; and Bristol had only a two weeks' supply remaining. On the 10th of November, the Board of Trade reported that it was unable to find forty merchant ships to bring wheat from Australia to the United Kingdom. American and Canadian wheat intended for Britain could not be sent: there were no ships for its transport.[95]

The shipping situation became so grave that British yards were no longer capable of replacing British losses in merchant ships. And the losses grew even worse in 1917. In the first four months of the year, Britain, its allies, and the neutrals lost over 2,350,000 tons of shipping. In April the United States declared war. The first American forces to enter the war zone ready for combat were the six destroyers of Commander Joseph K. Taussig's Desron 8 who reported to Vice-Admiral Sir Lewis Bayly, R.N. Flag Officer, Commanding at Bantry Bay, Ireland, on 4 May 1917. They had departed Boston Navy Yard on 24 April 1917 to answer the urgent appeal of Admiral Sims, senior U.S. naval officer present in London. This appeal reflected the

94. Despatch, Commander-in-Chief, Grand Fleet, H.M.S. Iron Duke to First Lord of the Admiralty, 29 October 1916, text in Joseph Davies, *The Prime Minister's Secretariat, 1916-1920* (Newport, Monmouthshire: R. H. Johns, Limited, 1951), pp. 75-77; see also, Arthur J. Marder, *From Dreadnought to Scapa Flow,* Volume III: *Jutland and After: May 1916-December 1916* (London: Oxford University Press, 1966), pp. 279-80.

95. Joseph Davies, *The Prime Minister's Secretariat,* pp. 69-72; "Statistical Review of the War Against Shipping," Director of Statistics, The Admiralty, December 1918, cited in Marder, *From Dreadnought to Scapa Flow,* Volume III, p. 270. A summary of all Allied and Neutral Shipping Losses to Enemy Action is included as an appendix in Joseph Davies, *The Prime Minister's Secretariat.* See also, *British Vessels Lost at Sea, 1914-18* a reprint of *Navy Losses and Merchant Shipping (Losses)* (H.M.S.O., 1919; Cambridge: Patrick Stephen, 1977).

desperate circumstances of Britain as a consequence of the German submarine campaign.[96]

The adoption of escort-of-convoy tactics and the addition of U.S. naval surface, submarine, and air units to the effort against German submarines reduced shipping losses to a point where they were no longer quite so critical.[97] But despite the measures adopted, shipping losses in 1918, up to the Armistice on 11 November, amounted to over 2,576,000 tons. The loss of allied and neutral shipping to enemy action in the course of the four years of war amounted to over 12 million tons of which 87 percent fell victim to German and Austrian submarines. British losses in shipping alone had amounted to nearly 8 million tons which represented three-quarters of the total tonnage in steamers that Britain had in 1914.[98]

The enormous loss in merchant marine tonnage in the course of the war was to have its long term effects on British shipping fortunes. Japan's merchant marine expanded during the war from just over a million tons to over 2,300,000 tons, yet Japan lost few ships in the war. Japanese tonnage would double again by 1931. The losses to British shipping in the war and the consequent diversion of merchant ships to support the war effort, detracted from the carrying trade. This left it to be picked up by the Japanese and the Americans; and, ironically, after the war, by the Germans.[99]

It might be supposed that the hard lesson taught by the German submarine in the Great War would have left a deep imprint on the British Government. Never again, one might have thought, would Britain permit itself to be exposed to such a hazard without having made adequate preparations. But that was not the case. The lesson seemed to disappear with the ending of the Great War only to be taught again when a new war broke out.

Great Britain had entered the Great War with 225 ocean-going and torpedo boat destroyers and had built 203 more in the course of the war. Aside from destroyer losses in the war, which amounted to sixty-seven, the

96. See J. K. Taussig, "Destroyer Experiences During the Great War," *United States Naval Institute Proceedings*, Vol. 48, December 1922, pp. 2105-40.

97. Sir Eric Geddes, First Lord of the Admiralty's report to the House of Commons on the seriousness of shipping losses and some measures being taken against German submarines is given, in part, in "Shipbuilding Near Losses," in the *New York Herald*, 15 December 1917, and reproduced in "Naval War Notes," *U.S. Naval Institute Proceedings*, Vol. 44, No. 1 (Whole No. 179), January 1918, pp. 180-81. The role of the U.S. Navy in fostering British adoption of the escort-of-convoy is described in Captain S. W. Roskill, R. N. (Ret'd.), "Capros not Convoy: Counter-Attack and Destroy," *ibid.*, Vol. 82, No. 10 (October 1956), pp. 1047-53, as well as in Rear Admiral William Sowden Sims, "The Victory at Sea, Part II: The Adoption of the Convoy," *World's Work*, Vol. 38, Oct. 1919, pp. 600-19.

98. *Jane's Fighting Ships, 1914* (London: Sampson Low Marston, 1914), p. 22. Of the 13 million 450 thousand tons of merchant shipping, 2 million 700 tons were in sailing vessels.

99. See, for example, Sir Archibald Hurd, "British Merchant Shipping Today," *The Journal of the Royal United Service Institution*, Vol. LXXXII, No. 525 (February 1937), pp. 32-52. Merchant ship tonnage is given in *Jane's Fighting Ships*, yearly.

Royal Navy had lost 457 inshore patrol vessels.[100] What was even more notable was that Germany had started the war with 28 submarines in home waters and had completed 367 submarines before the close of the war. In 1917 alone, with all of the expenditure of material on the Western Front, Germany completed 86 U-boats, or roughly one U-boat every five days. The German rate of submarine construction in the Great War might well have given the British Government future pause. Certainly after the conclusion of the Anglo-German Naval Agreement in 1935, granting Germany, in effect, parity with Britain in submarine tonnage, it might be thought that a new German submarine threat would be considered seriously enough to warrant some precaution. That is especially true after the Germans had demonstrated the capacity to produce a dozen submarines within three months of the signing of the Agreement. On the contrary, it was as though Great Britain did not find war a credible possibility. It was as though there could be no possible need for measures for the contingency of another submarine assault on Britain's lifeline to overseas. Yet it was not as though no one in naval circles had remembered the lesson of the Great War.

In 1939, on the outbreak of war, the Royal Navy had available worldwide, including Empire naval forces, 201 fleet and escort destroyers, sloops and corvettes. Only 150 destroyers and escorts were available for service in the Western Approaches and the North Atlantic. Within a year of the war's outbreak 22 destroyers had been lost.[101]

Germany began the war with 49 operational U-boats with additional boats working-up in home waters. The German Navy would add 172 new U-boats within a year of the outbreak of war. Most curious of all, the Admiralty did not receive permission to begin acquisition of a suitable anti-submarine escort vessel, adaptable to mass production, until after the Munich crisis. It was not until January 1939, that a design was settled on with the Smith's Dock Company, Ltd., in Middlesborough. The design of a whalecatcher was taken as the basis for construction of what was to be the *Flower*-class corvettes. The first orders for corvettes were not placed until 25 July 1939, forty days before war broke out. The first *Flower*-class corvette, H.M.S. *Carnation* (Pendant No. 00) was completed on 22 February 1940.[102]

Coastal Command of the Royal Air Force was hardly better prepared to take on the task of dealing with German submarines. Nineteen squadrons

100. Edgar A. March, *British Destroyers: A History of Development, 1892-1953* (London: Seeley Service & Co., Ltd., 1966), p. 238; H. M. Fleming, *Warships of World War I* (London: Ian Allen, Ltd., n.d.) pp. 133-81; and, Captain H. S. Lecky, R.N., "The Auxiliary Patrol in War," *The Journal of the Royal United Service Institution*, Vol. LXXVIII, No. 509 (February 1933), pp. 1-32.

101. Naval strength is included as an Appendix in Captain S. W. Roskill, R.N., *The War at Sea, Volume I: 1939-1945* in *The History of the Second World War United Kingdom Military Series* (London: H.M.S.O., 1954).

102. *Flower Class Corvettes, Ensign III* (Norwich: Bivouac Books, Ltd., 1973).

were available on the outbreak of war; only one of the eleven General Reconnaissance squadrons meant to patrol off-shore had up-to-date aircraft with a radius of action beyond 250 miles. Of the six flying boat squadrons for long-range maritime patrol, only two were equipped with the modern Sunderland flying boat.[103] This failure to equip more squadrons was not so much an oversight, although it reflected the same complacency about the German threat, as did the matter of corvettes. In the sudden haste to rearmament that overtook Britain in 1938 and 1939, Fighter Command and Bomber Command of the Royal Air Force enjoyed a far higher priority in the demand for new aircraft than did Coastal Command or the Fleet Air Arm. In the afterlight of the Battle of Britain, the ordering of priorities is understandable, even if the weaknesses of Coastal Command and the Fleet Air Arm were less than excusable.

Before the coming to power of the Nazis, there might well have been some basis for complacency in the matter of submarine warfare whatever clandestine preparations the German navy was making to maintain itself in respect to the U-boat. So long as Germany did not possess submarines there was hardly a reason for British concern. But when an avowedly revanchist regime came to power in Germany and when the British Government accorded that regime the right to parity in submarines with Britain, then it was a reason for concern, especially if anyone bothered to recall how close to defeat German submarine warfare had brought Britain in 1917. That Germany had been able to turn out one submarine every five days in 1917 and that in 1935 they gave evidence of possessing the same kind of capability, ought to have aroused some anxiety amongst prudent men, and especially so in a country that depended on its merchant marine to feed its people and to acquire the material with which to wage war.

Yet, in the first ten months of Hitler's war, the allies lost over 1,000,000 tons of shipping to German submarine attack. Within the following nine months (1 July 1940 to March 1941) the losses ran to over 2 million tons. In the seven months (January 1942 to July 1942) over 3 million tons; and an additional 4,326,000 tons in the ten months following.[104] Those losses were in addition to the ones suffered from Axis surface raiders, mines, and air attack, and of course do not include naval vessels sunk by submarines during the periods covered.

Looking back from this perspective in time, it may seem that the struggle to defend allied shipping from German submarines is somewhat inter-

103. Dennis Richards, *Royal Air Force, 1939-1945,* Volume I; *The Fight at Odds* (London: H.M.S.O., 1953) p. 56.

104. Jurgen Rohwer, *U-Boots: Ein Chronik in Bildern* (Oldenburg/Hamburg: Gerhard Stalling Verlag, n.d.), "Anhand. Deutsche U-Boot-Erfolge gegen Handeschiffe in sweiten Weltkreig," pp. 93-95.

esting, but hardly consequential for our times; after all we did win, did we not? Yet every ounce of human effort and every ton of material devoted to the struggle against the German submarine was effort and material not directed toward the defeat of the Germans. Every merchant ship sunk meant the loss of allied seamen and the expenditure of energy and substance for replacement. Every cargo lost at sea lengthened the war by some degree; it delayed the build-up of Allied forces for the reconquest of Europe. Every day the build-up in the United Kingdom was delayed was one more day the Danes, Norwegians, Dutch, Belgians, and French were held in merciless captivity. Each day of indecision was one more day that the killing machines in Dachau, Ravensbruch, Bergen-Belsen, and the other horror camps could digest their quotas of the innocent and defenseless.

III. Weakness, Forgetfulness and Misjudgment: The Beginnings of War

FORTUNATELY ONE SET OF ENTERPRISES—THE AIR DEFENSE OF GREAT BRITAIN—REFLECTED LESS INADEQUATE PREPARATION FOR WAR THAN THE REST. There were a number of reasons for that, most of which had little to do with ministerial concern for the defense of the British Isles or the possibility of another great war. Not the least of the reasons was that the visible element of British air defense, the aeroplane, seemed less costly than the equipment for armored divisions or the naval vessels for some remote and unlikely challenge to Britain's maritime lifelines.

The Perseverance of Air Defense

One of the things the Great War had produced was the famous air aces of both sides who seemed to epitomize all that was romantic, chivalrous, gallant, and heroic. The élan and accomplishment of the fighter pilots in their war presented a happy contrast to the grinding and brutal attrition of trench warfare and the frustrating and wearisome indecision of the war at sea. Many a Victoria Cross or D.S.O. was won in the mud of Flanders, on the fields of Artois and Picardy under circumstances too appalling to imagine, with a heroism too frequent to herald.[1] But those young men in their fragile aircraft dueled like mounted warriors of another age. They captured the imagination and added a flash of color and spirit to the otherwise grey tapestry of war. Few would remember the gunners of "L" Battery, Royal Horse Artillery, and their gallant stand to the last man and gun at Nery. But the names of the air aces were household words and their deeds were the stuff of legend for years to come. Von Richtofen, Georges Guynemer, Mick Mannock, Billy Bishop,

1. See for example, "Appendix III: List of Honours and Awards won by the London Scottish during the War," in Lt. Col. J. H. Lindsay, D.S.O., *The London Scottish in the Great War* (London: Regimental Headquarters, 1925); 1st Battalion of the London Scottish entered combat near Ypres in late October 1914, with a strength of around 1,200 men; 1st and 2nd battalions together lost 1,534 men killed and won 437 decorations, including two Victoria Crosses (Cpt. C. W. Train and Pvt. R. E. Cruickshank) and 19 D.S.O.s.

and Eddie Rickenbacker lent lustre to air warfare that would hardly disappear until our own times.[2]

The romance and excitement of aviation did not cease with the ending of the war. The U.S. Navy's NC-4 flight across the Atlantic in May 1919 was the beginning of a new era of aviation adventure. Aeroplanes and dirigibles flew from here to yon, exploring areas of the earth that had been almost inaccessible. Daring pilots tested the endurance of their aircraft flying non-stop, rising to record altitudes, travelling at ever faster speed. Trans-oceanic flights, around the world flights, flights non-stop across or the length of Africa, flights London to Basra, Singapore to London, set new records and made new heroes. Charles Lindbergh's flight alone, across the Atlantic, was an international event of aviation. The following year, Royal Air Force Squadron Leader Charles E. Kingsford-Smith and Flight Lieutenant Charles T. P. Ulm flew the *Southern Cross* 7,000 miles from San Francisco to Brisbane. The German dirigible *Graf Zeppelin* circumnavigated the globe. Civil and commercial aviation flourished as aeroplanes were employed for transport, to carry the mail, to explore and photograph remote regions of the world, to conduct scientific enquiry, in agriculture, for adventure, and for humanitarian purposes.

Each year at Hendon Aerodome, the Royal Air Force held a spectacular display of military aviation, aerobatics and formation flying. Tens of thousands of people would attend each display and other tens of thousands would see the display in newsreels at the cinema. Few would see the Royal Tank Regiment maneuver with their handful of tanks on Salisbury Plain or witness the battle practice of the Home Fleet, but thousands would see even an ordinary flight of a civil or military aircraft as it maneuvered over the English countryside.[3]

Then there were the advocates of "Air Power" who argued that the aeroplane would be decisive in any future war. Their writings would fuel the competition among the army, navy, and air force for the limited expenditures on defense. Douhet, Trenchard, Salmond, the American General Billy Mitchell, and figures less well-remembered served to keep public attention on aviation as an instrument of national power. H. G. Wells, in his book, *The Shape of Things to Come* (1933) that was made into a popular movie,

2. See for example, Captain Jacques De Sieyes, "Aces of the Air," *The National Geographic Magazine,* Vol. XXXIII (January 1918), pp. 5-9; and, Laurence La Tourette Driggs, "Aces Among Aces," *ibid.* (June 1918), pp. 568-80. Recall as well those magazines devoted to the real-life and fictional heroes of tigers in the air amongst which, were *Wings, The Lone Eagle, G-8 and His Battle Aces,* and *Flying Aces,* published in the United States.

3. See John W. R. Taylor and P. J. R. Moyes, *Pictorial History of the Royal Air Force* (New York: Arco Publishing Co., 1968) for descriptions of the R.A.F. displays at Hendon and for a brief review of other exploits that kept the Air Force before the public's notice.

represented those who used the threat and terror of air war to support pacifism and disarmament.

Remembrance

More than anything else, perhaps, was the deep impression left by the shock of German air attack on the British Isles in the Great War. In all, there were 57 bomber raids and 51 Zeppelin raids on the British Isles between 16 December 1914 and 17 June 1917, inflicting 4,882 casualties of which over 1,400 were killed; damage amounted in excess of three million pounds. The night of 28 January 1918, a single aircraft, a giant R-type bomber, bombed London after eluding the air defenses, and 38 people were killed by a single bomb in the shelter beneath Odham's printing works in Long Acre. The Zeppelins, the great Gotha and R-bombers, bombing sometimes by day and often at night, brought the war home to the British politician more than anything that transpired across the Channel. Their proven destructive capacity left an imprint in government circles and amongst the public that would be reinforced by the growing ubiquity of aviation in the post-war years.[4]

The shock of Zeppelin and bomber raids—particularly on London—and the pervasive threat against the morale of the British people, aside from the casualties and damage, caused the organization of air defenses in Great Britain. These air defenses were a direct response that was visible to the public in the form of anti-aircraft guns, barrage balloons, searchlights and fighter aircraft. By the end of the war, sixteen fighter squadrons were deployed in the homeland with a strength of 376 aircraft. When the Armistice came, there were 286 anti-aircraft guns deployed around London and an additional number along the coast from Chatham to Sheerness. Ground observers were posted to warn of incoming aircraft; hundreds of searchlights were deployed; and air raid precautions were instituted to get people to shelter when air raids threatened. The extensive defenses were built to meet the threat posed by a force of German bombers that never numbered more than about seventy, only about a third of which were ever available for a single attack. Indeed, the greatest number that had been available for a single air raid was forty aircraft.[5]

Air attack on England therefore was a matter within the not so distant past. From 1931 onwards, the notion of air attack on civilian populations

4. The raids to the middle of 1917 are listed in Arthur Banks, *A Military Atlas of the First World War* (London: Heinemann Educational Books, 1975), p. 284f. The particular raid that hit Odham's Printing Works is described in Francis K. Mason, *Battle Over Britain: A History of German Air Assaults on Great Britain, 1917-18 . . .* (London: McWhirter Twins Ltd., 1969), pp. 35-36. The political controversies ignited by the problem of air defense are recorded there as well as in John R. Bushby, *Air Defense of Great Britain* (London: Ian Allen, 1973).

5. Lieutenant-Colonel K. M. Loch, "Anti-Aircraft Defense," *Journal of the Royal United Service Institution,* Vol. LXXXII, No. 526 (May 1937), pp. 303-14.

was not just a holdover from the Gotha and Zeppelin raids. War in China, then Ethiopia, and then Spain, all featured the bomber aircraft as part of the panoply of combat. The air raids on Chinese, and especially Spanish, cities left little doubt about how bad war might become. From the very beginning of the Hitler regime, the German government began preparing the population against the possibilities of air attack. And this was certainly known in England.[6]

As might be expected, a considerable amount of attention, if not of money, was devoted to the problem of air defense for Great Britain. Intelligent analysis was made of the conduct of air defense in the Great War, and of the kinds of performance that could be expected of bomber aircraft. Those considerations, and others, gave some basis for estimating the requirements in fighters, guns, searchlights, and associated equipment and organization, should there be another war. Only those measures were taken that could be taken without the expenditure of substantial government monies. The Ground Observer Corps, for example, staffed by unpaid volunteers, was organized and even rehearsed in various air defense exercises. Plans were laid for the development of Air Raid Precautions with which to provide passive defense for the civilian population. During the Munich Crisis in September 1938, air raid shelters were prepared in London; some evacuations were carried out; and an issue of gas masks was prepared for the general population.

Forgetfulness

The weakness of the Royal Air Force became an issue in the House of Commons as early as 1933, at the behest of Winston Churchill and those few others who saw a substantial threat to England from the evident growth of German air power. Therefore, that aspect of air defense was another matter entirely.

Recalling that London alone had required 286 guns for its defense by the end of the Great War, it is notable that the Steel-Bartholomew Committee on Air Defense of Great Britain called for an establishment of 33 heavy anti-aircraft batteries or 254 guns plus searchlights. A 1935 Committee under Sir Robert Brook-Popham recommended an establishment of 58 heavy batteries or 464 guns and 2,400 searchlights. The Treasury modified the recommendation to 17 batteries (136 guns) to be acquired by 1940 with the rest to be made up by 1946. The rate of expansion of the German Air Force was such by 1936, when Royal Air Force Fighter Command was organized,

6. See "Air Notes, Germany," *Journal of the Royal United Service Institution*, Vol. LXXVIII, No. 512 (November 1933), pp. 865-66, which notes the formation of the Reichslufschutzbund e. V (German Air Defense League) under the German Air Ministry and the publication of the news-sheet, "Active and Passive Air Defense."

that no less than 1,200 heavy anti-aircraft guns would be needed, but by the following year only 146 such guns were available for home defense.

The Territorial Army, equivalent roughly to the National Guard in the United States, had the responsibility for providing the organization for gun defense, barrage balloons and searchlights. The Regular Army anti-aircraft artillery brigades would be required to defend the Field Army wherever it should be employed. In 1933, there were only ten anti-aircraft batteries whose personnel trained without pay save when they were in the two weeks' camp held during the summer. By 3 September 1938, the Dover Brigade which should have had four batteries comprising seventy-two guns, had only two batteries and a total of five guns. But then it had only 320 men rather than the over 1,600 required.[7]

The decision that had to be made as rearmament became pressing concerned which infantry divisions of the Territorial Army would have to be converted to anti-aircraft artillery divisions. Thus did the defense of the homeland bite into the forces that might otherwise have been available to strengthen further the British Expeditionary Force in France. There were delays in the ordering and manufacturing of new anti-aircraft guns; the first new ones were not ordered until 1937 and the delivery at no time met the modest schedules set in peacetime. By the time war broke, there were insufficient numbers of guns in the whole British Empire with which to defend London alone. Raw materials were scarce for all manner of weapons. When war did come, it was discovered that the Navy would require anti-aircraft defenses for its fleet bases at places like Scapa Flow, and the Navy had no guns to spare. Orders had been placed in 1937 for the excellent Swedish Bofors 40 mm. automatic anti-aircraft cannon. When war broke out Sweden refused to deliver the guns. No one seemed to know at the time that the German firm of Krupp through its subsidiary Rheinmetall-Borsig held controlling interest in the Swedish firm, so that weapon had to be manufactured in England instead. It was not that the Army had not been forward looking in the development of designs of weapons to meet air defense requirements. It was that even in so important a matter as the air defense of the homeland and its civilian population, about which there was little disagreement before the war, there was the same lack of urgency that pervaded the entire program of equipping His Majesty's armed forces for war. The procurement of equipment for air defense, before the war, was based not on the known dimension of the German air threat but on the basis of what could realistically be expected in the way of financial support from the Treasury and Parliament.

7. The territorial Army establishment in 1933 is given in "Army Notes: Territorial Army," *ibid.*, No. 509 (February 1933), pp. 191-96. The situation of the 12th Coer Brigade is described in *The Ironside Diaries, 1937-1940* (London: Constable, 1962), p. 60.

By July 1940, the opening of the Battle of Britain, there were only 316 heavy and 135 light guns with which to defend London and its eastern approaches from a German Bomber strength of nearly 1,000 operational aircraft.[8]

Despite the fact that the Royal Air Force was given priority over the other services in the various defense schemes after 1933, the acquisition of aircraft to strengthen British air defenses seemed hardly less leisurely than the equipment of the other services. The numbers that were given out at the time of the announcement of each scheme doubtless seemed impressive at the time. Delivery of aircraft was another matter. There were thirteen home-based fighter squadrons in 1933. In 1934, the Acting Prime Minister proposed doubling the size of the Royal Air Force to match the size of the French Air Force. By July of that year and the crisis in Austria, the scheme had been reduced to 60 per cent of the increase proposed in March of day and night bombers to be acquired by 1939. There were no increases in fighter strength included in that program.[9]

The Storm Begins

In 1936, another six fighter squadrons were added, a total of around ninety aircraft. By the end of the Munich Crisis there were 31 squadrons for Home Defence with the Hurricane fighter having been introduced into service between December 1937 and February 1938, into No. 111 Squadron. The first Hurricane order had been placed in June 1936. The Supermarine Spitfire—the star of the Battle of Britain—was first ordered for the air force in June 1936, and by August of 1938, a total of five aircraft had been delivered. Together, a total of 310 Spitfires and 600 Hawker Hurricanes were ordered in 1936. They were intended chiefly to replace the obsolete bi-planes then in service with Fighter Command.[10] By the outbreak of war, 497 Hurricanes had been delivered, enough to equip eighteen squadrons of Fighter Command; nine squadrons of Fighter Command were equipped with the Spitfire at the outbreak of war. Thus were 27 of the 36 squadrons of Fighter

8. Details on the development of A.A.A. equipment and related matters are in M. M. Postan, D. Hay and J. D. Scott, *Design and Development of Weapons: Studies in Government and Industrial Organization* in *History of the Second World War: United Kingdom Civil Series* (London: H.M.S.O., 1964), Chapter III: "The Problem of Anti-Aircraft Defense." Figures for number and deployment of guns in Anti-Aircraft Command are in Francis K. Mason, *Battle Over Britain.* The entire problem of air defense and its conduct is covered in General Sir Frederick Pile, *Ack-Ack: Britain's Defense against Air Attack* (London: George G. Harrap & Co., 1949). The matter of the Bofors gun is discussed in *The Ironsides Diaries, 1937-1940,* p. 128.

9. "Britain Will Build 460 planes by 1939: Baldwin Tells the Commons 41 Squadrons will be Added to the Air Force," *New York Times,* 20 July 1934, p. 1.

10. Expansion of Fighter Command is traced in Mason, *op. cit.,* p. 88f. Contracts for initial procurement of Spitfires and Hurricanes are mentioned in William Green, *Warplanes of the Second World War: Fighters,* Vol. II (Garden City, N.Y.: Doubleday & Co., 1961), pp. 57 and 92.

Command equipped with modern aircraft although it would eventually be decided that fifty-two fighter squadrons was an absolute minimum for the air defense of Great Britain. The 910 fighters ordered in 1936 and further orders seem to present a formidable array, yet Britain would lose 959 aircraft from the 10th of May 1940 to the surrender of France six weeks later; and in the Battle of Britain, starting a month after the Fall of France, another 915 aircraft would be lost. Those losses were in addition to the aircraft lost during the Allied attempt to defend Norway in April and May.[11]

Fifty-two fighter squadrons was a most realistic level of strength for defending the homeland. The problem was that the Government had made no allowance for aircraft with which to support France and the British Expeditionary Force, because, as has been noted, there were no plans for dispatching such an expeditionary force until quite late. In the event four fighter squadrons had to be sent to France as part of the Advanced Air Striking Force: 20 Gloster Gladiators—obsolete bi-planes, and 40 Hurricanes. These along with 552 French fighters, were to face 4,000 first line aircraft of the German Air Force of which 1,264 were fighters, 357 were dive bombers, and 1,120 were long range bombers.

On 10 May 1940 when the German Army began the conquest of Holland and Belgium and the invasion of France, the German Air Force attacked airfields throughout these countries as the first step in gaining air superiority on the battlefields. They succeeded with admirable precision in destroying much of Allied air strength in the first day and continued the work over the following days. Four more fighter squadrons were hurriedly dispatched from England plus 32 Hurricanes as replacements for the obsolete Gloster Gladiators in the Air Component of the B.E.F. By the end of the first week, the Dutch Air Force, the Belgian Air Force, and the French Air Force were all virtually out of action. The only fighters left to the Allies were in Fighter Command, based in Britain and dedicated to the air defense of the homeland, plus a rapidly dwindling handful in the Air Component of the B.E.F. and the Advanced Air Striking Force. The situation proved so grave in terms of available fighters that the Air Officer Commanding-in-Chief, Fighter Command, Hugh C. T. Dowding, threatened to resign if more fighters were sent to France from England. That was on the 15th of May, by which time the state of affairs on the ground and in the air in France presaged a sweeping German victory. Fighter Command strength had dropped to 36 squadrons in England, ten squadrons or their equivalent in fighters having been sent to France since the 10th of May. And the French were pleading for another ten squadrons of fighters to be sent from England.[12]

11. Denis Richards, *Royal Air Force, 1939-1945*, Volume I: *The Fight at Odds*, pp. 150 and 190.

12. Marshall Dowding's pleas to the British Cabinet on 15 May against further wastage of fighters

Air Chief Marshall Dowding's letter to the Air Ministry and ultimately to the War Cabinet minced no words:

> Once a decision has been reached as to the limit on which the Air Council and the Cabinet are prepared to stake the existence of the country, it should be made clear to the Allied commanders on the Continent that not a single aeroplane from Fighter Command beyond the limit will be sent across the Channel, no matter how desperate the situation may become.
>
> I believe if an adequate fighter force is kept in this country, if the Fleet remains in being, and if Home Forces are suitably organized to resist invasion, we should be able to carry on the war single-handed for some time, if not indefinitely. But if the Home Defence Force is drained away in desperate attempts to remedy the situation in France, defeat in France will involve the final, complete, and irremediable defeat of this country.[13]

Despite the desperate circumstances of Fighter Command at home, a further four squadrons were sent to France to operate from French airfields, while squadrons based in England continued to operate at the limits of their range. They supported the B.E.F. and the remaining elements of the French Armée du Nord, which together were falling back toward the Coast of France. Some 455 British pilots were lost, leaving Fighter Command 362 pilots below the required establishment. By the 1st of August, amidst *Adlerangriff,* the German daylight assault of England, Fighter Command had 719 aircraft, of which only 630 were Spitfires and Hurricanes.[14]

Despite the heroic efforts of Fighter Command, Anti-Aircraft Command, and the Air Raid Precautions Organization, there were over 16,000 casualties from air raids on England, between 18 July and 19 September 1940, of which 3,468 were killed and 12,590 were seriously injured.

The Battle of France was lost because the Allied armies on the ground were too weak to hold the enemy. Part of the reason for this was that there were too few troops trained and fully equipped in the British Expeditionary Force to contain the German attack into Belgium—too few, a matter of sheer numbers. The five divisions of the B.E.F. sent forward into Belgium along with the seven divisions of the French Seventh Army had to face portions of

---

in France and his blunt assessment of the peril facing England if Fighter Command were depleted further in a vain attempt to save the French, is in Francis K. Mason, *Battle over Britain,* p. 115.

13. Letter, Headquarters, Fighter Command, Royal Air Force, Bentley Priory, Stanmore, Middlesex to the Under-Secretary of State, Air Ministry, London, W.C. 2, 16 May 1940, text in Derek Wood & Derek Dempster, *The Narrow Margin,* pp. 191-92.

14. Basil Collier, *The Defence of the United Kingdom* in *History of the Second World War Series* (London: H.M.S.O., 1957), Appendices, as cited in Roger Parkinson, *Summer 1940* (New York: David McKay Company, Inc., 1977), p. 222.

two German Army Groups, comprising 72 divisions (of which ten were armored divisions), supported by airborne troops and with a general reserve of 46 divisions. The French Army had no disposable reserves while of the B.E.F.'s ten divisions, five were in the line, one in G.H.Q. reserve and three still being trained and equipped, although already in France.[15]

One should recall that the British Government had decided in April 1938 that the Army's role in a continental war would be limited to home defense; the field force to be formed of five divisions would be equipped for imperial defense, not for war on the Continent. There was no provision made at the time for reinforcement of the field force and the Territorial Army was to have only training equipment. The events of 1938 in Austria and Czechoslovakia had modified the Government's view to the point that the French were informed that Britain would initially send two divisions to the Continent in the event of war, but that an additional two divisions could be sent out only after a further eleven months. With the German absorption of Czechoslovakia in March 1938, it was concluded that Britain's initial force on the Continent would have to be four divisions. Within a month of the outbreak of war, four Regular Army divisions had been dispatched to France. By the end of 1939, a fifth Regular Army Division had been formed in France; by April five territorial divisions had arrived.

Day after day, and night after night, the bombers came, until finally the enemy turned away to seek easier prey. Unyielding and implacable the British people stood—behavior quite inexplicable, and irrational to the sophisticates of our more enlightened times. Like a great weapon, master-forged, with the pilots and aircraft of the Royal Air Force its cutting edge, but its heft the millions of unnamed citizens who did what was expected and more: soldiers, sailors, airmen, and civilians; policemen, firemen, ambulance drivers; nurses, doctors; ground observers, fire watchers, air raid wardens. Mr. Dooley might have said they were "dumb lucky" and they were in a way. Radar at the Chain Home and Chain Home Low stations was developed on a fiscal shoestring, but it came in time to give warning to the fighter control centers of No. 11 Group. These fighters would not have to scramble until the enemy aircraft were within reach of the limited endurance of their Spitfires and Hurricanes. An aircraft industry finally tooled-up to more than replace the daily wastage of aircraft. And, miraculously the German Air Force did not knock out the one factory where all the Rolls-Royce Merlin engines were

15. B.E.F. dispositions and organizations are given in Ellis, *The War in France and Flanders, 1939-1940,* Table, p. 47 and Appendix I; German Forces' disposition are given in Ulrich Liss, *Westfront, 1939-1940,* in series: *Die Wehrmacht in Kampf,* Band 23 (Neckargemund: Kurt Vowinckel, Verlag, 1959), pp. 140-1 and *Karte* 10: "Lage West vom 10.5.1940, 0,000 Uhr."

produced for both Hurricanes and Spitfires. It was a victory won by the narrowest margin. Yet it was a costly one.

The Battle of France had been lost partly because there were not enough aircraft to support the Allied armies on the ground. The disparity in aircraft numbers became painfully evident once the fighting started.[16]

One of the Territorial Divisions, the 51st (Highland) joined French forces in the Saar front. Bear in mind that the divisions of the Regular Army had to be filled up to war strength with officers and men from the Reserve; and that all the divisions, whether Regular or Territorial, had to undergo training for combat, even though they might be in tactical positions awaiting the German attack.

The most significant weakness in Britain's war preparations was in armor. It had been proposed to form two armored divisions in 1937; one such division was ready for dispatch to France by 10 May 1940, when the storm broke. Elements of that division, the 1st Armoured, landed in May and June to be consumed in the fighting on the Somme, and in the defense of Calais. The division was without its artillery and lacked one of its Tank Regiments. There was a shortage of wireless equipment, no bridging equipment, and no spare tanks with which to replace battlefield losses. The only effective use of British armored units was that in which 74 tanks of the 4th and 7th Royal Tank Regiment took part in a counter-attack against two German Panzer divisions at Arras on 21 May. The odds were about five-to-one in favor of the Germans. There was no air support for the British effort and no way of salvaging the tanks damaged in battle. Yet even that small number of British tanks held up the German advance and contributed to the success of the B.E.F.'s withdrawal to Dunkirk.

Like the Battle of Britain, the retreat to Dunkirk was conducted with immense skill and courage by units, many of which had not yet been fully trained for combat. These were as yet not fully-equipped lacking ammuni-

16. See for example, Admiral Stansfield Turner, "The Naval Balance: Not a Numbers Game," *Foreign Affairs,* Vol. 55, No. 2 (January 1977), pp. 339-54; by a happy coincidence Admiral Turner became Director of the Central Intelligence Agency. He says, in effect it is not that the Soviet Union has a larger fleet, but the United States has a smaller fleet. Since the United States, has lost its superiority over the Soviet Union in naval forces, it is no longer a question of who has the largest fleet, but rather who has something called "sea control capability." Daniel Yergin, "The Arms Zealots," *Harpers,* June 1977, pp. 64-76, points out it is really only a question of a lot of misguided folks on the "Right" who do not know that "much American military technology is simply beyond Russian capabilities"; in effect, less is better. And: "The Warnke Arithmetic," *The Washington Post,* 9 May 1977, p. A10: "If Mr. Warnke is defeated, the Administration's Arms Control hand will have been materially weakened and that of the Russian Hawks correspondingly strenghthened." Or: "Soviet capabilities should not be interpreted in a totally, offensive, threatening light," in Dennis Ross, "Rethinking Soviet Strategic Policy: Inputs and Implications," ACIS Working Paper No. 5, Center for Arms Control and International Security, University of California, Los Angeles, June 1977. The gist is that when the enemy gets to be too strong for you, just re-think what his strategy might be until you come up with one that is not threatening. Consultation with Soviet military planners is not included in the analysis.

tion and supplies. But worst of all, they were left without fighter cover to defend against German air attack, and bomber cover to disrupt German advances. The necessity to retain in Britain a minimum fighter force for home defense left little to spare for operations in support of the B.E.F. during the retreat to and the evacuation from Dunkirk. This cost thousands of casualties in killed, wounded, and prisoners, in addition to the loss of the entire equipment of the B.E.F. in France.

The evacuation of the B.E.F. and French forces from Dunkirk was a miracle of improvisation. It was carried out under constant air and eventually artillery attack with only nominal air cover. The plans for the evacuation were dictated by that which could be spared without jeopardizing Home Defense. Even so thirty fighters were lost over Dunkirk in a single day (1 June 1940) in an effort to give some cover to the evacuation.

Misjudgment

Here as elsewhere, it had been a case of too little and too late. Courage, determination and willful sacrifice were the only commodities not scarce amongst those ordinary citizens who bought time with their own persons to keep disaster from becoming complete defeat. How, one might ask, could a democratic government permit the safety of the people it ruled to be so jeopardized that only a tax exacted in blood and pain would buy national salvation?

How could such a government look on complacently while Germany rearmed "secretly"? How could such a government not take some minimal precautions? How could those who bore the responsibility for the safety of the kingdom watch idly while Hitler avowedly prepared Germany for war? What comforting illusions held decent men enthralled while the storm gathered?

Disarming as Strength

One British writer suggested in 1933 that "the best means of ensuring peace is to be found in a healthy balance of power, and the resuscitation of German sea power will contribute decisively to that end."[17] Acting Prime Minister Stanley Baldwin's statement to the House of Commons in July 1934 supporting the Government's policy of acquiring an additional 460 aircraft for the R.A.F., included the comment that: "There is no cause for panic of any kind. So far as I can see," he said, "there is no risk in the immediate

17. Rear Admiral Gadow, (Ret'd) of the German Imperial Navy, "Naval Problems of Today," *Journal of the Royal United Service Institution*, Vol. LXXVII, No. 512 (November 1933), pp. 711-21. Passage cited is in text. British author is not identified.

future of the peace being broken. . . . It is even possible that had our scale of armaments been higher we should have been better able to influence the course of the disarmament conference."[18]

These words were voiced one week after the Nazis had assassinated the Austrian Chancellor and attempted to seize the government by force. It was only two years and two months away from the invasion of Ethiopia by Italy. Earlier, in the House of Commons, Sir John Simon had replied to Churchill's violent criticism of the Government's devotion to disarmament by allowing that in rejecting disarmament the alternative was unregulated competition in armaments throughout the world: "An appalling prospect."[19] Early in 1936, a Committee on Defence Policy and Requirements, chaired by Stanley Baldwin, endorsed the view that in the light of the international situation, there should be "a far more effective standard" of preparedness for defense over the following five years, but that to organize for war in peacetime "is unthinkable in a democratic country like ours." It was decided that there should be developed a "shadow armament industry" but one that would not interfere with normal trade.[20]

Misreading the Nature of the Nazi Regime

One man who, as much as any, worked tirelessly and earnestly for peace was the British Ambassador to Berlin from 1937 to the outbreak of war. Sir Neville Henderson expressed an unfailing sympathy and understanding toward the German people and their condition. Henderson's ambivalence toward the Nazis, whom he thought to be at once horrible, yet some of whose measures he commended to the attention of the British people, allowed him to state:

> it would be better if people in England laid less stress on the Nazi dictatorship and paid more attention to the great social experiment which was being tried out in Germany, [as] they might learn some useful lessons . . . there are sermons in stones and good in everything; and, there are, in fact, many things in the Nazi organization and social institutions, as distinct from its rabid nationalism and ideology, which we might study and adapt to our own use with great profit to the health and happiness of our own nation and old democracy.

But even he would write, in his annual report on Germany for the year 1937, of the extent of German military preparations:

> The air force continues to expand at an alarming rate . . . the mobilization of the civilian population and industry *for war,* by means of

18. "Baldwin's Speech on Air Forces," *The New York Times,* 31 July 1934, p. 2.
19. Martin S. Gilbert, *Winston S. Churchill: The Prophet of Truth*, pp. 508-9.
20. *Ibid., pp.* 704-5.

> education, propaganda, training and administrative measures has made further strides. Military efficiency is the god to whom everyone must offer sacrifices. It is not an army but the *whole German nation that is being prepared for war.*[21]

On the occasion of a great hunting exhibition in Berlin in November 1937, General Goering, as Game Warden of the Reich, was the host to representatives of those European countries in which hunting was a traditional sport. Lord Halifax, Lord President of the Council, visited Germany in his private role as Master of Foxhounds. He was perhaps more like a hare amongst the jackals, but it was considered an opportunity for the British Government to pursue the improvement in relations with Germany which was at the heart of British policy. Having visited Der Fuehrer at Berchtesgaden on the 19th, he brought back to England some hopeful impressions in respect to the prospects for European disarmament, and the lack of prospects of a war in Europe. Lord Halifax concluded that "the Germans had no policy of immediate adventure . . . they were too busy building up their country." "He would expect," he said, "a beaver-like persistence pressing their aims in Central Europe, but not in a form to give others cause—or probably occasion—to interfere." Hitler had indicated, however, an interest in the abolition of bombing aeroplanes and Lord Halifax had the impression that it would not be too difficult to reach some basis of understanding on Central and Eastern Europe. The Halifax trip and its results moved the Foreign Office to state that: ". . . if we wish for a general settlement with Germany, it will be for us, and not the German Government to take the next step of putting forward some concrete proposals. . . . It is important, if we are really anxious to prevent the hopes created by the recent conversations from evaporating, that there should be no long delay."[22]

Czechoslovakia

The hopes expressed for diasarmament were a recurring theme of the time; they were more than enough, along with budgetary considerations, to slow the as yet leisurely pace of British preparations for defense. The siren call of disarmament would not be stilled until 15 March 1939, when German troops occupied the remnant of Czechoslovakia in willful violation of the Munich Agreement. Just two weeks before Lord Halifax's visit to Berchtesgaden which had raised such hopes for peace, Hitler addressed the Chiefs

21. Italics added. Sir Neville Henderson, *Failure of A Mission: Berlin 1937-1939* (New York: G. P. Putnam's Sons, 1940), pp. 98-99.

22. The Halifax trip is described in Sir Neville Henderson, *ibid.*, pp. 93-95; Lord Halifax's impressions of the meeting with Hitler along with the Foreign Office response is given in Ian Colvin, *The Chamberlain Cabinet* (New York: Taplinger Publishing Co., 1971), pp. 51-52 and 82.

of the three services, and his Ministers of Defense and Foreign Affairs, in a meeting at the Reichschancellory. He said:

> The German problem can only be solved by force and this is never without great risk . . . we are left to reply to the questions "when" and "how." . . . [After the period 1943-45] we can only expect a change for the worse. The re-arming of the Army, the Navy, and the Air Force, as well as the formation of the Officers' Corps are practically concluded. Our material equipment and armaments are modern, with further delay the danger of their becoming out-of-date will increase.[23]

In March 1938, German troops occupied Austria; that was the 12th, and the British Cabinet met that afternoon to discuss the event. The Prime Minister, Neville Chamberlain warned that the impression ought not to be given that the country was faced with the prospects of war in a few weeks. In Cabinet on the following Monday, it was agreed that in referring to the event in the House of Commons, only the methods used to take Austria ought to be condemned and that "no statement ought to indicate that events were leading to war."[24]

Despite the uncommonly strong faith in the prospects for peace, Prime Minister Chamberlain was faced, in the fall of the year, with the German threat to make war, if Czechoslovakia were not forced to cede its Sudeten territory to the Reich. Hitler never masked his intentions to go to war if German demands went unsatisfied. Herman Goering spoke to the British Ambassador in September, after the British Prime Minister had already agreed that the matter of the Sudetenland would be settled, at Hitler's insistence, "on the basis of self-determination." Goering warned the British Ambassador: "If England means to make war on Germany, no one knows what the ultimate end will be. But one thing is quite certain. Before the war is over there will be very few Czechs left alive and little of London left standing." After this warning, Goering "gave fairly accurate details of the numbers of modern anti-aircraft guns we possessed at the moment as well as of the unpreparedness of England's air defenses generally."[25]

The Czech Government agreed to the principle of self-determination in the transfer of the territory in question. Hitler then demanded its immediate cession and occupation by German troops. This demand, if not satisfied by 1 October (it was then 27 September), would be carried out with himself leading the Army.[26]

23. "NOTES on the Conference in the Reinchskanzlei on 5 November 37 from 1615-2030 hours," Document No. 386-PS in *International Military Tribunal.*

24. Ian Colvin, *op. cit.*, p. 106.

25. Sir Neville Henderson, *Failure of a Mission*, p. 156.

26. John W. Wheeler-Bennett, *Munich: Prologue to Tragedy* (London: Macmillan and Co., Ltd., 1948), p. 149.

On 1 October 1938, German troops began the occupation of the Sudetenland with British officers present to help assure that the provisions of the Munich agreement were complied with by the Czechs within the ceded territory.[27] In the pursuit of "Peace for Our Time," Czechoslovakia had been deprived of the territory containing its splendid fortifications, much of its economic potential, and humiliated into the bargain. The loss of the fortifications meant there could be no resistance to any further demands by Germany. Czechoslovakia had been sacrificed under the illusion that peace would thereby be saved. Hitler said of the events of September and October that it had been the result of the superb work of the German press in publicizing the military pressure being exerted against Czechoslovakia. He knew, he said, that the pressure would "destroy the nerves of those gentlemen in Prague." "It is a fabulous success," he said:

> so great that our present day world is hardly able to assess it. I myself became most aware of the grandeur of this success for the first time when I stood in the middle of the Czech fortified line. Then and there I realized what it is to take possession of fortifications representing a front almost 2,000 kilometers long without firing one single shot of live ammunition. Gentlemen, this time, by means of propaganda in the service of an idea, we have obtained 10 million human beings with over 100,000 square kilometers of land. That is something really magnificent.[28]

Back in London, at Number 10 Downing Street, on 31 October 1938, a somewhat different view was being taken of events by the resident of that address:

> There has been a good deal of talk in the country and in the press about the need for rearmament by this country. In Germany and Italy it was suspected that this rearmament was directed against them, and it was important that we not encourage these suspicions.
>
> A good deal of false emphasis has been placed on rearmament, as though one result of the Munich Agreement had been that it would be necessary for us to add to our rearmament programmes. Acceleration of existing programs was one thing, but increases in the scope of our programme which would lead to a new arms race was a different proposition. . . .[29]

In a statement on British foreign policy, the same day, the Prime Minister expressed the hope that "it might be possible to follow up the Munich

27. "An Observor in Czechoslovakia During the Crisis," *Journal of the Royal United Service Institution,* Vol. LXXXIV, No. 525 (February 1939), p. 175.

28. "Hitler's Secret Address to Representatives of the German Press," Munich, 10 November 1938, from *Es spricht der Fuehrer,* edited by Hildegard von Kotze and Helmut Krausnick, as cited in Z. A. B. Zeman, *Nazi Propaganda,* second edition (London: Oxford University Press, 1973), Appendix B.

29. Neville Chamberlain's statement in Martin Gilbert, *Winston S. Churchill: The Prophet of Truth,* p. 1014.

Agreement by other measures . . . that one day we should be able to secure limitations of armaments. . . ."[30]

As for defense, it was agreed that the Royal Air Force's notion of possessing air parity with the German Air Force was not to be taken to mean that Britain would have an air force of equal size and striking power to that of Germany, but rather that "parity" should be defined as "effective deterrent strength," a euphemism meant to disarm those who thought the air force under-strength for its task of defending the homeland.[31]

Ten days before, Hitler had directed preparations of plans for seizing that part of Czechoslovakia not yet in German hands. In his directive to the *Wehrmacht* Hitler said:

> The future task of the armed forces and the preparations for the wars resulting from these tasks will be laid down in a later directive. Until this directive comes into force, the armed forces must be prepared at all times for the following: (1) period for the liquidation of the remainder of Czechoslovakia; (2) period for the occupation of Memelland.[32]

As Churchill had warned, in the midst of the Czech crisis: "The sequel to the sacrifice of honour would be the sacrifice of lives—British lives."[33]

To those who were not blinded by the bright chimera of everlasting peace, or led on by the enticing mirage of universal disarmament, the vicious pogrom against the German Jews, started on 9 November 1938, left no doubt. The savage campaign against the Jews and all things Jewish was arranged to occur "spontaneously," with clear directives as to the manner in which the police, the SS, and the Gestapo were to supervise:

> Only those measures are permitted which in no way endanger the security of German life or property. For example, synagogues may only be set on fire if there is no danger of fire spreading to adjoining properties. Business, apartments, and houses of Jews may only be destroyed, not plundered. The police are responsible for supervising the execution of these orders. . . .[34]

The damage done to property was so excessive and looting was so widespread in the staged disorders that Goering proposed the Jews should be fined 250 million dollars so that German insurance companies could be compen-

30. Ian Colvin, *The Chamberlain Cabinet,* p. 173.

31. *Ibid.,* p. 173.

32. *International Military Tribunal Document,* C-136, as cited in John W. Wheeler-Bennett, *Munich: Prologue to Tragedy,* p. 195.

33. Martin Gilbert, *op. cit.,* p. 989.

34. See for example, Berlin Nr. 234 404 9.11.2355, An allé Stapo-Stellen und Stano Leistellen, An Leiter oder Stellvertreter [from] Gestapo II Muller, in Dr. Kurt Zentner, *Illustrierte Geschichte des Dritten Reiches,* p. 191; and, G. S. Graber, *The History of the SS* (New York: David McKay Company, Inc., 1973), pp. 95-103.

sated for the losses claimed by those covered by insurance. In a speech before the Reichstag on 30 January 1939, Hitler prophesied the elimination of the Jewish people from Europe.[35]

The British Ambassador in Berlin concluded that Reichskristallnacht, as the pogrom was called because of the amount of broken glass in the streets afterwards, had hampered the conciliatory efforts of the Czech government for better relations with Germany by encouraging the anti-German sentiment in Czechoslovakia.[36]

While the horrors inside Germany certainly discouraged the more fastidious of the appeasers, Hitler was at pains to continue to hold out the prospects of peace to those who would listen. In the Reichstag, on 6 November 1938, Hitler said: "As a peace-loving man, I have endeavored to give the German people those arms which are calculated to urge others to keep the peace. . . . All we desire is to live in peace, to go on with our work. . . ." Von Ribbentrop, the German Foreign Minister, told the Foreign Press Association in Berlin on the 7th of November that:

> Mr. Chamberlain and Lord Halifax have with wise insight given a clear rebuke to all these British war agitators and their endeavors to drive the nations apart. M. Daladier, the French Premier and his foreign minister, M. Bonnet, have likewise made speeches in the last few weeks which have been well received in Germany.

In a speech at the New Year's reception of the Diplomatic Corps in Berlin on 12 January 1939, Hitler said, in commenting on the Munich Settlement, that:

> . . . it was possible to achieve the peaceful settlement so much desired by us all . . . due not only to a wish for peace and to a sense of responsibility on the part of the governments concerned . . . the Powers have thus made a real contribution not only to the safeguarding of European peace but also to the creation of a sounder and happier Europe. In my opinion this development justifies the hope that in the future the insight of leading European statesmen will succeed in giving Europe a peace which will do the highest possible justice to the natural and legitimate claims of all peoples.[37]

Hitler explained his emphasis on peace, in his public utterances, when he spoke *in camera* to the representatives of the German press:

35. "Hitler prophezeit die Vernichtung der judischen Rasse in Europe," Reichstag, 30 January 1939, in *Der National-sozialismus Dokumente 1939-1945*, edited by Walter Hofer (Frankfurt an Main: Fisches Bucherei, 1957), p. 277.

36. Henderson, *Failure of a Mission*, p. 178.

37. These speeches with others are reproduced in *Documents on the Events Preceding the Outbreak of the War*, Compiled and published by the German Foreign Office (Berlin, 1939).

> The prevailing circumstances have obliged me to speak, for a decade or more, of almost nothing but peace. Only, in fact, by continuously declaring the German desire for peace and Germany's peaceful intentions was I able, step by step, to secure freedom for the German people and to provide Germany with the armaments which have, time and time again, always been the essential precondition for any further move.[38]

Brutality, consummate and manifest terrorism, and the promise of everlasting peace to those who will submit themselves without resistance, is the elixir of aggression, casting a trance over those who will imbibe, however sensible they may be in other matters. In reply to a particularly bellicose speech of the German Chancellor in the Reichstag at the end of January 1939, Prime Minister Chamberlain confided that he had gotten the impression, "that it was not the speech of a man who was preparing to throw Europe into another crisis." It seemed to him that there were "many passages in the speech which indicated the necessity of peace for Germany as well as other countries."[39]

On 2 January 1939, the *Daily Express* had written that "there will be no Great War in 1939." Indeed it seemed to some that a "Golden Age" had arrived now that the Czech matter was settled. A joint statement was issued by a group of English notables in education and other such hallowed pursuits to all men of goodwill abroad. And this statement appealed particularly to the leaders and people of the German Reich to "lay the spectre of war and enmity between nations" while the Prime Minister let it be known that "Europe was settling down to a period of tranquility, and that the Government was therefore contemplating the possibility of a general limitation on armaments."[40]

The Prime Minister had written to his sister on the 19th of February that:

> I myself, am going about with a lighter heart than I have had for many a day. All the information I get seems to point in the direction of peace & I repeat once more that I believe we have at last got on top of the dictators. Of course that doesn't mean I want to bully them as they have tried to bully us; on the contrary I think they have had good cause to ask for considerations of their grievances, & if they had asked nicely after I appeared on the scene they might already have got some satisfaction.[41]

Sir Samuel Hoare, the Home Secretary, told his constituents in Chelsea of the "Golden Age" that had just started now that the long period of

38. Z. A. B. Zeman, *Nazi Propaganda*, p. 213.
39. *House of Commons Debates*, 31 January 1939, col. 81 as cited in John W. Wheeler-Bennett, *Munich: Prologue to Tragedy*, p. 328.
40. The appeal was carried in *The Times*, 27 January 1939; the Prime Minister's statement is cited along with the appeal in Wheeler-Bennett, *op. cit.*, p. 329.
41. Martin Gilbert, *Winston S. Churchill: Prophet of Truth*, p. 1041.

preparations (armaments) had come to an end. That was the 10th of March. The Germany Army invaded Czechoslovakia on the 15th.[42]

Poland—Norway and Denmark

The hopes for peace lay in ruins and war came in September with the German invasion of Poland. Yet even that did not entirely convince the incredulous. The German Army, Air Force, and Navy, with their old ally of the days of secret rearmament, the Red Army, conquered Poland in a ruthless campaign lasting six weeks. The Royal Air Force bombed Germany with leaflets instead of bombs. The aircraft of Bomber Command and Coastal Command were forbidden to attack German merchant ships at sea even if those ships fired upon the aircraft. It was also forbidden to attack enemy warships in dock or berthed alongside quays because it might inflict damage on civilian installations.[43]

This attention to the niceties left German warships and merchantmen with little damage but cost the Royal Air Force unnecessary casualties. The German Air Force did not feel so compelled to exercise such restraint against British shipping and warships. Only the invasion of Norway and Denmark with the severe allied defeat suffered in the air, ashore, and in Norwegian waters, convinced the British government of the danger to Britain of adhering to rules that none but they would observe. All this offered one more reflection of the lack of preparation for war. Even by the time of the German invasion of France, there was such a shortage of service rifles for the Army and Home Defence that 500,000 obsolete Enfield rifles had to be procured from the United States along with 129 million rounds of ammunition, 80,583 machine guns and 20,000 revolvers, not to mention quantities of automatic rifles, mortars and artillery pieces. And that was eight months *after* the war had started and four years after British rearmament was haltingly begun. By November 1940, the financial burden of purchasing abroad those arms and tools which should have been readied in peacetime was so heavy that $335,000,000 worth of investments in the United States had been liquidated to finance purchases in the United States; 4,500,000,000 dollars in cash and gold had been expended on arms purchases from abroad—an amount equivalent to one-half of the U.S. federal budget for 1939. British financial reserves were down to the equivalent of 2 billion dollars and Britain required much, much more just to continue the war as well as to prepare for the winning of it.[44] In 1929, Winston Churchill had warned of the dangers

42. Roger Parkinson, *Peace for Our Time,* p. 106; and Wheeler-Bennett, *op. cit.*, p. 329-30.

43. Captain S. W. Roskill, *The War at Sea,* Volume I, pp. 143-44; and, Denis Richards, *Royal Air Force, 1939-1945,* Volume I: *The Fight at Odds,* pp. 44-47.

44. British figures from Winston S. Churchill, *The Second World War,* Volume II: *Their Finest*

of another war that would bring ruin upon Britain, even if she should be victorious.[45] It appeared as though the British Government would do all in its power to make the prophecy of Churchill's words come true. It was the British people, who with their allies had been victorious over Germany in 1945, that still suffered rationing of food and other wartime stringencies well into the 50s. It was the Germans and the Japanese, the defeated peoples, who would prosper at the hands *of the British* and the Americans.

The Old Queen had said it in 1879:

> One great lesson is again taught us, but it is never followed: NEVER *let the Army and Navy* DOWN *so low* as to be obliged to go to *great expense in a hurry*. . . . If we are to maintain our position as *a first rate Power*—and of that no one can doubt—we must with our Indian Empire and large colonies, be *prepared for attacks* and *wars somewhere or other* CONTINUALLY. And the *true economy* will be to be *always ready*.[46]

Great Britain was a small country in area and population that had become a great power through the exertions of its people in commerce and war. It could remain a great power only if it remembered the penalty exacted by weakness. It was certainly not unreasonable for Britain's political leaders to value peace after the terrible price paid during the Great War. To assume that no future price would be necessary was unworthy of the leaders of that nation. Britain, indeed, had for three centuries and more only secured the safety of its realm through the skill and courage of its seamen and soldiers.

Germany had, in World War I, destroyed the Russian Empire; it had very nearly defeated France in 1914, and had fought on for four more years, to be brought to a military draw only with the intervention of the United States. Could one really expect that that Germany would, after such enormous exertion, forswear forever its drive to dominate Europe, that drive that had led to the Great War in the first place? The peace of Europe at best had never been a sturdy thing. Was it suddenly to become less flimsy just because such an awful price had been paid? To let the Germans rearm and then to appease was folly. When appeasement stems from weakness and not strength, it is not kindness but fear that calls the tune. Only the strong can afford to be kind.

These events illuminate the follies of those decent, well-meaning men who, parsimonious while there was yet time, had to become profligate when time ran out. At Munich, they traded the freedom of the Czech peoples for

---

Hour (Boston: Houghton, Mifflin Company, 1949), pp. 557-58. U.S. figures in *Historical Statistics of the United States, Colonial Times to 1970*, Part II (Washington, D.C.: U.S.G.P.O., 1975).

45. Martin Gilbert, *Winston S. Churchill: The Prophet of Truth*, p. 123.

46. Queen Victoria to Lord Beaconsfield, 28 July 1879, cited in Wheeler-Bennett, *Munich: Prologue to Tragedy*, p. vi.

the goodwill of the German dictator, who, after all had none. The pennies saved on defense while Germany was evidently preparing for war had to be spent a thousand times over and more, just to keep England from being taken. The treasure of British blood and life had to be squandered in Flanders, Artois, and Picardy, in Norway, the Channel, and the skies over England, and in the cities and towns of the homeland, just to buy the time to get half-ready. How could such good men be so blind to the menace of German intentions? How could that blindness persist when those intentions became coupled to German preparations for war by a regime whose stock-in-trade was ruthlessness and brutality? How could such men remain deaf for so long to the warnings of those, no less good than themselves, who shouted of British military weakness, and of the dangers that faced Britain and Europe?

When one asks if the United States ought to be preparing for war, it is not intended to draw a parallel between the position of the United States today and that of England in 1939 and 1940. In those years, there was the Empire beyond the seas for Britain to call upon for help. There was the United States which, however reluctantly, would find its interest compelling enough to become the Arsenal of Democracy. And above all, there was Winston Churchill whose resonant tones bespoke the British peoples' defiance in defeat and resolution in war. There was the incomprehensible courage and determination of those people in the face of terrible danger and near catastrophe. But there also are lessons to be learned from the events of those distant days.

Narvik, Singapore, Corregidor, Dunkirk, Crete, Tobruk, the Rifle Brigade at Calais, gallant *Houston* and *de Ruyter, Hood, Prince of Wales* and *Repulse,* Hickam, Clark, and a score of other names now barely remembered mark well where the democracies paid their price for carelessness, unwisdom and good nature in permitting the wicked to exercise unbounded ambition, until it was nearly too late. What a rare accountant it would be who could balance the books on the tax in blood and treasure paid by the peoples of the democracies because they permitted their leaders to ignore those strategic considerations, neglect of which can only lead to defeat and submission.

Events in Europe moved swiftly after 1936. If they left democratic politician and public alike confused and uncertain, those with an eye to strategic values could only find them ominous. The German re-occupation of the Rhineland and the construction of the Siegfried Line on Germany's Western frontier covered the Nazi political campaign to incorporate Austria into the Third Reich. German troops in Austria outflanked the southern end of the Czech fortifications, while to buy peace, a British Prime Minister assisted Herr Hitler in detaching the Sudetenland from Czechoslovakia. That transfer of territory placed the Czech fortified line in German hands, leaving Czechoslovakia at once demoralized and unable to resist the German occupation when it came five months later.

The occupation of Czechoslovakia permitted German troops to deploy on the southern border of Poland. The *coup de grâce* against Poland was presaged by the Nazi-Soviet Pact of August 1939, wherein the two dictatorships agreed to a line of partition of that unfortunate country. The reward of Eastern Europe as a sphere of Soviet influence purchased a friendly neutrality so that Hitler could turn his strategic attention to the conquest of Western Europe. Hitler's recognition of Eastern Europe as a Soviet sphere of influence was a short-term convenience since he intended to conquer Russia one day anyway. For the Soviet Union, it was a bird in the hand, legitimatizing Soviet rights to the territory, rights not yet renounced even in this latter day of "national liberation."

Events in Europe moved with stunning swiftness beginning with the seizure of Denmark and Norway on 9 April 1940. Within only seventy-two days Denmark, Norway, Luxembourg, Holland, and France had fallen to the Wehrmacht. France, America's oldest ally with its great army and superb fortifications, had fallen in six weeks.

What to Americans had been merely one more of those nasty wars, which Europeans seemed incapable of avoiding, was now a matter of deep strategic concern. For twenty years the United States had worried that the British Fleet should conform to the strictures of the Washington Naval Treaty in the interest of universal peace. Now, it was a question of whether that fleet would fall to the Germans. Italy had finally joined the war on France, and the fate of the French Fleet remained in question. The safety of the Western Hemisphere now turned on whether Britain would fall, and the combined naval forces of that country, Germany, France, Italy, and Germany's eastern Ally, Japan, might be turned against the United States. The fall of France marked the beginning of serious mobilization for the United States.

The fall of France had almost immediate strategic consequences in the Far East. On June 21, France surrendered to the German Army. On the 6th of August, Japan demanded the right to control the airfields of French Indo-China and to move troops into northern Indo-China. German pressure on the "Vichy" government in France and Japanese threats to the Governor-General of Indo-China forced France to concede. Japanese forces moved into the northern provinces of the colony on the 23rd of September. On 8 December 1941, from the airfield at Saigon the first air attack against Singapore was launched; the Fifth Japanese Imperial Guards division moved from southern Indo-China against Siam at the same time; Hainan Island and Cam Ranh Bay were the sites where Japanese forces marshalled to invade the Netherlands East Indies. The British forces were stretched thin to defend England, to fight in the Middle East and in the Mediterranean, and to face growing punishment from German submarines and surface raiders in the North Atlantic. No resources could be spared to block the Japanese move into Indo-China in

September 1941, and the situation grew worse. In March of that year, Japan and the Soviet Union concluded a non-aggression pact, the effect of which was to free Japan to turn her attention to the liquidation of the British, French, and Dutch Empires in the Far East, and to move against the Philippines. The fall of France, the Low Countries, Norway and Denmark, the entry of Italy into the war on the side of Germany and the eventual occupation of Yugoslavia and Greece, shifted the strategic balance almost decisively against the democracies. Only a stubborn, unyielding Britain led by that bulldog of defiance, Winston Churchill, and Hitler's manic hatred for the Slavic peoples, bought time for those who had been half-blind to become half-ready.

IV. Czechoslovakia—1968: Strategic Implications

STRATEGIC INFERIORITY IS THE HANDMAIDEN OF DEFEAT. However, the lessons taught by those now distant events lie unlearned or half-forgotten. To wait until war has come before gaining strategic superiority is to entertain the false hope that the enemy will go easy until we can get ready; or that they will follow only those courses of action that play to our strengths. One may not count on that kind of indulgence; especially when one is matched against a ruthless totalitarian regime with pretensions to world domination. The day has already passed when we could claim that the security of the United States rests solely in its own hands. Debates on military matters in the United States do not turn on questions about the American capability to win a war, but on the assumption that there will not be one.

The Balance of Power

In 1965, the Secretary of Defense assured us that the Soviet Union had given up any notion of attempting to achieve a strategic nuclear force as large as that of the United States.[1] His comments were found assuring, as they seemingly portended the continued strategic nuclear superiority of the United States. But within two years the Soviet Union had almost doubled its ICBM force and within five years had only four fewer ICBMs deployed than the United States. By 1970 when the Soviet Union had 250 more ICBMs deployed than the United States, one was assured on all sides that the United States enjoyed such technological superiority that mere numbers could not be taken as an indication of who enjoyed nuclear superiority. This argument claimed the issue was so complex that ordinary folk could easily be misled if all they did was count things like missiles, *Hotel*- and *Dixie*-class submarines, and nuclear throwweight. Beyond that, strategic parity, as it now came to be called, was a terribly good thing because it assured the Russians that we were not going to fling NATO's 20-odd under-strength divisions on the 200

1. "Is Russia Slowing Down in Arms Race—Interview with Robert McNamara, Secretary of Defense," *U.S. News and World Report,* 13 April 1965.

divisions of the Warsaw Pact. Further, it was clear to those who were willing to see, that all the Soviet Union desired was "strategic stability" because they had the nagging problem of cutting defense expenditures in order to supply the omnivorous demands of the Russian consumer for automobiles, refrigerators, television sets and embossed stationary, not to mention tactical aircraft, new tanks, bomb shelters, armed helicopters, and other such comestibles so sought after by shoppers the world around.

It is a curious arithmetic indeed whereby the United States can remain the preeminent military power in the world, while cutting its fleet carriers from 58 to thirteen, reducing its force of attack submarines, cutting its general purpose naval forces, dropping its Army's manpower to 785,000 men and women, retiring all its surface-to-air missiles in CONUS (save for a handful in Florida), and cutting its USAF interceptor squadrons to 6. And America has done this while the Soviet Union increased its Army, Navy and Air Force General Purpose Forces, which were already larger than those of the United States, while deploying more ICBMs, MRBMs, and submarine launched ballistic missiles. We are also told that this shift in the relative forces has allowed the Soviet Union barely to achieve parity. In 1970, the U.S. had over 3,161,000 people in its armed forces while the Soviet Union had 3,305,000 plus 205,000 border guards and KGB troops. In 1977, the U.S. had 2,088,000 people in the service while the Soviet Union had 3,675,000 in the service plus over 450,000 border guards and KGB troops.

It must be exceedingly difficult for those who serve in the armed forces to make sense of current defense policy—or for that matter, that policy in force for the past couple of decades. On the one hand, our shortages of equipment and replacement parts, aging material and strict economy in all matters, particularly operational training, stand in contrast to an enemy who on the other hand seems to draw on an unexhausted treasury to supply himself with far more than enough of everything. This situation seems hardly to suggest that the safety of the United States rests in its own hands. But one is told that it requires a terribly sophisticated and cosmopolitan mind to grasp the subtleties of defense policy; such minds seem only to abound in Congress and elsewhere amongst those who have the constitutional obligation to provide for the safety of the country. It is difficult for those who may have to spend themselves for that safety to challenge the august personages who say everything is just fine. All those ponderous words and phrases like "sufficiency," "deterrence," "qualitative superiority," "essential equivalence" "mutual assured destruction" and the rest are obscure in meaning and even when explained, leave the ordinary sensible mind with the impression of flim-flam. To be tempted into asking some simple question like "who's going to win if there's a war?" is to brand oneself pitifully naive, at best, or at worst, a throwback to some earlier days when wars were won by the side that was strongest and best prepared to wage war. What is worse: one may well be engulfed in a flow of gummy and euphoric rhetoric designed to demonstrate the implausibility of war, the exceptional goodwill of the enemy and the futility of ordinary minds attempting to grasp anything more complex than the duty roster or watch list.

Examining the strength returns of the Soviet armed forces, and that of their allies, and of the Peoples Republic of China, does give one distinct impression: they have more of everything with which to wage war, than we in the United States and our allies have with which to defend ourselves. Of course, the reply is that differences in numbers are not that significant, it is really quality that counts and the way you use your weapons and equipment that is important. And it is certainly true, the Japanese had fewer planes in the air over Pearl Harbor than the United States had on the ground. But the tragic result at Pearl Harbor stemmed from the fact that the Japanese came prepared to wage war while the United States was still at peace; and, the Japanese planes were in the air where their combat characteristics could be employed effectively while the U.S. planes were on the ground where their combat characteristics were unemployable. The battle in the sky over Ford Island, Hickam and the rest was won because the Japanese were superior in numbers where it most counted. Using that superiority in numbers, the Japanese eliminated whatever strength might have been brought to bear against them to prevent the accomplishment of their objective: the destruction of that part of the Battle Force and Scouting Force of the Pacific Fleet in harbor on the day of the attack. It is notable that the outcome of that particular engagement was the immediate strategic superiority of the forces of the Empire of Japan in the Western Pacific and the expansion of their freedom of action.

No, to repeat, the situation in which the United States finds itself today is not that of Britain in 1940. There is no Britain with its Churchill to hold the fort while we Americans get half-ready. There is no American Empire to which the U.S. Fleet may retreat while the other democracies of the world prepare to deal with the foe. There will be no distant and protected arsenal of democracy upon which the United States can draw to remedy these deficiencies in military strength created by the disbelief in war or the unwillingness to see the menace.

Those few remaining democracies in the world today must look ultimately to the United States for defense; we may not look to them for ours. If the United States permits itself to be defeated by today's tyrannies, there will be no democracies remaining that are strong enough to fight on until the tyrannies are defeated. The balance of power has already set against the democracies through costly accommodation that seemed necessary at the time; through misplaced optimism about the magnitude of the threat;

through the sheer folly of those who suppose that the imperatives of strategy do not apply during times of peace.

Czechoslovakia—1968

The erosion in that balance of power began with the necessary accommodation of the Soviet Union in the matter of Eastern Europe. Had Britain and the United States not helped the Soviet peoples to fight on against the Nazis, Germany could not have been defeated by 1945; and the full power of the German Army and Air Force would have been waiting in France to contest the entry of British and American armies onto the continent. The price for the early liberation of Western Europe was acquiescence in the Soviet occupation of Eastern Europe. Whatever illusions there may have been that the countries of Eastern Europe, once freed of their Nazi jailers, would be treated by the Soviet Union to restoration of democratic government—as in the manner of France, Belgium, the Netherlands, Norway, and Denmark in the West, not to mention the fate of West Germany and Japan—were surely dispelled by the Communist seizure of power in Czechoslovakia in 1948.

The Soviet Union's intent to hold Eastern Europe as its own pasture was manifest with the forcible suppression of dissent in East Germany in 1953, in Hungary in 1956 and in Czechoslovakia in 1968. Perhaps Czechoslovakia in 1968 marked an important strategic change in respect to the defense of Western Europe. Instead of Soviet troops acting alone against a potentially dissident regime, it was a Warsaw Pact Army with Soviet ground and air elements, an East German motorized division and an armored division, Polish troops, Hungarian forces, and elements of the Bulgarian army, all under the command of a Soviet General.[2] This action demonstrated the capability of the Soviet government to call upon members of the Warsaw Pact to send their forces to enforce measures taken to safeguard purely Soviet interests. The upshot was to leave an additional five Soviet Divisions facing NATO on the Central Front from Czechoslovakia. This was in addition to the Groups of Soviet Forces in East Germany, the East German Army, and the ten divisions of the Czech Army.

The Soviet reaction to what was hardly more than a nominal challenge to Russian authority in Eastern Europe, was fully consistent with what had happened in East Germany in 1953 and Hungary in 1956. That reaction should not have come as a shock to anyone conversant with the nature of

2. "Czechoslovakia," in *Strategic Survey 1968* (London: Institute for Strategic Studies, 1969), pp. 19-22.

totalitarianism. Yet the possibility that the Soviet Union might employ its armed might to suppress Czech dissent was treated with an incredulity borne of optimism—an incredulity that would have done credit to British politicians of thirty years before.

Misperception: The "Softer-Line" Argument

When the Soviet invasion was only a month away, authoritative observers reported how the Soviets were adopting a softer line: that Communists in Eastern Europe were adhering to the Czech cause; and that "Moscow had made a historic mistake . . . when it attempted its crude intervention in Czechoslovakia's internal affairs."[3] One *New York Times* columnist, writing only nineteen days before the Soviet invasion, drew on his knowledge of recent history to remark:

> But this is not 1956 or Hungary, even with the disregard of world opinion it [the Soviet Union] has so often shown when its real interests are at stake. Moscow has a weak position in internal Czech politics and no good opportunity to impose by force or by coup a more malleable regime with a chance of standing on its own feet. . . .
>
> But that the Soviets, who have the power to crush the Czechs almost overnight, do not appear willing to do so, and that Dubcek went to Cierna so truly representative of his country's will, teaches the equally useful lesson that the conjunctions of ideas and circumstances can be more powerful than armies.[4]

On the 2nd of August, the *New York Times* prophesied authoritatively: "The Soviet Union is not about to invade Czechoslovakia." Further, it said: "It is only because he had a united nation behind him that Mr. Dubcek was able to deal with the Russians as equals and to demand as well as to offer concessions. The lesson will not be lost on other peoples in eastern Europe."[5]

On the 3rd of August, the *New York Times* told its readers of the contrast between Dubcek's reassuring the Czech people by radio and the silence of the Soviet Government in respect to explanations to the Soviet peoples: "The contrast suggests how far and how positively Czechoslovakia has moved from its former status of a satellite state ruled by an all-powerful totalitarian dictatorship."[6]

On the 5th of August, the *Times* found that:

3. "Soviets Reported To Send Czechs Softer Message; Dubcek Calls Meeting Today to Win Backing of Central Committee of the Party," *New York Times,* 19 July 1968, p. 3; Harry Schwartz, "Czechoslovakia Gains Allies in the Communist Camp," *ibid.*, 22 July 1968, p. 34.

4. Tom Wicker, "In the Nation: Reflection on Cierna," *New York Times,* 1 August 1968, p. 28.

5. "From Cierna to Bratislava," *New York Times*, 2 August 1968, p. 30.

6. "Stirrings of Democracy," *ibid.*, 3 August 1968, p. 24.

> The suppressionist elements in the Kremlin leadership and their neolithic allies in Eastern Europe have suffered a massive defeat. . . .
>
> The consequences within the Communist world of this successful defiance of attempted Muscovite dictation are likely to be profound. But even more significant is the impetus that the Kremlin's final decision to follow the road of reason and tolerance must give to the effort to strengthen the major foundations of world peace through an improved climate for Soviet-American cooperation.[7]

The *Times* did not explain what had happened to the "suppressionist elements in the Kremlin," or to their "neolithic allies." It was left to be inferred that they were now passé, replaced by their kinder and more tolerant colleagues.

The Moscow correspondent of the *Times* reported on the 6th of August that: "The spectre of 'counterrevolution' in Czechoslovakia that evoked cries of outrage and alarm from the Soviet Union seems to have disappeared into the mists of unhistory"; while: "Mass propaganda rallies throughout the country to stir up hostility against the Czechoslovak liberation program have ended."[8]

At the same time, the correspondent in Prague reported that the Soviet Union had been forced to accept a "humbling reversal of Soviet policy in front of the countries that had supported Moscow's earlier tough line on Czechoslovakia."[9]

The *Times* correspondent in Berlin reported: "The compromise on Czechoslovakia reached Saturday by the leaders of the six European Communist countries has forced the East German regime to shift its public stand." Herr Ulbricht, doubtless one of the "neolithic leaders" previously mentioned by the *Times,* was now faced with the prospect of having to moderate his internal policies or else adopt an even harsher line.[10]

Mr. Sulzberger at the *Times* pointed out the marvels of the new age that was dawning:

> Europe's political map has certainly been changed by the Czechoslovakian revolt against outside dictation and it is even possible the techniques and administration of Soviet Communism may ultimately be altered. Maybe the loudest echo will eventually resound in the Soviet Union. Russian Communism doesn't like to be led by failures, as Khrushchev found out after being faced down over Cuba. Brezhnev

7. "Face Saving at Bratislava," *ibid.,* 5 August 1968, p. 38.
8. "Press Attacks Abandoned," *ibid.,* 6 August 1968, p. 1.
9. "Bratislava Conference Put Soviets in an Awkward Spot: Brezhnev Backed Down," *ibid.,* 6 August 1968, p. 1.
10. "German Reds End Attack on Prague: Accords at Bratislava Brings Shift in Party's Stance—Ulbricht is Silent," *ibid.,* 7 August 1968, p. 1.

> allowed himself to become the symbol of a diehard line on Czechoslovakia and therefore may suffer personally for its lack of success.

And of course, best of all: "There seems to have been no permanent damage to the patient search for better relations between the White House and the Kremlin. Indeed, if the hard-liners really fade from dominant positions in the Kremlin, the search may be encouraged."[11]

On the 8th of August it was reported that Tito, that harbinger of all movements toward freedom and democracy, was to visit Czechoslovakia to be "received by an enthusiastic welcome."[12]

Not to be outdone in euphoria by the *Times,* the *Economist* in London, wrote:

> The democratic world has only just avoided a second Munich involving the same small country; and that only because the dominant faction among the present Russian leaders turns out to be a more rational group of men than the leaders of Nazi Germany.[13]

It was to the *Economist,* one more manifestation of the "thawing out of the cold war."

On the 12th, the *Times* asserted that "For Those Under 30, Prague Seems the Place to Be This Summer." As a graduate of the Harvard Law School put it so well, with that acute perception of the legally trained: "The Czechs are the good guys this year." A veteran of the French student riots observed: "How beautiful this is. To give a human face to modern society. That is exactly what we wanted to do in Paris this spring."[14]

There were those, of course, who urged some swift action by the United States. One such, a professor from a famous university, pointed out the obvious course of action for the government:

> The United States should match the weakening of Soviet influence in Czechoslovakia by an action that would reassure Moscow about the West's intentions. The proposal for a withdrawal of American troops from a substantial part of West Germany, especially its southern portion, would represent such a reassuring gesture. Such a move would not only save the Czechoslovak democratization program and further encourage the liberalization of eastern Europe, but also initiate the long-overdue military disengagement on the continent.[15]

11. C. L. Sulzberger, "Foreign Affairs: A New Little Entente," *ibid.*, 7 August 1968, p. 38.

12. "Tito Is Now Expected in Prague Tomorrow," *ibid.*, 8 August 1968, p. 8.

13. Brian Beedham, Foreign Editor of *The Economist,* "An Omen of the 1970's," *San Francisco Chronicle,* 12 August 1968, p. 12.

14. "For Those Under 30, Prague Seems the Place to Be This Summer," *New York Times,* 12 August 1968, p. 13.

15. "U.S. Troop Withdrawal Urged," Letter from Assistant Professor Vojtech Mastny, Columbia University, New York, to the Editor of the *New York Times,* dated 26 July 1968 in *New York Times,* 31 July 1968, p. 36.

A week after the meeting of the leaders of the six communist states at Bratislava, where Czechoslovakian reforms were discussed with the leaders of the Czech government and Communist Party, the editors of the *New York Times* were truly rhapsodic in describing the consequences of the meeting:

> The defeat Moscow and its allies suffered in their recent confrontation with Prague inevitably forced a rethinking of attitudes on many issues. This rethinking could produce changes making positive contributions and helping to ease present areas of world tensions. There are no guarantees of course, but evidence that some rethinking is taking place comes from the first shock waves that are already spreading in the wake of meetings at Cierna and Bratislava.

The *Times* seismic analysis continued with reflections on the "conciliatory line" that the East German leader, Walter Ulbricht, a notorious hard-liner, had adopted toward the Czechs. It said further that, with the Tito visit with the Czech leaders, a "new Prague-Belgrade axis" now existed, and asserted: "But no observers of Eastern Europe's contemporary political scene can doubt that their meeting was a celebration of victory. . . ."[16]

Around midnight of the 20th-21st of August, Warsaw Pact Airborne troops seized the Prague main airport and the other principal airports in Czechoslovakia while ground troops invaded the country. One U.S. senator and aspirant to the presidency nobly masked his shock at the outrage and said: "I do not see this as a major world crisis. It is likely to have more serious consequences for the Communist Party in Russia than in Czechoslovakia."[17]

Others less quick to recover, depended on the wisdom of the "experts" on Soviet Communism:

> Some of the best informed students of Soviet Communism agree that the Russians, by invading Czechoslovakia, have prepared the ruin of the international Communist movement . . . what remaining moral authority the Soviets still possessed in the Communist world has now gone—altogether.[18]

Joseph Kraft gave the whole thing an optimistic turn, with his impression that Brezhnev and Kosygin had tried manfully to move the inert mass of Russian and Communist bureaucracy to adjust to the transformations sweeping the world," but that the *apparatchiks* in Moscow had undone their work, and the tanks had rolled. He suggested that perhaps the United States had not gone about the matter of détente in the right way, but that there

16. "Shock Waves After Bratislava," *New York Times,* 12 August 1968, p. 32.
17. "Crisis Not Major, McCarthy Asserts," *Los Angeles Times,* 22 August 1968, p. 1.
18. "What Russians Blew," *San Francisco Chronicle,* 23 August 1968, p. 44.

must not be a yielding "to the instinct to cast aside now and forever, the possibilities of détente."[19]

Others pointed out how the invasion of Czechoslovakia had undermined the no. 1 position and raised the level of world distrust of the Soviet Union.[20]

Soviet Military Strength is Political Weakness:
The Anti-Cold War Argument

By the 23rd of August, with Warsaw Pact troops securely in control of Czechoslovakia and the rounding up of Czech malcontents well under way by the Czech and Soviet secret police, the *Times,* carefully avoiding any use of the rhetoric of the "Cold War," was able to see some light at the end of the tunnel:

> The reality, in short, is that no act of the Soviet Government—not even the subjugation of Hungary—has even been condemned with such near-unanimity on both sides of the Iron Curtain as this week's unprovoked, brutal violation of small, defenseless Czechoslovakia. . . . Already the Soviet Union has paid a heavy price in prestige and world respect for this blunder. But there is still time to cut those losses by evacuating Czechoslovakia promptly and permitting the people and the duly elected leaders of that country to decide their own fate.[21]

James Reston took comfort in the view that while the "men in the Kremlin can bully and betray an ally . . . this squalid business in Prague is not a sign of Soviet strength but a dramatic confession of moral and political weakness . . . in the long run Prague may very well inspire, even in the Soviet Union, the spirit of freedom Moscow is trying to smother."[22]

On the 24th of August, the *Times* spoke lovingly of the "outraged conscience of mankind," on the occasion of the Czech President's visit to Moscow, and of the "political debacle" the Soviet Union had brought upon itself. "By receiving Mr. Svoboda," the *Times* said:

> the Kremlin has shown that it feels the full impact of world and Czechoslovak opinion, and is frantically seeking some accommodation that will save face and cut some of this week's enormous losses in world respect.[23]

To Max Lerner, it was all a manifestation of the weakness of the Soviet "Empire," and the sounding of its ultimate end: ". . . the Soviet rulers and

19. Joseph Kraft, "A Better Road to Detente," *Los Angeles Times,* 23 August 1968, p. 5, pt. II.
20. Royce Brier, "Russ Throw Away Toil of Years," *San Francisco Chronicle,* 23 August 1968, p. 44.
21. "Communists and Prague," *New York Times,* 23 August 1968, p. 36.
22. "Tanks and Ideas: Moscow's Fatal Weakness," *New York Times,* 23 August 1968, p. 36.
23. "The Svoboda Mission," *ibid.,* 24 August 1968, p. 28.

their proconsuls in the other capitals have underestimated the cost of their military victory."[24]

There were more somber views expressed, of course, including that of the Soviet official reported to have said that it was not the failure of the Western Allies to warn the Russians off Czechoslovakia that had permitted the invasion to go on; no such warning would have been heeded, he said, even if the West had threatened war.[25]

While the downfall of the Soviet regime as a consequence of the Czech invasion was awaited with hope and optimism in some quarters, there were other and more pessimistic implications of the invasion, aside from the consequences for those Czechs who had thought the Czech regime could be liberalized in the face of Soviet opposition. Some of the Soviet paratroopers who jumped into Czechoslovakia, expressed their disappointment at discovering they were seizing a Czech airfield instead of one outside of Munich.[26]

The *Times* nowhere explained its deep and abiding concern that the Soviet Union should enjoy the respect and good opinion of the world, nor how the set-back the Soviet Union was seen to have suffered in Czechoslovakia was calculated to sweeten the Soviet temper.

In a second editorial on the 24th of August, the *Times* pointed out to the United States government that, the Czech invasion notwithstanding, Washington should not end its search for agreements with Moscow that "can make an explosive world marginally safer . . . it will serve the supreme long-run cause of peace if the two super-powers can continue, despite profound differences, to work out enforceable agreements in critical areas of mutual interest and worldwide concern." Presumably the freedom of Czechoslovakia ought once again not be an obstacle to "Peace for our Time."[27]

George Kennan, former Ambassador to the Soviet Union and *doyen* of commentators on Soviet practices, given some time to reflect on the Soviet invasion of Czechoslovakia, allowed as how it was the United States that had been at least partly at fault:

> We might, it seems to me, have at least proposed some modification of our military position in Germany as *quid pro quo* for Soviet forebearance in Hungary or in Czechoslovakia, as the case may be. We could have proposed, for example, a withdrawal of American forces from Bavaria or some other area in return for Russian withdrawal from Czechoslovakia.[28]

24. Max Lerner, "The International Jungle Still a Place of Savagery," *Los Angeles Times*, 23 August 1968, p. 5, pt. II.

25. Soviet Embassy, Washington, D.C., 19 September 1968.

26. General James H. Polk, U.S.A. (Ret'd), "Reflections on the Czechoslovakian Invasion, 1968," *Strategic Review*, Vol. V, No. 1 (Winter 1977), pp. 30-37.

27. "Next Steps for the U.N.," *ibid.*, p. 28.

28. "Send 100,000 GIs to Germany Kennan Urges," *San Francisco Examiner & Chronicle*, 23 September 1968, p. 2, section A.

It was, however, not entirely clear how the weakening of the NATO Central Front would moderate Soviet resistance to liberalization of the Czech regime. But then, in writing from his post in Czechoslovakia in 1938, after the German occupation of the Sudetenland, Mr. Kennan had taken comfort from the fact that "no ill wind can fail to blow good," and hoped that as a consequence of the Nazi action, there would be "greater economic security and greater racial tolerance" in what remained of the Czech nation. Admitting that the "adjustment"—his word for the Nazi depredations fostered at Munich—was in a "painful and deplorable form," yet, he found:

> . . . it has relieved the Czechoslovak states of liabilities as well as assets. It has left the heart of the country physically intact. Finally, and perhaps most important of all, it has preserved for the exacting tasks of the future a magnificent younger generation—disciplined, industrious and physically fit—which would undoubtedly have been sacrificed if the solution had been the romantic one of hopeless resistance rather than the humiliating but truly heroic one of realism. . . .

Beyond that, he found, "no indications of any desire on the part of Hitler to make Germans out of the Czechs. Their role is that of a vassal—and the vassal's role has always been easier to execute than that of the independent younger brother."[29]

By November 1968, the *New York Times* concluded that while it seemed true to say that conditions in Czechoslovakia were not at all pleasant for those who had enjoyed the "Prague spring," still, "Moscow can have no illusion that it is gathering anything but a harvest of hate from the seeds planted by the treachery of last August." But, the *Times* warned:

> It would be tragic if NATO's response to the new Soviet militancy were merely negative, signalling a return to the inflexible attitudes of the Cold War. . . .
>
> The West must continue to encourage in every possible way that growing body of opinion in Eastern Europe, and in the Soviet Union itself, that yearns for peaceful engagement.[30]

Yet one observer, more candid than others, recalled his pre-invasion optimism with a note of regret and a certain sadness:

> I have to confess that within the last six months I have predicted in public, not once but several times, that the Russians would not do the kind of thing that in August they did. This is one of the "uses of power"

29. George F. Kennan, *From Prague After Munich, Diplomatic Papers 1938-1940* (Princeton: Princeton University Press, 1968), pp. 5 and 9.

30. "Post-Invasion Prague . . ." and ". . . and the NATO Response," *New York Times*, 18 November 1968, p. 46.

> . . . that I might have stood here and depreciated in public if it had not already occurred to contradict me. I do not know where I went wrong. . . .[31]

What an irony it is that a totalitarian regime where there is no freedom at all can see the danger presented by those who profess to cherish their freedom beyond all other things, while those who profess to cherish freedom can see no danger at all.

Strategic Implications

But even in 1968, there seemed to be little inclination to draw any strategic inferences from Warsaw Pact Operations in Czechoslovakia.[32] The Soviet Union's use of the military power at its command to discipline those Czechs who had challenged Moscow's authority seemed to carry no lesson for those who might one day find themselves in a similar position. The fact that the Soviet Union increased its regular strength at the West German border by another five divisions while demonstrating that a Soviet general could call upon East German, Polish, Hungarian and Bulgarian forces to act alongside Soviet units seemed not alarming at all. The Czech invasion came at a time when the United States was carrying out a reduction of its forces in Western Europe. In 1961, at the time of the Berlin Crisis, U.S. Army forces in West Germany had numbered 273,000. By 21 August 1968, that number had been reduced by 70,000 and tactical fighter strength had been reduced by five squadrons.[33] The reductions scheduled long before the Czech invasion continued to be carried out despite the invasion.[34]

America's Military Retrenchment

Senator Mike Mansfield, the former Democratic majority leader, introduced a Senate resolution supported by 43 other Senators, in January 1967, to withdraw most of the troops stationed in Western Europe. He argued that relations between Western and Communist Eastern Europe had improved and that: "A substantial reduction of United States forces permanently stationed in Europe can be made without adversely affecting either

31. Thomas C. Schelling, "The Use of Force in the Nuclear Age," Tenth Annual Conference of the Institute for Strategic Studies, 21 September 1968.

32. "History Has a Lesson to Teach—On the 10th anniversary of Soviet invasion of Czechoslovakia," *Peking Review*, No. 34, 25 August 1978, pp. 21-22.

33. "Europe Armies: U.S. Forces at Low Ebb," *Palo Alto Times*, 21 August 1968, p. 5; "U.S. Strength at Low Ebb in Europe," *San Francisco Chronicle*, 21 August 1968, p. 13.

34. "NATO Dwarfed by Soviet Strength," *Philadelphia Enquirer*, 30 September 1968, p. 1.

our resolve or ability to meet our commitment under the North Atlantic Treaty."[35]

Senator Mansfield and some of his colleagues would continue to urge the withdrawal of U.S. forces from West Germany right up until the Soviet invasion of Czechoslovakia. Two days after the invasion the Senator was asked for his view of troop withdrawal in the light of that event. He allowed that perhaps the United States ought to wait and see what was going to happen before proceeding with the withdrawal. Three weeks after the invasion the Senator concluded that matters in Europe had settled down sufficiently to permit U.S. troop reductions.[36]

The Improved Viability of the Warsaw Pact: Beginning of a Pax Sovietica?

The Soviet Union demonstrated in Czechoslovakia that it could call on other members of the Warsaw Pact to discipline a fellow member; it demonstrated the pliability of the Czech armed forces to Soviet control—the Czech army did not move from its barracks during the invasion in 1968; and it demonstrated the close relationship between the Czech secret police and the Soviet KGB. Beyond that and more significant for the defense of NATO, the Soviet Union showed that it could increase its forces facing NATO without any commensurate military response from NATO.[37] After 1968, five Soviet divisions remained stationed in Czechoslovakia, of which two were tank divisions and three were motorized rifle divisions. Far from demonstrating any distrust of the Czech armed forces, the Soviet Union has permitted the Czech defense budget to increase by 66% while the Czech Army maintains in combat units 2,000 tanks (400 more than the U.S. Seventh Army in Europe possesses in its combat units and in its depots as stockpile for units that might be deployed from the United States).[38]

35. Text cited in "Mansfield Plans New bid to Bring GIs Home: Will Reintroduce Resolution Calling for Pulling 320,000 Servicemen from Europe," *Los Angeles Times,* 10 July 1969, p. 4.

36. "Mansfield Will Press U.S. Troop Cut in Europe," *New York Times,* 11 January 1968, p. 3; two days after the invasion: "Pressure to Cut U.S. Forces in Europe Eases; Mansfield Says Events Prompt Delay; Previously Planned Withdrawal to Go On," *Los Angeles Times,* 23 August 1968, p. 6; and, three weeks after the invasion: "Europe Troop Cuts Sought by Mansfield," *ibid.,* 14 September 1968, p. 10; and so on. "Mansfield Asks Troop Cut Again," *Baltimore Sun,* 14 September 1968, p. 1; "Mansfield Again Urges U.S. Troop Cut in Europe," *New York Times,* 2 December 1969, p. 2; and, "Mansfield Will Try to Cut U.S. Europe Forces," *Los Angeles Times,* 5 December 1970, p. 16.

37. "Russians Building Camps Near West Germany," *New York Times,* 25 September 1968, p. 4: "The presence, so close to towns like Neustadt and Regensburg, has shifted the balance of strategic military power in Europe."

38. Czech defense budget given in *The Military Balance, 1967-1968* (London: The Institute for Strategic Studies, 1967), p. 3 and *The Military Balance, 1976-1977* (1976), p. 12. Czech tank figures may be found in the same place where they are listed at 3,300. Figures in text are derived from Table of Organization and Equipment for Soviet Motorized and Tank divisions given in "American and Soviet Armed Services Strengths Compared 1970-76," in *Congressional Record—Senate,* 5 August 1977, S14063-S14081. See also, John M. Collins, *American and Soviet Military Trends Since the Cuban Missile Crisis* (Washington, D.C.: Georgetown University, 1978), p. 199.

The liberal West devoted little attention to the suppression of even the modest liberty essayed by the Czechs in 1968. The material shift in Soviet deployment of motorized rifle and tank divisions to the disadvantage of NATO called forth little response save suggestions to adopt measures that could only worsen NATO's capability. Yet it cannot be said that all has been forgotten. No indeed, there obviously remains some nagging disquiet to disturb the easy acceptance of a *Pax Sovietica.* How else could one explain the eager pursuit of whatever Western rationalization of Soviet behavior will put consciences to sleep. What better place to find such rationalizations than in that land where dwelt the architects of the Czech betrayal of 1938. The editor of the *Evening Standard* (London) seized the occasion of the tenth anniversary of the Soviet invasion of Czechoslovakia to explain the benefits to the world of that Soviet action: "The Russians argued [and to this extent rightly] that had matters continued in Czechoslovakia, central Europe could have broken up once again into its pre-war nationalist groupings with similar border tensions and flashpoints."

And, of course, it is true that pre-war Europe was one large bundle of border tensions and flashpoints. There was the Austrian border with Germany, the German border with Czechoslovakia, and ultimately the Polish border with Germany. But only the Poles had the extraordinary bad taste to attempt to defend their border against Germany. All the rest managed to accommodate Germany, some with the help and inspiration of the liberal West. At least neither Austria nor Czechoslovakia had such fanatic dedication to independence as to cause a war over a mere invasion of their national territory. So, for the editor of the *Evening Standard* to assert that Czechoslovakia, as an independent state, was ruled in 1938 and again in 1968 by a "Jewish-Czech clique," was only a rhetorical device to justify the statement that "it is desirable that some Soviet influence over Czechoslovakia continues" and that it is better for the West "to stare the Russians directly in the face." After all, as the editor pointed out, those manifestations in Czechoslovakia prior to the Soviet invasion and similar manifestations elsewhere in Central Europe create instability that is not necessarily "in the interest of European security. . . ." For: "If freedom comes to the victims of Soviet imperialism in Eastern Europe, it is more likely to come from relaxation within the USSR than through the activities of a Dubcek." The editor considered those who took exception to the *Evening Standard*'s statements to be guilty of "extraordinary outbursts" and their objections to be "nonsense."[39] It should be noted that the *Evening Standard* withdrew, in its later editions of the article on Czechoslovakia, the phrase, "Jewish-Czech ruling

39. "The Appeasers, 1938-1978," *Daily Telegraph* (London), 25 August 1978; "How Czechoslovaks Are Paying the Price," *ibid.*, 25 August 1978: A letter from the editor of the *Evening Standard* to the editor of *Daily Telegraph;* and, '"Standard" Apologizes for Remark," *Daily Telegraph*, 25 August 1978.

clique," as being "offensive." One cannot say that the *Evening Standard* values freedom beyond all else; one can say that it values "stability" above liberty so long as freedom of the press is not the case in point. Champions of stability will, wherever they are, understand the point made by the old/new appeasers: stability is too sweet to permit its being hazarded by malcontents seeking political freedom; far better the peace of surrender than the penalties of resistance.

But then one need not even consider such alternatives if there is no significant shift in the strategic position of the Soviet Union in relation to that of the West. Everyone knows, save perhaps a handful of worriers here and there, that the Soviet Union is not going to go to war; and the Soviet Union is certainly not going to go to war if the strategic advantage in such a war should lie with the Western powers. Those two fashionable "truths" along with the coterie of accepted wisdoms that support them dominate intellectual discourse about the relations between the Soviet Union and the democratic powers of the West. So long as any Soviet action wherever it takes place is classified as political and not strategic, the preferred truths can be affirmed. Thus the invasion of Czechoslovakia promoted "stability" in Eastern Europe and was therefore exclusively a political act with no military implications, despite the strategic residue left behind in the form of five additional Soviet divisions stationed on the border with West Germany. No military implications were drawn from the fact that the Soviet Union could call upon the armed forces of some members of the Warsaw Pact to discipline a fellow member who deviated from the path of true socialism.

Although Soviet strategists and politicians may see war and politics as two sides of the same coin, or as Lenin said in full agreement with Clausewitz, "war is simply the continuation of politics by other [i.e. violent] means,"[40] Western thinkers may not concede that point. Such a concession would implicitly force acknowledgement that there is a deadly struggle between the Soviet Union and the West rather than a well-mannered competition that can lead nowhere but to improved relations:

> There appears to be more realism now, more appreciation that détente is not a fixed condition but a slow process of improving relations during which the political and ideological competition still goes on. It is all to the good that the two sides still want to keep that competition within bounds and are drawing back from the recent mood of confrontation.[41]

Reluctance to discern the strategic implications of political acts between totalitarian states and democracies is an aspect of the incredibility with which

40. *Marxism-Leninism on War and Army* (Moscow: Progress Publishers, 1972), the American edition published by U.S. Government Printing Office, 1976, under the Title, *Marxist-Leninism on War and Army (A Soviet View)*, p. 7.

41. "Detente on the Mind," *The Christian Science Monitor*, 2 October 1978, p. 24.

war is viewed within democratic societies. In June 1935, when Great Britain and Germany concluded their naval agreement permitting Germany to build submarines, it was a mere political act on the part of Great Britain, aimed at mollifying the dictator of Germany. From the viewpoint of Britain, there were no strategic implications bearing on the defense of the United Kingdom or on Germany's capability to wage war: if appeasement were successful, there would be no war. To Germany, the reconstruction of the navy's submarine arm was a prerequisite for waging war against Great Britain. Britain's voluntary acceptance of a German submarine construction program under the assumption that no more than German pride was at stake, was a lot like giving a dog back its teeth so it would stop trying to bite people. The British effort to help Germany regain its "rightful place" in the community of nations obscured the political fact that Germany was now rearming with Britain's blessings, and the strategic fact that Germany would now equip itself with the one weapon that had very nearly cost Britain the war in 1917. It can be seen that there was both shortness of memory and neglect of strategy in British policy; both were a consequence of the failure to appreciate that politics and war are the same thing and therefore strategy is at the heart of every important diplomatic negotiation. What seemed a diplomatic triumph for British appeasement in 1935, in fact, granted Germany a strategic advantage for which Britain would pay dearly when war came.

V. The Cuban Missile Crisis—More Military than Political

SHORTNESS OF MEMORY ABOUT PAST EVENTS, AND THE NEGLECT OF STRATEGY ARE THE EVIDENT CONSEQUENCES OF THE RELUCTANCE TO BELIEVE WAR POSSIBLE. For if war is not possible there is no reason to bother with matters of strategy. The crisis over Cuba provides an illustration of the reluctance to consider war a possibility and of the consequent neglect of strategy on the part of the Western Democracies.

The Cuban Missile Crisis

Initial Misreading

A pervasive optimism dominated the American view of Fidel Castro when he came to power in Cuba in 1959. Fidel Castro, it seemed, would end the embarrassment of the United States stemming from the existence in Cuba of a repressive regime ruled by a petty tyrant. Here was a man of the people leading a spontaneous rebellion in the best tradition of the Green Mountain boys with a special fillip: the man had been to the university. So one had not only a man of the people, but an "intellectual" as well. Lionized on American television as a great freedom fighter, as a latin Robin Hood, the new leader of Cuba could only be a champion of the poor and oppressed. That he might be a Communist was dismissed as a fear typical of those who had brought poor Alger Hiss to a bad end; who had enmeshed the United States in a "Cold War" with the champions of progress in the Kremlin. It was typical as well of those who had cast doubt on the liberal instincts of the agrarian reformers who had come to rule China. Even a man with the best credential of anti-Communism, the deputy director of the Central Intelligence Agency, could find no blemish of Communism on the character of the new Cuban dictator.[1]

1. "Castro is not a Communist . . . the Cuban Communists do not consider him a Communist party member or even pro-Communist. . . . It is questionable whether the Communists desire to recruit Castro into the Communist party, that they could do so if they wished or that he would be susceptible to

Despite the hopes of some Americans that Castro would lead his nation into the ranks of the liberal democracies,[2] *Pravda,* on 15 April 1962, noted that "the heroic people of Cuba" had "embarked on the path of building socialism."[3]

Months before the existence of a crisis became publicly apparent, the Warsaw Pact powers, led by the Soviet Union, had begun shipping arms into Cuba; some reports suggested that as much as 800,000 tons of military equipment and supplies had arrived in Cuba by the time the United States imposed a naval blockade.[4] Indeed, the crisis did not come because the Soviet Union was shipping arms to Cuba or because it had stationed members of its own armed forces in the island in clear violation of the Monroe Doctrine. It came because unambiguous evidence was offered by the Russians that they were emplacing in Cuba SS-4 ballistic missiles capable of carrying one megaton warheads. In addition, they had deployed squadrons of Ilyushin II-48 medium bombers. On 22 October 1962, President Kennedy announced the imposition of a naval "quarantine" against Cuba because of the presence on the island of medium range ballistic missiles; the preparation of sites for intermediate range ballistic missiles; and the assembly of Soviet jet-bombers capable of attacking the United States with nuclear weapons.[5]

Soviet Duplicity and Military Overtness

The Soviet Foreign Minister, Andrei Gromyko, had assured the United States that the Soviet Union was not establishing a military base in Cuba. Such assurance was given notwithstanding the shipments of military equipment, and the evidence of the presence of Soviet strategic missiles revealed by aerial photographs as early as 14 October, eight days before the Cuban missile crisis was announced by the President. It was a strange anomaly indeed. The Foreign Minister of the Soviet Union denied that his country had any intention of doing what in fact it was doing. Yet the missile sites were being prepared and the missiles erected with absolutely no attempt either to conceal the offending activity, or to render its nature ambiguous. The missiles themselves had been identified in military parades in the Soviet Union so that it was impossible to mistake them for anything but what they were.

Communist discipline if he joined." See Roger W. Fontaine, *On Negotiating with Cuba* (Washington, D.C.: American Enterprise Institute, 1975), p. 44, which cites Senate hearings containing the Deputy Director's testimony.

2. See for example, statement of the U.S. Ambassador to Cuba: "This establishment, would, I thought, confine the new government and the leaders from the Sierra Maestra including Castro, within democratic patterns of behavior." Cited in Fontaine, *ibid.*, p. 42.

3. *Current Digest of the Soviet Press,* 9 May 1962, pp. 9-12, cited in Fontaine, *ibid.*, p. 41.

4. "Exiles Report Cuba has 15 Rocket Sites," *The New York Times Western Edition,* 25 October 1962, p. 12.

5. *Britannica Book of the Year, 1963* (Chicago: Encyclopaedia Britannica, Inc., 1963), pp. 303-4.

Here was the Soviet Army, past master of camouflage and deception, unable to hide a handful of missiles and their ancillary equipment. This was the same Soviet Army that, in the offensive to liberate Byelorussia in 1944, was able to conceal the concentration of 2.5 million troops, 4,000 tanks, and 24,000 mortars and artillery pieces from the German troops they were about to attack. The same Soviet Army had taught the North Koreans how to build bridges underwater to achieve surprise against United Nations troops fighting to defend South Korea.[6]

Even a superficial inspection of the series of aerial photographs taken by U.S. reconnaissance aircraft could hardly fail to reveal the nature of the installations and the identity of the weapons being emplaced. The *Sandal* or SS-4 missile, seventy-two feet long, had been displayed to the public in Moscow, for the first time, in November 1960, two years before the crisis. The other missile, called the *Shyster,* had been displayed in 1959.[7] The trailers upon which to carry the missiles, the prime-movers used to haul the trailers, the erectors for setting the missiles in place, all revealed themselves to the most casual inspection. Further, no attempts were even made to conceal the necessary support troops.[8]

The nature of the Soviet regime makes it difficult to imagine that the nuclear weapons were merely included by some minor functionary in the inventory of arms shipped to Cuba. To the contrary, it would seem that the deployment of nuclear weapons in Cuba was decided at the very highest level of government and only after the most careful review of the possible responses. Surely the possibility must have been explored that nuclear missiles in Cuba would arouse the United States to take some kind of action. At the same time, if it were accepted by the Soviet leaders that the United States would take exception to nuclear missiles in Cuba, then why were there no efforts exerted either to conceal the installation of the missiles or, at least, to render the installations sufficiently ambiguous so that aerial photographs would have revealed something that might be missile installations but that

6. The deception in the campaign to liberate Byelorussia is described in Earl F. Ziemke, *Stalingrad to Berlin; The German Defeat in the East in Army Historical Series* (Washington, D.C.: Office of the Chief of Military History, 1968), pp. 314-15; the underwater bridges and their use by the North Koreans and by the Soviet Army is described in Roy E. Appelman, *South to the Naktong, North to the Yalu* in *United States Army in the Korean War Series* (Washington, D.C.: Office of the Chief of Military History, 1961), pp. 345-46 and elsewhere.

7. See *Handbook on the Soviet Armed Forces, July 1969,* Defense Intelligence Agency, AP-220-3-19-69-INT, and p. 230 for *Sandal* and p. 229, for *Shyster.*

8. Numerous photographs of the installations are in "Russia Avoids Early Chance to Test U.S. Determination in Cuban Arms Blockade," *Aviation Week and Space Technology,* Vol. 77, No. 18, pp. 27-30; "Photos Documented Cuban Arms Buildup." *ibid.*, p. 31-34; and, "Latest Photos Show Speed of IRBM and MRBM Buildup in Cuba," *ibid.*, No. 19, 5 November 1962, pp. 30-34. A picture of one of the MRBM's similar to those deployed into Cuba, is shown when the missile was on parade in Moscow, on p. 24.

might be something else as well? Various kinds of Soviet arms had been coming into Cuba for months before the missile crisis, and the United States had done hardly more than half-heartedly support a handful of Cuban exiles in their abortive attempt to launch an anti-Castro invasion. There could certainly have been no question in the mind of the Soviet government that the United States would reconnoiter Cuba from the air. After all the Soviet Union had shot down a number of U.S. reconnaissance aircraft approaching or flying over Soviet territory in the past. Why should the Soviet government believe the United States would not routinely photograph Cuba from the air and thereby discover the missiles so obviously being emplaced? Cuba, a traditional interest of the United States, only ninety-odd miles from the American mainland, was certainly a center of controversy and discussion within the United States since Castro's seizure of the Cuban government and avowal of communism.

The Soviet Gamble: Political or Military?

Why should the Soviet Union wish, in effect, to create a *cause célèbre* with its ballistic missiles? As the *New York Times,* expressed it:

> Like a thunderbolt piercing a murky sky, the revelation that Premier Khrushchev is converting Cuba into a potential offensive nuclear base against the United States and the whole Western Hemisphere casts a lurid light on the present crisis. This is no longer a bearded Cuban revolutionary fulminating against us. This is Soviet Russia stretching out its nuclear arm across the Atlantic to confront us with a deadly challenge.

And the *Times* went on to point out that "Cuba's subjugation to Soviet control is merely the latest step in a long list of Russian aggressions stretching back over a quarter-century." The *Times* said: "This record has made Soviet Russia the largest and most oppressive colonial empire in history and puts the present Soviet challenge in its true light." But even the *Times* would ask why Khrushchev who "has given the impression of one who carefully calculated possible gains and possible losses before taking a step," should have "taken such an enormous risk."[9]

And indeed, that is *the* question. Why should the Soviet Union have taken such a risk without any apparent attempt to mitigate the risk by obscuring the nature of its actions? There was perhaps a clue further on in the *Times* editorial: "But we cannot and will not permit this direct provocation by the Soviet Union—*more political than military*—in upsetting the long-

9. "The Soviet Challenge in Cuba," *The New York Times Western Edition,* 25 October 1962, p. 10.

established *status quo* in this hemisphere by creating a potentially offensive nuclear base on our very borders."[10]

But the missiles were a *military* provocation, as the other Soviet arms supplied to Cuba earlier should have been. The willingness of the *Times* to see a distinction between political and military acts, however, overlooked the fact that to those who govern the Soviet Union, politics and war are but two sides of the same coin. Viewed in that light then, the Soviet provocation had several components. The introduction of the missiles into Cuba focused American attention on Cuba in a fashion that neither Castro's being a communist, nor the supply of conventional arms to Cuba by the Soviet Union, had been able to accomplish. The direct and totally unambiguous military threat against the continental United States posed by the Soviet rockets in Cuba forced the United States to seek a diplomatic accommodation with the Soviet Union over Cuba. Within six days after President Kennedy announced the imposition of the naval quarantine, the Soviet Union, without even testing the quarantine, began dismantling the rocket bases and gave an assurance that the rockets would be shipped back to Russia. In return for that assurance, the President gave a solemn undertaking that the United States would lift the naval quarantine and that the "United States would join with other nations of the Western Hemisphere in providing assurances against an invasion of the island."[11]

Premier Khrushchev took note that the Cuban people wanted nothing more than "to build their life in their interests without external interference"; that they wanted to be masters in their own country and to "dispose of the fruits of their own labor." In his message to President Kennedy, the Soviet Premier went on to explain that he had instructed his officers in Cuba to proceed with the dismantling of the installations that had caused the trouble. He then made a plea to the President to halt reconnaissance flights over Cuba:

> We are interested that there should be no war in the world and that the Cuban people should live in peace. But besides Mr. President, it is no secret that we have our people on Cuba.
>
> Under a treaty with the Cuban Government we have there officers, instructors who teach Cubans, mostly plain people: specialists, land reclamation specialists, plain workers, tractor drivers and others. We are concerned about them.
>
> I should like you to consider Mr. President, that violation of the air-space of Cuba by American planes could also lead to dangerous conse-

10. Italics added.

11. "U.S. and Soviets Reach Cuba Accord; Kennedy Accepts Khrushchev's Vow to Remove Missiles as U.N. Observes," *The New York Times Western Edition*, 29 October 1962, p. 1.

> quences. And if you do not want this to happen, it would be better if no cause is given for a dangerous situation to arise.

As though to sympathize with the difficult position of the President, the Premier went on to say:

> Mr. President, I trust your statement, but on the other hand there are irresponsible people who would like to invade Cuba now and thus touch off a war. If we do take practical steps and proclaim the dismantling and evacuation of the means from Cuba, in doing so, we at the same time want the Cuban people to be sure that we are with them and do not absolve ourselves of responsibility for rendering assistance to the Cuban people.[12]

And indeed, it is difficult to imagine a more gentlemanly accommodation than that made to resolve the crisis created by the Soviet Union's emplacement of nuclear weapons in Cuba. It was almost as though there had been a dreadful misunderstanding between the United States and the Soviet Union that the Soviet Union managed to clear up by its quick willingness to concede that rockets in Cuba were offensive to the United States and that their withdrawal would therefore allay the concern of the American government.

The American Response: Political Victory and (Unacknowledged) Strategic Defeat

The effort on the American side to de-couple the political from the strategic and to see the Soviet action as chiefly political relegated the strategic significance of Cuba to a mere footnote in the entire affair. The unwillingness to perceive strategic significance in Soviet military operations in Cuba reflected the reluctance to see war as a credible outcome of Soviet policy toward the democratic world. The Communist leaders of the Soviet Union might see politics and war to be inseparable parts of the struggle for supremacy over the West. But such, however, was not a palatable view to those who suppose that all international relations reflect a common desire for stability and peace; or those who wistfully hope that a Communist dictatorship, wherever established, will eventually evolve into a democratic society if given half a chance.

America Wins the Cold War: The Origins of Détente?

The fashionable view was that the United States had won a victory over the Soviet Union in Cuba. This victory ended the Cold war, opened all manner of opportunities for détente and arms control agreements and even

12. "Text of Khrushchev's Message On Cuban Missile Crisis, Airspace Violations," *The New York Times Western Edition,* 29 October 1962, p. 4.

caused the downfall of Premier Khrushchev. But this fashionable view simply and grossly ignored the strategic advantage that the Soviet Union had won in the missile crisis.[13]

President Kennedy, on his part, saw the ending of the crisis, "not as a victory but merely as an honest accommodation," while rejecting "the conclusion of the hardliners that the way to deal with Moscow everywhere in the world is to be tough."[14]

The *New York Times,* in a flash of instant optimism, celebrated "The Triumph of Reason":

> Reason prevailed and the threat of mutual thermonuclear annihilation began to fade when Premier Khrushchev agreed to dismantle his offensive bases in Cuba and ship his missiles back to the Soviet Union. The Soviet ruler's step was, as President Kennedy observed, a statesmanlike decision and an important contribution to world peace.

While the *Times* fell short of suggesting that the Russian Premier might be considered a candidate for a Nobel Prize for his contribution to world peace, it did suggest that there was now real hope for détente in Europe, nuclear disarmament, and similar good things. Indeed, the *Times* said: "The vision is almost too idyllic to be real, but it injects new vigor and hope into the pursuit of a peace of benefit to all mankind."[15] Thus what had at first appeared to the uninitiated as a blatantly warlike act on the part of the Soviet Union, now came to be seen in its true colors—as a prologue to world peace. The Soviet Union, having received its due in Cuba, would now become a force for moderation in the world.

The conventional view of the missile crisis argues that the Soviet leaders had made a dreadful error in underestimating the United States's willingness to defend its vital interests. Henry Kissinger, for example, while suggesting that the vacillations of the United States toward Soviet gambits in the past had, perhaps misled the Soviet Union, concluded that "it was difficult to explain Soviet actions except as a colossal blunder. The Russians clearly

13. See for example, Max Frankel, "Where Do we Go from Victory?," *The Reporter,* 22 November 1962, pp. 24-26; and, Henry A. Kissinger, "Reflections on Cuba," *ibid.* pp. 21-23. For more recent evidence of the notion of the fashionable view see, "Open-Skies Proposal: Eisenhower Paved Way for Strategic Arms Talks: In the Cuban Crisis, Khrushchev Learned the Limits of Nuclear Power," *Los Angeles Times,* 9 January 1978, p. 1. Quite naturally, textbooks on American foreign policy purvey the fashionable view: see for example, Walter LeFeber, *America, Russia and the Cold War* (New York: John Wiley & Son, 1976), p. 26f. and John Spanier, *American Foreign Policy Since World War II* (New York: Praeger, 1977), pp. 152-55. See also Ronald Steel, "The Kennedys and the Missile Crisis," in *Readings in American Foreign Policy: A Bureaucratic Perception* (Boston: Little, Brown, and Co., 1973), pp. 202-20; "Kennedy had pulled off the greatest coup of his career—the first, and one hopes, the last military victory of the nuclear era."

14. "The President's View: Kennedy Rejects Thesis That Outcome On Cuba Shows 'Tough Line' is Best," *ibid.,* p. 1.

15. "Triumph of Reason," 29 October 1962, p. 14.

misjudged the character of the President and the mood of the country." Kissinger dismissed the possibility that the installation of missiles in Cuba might have had strategic or military significance to the Soviet Union since:

> If the Soviets felt that missiles based on Cuban territory were necessary to redress the overall strategic balance, then the Soviet arsenal of intercontinental missiles must be much smaller than had been generally believed. If, on the other hand, the Soviets consider their arsenal to be adequate, then nuclear bases in Cuba were irrelevant to the security problem in Cuba. Given the vulnerability of these bases, it is difficult to understand to what military problem they were addressed.

He concluded therefore, that: "The chief benefit the Soviets would have obtained from these bases was *political,* not military."[16]

But withal, the future Secretary of State concluded that having cleared the air, as it were, it was now possible to contemplate the pursuit of some kind of settlement with the Soviet Union that would be tolerable to American and allied interests. "Responsible Russians should be given every chance to understand that the obstacle to coexistence is the Communist quest for world domination. On such a basis negotiations are highly desirable."

An American Defeat?

A far less fashionable view, and one that did not long endure, was that the United States had been had in the Cuban missile crisis. Charles Burton Marshall, quoting Goethe, wrote: "In the long run, over-great goodness, mildness, and moral delicacy, will not do, while underneath there is a mixed and sometimes vicious world to manage and to hold in respect." Beyond that Marshall found:

> The paeans occasioned by Soviet agreement to dismantle baffle me. Only by focusing narrowly on the issue of missile deployment can one call this a retraction on the part of the Soviet Union. Our President's avowal on April 20 last year, of resolve never to abandon Cuba to Communists had been publicly put aside—no mean feat of word-swallowing. By contrast, the Soviet pledge to shelter the Cuban regime is now redeemed. Cuba is now unmistakably a Soviet protectorate.

Mr. Marshall concluded:

> We have negotiated on this basis with the Soviet Union. Communist power is ensconced in the Western Hemisphere. We have in effect legitimized this. We have joined in invoking UN blessings on the arrangement.
>
> One must await what events may disclose as to the power of precedent in the pattern—what other positions may go in a sequence of seeing a

16. Henry A. Kissinger, "Reflections on Cuba," pp. 21-24. Italics added.

> Communist regime put into power by whatever means, having the stakes raised then guaranteeing the position in return for having the stakes lowered. As a gain, Cuba is somewhat akin to the victory at Ausculum: a few more such would be our undoing.
>
> A disposition to view the development as giving promise for negotiating a general détente seems borrowed from fantasy. . . . "If you believe that, you can believe anything."[17]

Mr. Marshall's view was a minority one, hardly to be noticed amongst all of the optimism generated by the willingness of the Soviet Union to be so exceedingly conciliatory in responding to the American anxiety about missiles in Cuba.

America as Aggressor?

The British foreign office, in the best tradition of 1938, saw the affair as an unmistakable opportunity to begin negotiations on the halting of nuclear testing in the atmosphere and on general disarmament. And indeed, by the end of the following year, a Test-Ban Treaty had been negotiated—*after* the Soviet Union had detonated a 50 megaton weapon in the atmosphere in violation of the test moratorium that had been declared by both the United States and the Soviet Union.[18]

There were, of course, those in the United States who saw the American "quarantine" on ships carrying missiles to Cuba as an unwarranted and warlike action on the part of the United States. The Student Peace Union called upon its 15,000 members to demonstrate in Washington against the American blockade.[19] Members of the academic community responded to the crisis in their traditional way and with the clarity of visions usually reserved for more recondite and less pressing matters. In "An Appeal to President Kennedy and Comrade Khrushchev," they informed the two that "we cannot believe that the Soviet Union wants war; rather we regard the provocative buildup of missile bases in Cuba as the culmination of a long history of mutual acts of cold-war antagonism." The professors went on to admonish the United States for its military bases overseas, pointing out what an impact such bases have "on Soviet attitudes and policies."[20]

17. Charles Burton Marshall, "Afterthoughts on the Cuban Blockade," *The New Republic,* 20 November 1962, pp. 18-20.

18. "Britain Sees Cuba As Key to Arms Cut," *The New York Times Western Edition,* 29 October 1962, p. 1.

19. "March by Students to Assail Blockade," *The New York Times Western Edition,* 25 October 1962, p. 1.

20. See advertisement in *The New York Times Western Edition,* 29 October 1962, p. 9: "The Cuban Crisis Advertisement Committee, P.O. Box 273, Lexington, Mass.—. . ." appeared over the signatures of approximately 500 faculty members of American colleges and universities.

In an even more forthright "Appeal for Peace," a small galaxy of movie stars, clergymen and thinkers (thirteen in all), bought themselves a quarter page of space in the *Times Western Edition* to urge the United States to assure the Soviet Union it was not going to invade Cuba.[21] By a happy coincidence, the terms for ending the crisis put forth by these notables, were the same as those put forth by Premier Khrushchev in his letter to President Kennedy on 28 October 1962.[22]

Cuba: Strategic and Geo-Political Implications

It cannot be that those who are constitutionally responsible for the safety of the United States are so badly schooled in geography and the principles of strategy that they are unable to understand what Cuba can be as a consequence of the Soviet missile gambit? Are those who must deal with the altogether Borgian politics of the Soviet Union so untutored in strategy that they cannot grasp what was gained by the "Missiles of October?" Can those sophisticated circles in Washington entertain the conviction that the Soviets are a bunch of clodhoppers from the steppes, incapable of doing strategic sums or working the simple formulae of enemy capabilities and vulnerabilities? Surely it must be reluctance to believe in the possibility of war and euphoric optimism about the benign evolution of Soviet policy that have deadened sensitivity to strategical considerations.

Suppositions that the Soviet Union had suffered a major defeat in Cuba when the Russian missiles and medium bombers were removed and that the "humiliation" suffered by Russia in that affair had played a part in the removal from office of Premier Khrushchev may have been comforting at the time. But, where Cuba is concerned, events since then provide no comfort.[23] Such an ill-founded view reflects an ignorance of history and a neglect of strategy.

Long before this republic was founded, Cuba compelled the strategic attention of those who would rule in North America. The island is so located as to provide the means for commanding the sea routes via the Florida Straits, the Windward Passage, the Yucatan Channel, and the Old Bahama Channel

21. "Negotiations, Not War," *The New York Times Western Edition,* 29 October 1962, p. 4.

22. "Text of Khrushchev's Message on Cuban Missile Crisis . . .," p. 4.

23. "Khrushchev's role in the Cuban crisis in 1962, was also widely criticized at home and among several Eastern European Communist countries." *Britannica Book of the Year, 1965*, p. 830; "By October 28 the crisis was over, and Khrushchev faced the hard task of reconsidering his whole strategic position in the light of his unsuccessful attempt to reduce the Soviet missile gap geographically," Malcolm Mackintosh, *Juggernaut: A History of the Soviet Armed Forces* (New York: The Macmillan Company, 1967), p. 301; ". . . the Soviet Politbureau. Khrushchev, who had been criticized for the *humiliating* outcome of the confrontation with the United States over Cuba . . .", Richard Pipes (ed.), *Soviet Strategy in Europe* (New York: Crane, Russak and Company, 1976), p. 108 (Italics added.)

off the Great Bahama Bank. In 1762, during the French and Indian War (Seven Year's War), it was the British capture of Havana that, in one blow, "crippled Spanish power in the West Indies" and cut the communications between old and new Spain.[24] It was clear to those who had initiated the expedition against Cuba, as well as those in command of it, that the possession of Havana as a military and naval base granted the strategic freedom to operate against French and Spanish positions in Louisiana and Florida.[25]

Thomas Jefferson, in 1812, wrote of the importance to the United States of maintaining "the meridian of the mid-Atlantic," as the "line of demarcation between war and peace, on this side of which no act of hostility should be committed. . . ." He observed elsewhere that, "Cuba alone seems at present to hold up a speck of war to us. Its possession by Great Britain would indeed be a great calamity to the United States."[26]

Furthermore, whenever Cuba has been in the hands of a weak regime or one hostile to the United States, American interests have been threatened. In the 1820s, when Cuba was ruled ineffectually from Madrid, pirates operating from the island's innumerable inlets and bays preyed on American and foreign shipping in the Gulf of Mexico and the Caribbean. In 1822, the U.S.S. *Enterprise* landed marines and sailors at Cape Antonio to pursue pirates taking refuge ashore; the U.S.S. *Peacock* captured a pirate ship west of Havana; and the U.S.S. *Alligator* fought an engagement against several pirate schooners in the harbor of Mantanzas. Again in 1823, a squadron based on Key West under command of Commodore David Porter pursued pirates ashore and afloat in and around Cuba and Puerto Rico.[27]

In the course of the Civil War, Union naval operations against the Confederate States aimed at preventing the entry of materials from abroad with which the Confederacy could continue the war, and the dispatch of Southern goods with which such materials could be purchased. Confederate raiders like the C.S.S. *Sumter* under Commander Semmes and Confederate and foreign blockade runners found Cuban harbors to be not unsympathetic havens in their efforts to elude the ships of the Union Navy.[28]

24. *The Seige and Capture of Havana, 1762*, Publications of the Navy Records Society, Vol. 114 (London: Spottiswoode, Ballantyne and Co., Ltd., 1970), p. xxxiv.

25. For example, see Letter, Admiral Sir George Pocock in H.M.S. *Namur* to John Cleveland, First Secretary to the Board of Admiralty, 9 October 1762, Document No. 525, *ibid.*, pp. 298-304.

26. Letter, Thomas Jefferson to Doctor John Crawford, 4 January 1812; and, Letter to James Monroe, 28 July 1824, as cited in Gilbert Chinard, *Thomas Jefferson, The Apostle of Americanism* (Ann Arbor: The University of Michigan Press, 1957), p. 182, f. 1. and pp. 485-86.

27. *Chronology of the UNITED STATES MARINE CORPS, 1775-1934*, Historical Branch, G-3 Division, Headquarters, U.S. Marine Corps, Washington, D.C., 1965, pp. 65-66; and, Archibald Douglas Turnbull, *Commodore David Porter, 1780-1843* (New York: The Century Co.), pp. 225-56.

28. *Civil War Naval Chronology, 1861-1865* (Washington, D.C.: Naval History Division, Navy Department, 1971), p. 1-18 and elsewhere. Blockade-running from Havana and Nassau is referred to in James Russell Soley "The Blockade and the Cruisers," in *The Navy in the Civil War* in Series: *Confederate Military History* of which this account is in Volume VII (Secaucus, N.J.: The Blue and Grey Press, n.d.), pp. 145-46.

Havana became a great entrepot for the accumulation and dispatch of war goods and other supplies for importation into the Confederacy. While the Spanish authorities in Cuba behaved correctly, under pressure from the Union, refusing Confederate raiders the right to dispose of prizes in Cuban ports, the Cuban and West Indian connection with the Confederacy remained as weak points in the Union Blockade until the Gulf Coast was secured for the Union.

Once again, in 1917, while the United States was preoccupied with events elsewhere, Cuba drew attention and military resources away from the principal theater of war. In February 1917, before the United States entered the war in Europe, revolts broke out in Oriente Province threatening the production of sugar, a commodity upon which both the United States and the Allies were dependent. Elements of the Atlantic Fleet landed Marine detachments which, along with other Marines from Guantanamo Bay and stateside, protected the sugar mills while the Cuban Army operated against the rebels. As the unrest subsided most of the Marines were withdrawn, to be prepared for transfer to France where the United States had entered the war. But the strategic importance of Cuba with its sugar production had not escaped the notice of the German government. In August, German agents encouraged Cuban rebels to disrupt the production of sugar in Oriente Province, forcing the deployment of the 7th Marine Regiment back into Cuba to protect sugar production. Cuba, like Waziristan, Mexico, and Ireland was a place where the Central Powers hoped to tie down Allied military forces to prevent their deployment into France where the decisive battles to defeat Germany had to be fought.[29]

For the United States, the disturbances in Mexico, spilling as they did, at times, over the border, threatened not only American interests in Mexico itself, but the safety of American citizens on American territory. American responsibility for good order in Cuba, as mandated by Act of Congress in the Platt Amendment to the Army Appropriations Bill of 1901, was a constitutional obligation under ordinary circumstances. It became a strategic imperative when the United States faced war in Europe.

It is the very essence of strategy to force one's enemy to defend that which he has no choice but to defend in areas away from the principal theater of war, while one's own forces concentrate to achieve a decision in that theater of war

29. The German effort in Cuba is cited in Captain Harry A. Ellsworth, *One Hundred Eighty Landings of United States Marines, 1800-1934* (Washington, D.C.: Historical Section, Headquarters, U.S. Marine Corps, 1934), p. 84; and see, Robert Debs Heinl, Jr., *Soldiers of the Sea: The United States Marine Corps, 1775-1962* (Annapolis, Md.: U.S. Naval Institute, 1962), p. 233. For German and Turkish encouragement of unrest in Waziristan and elsewhere on the Northwest Frontier of India, see, for example, Brigadier-General C. A. L. Graham, *The History of the Indian Mountain Artillery* (Alderson: Gale & Polden, Ltd., 1957), p. 199. German involvement in the Mexican revolution is described in Barbara W. Tuchman, *The Zimmermann Telegram* (New York: The Viking Press, 1968), Chapters 6 and 7. German involvement in the Irish troubles is suggested in Geoffrey Household's "Foreword" to Erskine Childers, *The Riddle of the Sands* (Harmondsworth, Middlesex: Penguin Books, 1978), p. 13.

where the outcome of battle will decide the outcome of war. Whether German-supported insurrections in Cuba and Mexico were successes or failures was less important than the fact the United States forces would have to be deployed in the Western Hemisphere as a consequence. Consider that in 1916, when the United States was about to enter the war in Europe, the total Armed Forces of the United States was 179,376, of which there were only 119,000[30] in the Army and Marine Corps. Every cavalry, infantry, or Marine regiment that could be tied down on the Mexican border or in Cuba was one that could not be sent to France. Every destroyer, cruiser, or battleship that had to be deployed in the Gulf of Mexico or the Caribbean, was one less with which to convoy troops and supplies to France in 1917, the year of the greatest Allied shipping losses to German submarines in the Atlantic.

It could hardly be unexpected that Cuba would be one of the sites where Germany would attempt to influence the outcome of the war in Europe. German military leaders were bereft of neither strategic insight nor geographic knowledge. Their quick recognition of the merit in the writings of the American naval strategist, Alfred Thayer Mahan, certainly gave evidence of this.[31]

Mahan had written in *Harper's New Monthly Magazine* (June 1897): "Cuba has no possible rival in her command of [the] Yucatan Passage just as she has no competitor in point of natural strength and resources, for control of the Florida Strait which connects the Gulf of Mexico with the Atlantic."[32] In his book, *The Interests of America in Sea Power, Present and Future,* published in Boston in 1897, Mahan wrote of the importance of Cuba to the control of the Caribbean and the Gulf of Mexico. Not only could Cuba command the entrance of the Gulf of Mexico from the Atlantic via the Florida Straits, but also the entrance of the Gulf of Mexico via the Yucatan Channel from the Caribbean. The Gulf of Mexico, at the mouth of the Mississippi, he pointed out, is where all the exports and imports of the Mississippi Valley that are transported by water meet. In respect to these, as well as to the traffic in and out of Galveston, Mobile, and the Mexican ports, Cuba had a preeminent intrinsic advantage:

> Regarded, therefore, as a base of naval operations, as a source of supply to a fleet, Cuba presents a condition wholly unique among islands of the Carribbean . . . such supplies can be conveyed from one point to the

30. See Table: "Military Personnel on Active Duty: 1789 to 1970" in *Historical Statistics of the United States: Colonial Times to 1970*, 93rd Congress, 1st Session, House Document No. 93-78, part 2 (Washington, D.C.: U.S. Bureau of the Census, 1975), p. 1141.

31. See, for example, reviews of Mahan's first two books in *Litarisches Zentralblatt,* 29 May 1897 and 28 April 1900, cited in William L. Langer, *The Diplomacy of Imperialism, 1890-1902* (New York: Alfred A. Knopf, 1951), p. 429. This work also discussed Mahan's influence in England as well as Germany.

32. "Strategic Features of the Gulf of Mexico and Caribbean Sea."

> other, according to the needs of a fleet, by interior lines, not exposed to the risks of maritime capture. The extent of the coast-line, the numerous harbors, and the many directions from which approach can be made, minimize the danger of total blockade to which all islands are subject.[33]

It would be dangerous to suppose that the intrinsic importance of Cuba and the seas it helps to contain would have escaped the consideration of those abroad who interest themselves in the strategic circumstances of the United States. Admiral of the Fleet of the Soviet Union, S. G. Gorshkov, has written in his book, *Navies in War and In Peace,* that Mahan is the premier theorist of American seapower. He notes also that the expulsion of Spain from Cuba "granted the United States the dominant position in the Caribbean" thereby ensuring American control over the approaches to the Panama Canal from the Atlantic. The Admiral observed further that the completion of the Panama Canal (in 1915) "was an important step for subsequent expansion [*sic*] into China and Southeast Asia."[34]

Soviet Strategic Analysis

It ought not to be surprising that Soviet leaders might be quick enough to grasp the strategic importance of any particular geographical area. Despite the appearance that Soviet leaders speak like politicians on campaign, they conduct policy as though the principles of war and the requirements of strategy were their guide. When the Libyan monarchy was overthrown by a military *coup d'état* in October 1969, the United States and Great Britain withdrew from their bases in that country at the request of the new government. *Pravda* observed the occasion with the comment:

> Liquidation of the [American] Bases in Libya would without doubt narrow the opportunities of American military circles for operations in the Mediterranean, the Near East, and Africa.[35]

The clarity of *Pravda*'s strategic perception seemed to be confirmed in the October 1973 war between the Arabs and Israel, with the Soviet Union threatening to intervene in order to save the Egyptian Third Army after the Israeli armor crossed the Suez Canal and began to roll up Egyptian air defenses and lines of communications on the West Bank of the Suez Canal. Admiral Zumwalt, who was Chief of Naval Operations at the time, has said that the United States forced Israel to permit the relief of the Egyptian Third

33. Cited in John D. Hayes, "The Soviet Navy in the Caribbean Sea and the Gulf of Mexico," *Interplay*, January 1971, pp. 5-9.

34. Admiral of the Fleet S. G. Gorshkov, *Navies in War and in Peace,* of which Chapter 3, appears in *U.S. Naval Institute Proceedings*, Vol. 100, No. 3 (Whole No. 853), March 1974, pp. 52-62.

35. *Pravda,* 3 November 1969, p. 5, in *The Current Digest of the Soviet Press,* Vol. XXI, No. 44, p. 25.

Army and to halt Israeli operations on the west bank of the Canal because the Soviet Union threatened to send in Russian forces if Soviet demands were not met. The Russians had "much greater capability to bring into the area" than the United States, and they were able to use airfields in Egypt, Syria, Yugoslavia and the Soviet Union.[36] The United States could employ only its carrier-based aircraft against such a Soviet threat and those aircraft carriers could not be expected to operate successfully in an area where the enemy enjoyed land-based air superiority.

It is notable that it was Israel that had to withdraw its forces from across the Canal and that it has been Israel that has been forced to concede territory to Egypt as a consequence of the war in 1973. The loss of the American bases in Libya not only denied the United States the capability to prevent Soviet intervention against Israel, it also meant that the United States had to airlift supplies directly from the United States to Israel while the Soviet Union could and did, overfly Turkey, Greece, and Yugoslavia with its own airlift of supplies to the Arabs. Beyond that, the United States could mount no significant military threat to Egypt to pressure that country to abandon its attacks across the Canal, but only threaten its ally Israel with the cut-off of military supplies if Israel did not bow to Soviet demands.

The ability of *Pravda* to grasp the strategic significance of the U.S. bases in Libya, while the United States Government apparently could not, suggests an ominous divergence of view between the Soviet Union and America on the relationship of geography to strategy and of strategy to politics.[37]

But then *Pravda's* sally on the Libyan bases may not have been merely a journalistic shot in the dark. The U.S. Sixth Fleet Commander reported in January 1979 that: "The massive flow of sophisticated Soviet weapons into Mediterranean nations, *especially Libya,* could change the balance of power in that area . . . at least 200 advanced Soviet aircraft, among them the MiG-25, are in Libya, with others in Syria and Algeria." Whatever advantage the

36. See "U.S. Hand Forced in '73 Mideast War: 'Savage' Soviet Note to Nixon Reported," *Los Angeles Times,* 31 July 1975, p. 4. Some details of the Israeli operations on West Bank of the Suez Canal and of the state of the Egyptian Third Army are given in *Strategic Survey, 1973* (London: International Institute for Strategic Studies 1974), pp. 28-29 and elsewhere.

37. In a conversation with a civilian official in the Defense Department at the time of the Libyan *coup d'état,* this author suggested that U.S. withdrawal from the bases in Libya would alter the strategic circumstances of the United States in the Eastern Mediterranean. The reply was that Wheelus had only been used by the Air Force to base fighter bombers for bombing practice in the desert and that could be carried on as easily at airfields in Spain. Since that time, Libya has become a site for Soviet Arms depots and apparently a partner with the Soviet Union in certain military enterprises in Chad. See "Qaddafi's Secret Base in Chad" in *Foreign Report* No. 1509 (26 October 1977), p. 4; and, report in the *Sunday Telegraph* (London), 21 September 1975, "Soviet weapons and Russian personnel to handle them are flowing into Libya at such a rate that the country seems destined to become Russia's main base for operations in the Mediterranean area . . ."; cited in Ian Greig, *The Communist Challenge to Africa, p.* 92.

Sixth Fleet enjoys from its two carrier air groups "would be lost if the Soviet Union could use the weapons it has supplied to Syria and Libya."[38]

If the strategic significance of air bases in Libya could be self-evident to the Soviet Union, is it really possible that the strategic significance of Cuba would have escaped the notice of those in the Soviet Union who plan for war? The Libyan bases fell to the Soviet Union by default. The Soviet Union, according to conventional wisdom, risked war to secure its position in Cuba. Surely there must be a warning in that somewhere.

Reliance on American Naivete and Optimism

On 19 September 1962, the Senate Foreign Relations and Armed Services Committees unanimously approved the text for a Joint Congressional Resolution, citing the Monroe Doctrine of 1823 and the Rio Treaty of 1947, and resolving that the United States is determined: "To prevent in Cuba the creation or use of an externally supported military capability endangering the security of the United States."[39]

In November 1964, when *The Military Balance, 1964-65* was published in London, Soviet forces in Cuba were reported to number 3,000. They presumably were present to oversee the manning of coastal defense missiles having a range of 25 miles and 24 anti-aircraft missile sites; and, to instruct in the use of the various naval vessels, aircraft, and armor given the Cubans by the Russians. By 1968, the total number of Soviet personnel stationed in Cuba was reported to be about 1,000, a figure which presumably remained about the same until 1976 after which time *The Military Balance* ceased to report the presence of Soviet forces in Cuba.[40] But by that time Cuban forces were reported to be in the Congo, Ethiopia, Guinea, Mozambique, Sierra Leone, Somalia, Tanzania, Uganda, South Yemen, and Zambia,[41] so the continued presence of Soviet forces in Cuba presumably had receded into insignificance: Cuba had become in its own right a military power in the world.

In that entirely hopeful period before the June War in the Middle East in 1967, the *New York Times* discovered that Cuba was playing an active role in "the fragmentation of the world Communist movement," over the matter of

38. "Flood of Soviet Arms to Mediterranean Area Cited," *Los Angeles Times,* 12 January 1979, p. 16. For earlier reports of Russian bases in Libya, see "Soviet Pact with Libya, Reported: Russ to Get Bases in Return for Arms," *Los Angeles Times,* 23 May 1975, p. 1; and, "Price Tag on Reported Soviet-Libyan Military Pact Seen as Only $1 Billion," *ibid.*, 29 May 1975, p. 20.

39. "Text of Senators' Cuba Resolution," *Los Angeles Times,* 20 September 1962, p. 22.

40. Soviet military forces present in Cuba were reported in *Military Balance* published annually by the Institute for Strategic Studies (later the International Institute for Strategic Studies) in London, for 1964-65 and 1965-66 under Cuba. In 1966-67 and until reports of them ceased, Soviet forces in Cuba were reported under the Soviet Union.

41. *The Military Balance, 1978-79,* p. 74.

whether or not Communism meant "adherence to the guerrilla struggle," and "the revolutionary line." Castro disapproved, it seemed, of the "efforts of the Soviet Union and Eastern European countries [formerly called satellites] to improve relations with non-Communist states in Latin America." It was even suggested that Havana might demand a veto over such efforts. As the *Times* pointed out with its customary optimism:

> Under Stalin, of course, such insolence from a national Communist leader would have meant swift excommunication. Today, because of the Chinese challenge and the general disorder in World Communism, Moscow is more cautious in its dealings with its satellites. . . . If Castro can make his deviation stick, he will encourage new diversity and division within the Communist camp.[42]

Such optimism, of course, was voiced before Warsaw Pact troops invaded Czechoslovakia to redress the wrongs of Czech deviation. Yet, a notable admission in the *Time's* editorial was that Castro's position in the Western Hemisphere was "so important to the Russians" that "he can do as he pleases and still be sure of Russian support." The nature of the importance was not, however, indicated.

Closer Soviet-Cuban Collaboration

The possibility that Cuba might become a base for Soviet military operations in the Gulf of Mexico and the Caribbean after the rockets and medium bombers had been removed was, of course, hardly worth considering. Still, in July 1969, a Soviet naval squadron called into Havana, where its sailors were to help in the harvest of Cuban sugar cane. The Cuban news magazine *Bohemia* said that the visit "constitutes another example of revolutionary solidarity that in spite of its short duration—one week—will heighten the enthusiasm of the armed forces and their combat preparation."[43] The squadron included a guided missile cruiser equipped with missiles capable of delivering a nuclear warhead to a range of 450 miles, a frigate, a destroyer, two diesel-power submarines and some logistical-support ships. The *New York Times* found the visit to be "an attempt by Moscow to show the world . . . that there had been a big improvement in relations with Havana."[44] In November, the Soviet Minister of Defense, Marshall Grechko, visited Cuba in connection with delivery of the "newest weapons and equipment" to the Cuban armed forces. This action was meant to enhance the "comradeship in

42. "Castro's Deviation," *New York Times,* 19 March 1967, p. E. 14.

43. Bohemia cited in "Visiting Soviet Sailors to Harvest Cuban Sugar," *The Evening Star* (Washington, D.C.), 18 July 1969, p. A-3.

44. "7 Soviet Warships Arrive For Week's Visit in Cuba," *New York Times,* 21 July 1969, p. 19; see also "Soviet Naval Visit to Cuba Shows New Policy Flexibility," *The Evening Star* (Washington, D.C.), 18 July 1969, p. A-3.

arms between the peoples and armies of the Soviet Union and the Republic of Cuba," according to *Red Star,* the Soviet armed forces newspaper. *Red Star* proceeded to describe the military assistance provided by the Soviet Union as embracing "all spheres of military construction."[45] It was suggested in some quarters around this time that Soviet control of the island of Cuba was increasing.[46]

Five months later, on 4 April 1970, Raul Castro Ruz, Deputy Prime Minister and Minister of the Revolutionary Armed Forces of the Republic of Cuba arrived in Moscow at the invitation of Marshall Grechko for "a friendly official visit." Having helped celebrate the centennial of Lenin's birth and the 25th anniversary of Soviet victory in the Great Patriotic War, Comrade Castro met with Comrade L. I. Brezhnev, General Secretary of the Communist Party of the Soviet Union, "to discuss the further development of Soviet-Cuban relations."[47] Two days later, on the 14th of May, Radio Havana reported that a Soviet naval squadron had stopped in the Cuban port of Cienfuegos "to refuel, resupply and rest."[48] Earlier in May a Cuban exile group in Miami had reported that Soviet troops were being landed in Cuba.[49]

On June 2, the *Los Angeles Times* reported in its "News in Brief" column, along with similar items *not* warranting attention elsewhere in the newspaper, that:

> The bulk of a Soviet naval flotilla is concentrating in the Gulf of Mexico after a visit to Cuba, the Pentagon said. A cruiser, destroyer and oiler are cruising about 260 miles west of Key West, Florida. Meanwhile two submarines were reported in the Yucatan Channel heading into the Gulf and a sub tender was said to be heading east, 180 miles south of the Windward Passage.

This was a news item of sixty-seven words ranking with an accident to a Philippine airliner and a prank played on music-loving citizens in a foreign city.[50]

For those who might have missed the item in *Time* magazine in July 1970, the *San Francsico Chronicle* gave a summary on page ten of its July 20, issue. *Time* had reported six flights by Soviet Tu-95 bombers into Cuba since April "probably for reconnaissance missions" and delivery of military sup-

45. "Russia Sending New Military Aid to Cuba: Western Experts Believe All Kinds of Weapons are Included in Shipments," *Los Angeles Times,* 3 December 1969, p. 12.

46. "New Troubles for Castro: Defectors Charge 'Sovietization' of Cuba: Grechko's Cuban Visit Marks a Warming Up of Moscow Havana Relations," *The Christian Science Monitor,* 3 November 1969, p. 1.

47. "Arrival of Raul Castro Ruz," *Pravda,* 5 April 1970, p. 4; "On a Friendly Visit," *Izvestia,* 5 April 1970, p. 2, in *The Current Digest of the Soviet Press,* Vol. XXI, No. 14, p. 15; and, "L. I. Brezhnev Meets with R. Castro," *Pravda,* 13 May 1970, p. 1, *ibid.,* Vol. XXII, No. 19, p. 14.

48. "Soviet Squadron refueling in Cuba," *Palo Alto Times,* 15 May 1970, p. 2.

49. "Russ Land Troops, Say Cuba Exiles," *Los Angeles Times,* 9 May 1970, p. 2.

50. *Los Angeles Times,* 2 June 1970, p. 2.

plies. Soviet *Komar*-class missile boats were reported operating off Key Biscayne, Florida.[51]

There was, of course, no alarm about these manifestations of Soviet activity in Cuba. The Subcommittee on Inter-American Affairs of the House Committee on Foreign Affairs did hold hearings in July and August on the matter and had concluded that "more than usual military and naval activity was taking place in Cuba." Robert C. Toth, a member of the *Los Angeles Times* bureau in Washington, observed that: "Cuba's role as a Soviet military station had been accepted de facto by the United States. Far from sounding the alarms that would have been heard five or ten years ago the United States has gone out of its way to play down the recent Soviet moves." "Why advertise our impotence?" Mr. Toth quoted one official's attempt to explain the "American silence." But Mr. Toth found that the Soviet Union was probably only "using the naval visits for purely selfish reasons—as a substitute for giving Castro more military aid."[52]

By the end of August, Soviet naval activity around Cuba had aroused some concern in Central America where it was reported that the topic was treated as front-page news in places like British Honduras and Guatemala. It was even reported in Washington, that "defense authorities have 'very real concern' over recent Soviet naval moves in the Caribbean."[53]

While never approaching the magnitude of the "missile crisis," the Soviet naval operations in the Gulf and Caribbean began to elicit some official attention in public at the beginning of September when the Secretary of Defense commented briefly on it in the course of discussing other issues related to U.S. policy.[54]

Ernest Conine, writing in the editorial pages of the *Los Angeles Times,* on 9 September 1970, remarked that:

> Russian warships have taken to steaming routinely around the Caribbean, and Cuba is emerging as an increasingly important base of Soviet military operations in the Western Hemisphere.
>
> . . . the temptation toward benign interpretations of Soviet intentions is made easier by Moscow's soft-sell diplomacy of late, with its emphasis on trade instead of violent revolution.[55]

Mr. Conine was, however, less optimistic about Soviet intentions, suggesting the possibility that they might promote a Communist seizure of

51. "A Report on Russ Action In Cuba," *San Francisco Chronicle,* 20 July 1970, p. 10.

52. "No U.S. Reaction This Time: Cuba: Russian Military Power Returns," *Los Angeles Times,* 26 July 1970, p. 2, section G.

53. "Soviet Ships Prowl Caribbean: Guatemala Honduras, Nicaragua Grow Uneasy," *The Christian Science Monitor,* 28 August 1970, p. 1.

54. "Caribbean Draws Russ Naval Ships," *Palo Alto Times,* 2 September 1970, p. 2.

55. "Soviet Power Draws Closer," *Los Angeles Times,* 9 September 1970, p. 6, pt. II.

power in Haiti or the Dominican Republic, "using their naval presence, and our reluctance to bring on a big-power confrontation, to inhibit the United States from direct counter-action."

Overt Naval Presence in Cuba: Intent and Response

By the end of September, there had been sufficient indications of Soviet naval activity in Cuba to interest various members of Congress. Senator Fulbright, while expressing doubt that the Russians were building a submarine base in Cuba, warned that if such a base were being built, the United States would not be able to bluff the Soviets into pulling out as it had in the 1962 missile crisis. "It was possible at that time to bluff them. I doubt it is possible now," the Senator said. The solution the Senator proposed, should the Soviet Union be behaving as charged, was to pursue the strategic arms limitation talks, the negotiations in Paris (on U.S. withdrawal from Vietnam), the Middle East negotiations, and the revival of United Nations influence.[56] Less sanguine members of Congress took a stronger line. Congressman Rivers, Chairman of the House Armed Services Committee, thought Soviet action warranted a prompt response, "military, if need be." "We cannot," he said, "live with this new Soviet threat on our doorstep. We cannot permit the cities of the eastern seaboard to become hostages of the Soviet Union." Senator Frank Church, arranged a *closed* hearing of his subcommittee on Western Hemisphere affairs because shipping and construction work in the area, "may have a military purpose involving the Russians."[57]

Meanwhile, the "White House," not the President, nor any named official, but someone who insisted on being identified only as a "White House source," warned the Soviet Union against building a strategic *submarine* base in Cuba. Emphasis seemed to be on the word "strategic." The use of the word seemed to imply "strategic" as in strategic nuclear weapons rather than "strategic" in the sense applied to the German submarine campaign against Allied shipping in two world wars, or in the sense employed by the United States in describing the U.S. submarine offensive against Japanese shipping in the Far East.[58]

While the *Washington Evening Star* reported on the 30th of September that: "Equipment specifically associated with the new Yankee class nuclear missile submarine is being installed at Cienfuegos on the south shore of

56. "Bluff Won't Eliminate Sub Base—Fulbright," *Los Angeles Times,* 28 September 1970, p. 6.

57. "Rep. Rivers Wants U.S. to Slap Down Red Base," *Palo Alto Times,* 29 September 1970, p. 6.

58. Thus: "A source in the intelligence community said that what the Russians appeared to be building was a rather limited facility, not a submarine base on the scale of American bases at Holy Loch, Scotland or Rota, Spain" (bases for the U.S. Polaris submarines which formed part of the so-called strategic nuclear triad, that is carrying strategic nuclear weapons.) See "U.S. Warns Soviet Not to Build Base for Sub in Cuba: Intelligence Indicates it May be Constructing Facility—1962 Warning Recalled: Data Remain Unclear," *New York Times,* 26 September 1970, p. 1.

Cuba." *The New York Times,* using the device of attribution to unnamed "American officials," professed its puzzlement that the White House would warn the Soviet Union on Cuba, since the United States "had only dated and dubious information."[59]

Contrary to the view of the dubious nature of U.S. intelligence, the Defense Department had reported in July the conduct of "scheduled" reconnaissance flights over Cuba, because of the Soviet presence, and such demonstrations of Soviet reach as naval cruises and long-distance bomber flights from the Soviet Union to Cuba.[60]

In the Hearings before the House Subcommittee on Inter-American Affairs, held on the 30th of September, officers from the Soviet Area Office of the Defense Intelligence Agency stated:

> Gentlemen, the third Soviet naval deployment to the Caribbean, in a little over a year, has apparently resulted in efforts to establish a Soviet naval facility at Cienfuegos, Cuba, which might support naval operations in the Caribbean area, including submarines.
>
> . . . The Combination of the submarine tender and the construction on Alcatraz Island appears intended to provide the Soviets with an increased capability to support their naval operations in the Caribbean area, including submarines.

It also emerged in the Hearings, which were not released for publication until a year later, that the Defense Intelligence Agency had detected in the Caribbean during May one Soviet *Echo*-class submarine and two *Foxtrot*-class submarines.[61] The *Foxtrot*-class vessel was a diesel-electric propelled attack submarine with a cruising range of 20,000 sea miles which carried twenty torpedoes. But the *Echo*-class submarine was nuclear powered and carried SS-N-3 cruise missiles in addition to torpedoes. The SS-N-3, or *Shaddock* cruise missile has a range of 450 miles and can carry a nuclear warhead of around one kiloton yield.[62]

The Economist in London found the entire affair of the possible submarine base at Cienfuegos to be perplexing, since the Russians had already modern-

59. "A-sub Equipment Installed in Cuba, New Data Shows," *The Evening Star* (Washington, D.C.), 30 September 1970; and, "Warning on Cuba Puzzles U.S. Aides—White House Data in Report on Base Termed Old," *The New York Times,* 30 September 1970. The text of both are in *Soviet Naval Activities in Cuba,* Hearings before the Subcommittee on Inter-American Affairs of the Committee of Foreign Relations, House of Representatives, 91st Congress, Second Session, September 30, October 13, November 19 and 24, 1970, but released on 26 September 1971. See also, "Doubt Cast on Sub Base Story," *San Francisco Chronicle,* 30 September 1970, p. 1.

60. "Pentagon Denies Sending More Flights Over Cuba," *Palo Alto Times,* 20 July 1970, p. 4.

61. *Soviet Naval Activities in Cuba,* pp. 1 and 10.

62. Soviet submarine characteristics are given in *Meyers Flottentaschen buch, 1969/70* (München: J. F. Lehmanns Verlag, 1970), pp. 178-79; Siegfried Breyer, *Guide to the Soviet Navy* (Annapolis: U.S. Naval Institute, 1970), pp. 280-93; *Understanding Soviet Naval Developments* (Washington, D.C.: Office of the Chief of Naval Operations, 1978), pp. 71-80. The SS-N-3, or *Shaddock,* is described in *The Military Balance, 1978-1979,* p. 81.

ized the port of Havana for Soviet naval use. Havana had been equipped in 1968 to handle up to 130 medium sized ships, with a floating dock, repair shops, and a long-range communication center manned by Russians.[63]

Izvestia, the Soviet newspaper, expressed Russian exasperation at the allegations that the Soviet Union "intended to create in Cuba a base for submarines equipped with missiles." In the first place: "It is a well-known fact that the Soviet Union altogether condemns the establishment of military bases by one state on the territory of another." Furthermore, *Izvestia* argued: "If Soviet ships and vessels pay official visits and put in on business in the ports of foreign states, including the Republic of Cuba, they do this with the consent of the governments of the corresponding states." The newspaper pointed out that there was a mutual understanding between the United States and the Soviet Union, in which the United States had promised not to permit an invasion of Cuba when the Soviet Union "announced [in 1962] that the arms that the U.S.A. characterized as offensive ones be withdrawn from the island." The blame for the "uproar" about "the alleged 'activism' of the Soviet Union in Cuba" rested with "ringleaders of the military-industrial complex in the U.S.A." "The handiwork of these circles is blatantly apparent in the fabrications and insinuations aimed both against the cause of peace and against the interests of the American people themselves."[64]

Izvestia's formal statement along with one issued by Tass, the Soviet news agency, on the 13th of October, helped to avoid any genuine crisis over the Cuban matter. The Soviet Union promised to "strictly adhere" to the Kennedy-Khrushchev Cuban missile agreement. According to the *San Francisco Chronicle* in a dispatch from the Times-Post Service, "the Kremlin declared it is not building a nuclear submarine base or any other kind of military installation in Cuba."[65] In another story in the *Chronicle,* this one from the *New York Times,* entitled, "Cuban Sub Base Grows Less Likely," the Defense Department was cited as saying that "new evidence from Cuba makes it appear less likely that the Soviet Union is planning to build a submarine base there." While it was true that there were "two-single story barracks, a soccer field, a tennis court, and an exercise area, there was no evidence that any Soviet naval personnel were ashore."[66]

While the Times-Post dispatch had said the Kremlin "declared it was not building a nuclear submarine base," *The Economist* of London noted that what the Kremlin had really said was "the Soviet Union has not built and is not building a military base *'of its own'* in Cuba."[67]

63. "Cuba: The Curious Affair of the 3 Barges," *The Economist,* Vol. 237, No. 6632, 3 October 1970, p. 3.

64. "Version or Diversion?" *Izvestia,* 10 October 1970, p. 2, in *The Current Digest of the Soviet Press,* Vol. XXII, No. 41, 10 November 1970, pp. 14-15.

65. "A Soviet Pledge on Cuba," *San Francisco Chronicle,* 14 October 1970, p. 1.

66. "Cuban Sub Base Grows 'Less Likely,'" *ibid.,* 14 October 1970, p. 30.

67. "Cuba: Thrice Denied," *The Economist,* Vol. 237, No. 6634, 17 October 1970, p. 32.

The State Department considered that to be a "positive statement" on the part of the Soviet Union. Besides that the Soviet ships had left Cienfuegos by that time.[68]

Unfortunately, four days later, the Soviet submarine tender put in at the port of Mariel, 25 miles west of Havana. Mariel had been the port through which, in 1962, the missiles had been landed and later disembarked. The Secretary of State met with the Soviet Foreign Minister on the 16th and 19th and "discussed Cuba," and the United States "considered the matter resolved." On the 2nd of November, Mr. Klein, the President's director of communications, told a news conference that the "last of the equipment has been pulled over the weekend." This was "a contention that intelligence photographs, now refute," as the *New York Times,* phrased it.[69]

By December, it was still not possible to say that the Soviet vessels had removed themselves from Cuban harbors or Cuban waters. But it was the contention that: "The strategic significance of a base in Cuba for missile submarines could easily be overstated." Meanwhile the United States had reassured the Soviet Union that they would not invade Cuba if the Russians stayed out.[70]

On 6 December 1970, Tass reported that three Soviet warships would make "business calls" at Cuban ports during the month. The group of warships would include a submarine, an anti-submarine vessel and a tanker. In its December 21 issue, *Aviation Week and Space Technology* offered photographs of what were described as "radioactive affluent barges used for disposal of salt-water waste from Soviet nuclear-powered submarines" while reporting the operation of Soviet long-range reconnaissance aircraft in and out of Cuba.[71]

However unclear, indecisive, or confused American policy was on the subject of a Soviet submarine base in Cuba, one conclusion did emerge. The United States gave explicit assurance of that which since 1962 had been only implicit: the United States would *not* invade Cuba. This promise was

68. "Soviet Ships," *Palo Alto Times,* 14 October 1970, p. 3.

69. The entire matter was reviewed in "Soviet Removal of Vessel in Cuba is Awaited by U.S.: Submarine Support Ship is Expected to Go as Result of an Understanding: Nuclear Arms at Issue: American Officials Hopeful Secret Talks Resolved Dispute Over Base," *New York Times,* 15 November 1970, p. 1.

70. Contention is in "U.S. Eyes Soviets in Carribean: Russian Naval Intentions Called Subject of Deep Concern," *The Christian Science Monitor,* 20 October 1970, p. 15. The continued presence of Soviet naval forces in the Cuban area are reported in "Russians in Cuba Under Watch," *Palo Alto Times,* 21 December 1970, p. 1; U.S. reassurances are in "U.S. Tells Moscow It Will Not invade Cuba If Russia Stays Out," *Los Angeles Times,* 14 November 1970, p. 1; "U.S. and Russia Swap Hands-Off Vow on Cuba," *San Francisco Chronicle,* 14 November 1970, p. 14; and, "U.S. Confirms Stand on Sub Base," *San Francisco Chronicle,* 18 November 1970, p. 12.

71. Cecil Brownlow, "Soviet Boost Caribbean Presence: Cuban base for Nuclear-powers: Submarines Readied, sea floor studied; Tu-95 recon aircraft arrive from Russia," *Aviation Week and Space Technology,* Vol. 93, No. 25, 21 December 1970, pp. 16-17.

coupled, at least in the public view, to Soviet promises to keep Russian military bases and offensive weapons off the island.[72]

Since the Soviet Union considered all Soviet weapons and bases to be defensive where the Socialist Motherland and its offspring were concerned there was really no problem. Recall that in the Cuban Missile Crisis, Khrushchev had undertaken to remove from Cuba, "the weapons you [President Kennedy] *describe as offensive.*" He had explained that the "Soviet Government decided to render assistance to Cuba with the means of defense against aggression, only with means for the purposes of defense. We have supplied the defense means which you *describe as offensive* means. We have supplied them to prevent an attack on Cuba."[73] Khrushchev may have fallen into disrepute for his sins against Socialism, but his sentiments had not. For the *Izvestia* statement of 10 October 1970, eight years after Khrushchev's statement, recalled that: "After President Kennedy gave an assurance that there would be no invasion of Cuba—either by the U.S.A. or any other country in the Western Hemisphere—the Soviet government announced that the arms that the U.S.A. *characterized as offensive* ones would be withdrawn from the island."[74]

A most intriguing metamorphosis had taken place. What the Defense Intelligence Agency had, at first, described to Congress as the construction of naval and ground facilities in Cuba which appeared to be intended to provide increased capability to support submarine and other naval operations, soon came to be described as "a rest and recreational facility for Soviet sailors whose ships visit Cuba." Such facilities—by definition—would not violate the Kennedy-Khrushchev agreement of 1962, which barred the Russians from establishing an offensive base in Cuba. After all, as it now appears, the crisis of October 1970 had just been about a little old soccer field![75]

Those Soviet vessels, including the submarine tender, that had aroused such unwarranted suspicions about Soviet intentions in the Gulf of Mexico and the Caribbean departed the area on 8 January 1971, the sports-loving Soviet sailors having doubtless tired of soccer for that season. Less than a month later, Tass reported the prospective visit of another squadron of Soviet naval vessels, including a submarine, a submarine tender, and a tanker.[76]

72. "U.S. and Russia Swap Hands-Off Vow on Cuba," *San Francisco Chronicle,* 14 November 1970, p. 14.

73. "Text of Khrushchev's Message On Cuban Missile Crisis, Airspace Violation," *The New York Times, Western Edition,* 29 October 1962.

74. "Cuba: Version or Diversion?" *Izvestia,* 20 October 1970, p. 2.

75. "How a Cuban Soccer Field Upset U.S.," *San Francisco Sunday Examiner and Chronicle,* 26 September 1971, p. 14.

76. "News in Brief," *Los Angeles Times,* 5 February 1971, p. 2; and "Three Russian Ships Heading for' business call' in Cuba," *Palo Alto Times,* 5 February 1971, p. 17.

On the 17th of February, the Pentagon announced: "A Soviet nuclear attack submarine has surfaced in Cuban waters." It was reported that President Nixon said: "the sub was being watched closely to determine if it was being serviced there or from facilities there." He said, further: "Such servicing would be a violation of an understanding under which the Russians have agreed to keep Cuba free of offensive weapons."[77]

On the 19th, authorities at Guantanamo Naval Base in Cuba reported that a Soviet intelligence ship was in the waters south of Cuba while two Soviet hydrographic survey vessels were operating off Trinidad. The former was said to be monitoring—to be conducting surveillance of electronic manifestations from U.S. naval vessels in the area. The nuclear attack submarine and its consorts, it was stated, would be under U.S. air and surface surveillance "when they leave Cienfuegos for visits to [other] Cuban ports."[78]

About a month later, three of the Soviet vessels were reported to have departed from Cuba. The only vessel that did not depart at this time was the submarine tender. As the brief news report said: "The Pentagon provided only the barest details of the Soviet ship movements in the Caribbean in contrast to the emphasis the Administration has placed on Russian naval activity in the past." Of course, the newspaper report itself was hardly prominent being sandwiched in between a report that Swedish teachers had returned to work after a strike and a photograph of two Highland soldiers bushwacked by the I.R.A.[79]

In May, *Pravda* reported:

> In accordance with a mutual arrangement, a detachment of Soviet warships, consisting of a submarine and an auxiliary vessel that are on a training cruise in the Central Atlantic, will pay a friendly visit to ports of the Republic of Cuba at the end of May and the beginning of June for the purpose of taking on supplies and granting a brief shore leave to the crews.[80]

Presumably, "taking on supplies" from Cuban ports, was not "servicing" of the ships, so there could be no question of a violation of the "understanding" of the year before. It certainly was not in any sense a provocation. Provocation was when a U.S. naval force appeared in the Baltic in the same month. The Baltic appearance, *Izvestia* said, was "provocational," whatever the U.S. Navy Department said about the visit being connected with a "courtesy visit" to the West German port of Kiel. It was shocking that:

77. "News in Brief," *Los Angeles Times*, 18 February 1971.
78. "Soviet Reported Tracking U.S. Ships in Caribbean," *New York Times*, 21 February 1971, p. 1.
79. "News in Brief," *Los Angeles Times*, 12 March 1971, p. 2.
80. "Visit to Cuba by Soviet Ships," *Pravda*, 22 May 1971, p. 5, in *The Current Digest of the Soviet Press*, Vol. XXIII, No. 21, 22 June 1971, p. 19.

> The cruise of the U.S. warships was undertaken precisely at a time when a growing tendency toward détente is observable in Europe. . . . The provocational nature of this voyage is also underlined by the landing of a military plane and helicopters from the aforementioned ships on the Danish island of Bornholm. This island, as is known, was liberated by the Soviet Army during the second world war; and the Danish government, in 1946 and again in 1961, gave assurances that only Danish troops would be maintained on Bornholm.[81]

Sauce for the goose was clearly not gravy for the gander. In September, doubtless to help celebrate the visit of Premier Alexei Kosygin to Cuba, the Soviet Union delivered five MiG-21 jet fighters to Havana abroad a Russian freighter. This brought to sixty-seven the number of such aircraft then in Cuba. The American government failed to point out that such offensive weapons in Cuba would violate the 1962 and 1970 agreements. Apparently, it was supposed that the new aircraft were no more than replacements for the older MiG-15s and MiG-17s that had been delivered earlier.[82]

If one were to have supposed that such Soviet-Cuban contacts were only casual, in the spirit of that cooperation pursued by nations having common sentimental devotion to a revolutionary tradition, such supposition might have been rendered suspect. Writing in *Pravda,* Carlos Rafael Rodriguez recounted the work of the Soviet-Cuban Intergovernmental Commission, of which he was chairman of the Cuban Section, as well as Minister of the Revolutionary Government of Cuba. The Commission, set up in 1970, coordinated Soviet-Cuban efforts in the industrialization of Cuba, including electrification, modernization of agriculture, the construction of industrial plants, the improvement of the Cuban merchant marine and the modernization of ports.[83]

On the occasion of the visit of L. I. Brezhnev to Cuba from 28 January to 3 February 1974, a joint Soviet-Cuban Communique was issued referring to the extensive past and future developments in Cuban-Soviet cooperation. In addressing a rally marking the visit of the Soviet leader to Cuba, his revolutionary colleague, Fidel Castro, paid tribute to the "splendidly equipped armed forces and military equipment obtained from the Soviet Union" and to the "Soviet specialists who amassed unparalleled experience in the heroic battles of the Great Patriotic War [who] have transmitted to us military knowledge that is making our revolutionary Armed Forces . . . an invincible bulwark of socialism on this continent."[84]

81. "Dangerous Visitors," *Izvestia,* 22 May 1971, p. 2.

82. "Cuba Receives Jet Fighters from Soviets," *Palo Alto Times,* 30 October 1971, p. 1.

83. Carlos Rodriguez, "Important New Stage," *Pravda,* 11 March 1972, p. 4, in *The Current Digest of the Soviet Press,* Vol. 24, No. 10, 5 April 1972, pp. 17-18.

84. An extensive description of Soviet-Cuban cooperation is given in "Visit of Friendship and

It may have been that by this time, the presence of Soviet warships in Cuban ports no longer elicited very much attention. It was, however, reported in September 1973, that an *Echo*-class nuclear attack submarine had sustained minor damage from collision with a Soviet cruiser just south of Cuba.[85] Readers of *Gramma,* the weekly Havana newspaper, were doubtless better informed about such matters. For that journal reported the "friendly, non-official visit to Havana of a Soviet flotilla of anti-submarine units, with a tanker, on March 1, 1975."[86]

In 1976, the August 29 edition of *Gramma* reported the visit of another Soviet flotilla which entered port three days after a Polish naval vessel carrying a Polish rear admiral entered the harbor. It was a notable event to have a naval unit from one of the other Warsaw pact countries visit the comrades of the Caribbean.[87] The courtesy was returned in September when Raul Castro attended the *SHIELD 76* maneuvers of the Warsaw Pact armies. He and his delegation of Cuban officers were the guest of the Polish United Workers Party, the Polish Government, and the Polish Ministry of Defense. It seems to have been a signal honor for Cuba to have its Minister of Defense attend the maneuvers. Mongolia, Vietnam, and Yugoslavia sent only senior military officers; the Soviet Union and the other members of the Warsaw Pact were represented by their respective ministers of defense.[88]

While Raul Castro was off with the Warsaw Pact, Cuba's Commander-in-Chief, first secretary of the Party, and prime minister, Fidel Castro, was paying his compliments to General Nikola Ljubicic, Secretary of Defense of the Socialist Federative Republic of Yugoslavia, on tour of Cuba with a military delegation from Yugoslavia.[89]

Cuba as Soviet Military Proxy

It might seem difficult to think of Cuba as a minion of the Soviet Union even after the integration of the country into the Council for Mutual Eco-

---

Brotherhood," *Izvestia,* 5 February 1974, p. 1 and elsewhere in the Soviet Press, all may be seen in "Brezhnev in Cuba, Talks with Castro," *The Current Digest of the Soviet Press,* Vol. XXVI, No 5, 27 February 1974, pp. 1-10, 31. See also, short article, "Brezhnev Flies Home After 6-Day Cuba Visit," *Los Angeles Times,* 4 February 1974, p. 4.

85. "Russian Sub, Ship Collides Off Cuba," in "News in Brief," *Los Angeles Times,* 6 September 1973, p. 2.

86. "Soviet Flotilla Pay Friendly, Non Official Visit to Havana," *Gramma* (Havana), 9 March 1975, p. 1.

87. "People of Havana Give Fraternal Welcome to Soviet Flotilla," and "Training Ship from Polish People's Republic Visits Havana," *Gramma,* 29 August 1976, p. 1.

88. "Division Commander Raul Castro is Guest at Shield 76 Maneuvers By Warsaw Pact Troops," *Gramma,* 19 September 1976, p. 1.

89. "Army General Nikola Ljubicic Leaves Cuba After Friendly Visit: Commander-in-Chief Fiedel Castro Bids Him Farewell at Protocol Residence," *Gramma,* 19 September 1976, p. 1.

nomic Assistance, that organization through which the Soviet Union appears to coordinate the economies of its various East European consorts. Those who viewed Cuba and Castro through sentimental eyes, would count it "a mistake, to exaggerate Cuba's dependence on the Soviet Union. . . ." An editor of the *Los Angeles Times,* for example, hardly a figure given to romantic notions about Latin American dictators, one would think, dismissed as a "cold-war cliché" that Cuba is a pawn of Moscow. He found it "thrilling to meet a teen-age son of [Cuban] peasants whose favorite poet is Walt Whitman," and "found it discouraging to be informed that ordinary Cubans need special permission from the government to read the *New York Times.*"[90] It was not just that Castro had made the trains run on time, or that Castro was willing to send Cubans to fight alongside Soviet, East German and Ethiopian soldiers to establish the right sort of regimes in Africa.[91] It was his love and encouragement of things like ballet that set him apart as a man of culture and refinement, who enters the Teatro Garcia Lorca "to a rousing ovation, in full military regalia." Indeed, a man of the people, who with an "indulgent smile and a masterful choreographic gesture, motioned everyone to be seated," after the second ovation. "Enough," he obviously wanted to say, "is enough."[92] Indeed, art knows no nationality.

The view of Havana as the cultural capital of the Antilles, providing rich artistic fare to the average Cuban cane-cutter—the music critic observed "nary a tuxedo, much less tails in sight"—reinforces the tendency to see Cuba as the champion of the poor nations of the "Third World." This makes it possible to write of Cuba, as the *Los Angeles Times* did in July 1977, as "menacing, helpful, subversive and benign." The *Times* editor clung to the good news that: "The stability that the Cubans have brought the new nation [Angola] is in many ways useful. . . . The most ambitious new military training exercise is taking place in Ethiopia, where the Cubans have undertaken to train the new people's militia with which the military dictatorship hopes to suppress the civil wars that risk the breakup of the Ethiopian nation." As the editor said:

> Most of the operations appear to be directed largely toward technical assistance. Many of the Cubans in Angola, for that matter, are fulfilling

90. Steve Wasserman, an editor of the "Opinion" section, after a three-week visit to Cuba, "Castro's Cuba and the Romantic Left: Cuba and the Romance of Revolution," *Los Angeles Times,* 17 September 1978, part VI.

91. See "East Germany's Menacing New 'Afrika Korps,'" *South China Morning Post* (Hong Kong), 30 July 1978, p. 2; and, "Russians Pull the Triggers in Eritrea," *ibid.,* 12 February 1978, p. 4.

92. Enraptured reviews of Cuban ballet are given in the following places, Martin Bernheimer, music and art critic, "Havana Turns Out for Terpsichere, Ballet in Cuba . . . almost as much a popular ritual as an artistic experience," *Los Angeles Times,* 2 November 1978, p. 1, part IV; "Ballet Fever Has Havana in a Buzz," 4 November 1978, p. 10, pt. 2; and, "An Ecstatic Public: A Cuban Mix of Cultures," *Los Angeles Times,* 10 November 1978, p. 1, pt. IV.

> administrative and health services left depleted by the Portuguese withdrawal. . . . In Somalia, Cubans are helping to develop sugar production . . . similar to American technical assistance, Peace Corps and military training.[93]

And certainly the Cubans were apparently a great success in training the Ethiopians to fight, for it was not to be long before those Ethiopians would, with their Soviet and Cuban brothers-in-arms, defeat both the Somalis and the Eritreans in what might have easily passed for a war, in other circumstances.[94]

The eagerness to see Cuban enterprises in Africa as good works is only a reflection of the reluctance to see Cuba for what it is: an active ally of the Soviet Union; and the island itself a defended, advanced base for the Warsaw Pact in the Caribbean and the Gulf of Mexico.

When it was reported in the fall of 1970 that the Soviet Union might be building a submarine base at Cienfuegos the Chairman of the Senate Foreign Relations Committee dismissed the matter: "It happens every year at appropriations time. Last year it was the SS-9 Missiles. Now it's a submarine base. They are hoodwinking the American people."[95]

Long after several Cuban Army victories in Africa, it could be reported:

> . . . military observers in Havana are more inclined to accept Castro's protests that his troops in Africa are actually serving more as police and technicians than as members of an impressive fighting machine. . . . The assertion that Cuban troops overseas are serving more as technical assistants than mercenaries wins support from observers here, who point out that the peacetime role of the armed forces of Cuba has been *largely a civilian police* function.[96]

This statement surely puts into perspective the situation in Cuba: an army, navy and air force of 159,000, equipped with the latest jet fighters, over 600 tanks, 400 armored personnel carriers, medium artillery, air defense artillery, torpedo boats, landing craft, fighter bombers; plus, 10,000 militia, all directing traffic, regulating vice and arresting criminals. It must be unusually safe in Cuba with one policeman for every 32 people. The view of the Cuban military units in Africa as a kind of Cuban Peace Corps and the Cuban armed forces at home as a Latin version of New York's finest is not one universally accepted, even outside of Africa. Comrade Ramon Sanchez-

93. "Cuba: A Bridge Too Far?" *Los Angeles Times,* 4 July 1977, p. 1, part II, "tuxedo" quotation from Bernheimer, *op. cit.*

94. "Ethiopia Confirms Cubans Are at Front," *Los Angeles Times,* 3 March 1978, p. 15; and, "Russians Pull the Triggers in Eritrea," *The South China Morning Post,* 12 February 1978, p. 4.

95. "Fulbright Hits at Sub Base Story," *San Francisco Chronicle,* 5 October 1970, p. 13.

96. "CIA Blamed for Rain on His Parade: Castro Shows Off Military, MiG-23s," *Los Angeles Times,* 11 January 1979, p. 16, part I.

Parodi, chief of Cuban diplomatic interests section in Washington, has noted with some pride the contribution made by the Cuban armed forces in Africa: "We are not acting as an expeditionary force, but as advisers, technicians, and troops. . . . We subordinate ourselves [to the Ethiopians]."[97]

In Africa itself, the Ethiopian Head of State, Lieutenant Colonel Mengustu told a rally in Addis Ababa: "The Cubans, renowned for shedding their blood anywhere and at any time for just struggle and cause, are bracing themselves with the Ethiopian's People's Army at the front line." The Somalis who were being defeated in the Ogaden, confirmed the martial nature of the Cuban forces at the front.[98]

The disarming notion that Cuba is merely paying off its debt to the Soviet Union by sending its troops to Africa and the Middle East to serve as "advisers and technicians," or in the "front-line" as suggested by Ethiopia and Somalia, is reinforced by the hopeful view that once the United States "normalizes" relations with Cuba, Cuba will cease to be consort to the Soviet Union in such adventures. The other attractive idea is that Castro is really not master in his own house, since he is really caught between "the old-line Cuban revolutionaries" or "hard-liners" and the "technocrats."

> Although Castro symbolizes the revolution by no means does he run a one-man show. Overtures to the United States last year and talks with Cuban exile leaders this year are said to be victories for Castro over the hard-liners around him.[99]

It should be recalled that once it was believed that Stalin was a "barrier" between the West and "the hard-liners around him."

The conviction that "Dr. Castro would like to get away from his over dependence on the Soviet Union" walks hand-in-hand with the belief that relations with the United States would improve if the Cubans could just resolve their internal bureaucratic and political struggles. As one unidentified American official who had been "close to the talks" during secret negotiations in 1974-75 expressed it:

> On the one hand you had the technocrats, who wanted wider contacts with the United States. On the other, you had the old-line Cuban revolutionaries who knew that improved relations with Washington would destroy some of their revolutionary elan. I believe that Fidel

97. "Cuban Aide Here Rebuffs U.S. Troops in Africa," *The Washington Post,* 15 February 1978, p. 1A.

98. "Ethiopia Confirms Cubans Are at Front," *Los Angeles Times,* 3 March 1978, p. 15. One may also see Hugh Thomas's view of "Cuba's Military Adventures," *The Christian Science Monitor,* 17 March 1978, p. 20-21.

99. "Most Better Off: Cuba Prepares for 20th Anniversary," *Los Angeles Times,* 13 December 1978, p. 1, Part IX.

couldn't decide which side of the argument to support, so he just let the contacts stop.[100]

What echoes from the past that one raised! The British Ambassador to Berlin, Sir Neville Henderson, for example, wrote of how Hitler's threat to go to war for the Sudetenland in the Fall of 1938, really stemmed from the treatment of the Czech rebuff to him in the American and European press. It served as an excuse, "for Hitler to come down on the side of his extremists and to approve once again solutions by force." And: "History will assuredly attribute a large share of the blame for September 1939 [the attack on Poland] to Ribbentrop; his successful intrigues against Neurath's visit to London were neither the first nor, unfortunately, the last instance of his sinister influence on the policy of his Fuehrer." And Herman Goering, that thorough-going good fellow who was "on the side of peace in 1938," had already expended his influence on behalf of moderation by September 1939.[101]

Fanciful preoccupation with what is seen as the inner struggles of ruthless dictators like Hitler and Castro and the search for manifestations of civility in those activities that know no international boundaries—the arts and science—all obscure the sinister meaning of such dictatorships.

The Effect of Cuba on the Balance of Power

The strategic fact is that the Soviet Union has been permitted to develop an advanced base in the Gulf of Mexico. It should not have escaped the notice of those who have the responsibility for the safety of the United States and of its people. Cuba is now a base for Soviet operations in Africa and the Middle East and has, from 1962 at least, become an instrument of Soviet policy in the world. Whether the Cuban dictator is a willing partner, a pliant tool, or a socialist brother-in-arms, makes little difference in counting the strategic consequence for the United States.

The fact is that the balance of power in the Gulf of Mexico and the Caribbean shifted markedly about 1962, to the disadvantage of the United States, and that shift continued. Those who prefer to see the consolidation of Communist power in Cuba as manifestations of the improvement of conditions in Cuba, merely confirm, without intending to do so, that such a strategic shift has taken place.[102]

100. "Secret '74-75 U.S.-Cuba Talks Revealed," *Los Angeles Times*, 30 March 1977, p. 4.

101. Sir Neville Henderson, *Failure of a Mission: Berlin, 1937-1939* (London: Hodder and Stoughton, Ltd., 1940), pp. 140-41, 69, and 83.

102. See for example, "Cuba Seems Bent on Warming to U.S.: Castro Rules Firmly But Some Changes Appear on the Horizon," *The Christian Science Monitor*, 4 January 1979, p. 7; "Castro's Cuba: Still Some Shortages but . . .," *ibid.*, 31 January 1979, p. 12-13.

Perhaps the Cuban people have come to accept the dictatorship, the alliance with the Soviet Union and a military role in Soviet schemes for Africa and the Middle East. If so, that change is as significant for Cuba's role in the Gulf, as Hitler's consolidation of power in the Reich was for Germany's role in Europe.

The fact that there was a Cuban missile crisis in 1962 ought to have been a sharp warning of the shift in strategic conditions in the Gulf of Mexico, and thus in the world. For the first time since the Civil War a major European power sent troops into an independent country in the Western hemisphere to establish a regime that would favor its own interests. Even the mere threat of such a thing happening in 1940, when it was thought the Nazis might attempt to support a coup in Brazil, was cause for the United States to plan for an expeditionary force to Brazil to prevent the extension of German power into the Western Hemisphere.[103]

The very fact that it would be accepted in 1962 that the Soviet Union had the right to establish a base in the Gulf of Mexico, so long as it contained no "offensive weapons" was itself a remarkable departure from the policies implied by the Monroe Doctrine. Insofar as the Soviet strategic gambit at the time did call forth fears of war with Russia, that should *itself* have inspired serious thought about the strategic significance of the event.

Yet in 1974 and 1975, during secret negotiations with Cuba to "normalize" relations, it was counted "an important step toward improved relations" when the Cuban government was said to have agreed to a "*reduction of Cuban subversion* in the Puerto Rican situation."[104]

It would certainly seem that an effort to subvert the government of an American territory would awake some deep speculation about the significance of a pro-Soviet regime in Cuba committed to such subversion, but willing to *reduce*—not cease, but *reduce* such subversion. Yet President Carter counted "Cuba's demands for independence for Puerto Rico" as one of the "irritants" in relations between the United States and Cuba.[105] It was not apparently

103. Skinner Watson, *The War Department: Chief of Staff: Prewar Plans and Preparations* in *United States Army in World War II* series (Washington, D.C.; Historical Division, Department of the Army, 1950), p. 95-96:

> As late as 24 May 1940 there was warning from London that 6,000 Nazis loaded aboard merchant ships were possibly headed for Brazil, there to be joined by the crews of other German merchantmen in harbor and employed by Nazi elements in Brazil as a means of seizing the government . . . the President directed the Chief of Naval Operations to devise plans for the moving of 10,000 troops to Brazil by air, to be followed by 100,000 to be transported by sea.

104. "Secret '74-75 U.S.—Cuba Talks Revealed," *Los Angeles Times,* 30 March 1977, p. 4. Italics added.

105. "Carter Cites Irritants That Block U.S.–Cuba Relations," *Los Angeles Times,* 8 February 1979, p. 13. See also, "Cuba and Puerro Rico: Solidarity in the Face of Yankee Imperialism," *Gramma* (Havana), 9 March 1975, p. 2.

even an irritant when the Soviet Union, Cuba's mentor in the world, campaigned for Puerto Rican independence.[106] And it was, no doubt, taken as a demonstration of the friendship that the Panama Canal Treaty was supposed to promote when the Panamanian dictator reaffirmed his support for Cuba on the question of Puerto Rican independence.[107] The important fact, however, is that the United States is compelled to negotiate with Cuba over the acceptable degree of Cuban subversion within a territory of the United States. That fact alone demonstrates the change in strategic circumstances in the Gulf of Mexico and the Caribbean. Were that not enough to suggest the role of Cuba in Soviet strategy, the constant presence off the U.S. Atlantic Coast of Soviet strategic bombers, Tupolev TU-95s, flying a regular route from Murmansk to their Soviet base in Cuba ought to tell us what Cuba is.[108]

Such aircraft as the TU-95 are capable of launching the AS-6 *Kingfish* air-to-surface cruise missile, or the AS-4 *Kitchen* cruise missile, capable of delivering a one megaton nuclear warhead to ranges up to 450 miles.[109] They are also capable of controlling and coordinating strikes by surface-to-surface missiles and submarine attacks against shipping and naval targets. In Soviet eyes, such extended range aircraft have a clearly defined role:

> Aircraft with extended range capabilities and speed can quickly strike enemy forces at sea. Aviation units and forces can be readily transferred from one area to another. For example, large groups of aircraft can be redeployed from one continent to another in less than a day, without any loss of combat effectiveness.[110]

Reluctance to consider any Soviet weapon or military vehicle based in Cuba as having a strategic role rather than a defensive one, is to play with words in order to seek definitions that are harmless or unprovocative. It seems that concern belatedly expressed about the introduction into Cuba of MiG-27 aircraft (MiG-23s adapted for ground attack) came from fear that the presence of those aircraft would disturb the administration's drive in Con-

106. As an example, see "The World of Capital in the World of Lawlessness: AMERICAN COLONY," *Izvestia,* 7 October 1978, p. 5, in *The Current Digest of the Soviet Press,* Vol. XXX, No. 40, 1 November 1978, p. 14.

107. "Panama's New Foreign Policy," *San Francisco Chronicle,* 20 July 1978, p. 20; but see also, "Panama Gets Into Close Step With Cuba Regime: Common Antagonism Toward U.S. Possible Spurs Bond Between Torrijos and Castro," *Los Angeles Times,* 22 September 1972, p. 12.

108. "Russian Plane Down Off Canada," *Los Angeles Times,* 6 August 1976, p. 2; "Soviet Plane Flies Over U.S. Ships 60 Miles From Florida," *ibid.,* 23 April 1977, p. 1; "Russian Planes Shadow Navy Vessels Off U.S.," *ibid.,* 15 October 1977, p. 21. The TU-95 is classified as a heavy bomber, comparable to the U.S. strategic bomber, the B-52. It has a maximum range of 8,000 miles and can carry a weapons load of 20 tons.

109. *The Military Balance, 1978-1979,* pp. 81-82. General Major N. Vishinsky, "Naval Aviation is Oceanic Aviation," in *Morskoy Sbornik,* No. 8, Paul J. Murphy (ed.), *Naval Power Policy* in Vol. 2 of *Studies in Communist Affairs* (Washington, D.C.: U.S.G.P.O., 1978), p. 181.

110. General-Colonel S. A. Bulyayev, "The Role of Aviation in Combat Operations at Sea Today," *Morskoy Sbornik,* No. 6, 1965, pp. 36-42, cited in *Naval Power in Soviet Policy,* p. 181.

gress for acceptance of SALT II, rather than any concern that the Soviet Union might be posing a threat to continental United States. While the Cuban dictator said the Soviet aircraft had been in Cuba since January 1978, U.S. aerial reconnaissance of Cuba was not resumed until the beginning of November, eleven months later.[111]

The Soviet press treated the matter with contempt saying any suggestion that the MiGs sent to Cuba violated the 1962 Soviet-American agreement was "groundless and provocative from start to finish." *Pravda* said of the MiG-23s: "In their main characteristics, these aircraft are of the same type which have been and are in Cuba and which have been and remain necessary to safeguard the legitimate interests of Cuba."[112]

Earlier, when it was reported that Soviet pilots were flying Cuban jet interceptors in Cuba, the news was received with the calmness typical of those who are secure in their own strength and determination. The Pentagon explained that for a number of years Soviet pilots had been flying as instructors in the Cuban air force and that the aircraft being flown were, in any case, "antiques" by present standards, with a combat radius of barely 300 miles; they could hardly reach beyond Miami and certainly would not be able to reach any important places in the United States. It was explained that one reason Soviet pilots were flying the interceptors for Cuban air defense was probably to free Cuban pilots "for duty on the battle front between Ethiopia and Somalia."[113] When the newer MiGs appeared in Cuba and were acknowledged to be present by the administration, the concern expressed was not whether the new Soviet interceptors in Cuba had any significance for the defense of the United States, but that the "MiGs-in-Cuba issue not be added to other objections being raised by U.S. conservatives to ratifying a SALT II treaty in the Senate." And indeed even Premier Kosygin admonished seven U.S. senators visiting Moscow at the time that the MiGs in Cuba should not be linked to SALT II.[114] And certainly no one would know better than the Soviet Premier whether or not Soviet pilots and fighter aircraft in Cuba would have any bearing at all on the strategic situation in the Caribbean and the Gulf of Mexico.

In March 1978, when reports came out of London that the Soviet Union was constructing a pen for nuclear submarines at Cienfuegos in Cuba and that

111. Castro's observation about the MiGs in Cuba is in "Why Cuba Will Open Jail Doors," *The Christian Science Monitor,* 24 November 1978, p. 4. Resumption of U.S. reconnaissance of Cuba is reported in "President Orders Cuba Overflights: Planes to Check on New Soviet MiG Jets," *Los Angeles Times,* 19 November 1978, p. 1.

112. Cited in "Cuba tight-lipped on U.S. accusations," *The South China Morning Post,* 19 November 1978, p. 1.

113. "Pentagon Calm at larger Soviet Role in Cuban air patrol activity," *The Christian Science Monitor,* 16 February 1978, p. 3.

114. "Keeping cool on MiGs in Cuba," *The Christian Science Monitor,* 5 December 1978, p. 1.

the Soviet Union had shipped strategic missiles to the island, it was strictly page 14 news, which both the State Department and the Defense Department were at pains to deny.[115]

It must have been most troublesome for those who have always regarded China to be ruled by men of great sagacity and perception when these men bespoke different interpretations of Cuba:

> As a matter of fact Cuba has become the Soviet Union's military springboard in the Caribbean. At present, more than 20 Soviet TU-95B long-range reconnaissance bombers are stationed at Cuban air bases. . . . Cienfuegos has become a base for Soviet naval task force maneuvering in the Caribbean. The Soviet Union has built many modern military bases and installations in Cuba. They include air force bases, nuclear-powered submarine bases and arms depots as well as command telecommunication centres. . . . The Cuban army's military guiding thought, the principles governing its build-up, its strategy and tactics, and its intelligence system have all been adapted to the advantage of the Soviet Union.[116]

Such an eccentric view of Soviet military power in Cuba is the product without doubt of Chinese anxiety about the million Soviet troops on the Chinese border and the Soviet presence in Laos and Vietnam. But such anxiety can often focus the mind quite sharply.

Of course, if the Soviet Union is not preparing for war, then the Soviet presence in Cuba and Soviet naval forces in the Gulf of Mexico and the Caribbean are hardly worth mentioning. But if the Soviet Union is preparing for war, it is a different matter indeed. For Cuba retains the same strategic position it always has had in respect to the Gulf and the Caribbean; and the Gulf and the Caribbean are on the southern flank of the United States.

The Soviet presence in Cuba and Cuba's status as a consort of the Soviet Union in Africa and the Middle East cannot reasonably be seen as merely a political consideration ranking with Soviet attitudes on human rights or Cuban support for Marxist regimes in Africa. It is a strategic fact. It bears on the capability of the United States to wage war on behalf of its allies in NATO and on the defense of the United States.

To understand how that can be, it need only be recalled how it was in the Gulf of Mexico and the Caribbean in the dark days after the Japanese attack on Pearl Harbor: in those months Hong Kong, Malaya, Thailand, and the Netherlands East Indies were conquered by Japan; the Philippines was in-

115. "Russ Building Nuclear Sub Base in Cuba, London Paper Reports," *Los Angeles Times,* 28 March 1978, p. 14; and "Russian Sub Pen in Cuba Reported," *San Francisco Chronicle,* 28 March 1978, p. 9.

116. "Cuba: From Economic Dependence to Political Submission," *Peking Review,* No. 50, 15 December 1978, pp. 26-28.

vested and seized by Japan; Allied naval power in the Far East was destroyed off Kuantan and in the Java Sea. Between January and August 1942, 263 Allied merchant ships totalling a million and a half tons were sunk by German submarines in the Gulf of Mexico and the Caribbean. In two weeks alone, in June, 13 ships were sunk in the Atlantic approaches to the Panama Canal. Forty-one ships were sunk in the Gulf of Mexico during the single month of May. In three months—May, June and July—16 ships were lost in the approaches to the Mississippi. Over half of the ships lost to German submarines in the period were tankers. On the 19th of May, one such tanker, the *Mercury Sun,* was torpedoed and sunk of Cape Corrientos, Cuba. The fuel oil it was carrying has been intended for the Fleet at Pearl Harbor.

It was not just the ships that were lost but Allied merchant sailors, navy gun crews, and the precious cargoes, all of which had to be replaced if the Allies were to wage war against the Axis. Every merchant ship lost had to be replaced by a new one, taking steel and labor from the construction of other war materials; and above all time, the one commodity that could not be replaced. How many of those twelve million Europeans who found death in Nazi extermination camps would have survived the war if the Allies could have been spared the loss of the million and half tons of shipping sunk in the waters of the Gulf and Caribbean between January and August 1942?[117]

And, of course, German submarines attacked shipping, during the same period along the Atlantic Coast of Florida, off the Carolinas and amongst the islands of the British West Indies, as well as in the rest of the Atlantic Ocean. Admiral Doenitz writing of what German submariners called the "Happy Time," summarized nicely the strategic concept of the campaign during this period when the United States was only just beginning to become prepared for war.

> For the conduct of U-boat warfare this granting of liberty of action in American waters held yet a further advantage. . . . As the attackers we held the initiative, and by rapid switches of the main weight of our attack from one focal point to another we could confuse and surprise the enemy. The Americans obviously could not provide adequate protection for all focal points at all times, and they would be compelled to follow us from one to the other. In this way it seemed likely that *we could compel the enemy to a real dispersal of his defensive forces.*[118]

117. Shipping losses are given by areas in which losses were sustained in Samuel Eliot Morison, *The Battle of the Atlantic, 1939-1943,* Volume I in the series *History of United States Naval Operations in World War II* (Boston: Little, Brown and Company, 1957), pp. 137-44 and in Appendix I; the German account of the campaign in the areas is given along with statistics of losses inflicted, Jurgen Rohwer, *U-Boote: Eine Chronik in Bilder* (Oldenburg/Hamburg: Gerhard Stalling Verlag, 1962), p. 34-36 and *Anhag.*

118. Admiral Doenitz, *Memoirs: Ten Years and Twenty Days* (London: Weidenfeld and Nicolson, 1958), p. 196.

The admiral was correct. Because the Americans were so desperately unprepared for U-boat attacks on coastal, Gulf, and Caribbean shipping, the Royal Navy had to transfer three of its hard-pressed escort groups to assist in the protection of shipping in U.S. waters. These had to come from those working the convoy routes in the Atlantic and in the Western Approaches of England.[119]

German submarines attacked with torpedoes and deck guns in surface actions. They also laid mines in heavily travelled shipping channels. The mere suspicion that a submarine was present in an area forced delays, re-routed merchant ships, and tied-up scarce air and naval units that might have been employed elsewhere against the Axis. A submarine-laid minefield for example would lie undiscovered until a ship entered it to be damaged or sunk. Then shipping had to be halted or routed elsewhere while the minefield was swept.

The formation of merchant ships into convoys afforded the most effective means of employing the limited number of escorts and aircraft available to protect shipping from attack. Convoying imposed delays on shipping because merchant ships had to be collected in a protected area in order to pick up the convoy escort, while the convoy could travel no faster than the slowest merchant ship in its midst. Once a sea area became thoroughly patrolled by air and surface forces and convoys instituted throughout the area, losses to submarines decreased. But if the precautions were relaxed, it could be expected that submarine attacks would be resumed. Only in July 1944, could air and naval forces in the Caribbean and the Gulf of Mexico be considered adequate to the threat posed by Axis submarines and that was the last month in which Admiral Doenitz deployed submarines into the area. And by July 1944, because of the allied invasion of France, the German submarine bases on the French Coast could not be used. New bases were established on the Norwegian Coast. It has to be noted that in the course of the anti-submarine operations in the area of the West Indies, Central America, and the Gulf of Mexico, Cuban, Brazilian, Mexican, Dutch, as well as British and American forces were employed against Axis submarines. Cuba, the islands of the West Indies, and the Lesser and Greater Antilles, were all in friendly hands during the time of the German submarine campaigns and the Allied counter-offensive in the area. The entire area was encompassed by Allied air bases, and by naval operating bases from which small craft could operate in defense of local traffic. There was no Axis submarine base in the region at which German submarines could seek shelter for refueling, re-victualling, and repair.[120]

119. Captain S. W. Roskill, *The War at Sea, 1939-1945*, Volume II: *The Period of Balance* in *History of the Second World War United Kingdom Military Series* (London: H.M.S.O., 1965), p. 102-3.

120. German submarine operations in the Caribbean Sea Frontier, the Panama Sea Frontier and

A handful of German submarines, never more than a dozen, operating from bases four thousand miles from Havana, Cuba, beyond air cover from the Luftwaffe, and beyond support from the German surface forces, with no command and communications facilities closer than St. Nazaire or L'Orient, to coordinate attacks, and with no German long-range aircraft to locate targets, tied down fleets of naval craft and squadrons of airplanes far from the theater of operations where the decisive battles for the liberation of Europe would have to take place.

If, as the Chinese insist and ordinary observation would confirm, Cuba has become an advanced base for Soviet air and submarine operations in the Caribbean, the Gulf of Mexico, the West Indies, and the southern Atlantic Coast of the United States, then the significance of the "Missiles of October" becomes apparent. Having introduced missiles and bombers into Cuba in 1962, and then negotiated their withdrawal as a *quid pro quo* for a guarantee that the United States would not invade Cuba, the Soviet Union gained a significant strategic asset to use in any future war with the United States. For, in effect, the United States granted to the Soviet Union the license to develop an advanced base from which Soviet and Cuban forces could wage war against the United States far from Europe and the Western Pacific where the decisive battles would take place.

In war, the purpose of grand strategy is so to deploy one's own forces as to deprive the enemy of his freedom to act effectively to carry out his policies: to gain the objectives of the war. To do so one must destroy the enemy's armed forces or their will to resist. The armed forces may be destroyed by forcing them to fight under circumstances of one's own choosing where one enjoys superiority in forces and superiority in strategic position.

---

the Gulf Sea Frontier during 1943 and 1944 are recounted in Samuel Eliot Morison, *The Atlantic Battle Won, May 1943-May 1945,* Volume X in *History of U.S. Naval Operations in World War II* (Boston: Little, Brown and Company, 1968).

VI. Grand Strategy—Cuba and Yugoslavia

NATIONS, WHO PERMIT THEMSELVES TO GIVE UP IMPORTANT STRATEGIC ASSETS TO PURCHASE THE GOODWILL OF DICTATORSHIPS in order to promote peace, will pay a dreadful price when war does come. They may even be defeated.

Endangering America's Southern Flank—Cuba

The ultimate in grand strategy is to confront one's enemy with such a preponderance of military power and such a superiority of strategic position that he has no hope of resisting; if he resists anyway, he will surely be defeated. In short, there comes a time when the imperatives of strategy can no longer be ignored in the interest of preserving international goodwill—a commodity that is scarce at the best of times and worthless when a nation's back is to the wall.

The easy surrender of Cuba, in 1959, to the control of a regime hostile to the United States and the license so quickly granted to the Soviet Union to convert Cuba to an advanced base for Soviet military operations in the Gulf of Mexico and the Caribbean will exact an awful penalty from Americans when war comes. Indeed, the alliance between the Soviet Union and Cuba has already had its fateful consequences in Africa and the Middle East. It cannot be that the Western Alliance has yet paid the final price for American liberality.

All along, it has been difficult for Americans to believe that Cuba and the Soviet Union mean any real harm to American interests in the Gulf and Caribbean. Each report of Soviet and Cuban military enterprise there or elsewhere has been excused or passed over with some optimistic rationalization.

The Implication of Submarine Warfare

In 1962, Soviet missiles and medium bombers in Cuba had caused a crisis; in 1970, the presence of Soviet submarines in Cuban harbors and Cuban waters had very nearly caused a crisis. In 1979, a Soviet submarine given to the Cuban navy would be only page five news in the *Los Angeles Times,* a newspaper that had headlined on its front page the crisis of 1962 and the near-crisis of 1970. The Defense Department report of the new Cuban submarine was a model of disinterest. Although expressing uncertainty about whether the submarine would be the precursor of an entire submarine squadron, "defense analysts," assured all that: "The 2,100-ton *Foxtrot* submarine, represents no serious threat to U.S. interests."[1] The Defense Department analysts did not comment on whether or not they thought the Soviets might have a submarine base in Cuba, nor apparently did any alert, investigative reporters. Perhaps the *Foxtrot* will be boxed-up and returned to Murmansk should it ever require repair, refueling, or rearming.

It would be nice to be able to charge the Soviet Union with treachery. Unfortunately, however villainous its intentions toward the United States, the Soviet Union has merely played along with the definition laid down by a succession of American administrations about what constituted "offensive" weapons in Cuba. While common sense might urge that a newer version of a type of vessel that had destroyed millions of tons of Allied shipping in two World Wars was hardly preeminently a defensive weapon, the evidently more agile minds of this generation of "defense analysts" have little difficulty in avoiding the conclusion that a Soviet attack submarine is indeed designed to attack.

One may consult the *Dictionary of Basic Military Terms,* compiled by the faculty of the General Staff Academy of the Armed Forces of the U.S.S.R. for the definition of a submarine:

> *PODVODNAYA LODKA* [submarine]—A combat vessel intended to cruise and conduct combat operations under water. A submarine is used to destroy surface warships, other submarines, and transport vessels, at sea and in bases (ports), and also *to demolish important installations in a wide coastal zone of enemy territory.* The basic combat feature of a submarine is the covert nature of its actions. According to their armament, submarines are divided into missile, torpedo, minelaying, and special categories. Special-purpose submarines include those in the radar-patrol, transport, amphibious-assault, and oil-tanker categories. According to their displacement, submarines may be classified as large, medium, or small; and according to their type of propulsion machinery, they may be identified as diesel-electric, gas-turbine, or atomic-powered.
>
> *PODVODNYYE LODKI FLOTA* [Fleet submarines]—One of the main branches of a fleet, which includes strategic formations and formations of submarines of various classes and sub-classes (or type). Fleet submarines are used to destroy enemy warships and transports, and to demolish installations on enemy territory, both independently and in

1. "Russians Beefing Up Cuba's Small Navy," *Los Angeles Times,* 11 February 1979, p. 5.

> coordinated action with other branches of the fleet. Fleet submarines may also be used to conduct reconnaissance, lay mines, land reconnaissance-sabotage groups clandestinely on the enemy coast, guide friendly strike forces to enemy targets at sea, transport personnel and important cargoes, etc.[2]

It might appear incredible that the regime in Cuba would tie its fate to that of the Soviet Union in any war between that power and the United States. But then Castro has seemed delighted to be able to send thousands of his soldiers to fight alongside Russians, East Europeans and Africans, in Angola and Ethiopia.[3] If the Soviet Union were to be defeated in Europe, then there seems little doubt that Castro would seek accommodation with the United States. Were NATO to be overrun, then there is equally little doubt that Castro would claim a Soviet reward for whatever contribution Cuba made to the Soviet victory.[4]

Cuba seems the principal agent of the Soviet Union and the "socialist commonwealth" in the councils of the non-aligned or "Third World."[5] In voicing approval of the results of the 1974 visit of Brezhnev to Cuba, the Politburo of the Central Committee of the Communist Party of the Soviet Union, the Presidium of the U.S.S.R. Supreme Soviet, and the U.S.S.R. Council of Ministers stated their view of Soviet-Cuban relations:

> The Soviet-Cuban Declaration signed by Comrades L. I. Brezhnev and Fidel Castro is a highly important document. It generalized the 15 year experience of truly international cooperation between the world's first socialist country and Latin America's first socialist state, and it outlines a broad program for the further planned development of political, economic, and cultural ties between the U.S.S.R. and Cuba, exchanges of experience in socialist and communist construction and coordinated actions in the struggle to strengthen the solidarity of the socialist commonwealth and the world Communist movement on the basis of the principles of Marxism-Leninism and proletarian internationalism.[6]

2. *Dictionary of Basic Military Terms: A Soviet View,* prepared by Colonel A. A. Oleynik, Faculty of the General Staff Academy of the Armed Forces of the U.S.S.R., translated by the D.G.I.S. Multilingual Section, Translation Bureau, Secretary of State Department, Ottawa, Canada (Washington, D.C.: U.S.G.P.O., 1976), pp. 161-62.
3. See for example, "Raul Castro Attack Aimed at Brzezinski," *Los Angeles Times,* 3 January 1979, p. 10.
4. See for example, "Caribbean Islands Build Cuban Ties," *The Christian Science Monitor,* 30 June 1975, p. 9.
5. "The African Expeditions: Cuban Army Fortifies Castro Third-World Role," *The Christian Science Monitor,* 21 March 1978, p. 5.
6. "In the Politburo of the C.P.S.U. Central Committee, the Presidium of the U.S.S.R. Supreme Soviet and the U.S.S.R. Council of Ministers: ON THE RESULTS OF COMRADE L. I. BREZHNEV'S VISIT TO THE REPUBLIC OF CUBA." *Pravda,* 7 February 1974, p. 1, in *The Current Digest of the Soviet Press,* Vol. XXVI, No. 5, 27 February 1974, p. 31.

In March 1974, within a few weeks of the Brezhnev visit to Cuba, Cuban military instructors arrived in Somalia, in the Cuban ship, *Vietnam Heroica.*[7] The following year, in December, it was finally acknowledged by the Secretary of State, that indeed Cuban troops were fighting in Angola, while *U.S. New and World Report* would tell of the presence of Cuban soldiers in Syria, South Yemen, the Congo, Equatorial Guinea, Guinea-Bissau, Sierra Leone, and Tanzania.[8]

It seems evident that from the Soviet perspective, Cuba is eventually to play the same role in Central America, the West Indies, the Gulf, and the Caribbean that the Socialist Republic of Vietnam is intended to play in Indo-China and the rest of Southeast Asia: the nucleus around which to organize a regional political and economic unit of the socialist commonwealth.[9] As the *Beijing Review* (Peking) sees it, Vietnam is now the "Cuba of Asia":

> The Soviet strategy in Asia is to put down a strategic cordon around the continent, stretching from the Mediterranean, the Red Sea, the Indian Ocean and up to Haisenwei [Vladivostok], and using the "Cuba of Asia," Viet Nam, as its hatchetman, seize the whole of Indochina to dominate Southeast Asia. . . .[10]

And now Fidel Castro, like some Ottoman Pasha, takes school children from their homes in Africa to be trained as so many Janissaries to serve the sultans of a new world empire.[11] The political and military role accorded to Cuba in the Soviet scheme of things leads to the conclusion that the island, under its present regime, is an important factor in Soviet strategic policy. It is evident that in any U.S.-Soviet war, among the first considerations for the United States would be the neutralization of the island to prevent its use as a base for Soviet-Cuban operations in the area. Yet the present condition of the armed forces of the United States lends no assurance that Cuba could be dealt with quickly or cheaply, nor without diverting important military resources from the principal theaters of war.

Cuba's relations to Soviet strategy is a peculiar one. Soviet and Cuban forces in the island resemble the Afrika Korps under Rommel in the Western Desert. If the Allies did not defend Egypt and the Suez Canal from German

7. Ian Greig, *The Communist Challenge to Africa: An Analysis of Contemporary Soviet, Cuban and Chinese Policies* (Richmond, Surrey: Foreign Affairs Publishing Company, 1977), p. 108.

8. "Cuba General Linked to Russ Angola Aid," *Los Angeles Times,* 2 December 1975, p. 11; see also, "Moscow's Next Target in Africa," *The London Sunday Times,* 20 February 1977, printed as "a paid advertisement" in *Washington Post,* 15 March 1977, p. A7.

9. "A Regional Leadership Role for Vietnam?: Southeast Asia: POSITIVE TENDENCIES," *Pravda,* 29 October 1978, p. 4, in *The Current Digest of the Soviet Press,* Vol. XXX, No. 43, 22 November 1978, pp. 8-9.

10. "Social-Imperialist Strategy in Asia," *Beijing Review,* No. 3, 19 January 1979, pp. 13-16.

11. "2,000 African High School Pupils Studying in Cuba," *Los Angeles Times,* 25 June 1978, p. 1.

attack those places would ultimately fall to the Axis, causing the loss of the Middle East, inflicting on the Allies an enormous handicap that might well have led to the defeat of an important ally, the Soviet Union. Yet when the English and Americans defeated the Afrika Korps, as they did in 1942, that did not automatically lead to the defeat of Germany. In the same way, Cuba as a Soviet base, during a war for NATO Europe, could not be ignored.

Perhaps a third of the petroleum imported by the United States moves along the route through the Yucatan Channel or the Florida Straits past Cuba to U.S. Gulf ports. By the end of 1979, 555,000 barrels of oil a day from the Alaska North Slope fields will have to come through the Panama Canal and into Gulf ports.[12] Every fifteen days, a 65,000 ton oil tanker unloads its cargo at the Tenneco oil docks on the Mississippi by New Orleans. There are eighty or so other crude oil docks between the Gulf and Baton Rouge that accept similar tonnages of oil.[13] And, New Orleans is only one of the Gulf ports through which oil moves into the United States. Almost 90 percent of the Bauxite consumed in the United States moves by Cuba from its sources in the West Indies, or South America. A host of other raw materials are transported by sea into Gulf ports or along the Southern Atlantic Coast of the United States.[14]

But it is not just the supply of essential raw materials that is at hazard from Soviet and Cuban operations in the waters adjacent to Cuba; nor is it merely that the protection of sea-borne traffic in those waters would require most of the surface and air units now operational in the U.S. Navy. While it is true that the Gulf and Caribbean are waters unusually favorable for operations of deep-diving submarines—the average depth of water is over 1500 meters while the currents and temperature gradients are less than favorable for sonar detection of submarines—there are as well a dozen or more oil and gas platforms in the sea off the mouth of the Mississippi alone. These are obvious targets for attack by light naval units such as the 26 *Osa*- and *Komar*-class fast patrol boats armed with *Styx* surface-to-surface missiles, missiles that can deliver a 720 pound warhead to a range of 43 kilometers.[15] That is aside from the threat posed by Soviet and Cuban aircraft and submarines.

12. "Congressmen Criticize California on Pipeline: Alternative Plans Face Same Obstacles," *Los Angeles Times*, 14 March 1979, p. 1.

13. "Tanker Traffic on Mississippi Spurs Fears of Explosion," *Los Angeles Times*, 21 January 1978, p. 2.

14. Typical figures on imports by sea are given in *U.S. Life Lines* (Washington, D.C.: Department of the Navy, December 1966).

15. Bathymetric and circulatory characteristics of the Caribbean and Gulf of Mexico are in *The Rand McNally Atlas of the Oceans* (New York: Rand McNally and Company, 1977), pp. 124-25. Location of oil and gas fields off the mouths of the Mississippi is in the same place, p. 127. The Cuban navy is described in *The Military Balance, 1978-79* (London: International Institute for Strategic Studies, 1978), pp. 73-74. The *Osa* and *Komar* boats are described in *Combat Fleets of the World, 1976/77* as well as in *The Soviet War Machine: An Encyclopedia of Russian Military Equipment and Strategy* (London: Salamander Books, Ltd., 1977), pp. 145-46.

As to the submarine threat, Admiral Sergei Gorshkov, Commander-in-Chief of the Soviet Navy wrote in his book, *Seapower of the State* (1976), the Soviet Union gave priority to the development of submarines because:

> they enabled our navy to increase its *attack* capabilities in the shortest possible time in order to pose a serious threat to the main forces of the enemy navy in the ocean theaters, and to do this at a cost of fewer resources and less time.[16]

Admiral Gorshkov's general conception of naval operations within which submarine operations are meant to fit, nearly echoes the words of Admiral Doenitz writing about the purpose of German submarine operations. Gorshkov says:

> To achieve superiority of forces over the enemy in the main sector and *pin him down* in the secondary sectors at the time of operations means to achieve sea control in a theater or sector of a theater—i.e. to create such a situation that the enemy will be paralyzed or constrained in his operations, or weakened and thereby hampered from interfering with our operation or our countering of his operation.[17]

It is not difficult to conceive the kinds of penalties that hostile forces operating from Cuban bases could exact from the United States in the course of a war with the Soviet Union, in the light of presently available Allied naval capabilities. In August 1942, the U.S. Atlantic Fleet had available 104 surface combatants including 77 destroyers, one fleet and seven escort carriers. The Royal Navy and the Royal Canadian Navy had deployed at the same time 113 destroyers and corvettes in the Western Atlantic. It took all of that plus aircraft of the U.S. Army Air Corps, Royal Air Force Coastal Command and Fleet Air Arm, plus Canadian ships and aircraft, to combat the operations of 140 German U-boats operational in the Atlantic, Gulf, Mediterranean and elsewhere of which perhaps a third could be expected to be on station along the convoy routes at any one time.[18]

In 1942, 22% of the ships carrying bauxite were sunk, 20% of the Puerto Rican merchant fleet was destroyed, and 3.5% of the available tanker fleet was lost every month, to German submarines. The United States would have

16. Cited in *Naval Power in Soviet Policy*, p. 17. (italics added)

17. Cited in *Naval Power in Soviet Policy*, pp. 11-12. (italics added)

18. U-boat statistics are given in Captain S. W. Roskill, *The War at Sea*, Volume II: *The Period of Balance* in *History of the Second World War United Kingdom Series* (London: H.M.S.O., 1956), p. 113 and Appendix K: "German U-boat Strength January 1942-May 1943." Royal Navy and Royal Canadian Navy Escorts deployed in the Western Atlantic 1 August 1942 is given in *ibid.*, Appendix G: "British Excort Vessel Strength and Dispositions," p. 457f. Total Allied Escort Strength for any period may be derived from Tables in Peter Elliott, *Allied Escort Ships of World War II* (Annapolis: U.S. Naval Institute, 1977). Strength of U.S. Atlantic Fleet in August 1942 is from Samuel Eliot Morison, *The Battle of the Atlantic, 1939-1943,* Appendix VI: "The Atlantic Fleet of the United States Navy, 5 August 1942." On station strength of U-boats as a fraction of operation strength of U-boats may be derived from information in Karl Doenitz, *Memoirs.*

to build and deploy 420 destroyer escorts in the Atlantic before merchant ship losses were down to only four merchant ships lost to every German submarine destroyed.[19]

Today, the United States Navy has 62 major combatant ships in its Atlantic Fleet plus five fleet carriers. That is ten fewer ships than there were destroyers in the Atlantic Fleet in 1942, when that Fleet could boast 104 surface combatants. The Soviet Union has in its active submarine force, 243 attack submarines of which 69 carry anti-ship cruise missiles in addition to torpedoes or mines. Of these, 150 are available for deployment in the Atlantic Ocean. There are, in addition, 117 attack submarines in reserve. Besides all of those submarines, there are ninety Soviet submarines capable of launching some 1,015 ballistic missiles directly against targets within the United States or Allied territory abroad. Those submarines alone can, if permitted to survive in a war, inflict enormous damage and immense casualties on the United States and its Allies.

What Cost Cuba?: Global War Implications

The coast of Cuba stretches for over 1,600 miles; it provides countless bays, inlets, and sheltered harbors along with scores of islands from which light naval force, and coastal and ocean-going submarines may operate. Were Cuba undefended, the problem of keeping such a coastline under watch to prevent hostile operations against U.S. merchant marine traffic or U.S. territory would be immense. But Cuba is not undefended. Before the Soviet Union sent in the twenty or so MiG-23 aircraft in 1978, the Cuban air force had seven interceptor squadrons or 118 aircraft with which to defend Cuba against attack from the air—one interceptor for every 370 square miles. By comparison, the United States has one interceptor per 20,000 square miles of territory when the 190 Air National Guard interceptors are counted along with the six Regular Air Force interceptor squadrons which operate 141 aircraft. Apparently only East Germany, Poland, and Czechoslovakia have a higher density of interceptors than Cuba in the Communist world. In the Free World only Israel and Switzerland have a higher density of interceptors than Cuba.[20]

In addition to its air defense squadrons, Cuba has 24 surface-to-air missile battalions with 144 launchers. The United States has four such bat-

19. *Hearings on Military Posture and H. R. 11500, Department of Defense authorizations for Appropriations for Fiscal Year 1977* before the Committee on Armed Services, House of Representatives, 94th Congress, Second Session, Subcommittee on Sea Power . . ., part 4, p. 147.

20. The Soviet Union deploys about one interceptor per 3,100 square miles; Poland with 420 interceptors has one per 290 square miles; Czechoslovakia with 240 interceptors has one per 250 square miles; East Germany with 270 interceptors has one per 160 square miles; Switzerland has 120 interceptors or one per 130 square miles while Israel has one per 29 square miles or a total of 275 interceptors. The United Kingdom has one interceptor per 980 square miles. Based on data in *The Military Balance, 1978-79* and *The Times Atlas of the World* (London: The Times Newspaper Ltd., 1968).

talions, one in Alaska and three in Florida. Besides the mobile artillery available to the Cuban Army for coastal defense, there are reported to be around 50 *Samlet* surface-to-surface coastal defense missiles. The United States has no coastal defenses. Withal, it should not be thought that neutralization of Cuba by maritime blockade or air attack would be a piece of cake. If there were no war anywhere else—if the Russians were not overrunning NATO or seizing Hokkaido at the time—the United States possesses the military and naval capability to secure Cuba. But then, if there were no war anywhere else at the time it could hardly be expected that any U.S. administration could find a cause for war on Cuba, since nothing that Cuba has done thus far under the Communists has provoked an American military response.

If the Warsaw Pact were to begin to overrun NATO Europe, the situation would be notably different. One could hardly expect any administration to be blind to the threat posed by Cuban and Soviet naval and air forces.

Yet the present state of the United States Armed Forces provides few capabilities for a president forced to dispatch naval air and ground forces to Europe, while dealing with equally pressing threats in the Gulf, Soviet submarine operations against the tanker traffic from Alaska, and actual or potential assaults on the Aleutians, Japan, and South Korea. Also looms the possibility of a nuclear attack on the United States itself, now deterred, as it is said, by the threat of U.S. retaliation.

An actual invasion of Cuba by U.S. forces would certainly be no more difficult than the Japanese seizure of Luzon in the Philippines in 1942 or the Allied occupation of Okinawa in 1945; the former required five months and the latter two and a half months. Capturing Okinawa cost the United States 49,201 casualties, of which 12,281 were killed. Thirty-six American ships were sunk and 368 damaged, and 763 aircraft were lost. More American surface ships were lost or damaged in the battle for Okinawa than there are surface combatants in the United States Navy today. The U.S. forces employed to seize Okinawa included three Marine divisions, and four Army divisions supported by at least sixteen U.S. fleet aircraft carriers, plus four British carriers of Task Force 57, and numerous escort carriers.[21]

The ground forces required for the capture of Okinawa, against a defending force of about 700,000 Japanese troops is one-half the size of that force the active Army now holds in strategic reserve in the continental United States for defense of South Korea, Japan, and NATO Europe. The number of

21. Forces in the assault on Okinawa are given in George Carroll Dyer, *The Amphibians Came to Conquer: The Story of Admiral Richmond Kelly Turner,* Volume II (Washington, D.C.: U.S.G.P.O., 1972), pp. 1063-1104; composition of the Fast Carrier Force and the British Task Force 57 are in J. Rohwer and G. Hummelchen, *Chronology of the War at Sea, 1939-1945* (New York: Arco Publishing Company, 1974), pp. 498-500 and 517-19. Casualties in the Battle of Okinawa are in *The Simon and Schuster Encyclopedia of World War II,* pp. 457-58.

aircraft carriers employed to support the capture of Okinawa equals the combined active and reserve carrier force of the U.S. Fleet today.[22] Of that force two carriers are in the Western Pacific and two in the Mediterranean. The seven carriers in reserve would require up to six months to activate.

There is no reason to assume that the capture of Cuba would be easy. Perhaps when the first American flag got ashore, resistance would collapse. But if, as some would suggest, the Cuban people have never been happier nor prospered more than they have under the communists, then they may well fight for their revolution and for their dictatorship.[23]

Amphibious operations against Cuba, to seize and occupy the island, would be the most obvious course of action. Such operations are the province of units like the two U.S. Marine Amphibious Forces. The Ist Marine Amphibious Force is at Camp Pendleton, El Toro, and Twenty-Nine Palms, California, and, the IInd Marine Amphibious Force at Camp LeJeune, Cherry Point, and New River, North Carolina, and at Beaufort, South Carolina. A Marine Amphibious Force includes one marine division of 18,000 men organized into 9 infantry, one tank, 3 artillery, an assault amphibious, a reconnaissance and an engineer battalion, plus one Marine aircraft wing with about 96 combat aircraft plus helicopter squadrons. To move the IInd Marine Amphibious Force from its present station to the zone of operations would require between thirty-six and seventy-two amphibious ships of which the Navy now has sixty-five. John Collins in his report to Congress on the status of U.S. and Soviet forces (1978) considered that the sea-lift for one Marine amphibious force would require "all but four operational ships scattered from Manila to the Mediterranean." The time for assembling the ships for an operation against Cuba might run to months.[24] How many surface combatant ships could the Navy spare from their principal roles of keeping the North Atlantic routes to Europe open and combating Soviet naval operations against the maritime flanks of NATO? At least one carrier task group—a carrier, one cruiser, three guided missile destroyers, three destroyers and one attack submarine—would be required to give distant cover to an amphibious landing in Cuba, in addition to a protective force of perhaps five frigates and two guided missile destroyers, to convoy the amphibious vessels on their way

22. There are thirteen carriers in the active Fleet today one of which has no air group assigned. Figures on Army units available in CONUS (Continental United States) and Hawaii are in *Manpower Requirements Report for FY 1979* (Washington, D.C.: Office of the Assistant Secretary of Defense, February 1978), pp. V17-V22.

23. See for example, "Cuba Seems Bent on Warming to U.S.: Castro Rules Firmly but some changes appear on Horizon," *The Christian Science Monitor,* 4 January 1979, p. 7; and, "Castro's Cuba: Still Some Shortages but . . .," *ibid.*, 31 January 1979, pp. 12-13.

24. Sea-lift requirements and composition of Marine Amphibious force are in *Manpower Requirements Report for FY 1979,* pp. V-1f. John Collins' report is in "American and Soviet Armed Services Strengths Compared, 1970-1976," *Congressional Record-Senate,* 5 August 1977, pp. S14063 and following. Amphibious ship strength for FY 79 is in *Manpower Requirements Report for FY 1979*, p. V-11.

into the landings. How many of the 22 mine clearance vessels now in the fleet could be spared from other equally pressing operations, to sweep for mines in the constricted waters approaching Cuba?

All of this, of course, is if the Marines were not needed elsewhere for something even more important. If the Soviet Union crosses the line in Germany some Thursday evening, it cannot be expected that those two Soviet motorized rifle divisions and the naval infantry brigade now deployed in the Murmansk region will not attempt to overrun or outflank the single Norwegian brigade group that defends the Norwegian border with the Soviet Union and covers the North Cape.[25] Nor may one expect that Soviet personnel present in Spitsbergen will not assist other Soviet forces to liberate those Norwegian islands.[26] It is between the North Cape and Spitsbergen that the Soviet Northern Fleet with its 120 submarines and 55 major surface combatants will move to enter the North Atlantic. The Marines, in 1978, were deployed into Jutland, Denmark as practice for operations in Northern Europe in Exercise BOLD GUARD 78.[27] Keeping the Skaggerak closed to the Soviet, Polish, and East German fleets is nearly as important as closing the route between the North Cape and Spitsbergen.

Secretary of Defense Harold Brown has said that the United States "would seek to increase" its troop strength in Europe by 150,000 men within two

25. Norwegian and Soviet strengths given in *The Military Balance, 1978-1979*. The Norwegian Army has 20,000 men. The two Soviet Motorized Rifle Divisions contain a total of 26,000 men. That Norwegian Brigade Group on the border with the Soviet Union has about 5,000 men. The Soviets dispose of 532 tanks in their two divisions. The Norwegian Army has a total of 186 tanks.

26. See "Soviets Amassing Missiles in stormy, northern waters," *The Christian Science Monitor*, 14 March 1979, p. 3; on Spitsbergen, see John C. Ausland, "Spitsbergen: Who's in Control," *U.S. Naval Institute Proceedings*, Vol. 104, No. 11 (Whole number 909), November 1978, pp. 63-70; see as well, the following: "Norway Ignores Recent Soviet Border Exercise: Assumes Russians Protesting Earlier Maneuvers by NATO's 'Polar Express'," *Los Angeles Times*, 23 June 1968, p. 15; "Major Global Operating Base: Soviet Builds Military Power Around Far-North Murmansk," *ibid.*, 14 October 1968, p. 1; "Norway Is on Watch At NATO's Frontier," *New York Times*, 4 July 1970, p. 2; "Norway Outflanked: Russia's Northern Fleet New Threat to NATO: A Decade of Expansion," *Los Angeles Times*, 2 May 1971, p. 1, section G; John Jorgen Holsti, "The Soviet Build-Up in the North-East Atlantic," *Survival*, Vol. XIV, No. 1 (January/February 1972), pp. 24-28; "Swedish Magazine Exposes Soviet N. Europe Schemes," Peking, New China News Agency Broadcast in English, July 1974, *FBIS, CHI*, 74-133, 10 July 1974, p. A14; "Die NATO-Nordflanke: Lebenswichtig, aber zunehmend verwundbar," *Wehr und Wirtschaft* (June 1974), p. 300; "Norwegians See Threat to Isles: Moscow's Intentions Over Spitsbergen Quesioned as Oil Talks Approach," *New York Times*, 25 November 1974, p. 9; "Five Soviet Wives Live On, Complicate Spitsbergen Isle, Massed Menace," *To the Point International* (Antwerp), Vol. 2, No. 9, 3 May 1975, p. 10; "Soviet Spy Plane Intrudes into Norwegian Airspace," *New China News Agency*, Peking, in English, 19 February 1975, *FBIS, CHI*, 75-35, 20 February 1975, p. A1; "Kremlin Sees Norse Isle as Vital: Russ Begin Spitsbergen Air Service," *Los Angeles Times*, 10 September 1975, p; "Penetrating Every Nook and Cranny," *Peking Review*, No. 15 (9 April 1976), p. 17; "Norway Wary of USSR Navy Buildup on Its North Flank," *Aviation Week and Space Technology*, Vol. 104, No. 21 (24 May 1976), p. 24; "Huge Russ Fleet Based Near Murmansk: Vessels Would Threaten NATO's Supply Lines," *Los Angeles Times*, 26 November 1976, p. 6, pt. 1-A; "Massive Soviet Base Built During Years of Detente," *Los Angeles Times*, 24 January 1977, p. 1.

27. Operation BOLDGUARD 78 is reported in *United States Military Posture for FY 1980*, Chairman of the Joint Chiefs of Staff, p. 45.

weeks of the start of any war. The equivalent of five divisions would have to be moved within that period, if there were sufficient air-lift to accomplish the movement, which at present there is not.[28]

The remaining Regular Army divisions in the United States, one in Hawaii, two on the West Coast—at Ford Ord, California and Fort Lewis, Washington—could be taken in hand and given amphibious training, something that could be accomplished in six months as soon as sufficient landing craft and other equipment were made available. The Ist Marine Amphibious Force on the West Coast might be available if nothing pressing were transpiring in the Pacific. Both Japan and South Korea rather depend on the commitments the United States has formally undertaken on behalf of their defense. They may be wrong to do so, of course, given the unfortunate outcome of the U.S. commitment to the defense of South Vietnam. But the installation of Soviet military and air facilities in the Southern Kuriles, the proximity of the Soviet Far Eastern Fleet and Air Forces in the Vladivostok region, and the newly-appreciated strength of North Korean forces lend little assurance that neither Japan nor South Korea would escape communist attentions were there to be a Warsaw Pact invasion of Western Europe.[29] If the Soviet Union exploits its wardship over Vietnam to base Soviet fleet units on the Vietnamese coast, at the former U.S. base in Cam Ranh Bay, Japanese maritime routes to Middle Eastern and Indonesian oil would be vulnerable to interruption.[30] U.S. ground, naval and air units deployed now on the West Coast and in Hawaii might well have their work cut out for themselves in the Western Pacific were there to be a war in Europe. That is, of course, if the Soviet Union is not tempted to restore Alaska to the possession of the "new Tsars" in order to prevent North Slope oil from reaching the bunkers of American ships; or, if the Soviets do not seize islands in the Aleutians, as the Japanese did during World War II, in order to mount a naval threat to North Pacific maritime communications. Then there is the security of the Pacific Coast of North America to be considered, where numerous lucrative targets exist for Soviet submarine attack. Since we have been assured of the good

28. "U.S. Has 'Airlift Deficit' for Europe War, General Says," *Los Angeles Times*, 27 March 1979, p. 6.

29. Such concerns are reflected in "Defense of Japan—White Paper on Defense (Summary)—", in *Defense Bulletin*, Vol. 2 (October 1978), Japan Defense Agency, Tokyo; and, in Korea: The U.S. Troop Withdrawal Progam, Report of the Pacific Study Group to the Committee on Armed Services, United States Senate, 96th Congress, 1st Session, 23 January 1979; and, in "Foreign Ministry Heading toward Lodging Strong Protest; Establishment of Military Bases (Soviet) on Northern Islands," *Asahi* (Tokyo), 30 January 1979, p. 1.

30. Reports of a Soviet squadron at Cam Ranh Bay as well as of the construction of a Soviet submarine base at Cienfuegos in Cuba are in the editorial: "The Soviet Push Is Too Pushy," *Los Angeles Times*, 4 April 1979, p. 6, pt. II. But see also, "Evidence of Russ Navy in Vietnam Told," *ibid.*, 14 September 1976, p. 12; and, "The Bear and Cam Ranh Bay," *Beijing Review*, No. 3 (19 January 1979), p. 16.

intentions toward the United States of the Panamanian dictatorship, at least we will not have to worry about U.S. acccess to the Panama Canal in times of acute crisis.

Three Marine regiments and assigned air groups would be deployed into Northern Norway and into Schleswig-Holstein to reinforce Danish, German and Norwegian forces, because present Warsaw Pact forces threatening the two areas now have a two-to-one advantage in manpower.[31] Three marine regiments is in fact the infantry force available to the IInd Marine Amphibious Force now on the east coast of the United States. But then, it does not seem likely that the IInd Marine Amphibious Force would be sufficient to secure Cuba in any case. Of course there are the eleven active army divisions in the United States some of which might be deployed against Cuba. None is trained for amphibious operations nor has any of the necessary equipment. Two of the divisions, the 82nd and 101st, are airborne, perfectly suitable for operations against Cuba, so long as the United States could gain air superiority over the island and so long as reinforcements could be landed across the beaches to deal with Cuban armor, a task for which airborne divisions are ill-equipped. But they, like the IInd Marine Division are slated for a role in reinforcing NATO.

Since Regular Army divisions and brigades are pretty well dedicated to covering contingencies in Europe and Asia, one must consider the use of the National Guard to deal with contingencies arising from Soviet and Cuban operations in the Gulf and Caribbean. None of the National Guard Divisions, of which there are six infantry and two armored, have had amphibious training nor have they the equipment for conducting landings-in-force on hostile shores. They could be trained and equipped for such tasks if they were not needed to reinforce the Regular Army in Europe or the Far East, and if they were not needed for post-attack recovery within the United States. Post-attack recovery would only be needful if there were a direct nuclear attack on the United States.

There are fifty-four Tactical Air Force squadrons in Continental United States, with a total of 1,290 aircraft of which 1,032 are fighter or attack aircraft. They could be employed against Cuba, save for those already designated as reinforcement in Europe. Defense Secretary Brown has said, however, that the number of American combat aircraft in Europe would be increased from 600 to 1,900 within a week "of the start of any war." Such an increase works out to about 54 squadrons, which is about what the Air Force

31. See "Aggregate *U.S. Projection* Force for the Northern Flank," in U.S. Projection Forces: Requirements, Scenarios, and Options, Budget Issue Paper For Fiscal Year 1979, Congressional Budget Office, Congress of the United States, April 1978, pp. 37-38.

has in the Continental United States.[32] Consequently nothing is left save the Air National Guard Squadrons for reinforcement in the Pacific. It also takes to Europe those two F-4 aircraft which each F-4 squadron in the United States had dedicated to the air defense of the United States.

There is always the B-52 strategic bomber fleet with its 316 bombers, a force to be reduced by sixty bombers under provisions of SALT II.[33] The B-52 fleet is one-third of the strategic "triad" for delivery of nuclear weapons, along with the ICBM force and the *Polaris/Trident* force to secure "nuclear deterrence." It is there to make believable the hope that the Soviet Union will believe that a Soviet nuclear first strike on the United States will be followed by a similar strike by the United States on the Soviet Union. The B-52s, according to present aspirations, will be configured to carry the new cruise missile—whenever those vehicles are manufactured and deployed to the strategic bomber squadrons. If the Soviet air defenses deployed in North Vietnam and in Egypt before the 1973 war are a measure of the potential effectiveness of Cuban air defense, also deployed by the Soviet Union, then neither the Tactical Air Force nor the Strategic Bomber Force, were it available, could be expected to eliminate Cuba as a threat in the Gulf. Nuclear weapons might be the solution, but that raises a host of other problems.[34]

For example, the comfortable *intelligentsia* of America, still offended that President Truman ordered nuclear attacks on Nagasaki and Hiroshima, rather than doing the manly thing by invading the Japanese Home Islands at the cost of perhaps 250,000 Allied casualties, entertains the notion that use of nuclear weapons, by our side, at least, is virtually a "war crime."[35] There is the further and very important consideration that using nuclear weapons on Cuba may well lend the Russians an excuse to do the same sort of thing against the United States—if indeed the Russians need such an excuse when they possess a notable, first-strike strategic nuclear capability.

There is no doubt that under the pressures of circumstances something would be done to neutralize Cuba, and the forces would be found somewhere to do it, but it would be costly to both Americans and Cubans.

32. Considering 24 aircraft to a squadron, the figure is given in *The Military Balance, 1978-1979*. Brown statement in "U.S. Has 'Airlift Deficit' for Europe War, General Says," *Los Angeles Times*, 27 March 1979, p. 6. *Number of Squadrons of Tactical Aircraft given Manpower Requirements Report for FY 1979*, p. V-23.

33. "SALT Would Scrap 60 B-52s," *Palo Alto Times*, 1 March 1979, p. 19. There are fifty B-52s used for training and 125 in storage. One can legitimately infer that those in storge have been cannibalized to keep the aircraft in active squadrons operational.

34. The Soviet built and manned air defenses along the Suez Canal, provided the cover for the Egyptian attack across the Canal, prevented an effective Israeli air riposte against the Egyptian attack, and cost the Israeli Air Force a quarter of its strength within the first few days of the 1973 war. Egyptian Air Defense was eliminated when Israeli armor finally crossed the Canal. Details are in *Strategic Survey, 1973* (London: International Institute of Strategic Studies, 1974), pp. 20-27, as well as in *International Defense Review* (Geneva), December 1973.

35. "Truman 'Acquitted' by Students in Hometown War Crimes Trial," *International Herald Tribune* (Paris), 15 March 1979, p. 3.

Cuba's strategic importance to the United States cannot compare to that of Western Europe, although Cuba as an ally of the Warsaw Pact can contribute to the defeat of NATO in Western Europe. Yet a U.S. conquest of Cuba could never compensate for an Allied defeat on the Continent, while Cuba's conquest by the United States would hardly be noticed by the Soviet Union were it to have won Western Europe.

The policy of the United States towards Cuba since the coming to power of Fidel Castro Ruz, proves exemplary of the strategic negligence that has been engendered by disbelief in the possibility of war, by optimistic views of Soviet capabilities and intentions, and by what one writer has called "ignorance as a strategy."[36]

However tiresome, the lesson is obvious. When the so-called strategic balance—that complex equation that measures the relative capability of one side or the other to win a war—is computed, each small increment of strategic advantage accruing to the Soviet side will, if it is not somehow compensated for by the West, add to the assurance of defeat for the Western Democracies. Cuba provides but one increment to be added to the additional five Soviet divisions deployed against NATO under cover of the invasion of Czechoslovakia in 1968. Deferral to the Soviet Union on what constitutes "strategic nuclear parity" in the SALT agreements is another. Loss of those electronic monitoring stations in Iran which erodes the U.S. early warning system is another. Reduction in the number of U.S. fleet aircraft carriers from 26 in 1962 to 13 in 1979 is another. Acceptance of Warsaw Pact superiority in manpower, tactical aircraft, tanks, and artillery opposite NATO's central front is yet another. Warsaw Pact civil defense preparations along with the training and equipment of Warsaw Pact forces to employ and to withstand nuclear, biological, and chemical attack is still another. Increase in Soviet capabilities to move troops by air and to support Soviet and Cuban forces at long distances is still another increment. And there are a hundred more that through ignorance or neglect are neither compensated for nor even considered.

The American government's treatment of Cuba's enlistment in the Soviet host as no more than an incident of nominal significance is hardly different from the treatment accorded to the matter of Germany's "secret" rearmament from 1919 until 1933. German rearmament proceeded with barely a murmur from the British Government until the Nazis came to power, then it was not reflected in Britain's military policy. It was as though Germany's preparations for war had started with Hitler and not fifteen years before. In like manner, the militarization of Cuba has proceeded apace for the past score of years with hardly a murmur from the United States and certainly without any

36. George F. Will, "Fear of Facing the Truth," *Newsweek,* 22 January 1979, p. 88.

reflection of that militarization in U.S. military policy. Indeed, quite to the contrary, the armed forces of the United States are smaller now than they were in November 1961, a year before the Cuban missile crisis. Then there were 967,000 soldiers in the army, but only 774,000 now. There were thirty-five fleet aircraft carriers and numerous lesser ones in the navy then, now there are but thirteen. The U.S. Navy could boast of 611 surface combatants then, but now there are only 172. Strategic Air Command had 1,600 long-range bombers; there are 432 now. Nineteen air defense wings with 1,425 aircraft guarded the skies of the United States against bomber attack, there now are six full-time and ten part-time interceptor squadrons or 331 aircraft to perform the same task. In 1961, the United States possessed hundreds of anti-aircraft missile launchers throughout the country with which to protect American cities from bomber attack. Now there remain but a handful, and those only in southern Florida and in Alaska. In 1969, a Cuban fighter aircraft flew into southern Florida without being detected until it landed at Homestead Air Force Base. In 1971, a Cuban aircraft flew undetected across the Gulf of Mexico to land at New Orleans. Congressional inquiry into how potentially hostile aircraft could enter U.S. air space without detection or interception elicited a reply from the Defense Department to the effect that "a potential attack on the southeastern United States is not a great likelihood."[37]

When Britain turned a blind eye toward German rearmament, there was the excuse, at least, that Germany was trying to keep the matter decently secret, that is, until the Nazis took off the wraps. The American Government has had no such excuse. What has been done in Cuba has been done openly, almost boastfully, as though it were important to the Soviet Government that the people of the United States know what is transpiring. Soviet ships and planes entering and leaving Cuba, Cuban soldiers fighting around the world, appear so commonplace that they are hardly ever mentioned in American newspapers, or on television or over the radio. The refusal of various American administrations to see any threat from Cuba's becoming a Soviet protégé reflects a cast of mind that simply rules out any consideration of the principles of strategy as they apply to the geographic and military situation of the United States. But if such a cast of mind dictates reluctance to see any peril to the United States from a situation that has grown up only 90 miles from the country's shores, how much more reluctant must those be who are constitutionally responsible for America's defense, to see peril in strategic changes occurring in more distant climes and under circumstances far less obvious.

37. "Critical Report: U.S. Air Defense Called Faulty," *San Francisco Chronicle*, 12 June 172, p. 9.

The Turning of NATOs Southern Flank—Yugoslavia

The case of Yugoslavia seems a most apt illustration of the "strategy of ignorance" or of the policy of reluctance to see changes in the strategic equation unfavorable to the Western Democracies. On 28 June 1948, the COMINFORM, a creature of the Communist Party of the Soviet Union, announced the expulsion of the Yugoslav Communist Party. Such action appeared to signal the beginning of Yugoslavia's break with the other Communist powers in Europe. Soviet exclusion of Yugoslavia from the Council for Mutual Economic Assistance (COMECON) in January 1949, occurred because of intense disagreement between the Soviet Union and Communist Yugoslavia. In December 1949, President Truman designated Assistant Secretary of State, George V. Allen, to be Ambassador to Yugoslavia. The *New York Times* reported the new ambassador's statement of U.S. policy toward Yugoslavia on 23 December 1949:

> The President confirmed that the United States is unalterably opposed to aggression wherever it occurs or threatens to occur. Furthermore, the United States supports the principle of the sovereignty of independent nations. As regards Yugoslavia, we are just as opposed to aggression against that country as against any other, and just as favorable to the retention of Yugoslavia's sovereignty. . . .[38]

The United States extended assistance to Yugoslavia under the Yugoslav Emergency Relief Assistance Act of 1950, credits through the U.S. Export Import Bank and financed rations for the Yugoslav Army to the extent of 16 million dollars under the Mutual Defense Assistance Act.[39] Great Britain undertook similar measures of assistance but on a scale smaller than that of the United States. By 1951, Yugoslavia had received over a quarter of a billion dollars in assistance from the United States and Great Britain. In June, the United States granted military assistance to Yugoslavia under a program that led eventually to the equipment of the Yugoslav air force with American fighter aircraft to the number of over 550, and of the Yugoslav Army with American tanks and artillery in large numbers. While neither the United States nor its allies expected that Yugoslavia, having broken with the Kremlin, would become less Communist, it was considered an important shift in the strategic situation and one that favored NATO. The signing of the Balkan Pact by Yugoslavia, Greece, and Turkey in February 1953, and

38. Cited in Richard P. Stebbins, *The United States in World Affairs, 1949*, published for the Council on Foreign Relations (New York: Harper & Brothers, 1950), p. 262. Chronology and events of the Soviet-Yugoslavia break are in successive volumes of *The United States in World Affairs* commencing with John C. Campbell, *ibid., 1948-1949* (New York: Harper & Bros., 1949). One may see also a rather thorough survey in Robert Lee Wolff, *The Balkans in Our Times* (New York: W. W. Norton & Company, 1967).

39. Richard P. Stebbins, *The United States in World Affairs, 1950*, pp. 292-93.

the addition of a military alliance in August 1954, seemed to place Yugoslavia, if not in the ranks of the West, at least definitely out of the ranks of the Soviets.[40]

Strategic benefits accrued almost immediately to the West with Yugoslavia at odds with the Kremlin. Infiltration of communists into Greece was halted, neutral Austria's southern border softened and eventually was lubricated by diplomacy. Best of all, the Soviet path to the Adriatic was blocked, enhancing the security of Italy, Greece, and even Turkey, leaving NATO supreme in the Eastern Mediterranean.

Reaffirming the Strategic Importance of Yugoslavia: Czechoslovakia, 1968

Following the invasion of Czechoslovakia, in August 1968, by Soviet, East German, Polish, and Hungarian forces, it appeared as though the Russians might attempt to extend the Brezhnev Doctrine to include Yugoslavia. "We will be another Vietnam," was the word in Belgrade.[41] The threat to Yugoslavia was considered so serious to the flanks of Western Europe that it "would create an international crisis with grave consequences," and NATO "could not remain indifferent to any development which endangers their security."[42] Dean Rusk, the U.S. Secretary of State, indicated that a Soviet invasion of either Austria or Yugoslavia would be regarded as "a grave act against NATO's defensive well-being."[43]

At the time it certainly appeared that there was genuine concern, both in Western Europe and in Yugoslavia, that the Soviet Union might seek by force to reincorporate Yugoslavia into the Soviet fold. The Yugoslavs themselves deployed troops to the frontier after the invasion of Czechoslovakia and initiated a new national defense plan emphasizing the participation of the general citizenry in resistance to any Soviet invasion. The Yugoslav army could not by itself hope to prevent a Soviet occupation of the country.[44]

The *Frankfurter Rundschau* wrote that NATO would have to "block the Straits of Otranto with the ships of the Sixth Fleet," and, "supply the Yugoslavs fighting in the mountains. . . . Yugoslavia would become a European Vietnam," if the Soviet Union invaded the country. "The occupation of Yugoslavia—unlike the occupation of Czechoslovakia—very definitely alters the military equilibrium of the region."[45]

Such a grave view of a Soviet military presence in Yugoslavia seemed consistent with the evident strategic importance of Yugoslavia—control of

40. Robert Lee Wolff, *op. cit.*, pp. 416-17.

41. "Fear of an Invasion Real in Yugoslavia," *Washington Post*, 16 September 1968, p. 15.

42. "NATO Issues Stern Warning to Soviets," *Washington Post*, 17 November 1968, p. 1.

43. "Rusk Places Yugoslavia in NATO Zone," *Baltimore Sun*, 16 November 1968, p. 1; and, "Rusk Warns Russia: Hands Off Austria and Yugoslavia," *Los Angeles Times*, 17 November 1968, p. 1.

44. "Yugoslavia Adopts New Anti-Invasion Program," *Los Angeles Times*, 27 September 1968, p. 11; see also, "Between East and West: the Yugoslav Army," *Armies and Weapons 35* (Zug, Switzerland) Vol. IV, Year V, 15 May-15 June, 1977, pp. 47-54.

45. The *Franfurter Rundschau* article (translated) appeared as "World War III: It Could Have its Beginnings in Yugoslavia," *Los Angeles Times*, 12 January 1969, p. 3, section G.

the Mediterranean. Certainly, the German invasion of Yugoslavia in 1941 had precipitated a military crisis in the Mediterranean for Britain. The German conquest of Greece and of Crete that followed the German occupation of Yugoslavia permitted bases in the Greek islands and the Balkans, and facilitated the Axis operation in Tripolitania, Cyrenaica, and Egypt. These operations were only brought to an end with the Allied invasion of North Africa, following the British Eighth Army's victory at El Alamein.

Yugoslavia and the Arab-Israeli War, 1973: A Soviet Démarche?

The grave view taken of any Soviet military intervention in Yugoslavia reflected the strategical importance of Yugoslavia to the security of Greece; to the continuance of Allied naval supremacy in the Eastern Mediterranean; and to the defense of NATO's southern flank. Any suggestion that Soviet military forces might actually be in Yugoslavia would, therefore, be expected to arouse consternation as well as intense concern in Washington and amongst the capitals of Western Europe.

In the event, any such expectation turned out to have been ill-founded. It was reported in November 1973 that:

> Soviet military movements involving Yugoslavia include the following:
>
> Transfer of an airborne division from Tula, in central European Russia, to a base near Belgrade, where they are on alert. Staff of the division is in Damascus. . . .
>
> Movement of a major air transport unit of approximately 30 aircraft from Prague to Belgrade. The units include at least one Antonov An-22 heavy logistic transport, but mainly An-12 cargo aircraft. It also includes about six Mil Mi-6 heavy helicopters.
>
> Establishment of a land rink [sic] from Hungary to the Yugoslav port of Rijeka. Heavy military supplies are moved from the port by ship to Alexandria, Egypt and to several Syrian and Algerian ports.
>
> Establishment of direct military cargo flights from a Soviet air base at Turkeve, Hungary, to Titograd, Yugoslavia. . . .
>
> The Soviets have been using the air and sea links, which were expanded in the period leading up to and during the war, for equipment drawdown from forces stationed in Hungary. T-54 tanks have been moving to the Middle East from Hungary via Yugoslavia. . . .
>
> The Rijeka facility under Soviet control, is handling an average of 60,000 tons of material per week. . . .
>
> The unit [airborne] that was moved is the same one that brought the vanguard of Soviet invasion forces to the Czechoslovak capital in August 1968. . . .[46]

46. "Soviet Yugoslav Buildup For Mideast Worries West," *Aviation Week & Space Technology*, 19 November 1973, pp. 13-15.

Surely, here was a page one story to seize the attention of managing editors, television and radio announcers, and distinguished news anchorpersons prepared to analyze the Soviet *démarche*. No. Not at all. If the Russians were back in Yugoslavia it was difficult to find any reference to it outside the pages of the trade journal of the aerospace industry. It was as though the event had never happened. It was as though the story of Soviet forces in Yugoslavia was so patently false that none would even lend it the credibility of a denial. And, indeed, to the casual reader who might have happened on the story in the aerospace magazine, there arose the temptation to dismiss it all as a sensational report without substance. The *New York Times* carried a front page story on the U.S. military alert of October 24, when the Soviet Union had threatened intervention in the Middle East war, if the Israelis did not stop attacking Egyptian forces in the Suez Canal Zone. However, the story mentioned not one word about Yugoslavia, although the most intimate details of Administration considerations, and of Soviet actions, were recounted with assiduousness.[47] While the *Times*' story reported that "the Soviet Air Force had pulled most of its large transports back from Damascus and Cairo to their home bases," it did not explain how the Soviet transports managed the trip home without flying over Greek, Turkish, or Iranian territory. There was certainly no mention of any flights using Yugoslav airfields. A glance at the atlas demonstrates how difficult it is to fly from either Egypt or Syria into Soviet territory without intruding over non-Soviet territory.

Routine practice amongst Communist states, when their airspace is violated dictates either forcing or shooting down the intruding aircraft. Yugoslavia, for example, forced an American C-47, en route to Vienna from Italy to land, and imprisoned the crew and passengers in August 1946; ten days later, on the 19th of August, a second U.S. transport aircraft was shot down by Yugoslav fighters causing the deaths of the crew and passengers. Between 1950 and 1969 twelve U.S. aircraft were shot down, in international airspace of North Korea, by Chinese, North Korean, or Soviet fighters, with the death of 109 Americans.[48]

As recently as 1977, Soviet fighter aircraft shot down a South Korean commercial airliner that had strayed off course into Soviet airspace.[49] There apears to be no instance where a Communist aircraft has been shot down when intruding into non-Communist airspace, except during the Korean and

47. "An Implied Soviet Threat Spurred U.S. Forces 'Alert,'" *New York Times*, 21 November 1973, p. 1.

48. Incidents described in Robert Lee Wolff, *The Balkans in Our Times*, pp. 31-32. And in, "Asian Spy Missions Kill 105 Americans," and "Soviet U.S. on Spy Plane," *Los Angeles Times*, 17 April 1969, p. 1.

49. "Russ Force Airliner Down: South Korea Jet Strays: All Aboard Reported Safe," *Los Angeles Times*, 21 April 1977, p. 1.

Vietnam wars. Two small Austrian aircraft, one in July 1973 and the second in September, were rammed by Czech fighters to force them down when they came close to Czech territory.[50] It would therefore not have seemed out of the ordinary, had Yugoslavia, presumably jealous of its territorial airspace, particularly where the Soviet Union was concerned, taken strong measures had Soviet military transports violated Yugoslav airspace during the 1973 war.

From all appearances then, the Soviet Union freely moved its military aircraft into Syria and Egypt in 1973, without the fuss of any challenge from those countries over which the aircraft needed to fly. While it was nowhere suggested that the thousands of tons of supplies and equipment given Egypt and Syria just prior to and during the course of the 1973 war might have been moved by parcel post, neither was it openly inferred that Soviet logistical lines crossed Yugoslav or NATO territory. If Soviet military cargo and troop transports flew without challenge into the war zone in the Eastern Mediterranean, such was not the case with the United States airlift to Israel. Six months before the Arab-Israeli War started, a U.S. Air Force, C-130 cargo aircraft on its lawful occasions in international airspace, was fired on by two Libyan jets off the coast of Libya. While it was assumed at the time that the firing had been inadvertent, the subsequent mining of Libyan coastal waters by the Libyan Navy, causing the loss of one small Greek vessel and damage to a second, appeared to presage the coming war in the Middle East. After the mining of the two Greek vessels the Libyan government warned shipping against entering certain coastal zones because of the minefields.[51] Whether the firing on the U.S. cargo plane was inadvertent or a warning about any future violation of Libyan airspace by U.S. aircraft, the United States took extreme care to confine its cargo aircraft, in flight to Israel, well within the international air corridor over the Mediterranean. Greek, Turkish, Iranian, and Spanish airfields were closed to U.S. cargo flights to Israel; they originated, instead, from the United States, with the Azores as a way station and with in-air refueling over the Mediterranean for those aircraft having too short a range to reach the Middle East without refueling.[52]

There was no particular reason why any NATO country ought to have lent landing facilities to U.S. transport aircraft supplying the besieged Israelis, since the European members of NATO could not be expected to share concern for Israel's survival in the face of the Arab oil embargo that was damaging Western Europe's economy. But surely the deployment of elements of the

50. "Czechoslovak Hostility Toward Austria Grows," *Los Angeles Times*, 16 December 1973, p. 7, pt. II.

51. "Libya Reportedly Sows Mines in Mediterranean Off Tripoli," *Los Angeles Times*, 8 September 1973, p. 1.

52. "U.S Trains G-5Refuelers," *Christian Science Monitor*, 9 October 1974, p. 5.

Soviet Armed Forces into Yugoslavia before the outbreak of the Middle-East war should have called forth some anxiety or at least comment. The apparent lack of concern therefore lent the impression that it had not happened.

Two years after the 1973 war, a public official in the United States openly acknowledged that Soviet forces had been in Yugoslavia during the Middle East War. Admiral Elmo Zumwalt, who had been Chief of Naval Operations during the 1973 war, explained why the United States had been forced to back-down:

> The United States had to back down in the face of a Soviet ultimatum, partly because Gorshkov [the Soviet Navy's Commander-in-Chief] had U.S. ships outnumbered in the Mediterranean, 98 to 65, and could have attacked U.S. carriers with airplanes flying in from four directions.
>
> Soviet planes had bases in Egypt, Syria, the Crimea *and Yugoslavia*—virtually surrounding the U.S. 6th Fleet in the Mediterranean, while we didn't have a single land base in the area because none of America's allies would allow their land or airspace to be used to help Israel.[53]

From that statement, which received no particular notice at the time it was made, it would appear that Sixth Fleet operational intelligence knew of the Soviet presence in Yugoslavia and that the U.S. decision to force Israel to relent in its destruction of the Eygptian Third Army was based in part on the knowledge of that presence. For, as Admiral Zumwalt said: "As the Israeli troops encircled Egypt's prized 3rd Army and threatened to annihilate it, Soviet leaders sent a 'savage' ultimatum to President Nixon to pull back the Israeli forces or else the Russian troops would rescue the Egyptians."

At this point it is interesting to recall President Tito's statements on the Middle East after a speech given at the National Press Club in Washington, D.C. in October 1971. Tito said that Leonid Brezhnev had told him "all Soviet military personnel would be withdrawn from Egypt and other Arab countries once a Middle East peace settlement was reached." Tito, acting as the pipeline to the American press for Soviet and Egyptian policy, explained that Soviet and Egyptian objectives included the withdrawal of Israeli forces from the Suez Canal to a distance of 36 miles, re-opening of the Suez Canal, the eventual withdrawal of Israel from the Sinai, and its re-occupation by Egypt.[54]

The one thing that would have frustrated Soviet and Egyptian policy was the Israeli crossing of the Suez Canal, that could have led to the destruction of the Egyptian 3rd Army while leaving Israel in possession of the Canal. The Soviet Union had trained and equipped the Egyptian Army so that it could cross the Suez Canal; Soviet personnel manned Egyptian air defenses and

53. "Soviet Navy Plans Better Than U.S., Zumwalt Says," *Washington Post,* 28 July 1975, p. A1.
54. "Tito Reports Soviet Pledge on Mideast," *New York Times,* 30 October 1971, p. 3.

aircraft to prevent the Israeli Air Force from interfering with the crossing; and, the Soviet government through the threat of military intervention against Israel, saved the Egyptian 3rd Army from destruction, thereby securing for Egypt both the Canal and a foothold on the Eastern bank. From that foothold, through the efforts of the American Administration, the Egyptians were able to insist on and win the eventual surrender of the Sinai to Egypt. The crucial factor was the Soviet air capability to prevent U.S. interference in any Soviet deployment against Israel; and that factor was introduced by the use of Yugoslavia as an advanced base for Soviet military power in the Eastern Mediterranean.

A Belgrade-Moscow Rapprochement

It seemed almost as though, unnoticed and certainly unremarked, Yugoslavia had slipped once more into the Soviet orbit. Such a view, in 1968, would have been deemed a major strategic disaster for the West. Now such a disaster seemed actually to have transpired, without comment, in the ensuing five years. Just as the "secret" rearmament of Germany, before Hitler ever came to power, slipped from the memory of the British Government when they came to deal with Hitler, so had the Soviet deployment of forces in Yugoslavia in the 1973 war left no evident mark on the consciousness of the American government. On the contrary, it is the impression of that government that nothing is even now amiss, where Yugoslavia is concerned. Drawing on statements by Secretary of State Cyrus Vance and White House foreign policy aide Zbigniew Brzezinski, the former speaking in Chicago on 1 May 1979 and the latter in New York on 2 May 1979, the *Christian Science Monitor's* Joseph C. Harsch concluded that "Moscow, has never yet, after some 30 years of trying, succeeded in coercing Yugoslavia back under Moscow's discipline."[55]

Yet Mr. Harsch, writing in 1976, after presidential candidate Carter had asserted that the United States would not go to war if the Soviet Union sent troops into Yugoslavia, demonstrated his grasp of Yugoslavia's strategic importance to the West:

> If the Soviets seized Yugoslavia they would then control the Dalmatian Coast with excellent warm water ports for their Mediterranean squadron and ample bases for their air fleets. Their propaganda would be just across the Adriatic from Italy. The southern flank of NATO would be exposed. All of Western Europe would be shaken and endangered. The only worse thing that could happen to Western Europe would be an actual Soviet invasion.[56]

55. Joseph C. Harsch, "Washington Looks Anew at the World," *The Christian Science Monitor,* 10 May 1979, p. 23.

56. Joseph C. Harsch, "The U.S. and Yugoslavia," *The Christian Science Monitor,* 2 November 1976, p. 27.

In December 1973, after the Soviet Union had used Yugoslavia as an advanced base for its operations in the Middle East War, Moscow offered an explanation why Yugoslavia was not, at the time, a member of COMECON or the Warsaw Pact: "Yugoslavia is a non-aligned country and that such a position *per se* excluded its membership in any bloc." The explanation was offered following the meeting at Kiev between Tito and Brezhnev, held 12-15 November 1973. Non-alignment was explained as "a policy line which is becoming even more significant, a fact which now in the Soviet Union is officially and vociferously recognized." Further, it was stated, ". . . strengthening of relations between the Soviet Union and Yugoslavia was not a unilateral process but rather the result of the general striving toward mutual understanding and extensive cooperation, which means it is mutually beneficial." The foundations for cooperation between the two countries included:

Their close historical destinies.

The common bases of their social order.

Their similar approaches to many international issues.[57]

The general striving toward extensive cooperation apparently included Yugoslav adherence to COMECON, because in January 1975, *Tanjug* (Belgrade), reporting the return to Belgrade of the Yugoslav delegation to a COMECON meeting in Moscow, cited Dr. Borislav Jovic, member of the Yugoslav Federal Executive Council, as head of the delegation, and as Yugoslavia's "permanent representative in the COMECON."[58]

Whether Yugoslavia had been "coerced" into adherence to COMECON, or had joined or had become a member spontaneously, is not clear. the U.S.S.R. trade representative to Japan in an interview with *Nikkan Kogyo* listed ten "formal government members" of COMECON: U.S.S.R., Poland, East Germany, Czechoslovakia, Hungary, Bulgaria, Rumania, Vietnam, Cuba and Mongolia. He then included Laos, Angola, Ethiopia and Yugoslavia as "observers."[59]

It is a curious fact that each of the "observer" members of COMECON *including* Yugoslavia, partake of the privilege of having either Soviet or Cuban armed forces on their soil; while all of the "formal" members enjoy the privilege of Soviet military units in their territory. Laos, for example, appears to have received, along with MiG-21 aircraft and Soviet armored equipment,

57. "Zhukov Answers Speculators," *Vjesnik* (Zagreb), 6 December 1973, cited in "Moscow TV on Yugoslavia and Warsaw Pact," Yugoslavia Media Translation, *Radio Free Europe Research,* No. 1943, 11 December 1973.

58. *Tanjug,* in English, 2106 GMT, 24 January 1975, in *Foreign Broadcast Information Service (FBIS), Eastern Europe,* Vol. II, 27 January 1975, p. I.

59. "Interview with USSR Chief Trade Representative to Japan V. B. Spandaryan; 30th Anniversary of Formation of COMECON . . .," *Nikkan Kogyo* (Tokyo), 24 January 1979, p. 4.

Soviet pilots and other military instructors. Laos has as well, some 10,000 regulars from North Vietnam, an "official" member of COMECON. Ethiopia and Angola, both "observer" members have between 17,000 and 20,000 Cuban soldiers each—the Cuban force in Ethiopia is primarily a combat unit; and, presumably both countries have a quota of Soviet military personnel, as well.[60]

Whether or not the distinction drawn between "formal" and "observer" membership in COMECON is an important one, the fact remains that the Soviet Union and Yugoslavia* have organized between themselves, the Soviet-Yugoslav Intergovernmental Committee on Economic, Scientific, and Technical Cooperation, the sixteenth session of which was held in November 1978.[61]

Commerce and Arms

It can be argued that such a trade as that carried on between Yugoslavia on the one hand, and the Soviet Union and the other official members of the COMECON on the other, need have no political or strategic implications for the West. After all Western Democracies trade with the eastern countries and with China, and none of those countries have become democracies yet nor are likely to do so as a consequence of trade with the West. But one knows that Germany, when that country was a socialist dictatorship, used trade as a device through which to tie lesser countries into the Nazi orbit. Indeed, Nazi plans for the unification of Europe were to be implemented through the purchase, by corporations within the Reich, of controlling interests in those enterprises within occupied countries which would fit into Hitler's scheme for the eventual integration of occupied Europe into the economy of the Greater Third Reich.[62]

An article written by the assistant director of the U.S.S.R. Academy of Sciences' Institute of Economics of the International Socialist System, describes the requirements for eventual unification of the economies of the various

* See Appendix A, "Soviet-Yugoslav Trade," pp. 286-87

60. See "Soviets Sends Laotian Reds Ten MiGs," *San Francisco Chronicle,* 8 October 1977, p. 10; "News in Brief," reports the Cubans in Angola and Ethiopia, *Los Angeles Times,* 16 May 1979, p. 2; see also for both, Laos and Ethiopia, *The Military Balance, 1978-1979.* And, see "Tugs at Laos: Communist Vie for Influence," *The Christian Science Monitor,* 12 December 1978, p. 7.

61. "Work Completed," *Pravda,* 28 November 1978, p. 4, in *The Current Digest of the Soviet Press,* Vol. XXX, No. 48, p. 23.

62. See for example: "A stronger sense of economic community among European nations must be aroused. . . . The economic consolidation of European countries should improve their bargaining position in dealing with other economic groups. . . . This united Europe will not submit to political and economic terms dictated to it by any extra-European body." From a speech by Walther Funk, Reichsminister of Economics, on the Economic New Order in Europe, 25 July 1940 (*Sudost Echo,* 26 July 1940); and, see: "It appears useful to take care that the title of economic enterprises which are located within one of the occupied countries will only be sold to German interests and in no case to citizens of another occupied country or of a third foreign power. . .," from "Memorandum by Goering on the Increased Participation by Germany in European Industry, 2 April 1940," both cited in *Documents on International Affairs, 1939-1940,* Volume II of *Hitler's Europe* (London: Oxford University Press, 1954), pp. 29-37.

COMECON countries. Thus: "The planned unification of national economies is leading to the gradual formation of a new economic community—an international complex that is the economic basis of the integrated commonwealth of socialist states." The writer suggested as one useful mechanism for furthering integration, the formation of "transnational" complexes: "these complexes consist of research and production association that has a network of branch plants in other countries. In cases of this kind, production and technical ties within the framework of the complex cease to be purely external and become a special form of internal ties." This is explained further:

> In principle, international research-and-production complexes can be based on international [shared] ownership, several ownership by the participating countries, national ownership by one country or a combination of forms of ownership.[63]

The assumption underlying this view seems to be the following:

> Socialist economic integration is the concrete path for the realization of the objective law of development of world socialism, of the historic tendency toward the creation of a new international division of labor, as a new world market, the new really unified world economy about which Lenin wrote.[64]

Given the apparent purpose of the Council for Mutual Economic Assistance headed by the Soviet Union and of which Yugoslavia is an "observer" member, it is not difficult to suppose that extensive trade between Yugoslavia and the Soviet Union is a function of more than just the simple joy that Soviet citizens take in Yugoslavian craftsmanship and manufacturing skill.

COMECON is presently financing the construction of a 4,000 megawatt nuclear reactor and planning the construction of a second similar reactor, both at Khmelnitsky in the Ukraine. They are to supply electricity to the new 750 kilovolt power grid also financed by COMECON. The extra-high voltage grid now extends from the Ukraine into Hungary and will eventually serve Yugoslavia as well.[65] Inclusion of Yugoslavia in such a project makes it seem as though Soviet-Yugoslav relations are expected to be more than casual over the coming years.

63. Yu Shiryayev, "Socialist Integration as a Process of Planned Unification of the National Economic Complexes of C.M.S.A. Countries," *Planovoye khozyaistvo,* No. 4 (April 1974), pp. 31-36; "Model Statutes on Conditions for the Establishment and Operation of Economic Organizations in O.M.B.A. Member-Countries," *C.M.E.A. Bulletin of Economic Information, 1973,* No. 4 (1973), p. 4, in *The Current Digest of the Soviet Press,* Vol. XXVI, No. 34, 18 September 1974, pp. 13-14.

64. Quotation is cited from "Class and National Consciousness," a pamphlet prepared for Soviet popular consumption, according to "Soviets Seek To further Long Time Dream of Unified Worldwide Socialist Economy," in *Soviet World Outlook,* Center for Advanced International Studies, University of Miami, Vol. 1, No. 9, 15 September 1976, pp. 10-12.

65. "Russia Turns to Nuclear Power as Oil Strains Show," *The Economist* (London), Vol. 271, No. 7082, 26 May 1979, pp. 105-8.

Trade need not impinge on politics or strategy unless it is intended that it should. But it seems possible to demonstrate that there is more than trade, high voltage electricity and natural gas in the relationship between Belgrade and Moscow. It will be recalled that the United States began to supply arms to Yugoslavia after the contretemps between the Soviet and Yugoslavian Communist Parties. That supply of arms was pretty well completed by 1961. Yet Yugoslavia is not the least well-armed power in the Balkans. It is the details that go to make up that fact which suggest that the relationship between Yugoslavia and the Soviet Union is more than the tie of sentiment between the motherhood of communism and the only "volunteer" communist state in the Balkans.

The number and variety of Soviet weapons and equipment and military material from other members of the Warsaw Pact, along with such hardware as the Yugoslavs themselves manufacture, make the Yugoslav armed forces one of the best armed in the area. That Yugoslavia should be well-armed if the principal threat to Yugoslav independence is the Soviet Union is of course not notable. But that Yugoslavia should be well-armed chiefly with Warsaw Pact weapons is indeed an anomaly. The types of weapons that have been furnished the Yugoslav armed forces by the Soviet Union are not such as to suggest that they are leftover from those days before Tito and Stalin had their disagreement. On the contrary many of the weapons or equipment are quite as modern as those deployed by the Soviet Union or the other members of the Warsaw Pact.

In a military parade in Belgrade in 1976, there appeared the heavy, mechanized portable bridge, the Soviet designation of which is TMM, borne on a truck manufactured in Yugoslavia. The bridge is standard issue in the Czech Army where it is carried on the TATRA 813 prime mover; in the East German Army where it is carried on the Soviet prime mover KRAZ-255B; and, in the Soviet Army where it is also carried on the KRAZ-255B.[66]

One could see also the Soviet folding, pontoon bridge (PMP) carried on a Yugoslav truck; the Soviet 130 mm. cannon, the Soviet air defense rocket, SA-3(GOA) on a Soviet ZIL truck, the Soviet ground-to-ground artillery rocket, FROG-7, and the Soviet long-range air defense missile, SA-6 (GAINFUL), on a tracked vehicle derived from the Soviet PT-76 amphibious tank. Elsewhere one may see photographs of Yugoslav artillery units armed with the 122 mm. M 63 (D-30) howitzer, the 152 mm. D-20 how-

66. See, "UdSSR Ubersetzmittel, TMM," in *Erkennungsbalatter,* Folge 211, in *Soldat und Technik* (September 1976); "Pioniere und Militartransportwesen der NVA," *Soldat und Technik* (November 1978), p. 596; and, "Ausrustung der Jugoslawischen Streitkrafte: Soveietsierrung der Waffenausrusteng und Lesitungen der einheimischen Rustungsindustrie" ("Equipment of the Yugoslav Armed Forces: Sovietisation of Equipment and Capability of the Domestic Arms industry") *Soldat und Technik* (February 1974), pp. 78-82.

itzer and the 100 mm. anti-tank gun, Model T-12A (the most modern version of that weapon). In addition, there are photographs of Yugoslav soldiers firing the hand-held STRELA air defense missile, and using the Soviet anti-tank guided missile, the SAGGER.[67] The hand-held Soviet anti-aircraft missile, SA-7 (GRAIL), as issued to Warsaw pact troops, to the Cuban Army and to pro-Soviet forces in Angola, is also an item of Yugoslav equipment.[68]

The Yugoslav navy, besides the vessels constructed in Yugoslav yards, is equipped with the *Osa*-class guided missile patrol boat, contributed by the Soviet Union, and the *Shershen*-class, fast torpedo boat, some of which came from the Soviet Union but most of which were produced in Yugoslav yards.[69]

The Yugoslav navy's hydrographic and oceanographic vessel, *Andreas Mohorovic* was built in the Polish yards at Giansk in 1971, and is a duplicate of the Soviet *Moma*-class of which the Soviet Fleet operates about thirty.[70]

While Yugoslavian yards constructed five submarines from 1957 through 1969, demonstrating the capability for design and construction of such vessels, as well as other types of warships, only within the last four to five years, have Yugoslav yards begun once again to produce vessels that are not strictly to Soviet design. The first of the Type 211 guided-missile patrol boats was floated in October 1976. Propelled by Rolls-Royce gas turbines and West German diesels, with Swedish anti-aircraft guns, it was however armed with the Soviet SS-N-11, surface-to-surface missiles, which replaced the SS-N-2 missiles on the later version of the *Osa*-class of Soviet guided missile patrol boats. That the Yugoslav boats would not use Rolls-Royce gas turbines does not represent a departure from Soviet usage since the Soviet Union has acquired Rolls-Royce gas turbines with which to equip gas pipeline pumping stations.[71]

Insofar as the Yugoslav navy would essay an eclectic design like that of the new patrol boats need not imply the independence of that navy from

67. These may be seen in successive issues of *Soldat und Technik*, for the years 1974 to 1979, as well as in "Between East and West: The Yugoslav Army," *Armies and Weapons*, Year V, Vol. IV, 15 May-15 June 1977, pp. 47-54. But see as well, "Jugoslawien: Nues Sowjetisches Wehrmatered," *Wehrtechnik* (May 1976), p. 48.

68. "Die Fliegerfaust, SA-7 (GRALL)," *Soldat und Technik* (November 1976), p. 605.

69. Jean Labayle Couhat (ed.), *Combat Fleets of the World 1976/77: Their Ships, Aircraft and Armament*. The edition in English of *Flottes de Combat* (Annapolis, Md.: U.S. Naval Institute, 1976), pp. 554. One may see a photograph of a *Shershen*-class in Yugoslav hands in "Mit sowjetischer Hilfe [With Soviet Help]," *Soldat und Technik* (May 1976), p. 206, while a list of states to which the Soviet Union has transfered *Osa*-class, guided missile patrol boats, including Yugoslavia, is given in "Die FK-Schnellobottee Ser sowjetischen 'Osa'-Klasse," *ibid.* (November 1976), p. 604.

70. *Combat Fleets of the World 1976/77*, pp. 441 and 556.

71. Description of the Type 211 patrol boat is given in "Hauprogram for Jugoslawiens Kriegsmarine: Hemuhung un mehr Unabhangigkeit von der Sowjets," *Soldat und Technik* (October 1976), p. 567. Further details are in "Jugoslacien mit neuen FK-Schnell hpoten: Rine Synthese ostilicher und ewropaischer Technologie," *ibid.* (March 1978), p. 154.

Soviet influence. It has been a practice of the Soviet Union to encourage the development of naval building capabilities on the part of Poland and East Germany so that the fleets of both countries contain ships that are constructed within their own yards as well as those that have been constructed in Soviet yards. Thus sister-ships of the Polish-built *Polnocny*-class and of the Soviet *Ropucha*-class have been built in Polish yards for both the Soviet Union and Poland. Poland and East Germany have each developed its own design of fast patrol boats while each also has Soviet-built ships on their naval lists. It is usual, however, just as in the Yugoslav case, that the main battery weapons with fire control, target acquisition, and early warning systems are of Soviet design and origin.[72]

Soviet practice seems to permit development of small arms and armored fighting vehicles and support-vehicles within the armies of the Warsaw Pact, although major weapons such as tanks and artillery pieces remain of Soviet design even when produced by those Warsaw Pact members capable of such production.

The Yugoslav Air Force, for its part, deploys a few of the F-84G fighters sent by the United States at the time of the break with the COMINFORM, a number of Soviet MiG-21 fighters, and some jet aircraft built to Yugoslav design in Yugoslavia, the Soko G2-A, *Galeb* and the Soko J-1, *Jastreb.* Yugoslav helicopters include three different Soviet types and the Westland Gazelle, built under license in Yugoslavia. Transport aircraft include old U.S. aircraft (C-47), a French *Caravelle,* one Boeing 727, and six different types of Soviet transport aircraft. Together with Romania, a member of the Warsaw Pact and COMECON, Yugoslavia has developed a multi-role-combat aircraft, the *Orao.*[73]

It is possible to dismiss the transfer to Yugoslavia of Soviet arms, military equipment, warships, and combat aircraft, as a kind of commercial neighborliness, and of a piece with industrial items furnished the Soviet Union by Yugoslavia, and therefore without political or strategic significance to the West. The Soviet view of trade in arms, does not dismiss such matters so lightly. A TASS report printed in *Pravda* takes exception to the idea that arms shipments are "a natural element of balanced political, trade, scientific, and cultural relations." TASS said:

72. See Siegfried Breyer, "Aufwertung der DDR-Marine im Warschaupakt: Sowjetische Fregatte der 'Koni'-Klasse ubergeben," *Soldat und Technik* (March 1979), pp. 138-41; "'Tomba'-Klasse, neuer sowjetischer Hilfssiffetyp: Polen starker fur sowjetischen Kriegsschiffbau eingesetz," *ibid.* (September 1977), p. 489; and, Polish, East German and Soviet sections in *Combat Fleets of the World 1976/77.*

73. *The Military Balance, 1978-1979* gives the inventory of Yugoslavia's Air Force; *Jane's All The World's Aircraft, 1977-1978* (New York: Franklin Watts, 1977), pp. 475-76, gives the characteristics of the *Galeb* and *Jastreb* in their various versions; and see, "Defense Secretary Views, New Yugoslav-Romanian Plane," Belgrade TANJUG Domestic Service in Serbo-Croation, 1035 GMT 15 April 75, *FBIS,* Vol. II, *Eastern Europe,* 16 April 1975, pp. 14-15.

> One can hardly view arms shipments in the context of ordinary trade. It is quite obvious that this is a political question. Arms deliveries, L. I. Brezhnev stressed, cannot be considered without taking into account the purposes for which such arms are being acquired.[74]

In January 1975, Belgrade Radio reported in Russian a story from the Austrian newspaper *Kurier* that included the following allegations:

> construction of a large airfield near Zabljak in Montenegro for the use of Soviet Antonov military transports;
>
> underground shipyards and docks had been built with Soviet aid near Split and Hercegnovi;
>
> a Soviet coastal battery had been set up in Rognoznica;
>
> a high Soviet military leader secretly visited Yugoslavia inspecting Yugoslav units near the Italian border;
>
> and, a unit of Soviet paratroopers was in training near Belgrade.

The allegations were dismissed by Belgrade Radio as directed "against the central issue of Yugoslavia's independence and nonalignment, independence in the military sphere," and asked: "Are these fabrications of *Kurier* not a method of casting doubt on the correctness of the principle of independence in general and the principle of nonalignment with blocs?" Whether the radio commentator was in fact Russian was not made clear.[75]

The Yugoslav government sent a note to Austria, on this occasion, charging Austria with a violation of the Austrian state treaty in permitting the "organized dissemination of various fabricated stories about Yugoslavia."

Yet the *International Defense Review* (Geneva) reported in 1976 that MiG fighter aircraft had used the airfield at Kragujevac, Yugoslavia to refuel on their way to Egypt in the 1967 Middle East war and that Soviet aircraft had used Yugoslav airfields in the 1973 war as well. The article reported further that Soviet military personnel were stationed at airfields at Sarajewo, Mostar, and Batanjnica near Belgrade; and, that the Soviet-built field at Petrovac near Skopje was equipped with "protective emplacements"; and the "recently built airfield of Zabljak can accommodate large Antonov transport aircraft." Other Soviet projects in Yugoslavia include a coastal battery at Rognoznica and a command centre at Valjevo in Serbia.[76]

In this light it is interesting to note the sharp denial made by the Zagreb newspaper, *Vjesnik* to a Reuter's story about NATO airplanes flying over Bulgaria and Yugoslavia:

74. "TASS REPORT," *Pravda,* 25 January 1979, p. 1, in *The Current Digest of the Soviet Press,* Vol. XXXI, No. 4, 21 February 1979, p. 18.

75. "Dozet Military Commentary Criticizes Austrian Press," Belgrade International Service in Russian 1430 GMT 26 Jan. 75, in *FBIS,* Vol. II, *Eastern Europe,* 27 January 1975, pp. I 2 and I 3.

76. Arel Horhager, "Yugoslavia's Defense: The Logic of Politics," *International Defense Review* (Geneva), Vol. 5 (October 1976), pp. 733-38.

> no passenger plane, even less a military plane is allowed to fly over Yugoslavia without its permission. . . . As is well-known Yugoslavia has not given such permission to the Atlantic Alliance [just as, by the way, it has not given it to the Warsaw Pact] . . . stories of phantom fleets in the Adriatic and of planes over Yugoslavia will very likely be followed by a third and fourth story. . . . Somebody obviously continues to wage a special war against Yugoslavia. . . .[77]

But, at the same time, the *Los Angeles Times,* observed in an editorial, that the Yugoslav press had unleashed "virulent attacks on the United States, and Tito has taken to ridiculing, for the record, the existence of any danger from the Soviet Union." "Recently," the *Times* said, "a Russian submarine and sub tender reportedly put into a Yugoslav port for 'repairs' raising concern in Western circles that the Soviet navy may be on the way to gaining a strategically important base there." The *Times* expressed disappointment over the matter:

> For years Yugoslavia has been a beacon of hope for those who, despite the Soviet invasion of Czechoslovakia, have remained faithful to the belief that communism can be made compatible with individual dignity and freedom. It is depressing to see Yugoslavia opting out of the experiment.[78]

When Laurence Silberman, former U.S. Ambassador to Yugoslavia, suggested in 1977 that "Yugoslavia had consistently sided with America's enemies in the world," and, "that Washington should re-examine its relations according to the United States' true interests," the Yugoslav government was outraged and the State Department "disassociated itself" from Mr. Silberman's views.[79]

Buried in the midst of a Congressional Research Service report was the news that in 1977, the Soviet Union continued to supply Egypt with weapons, ammunition, and spare parts. The source of information was said to be Israeli intelligence. The routes used for supply led through Czechoslovakia, Yugoslavia, and North Korea. It was said that American analysts agreed on the existence of the routes but disagreed with Israeli intelligence on their importance.[80]

77. "Vjesnik Scores Report on NATO Flights Over SRRY," *Vjesnik* (Zagreb) in Serbo-Croatian, 21 March 1975, p. 5, in *FBIS,* Vol. II, *Eastern Europe,* 27 March 1975, p. I 1.

78. "Tito Tightens the Screws," *Los Angeles Times,* 24 March 1975, p. 6, pt. X.

79. See "Yugoslavia," in *Report on World Affairs,* 1 January to 31 March 1977 (London: RWA), pp. 70-71; see also "President Tito Harshly Denounces U.S. Ambassador on Having Initiated 'Campaign' Against Yugoslavia," *New York Times,* 1 August 1976, p. 1; and Laurence Silberman did a series of articles for the *New York Times,* January to March 1977.

80. *The Soviet Union and the Third World: A Watershed in Great Power Policy?* Report to the Committee on International Relations, House of Representatives by the Senior Specialists Divisions, Congressional Research Service, Library of Congress, 8 May 1977, 95th Congress, 1st Session, p. 135; report cites, Drew Middleton, "Soviet Arms to Cairo Reported Continuing," *New York Times,* 2 February 1977, p. A6.

The fact that Yugoslavia, along with Czechoslovakia and North Korea, should be acting as freight-handlers for Soviet arms to the Middle East seemed to warrant no comment, as though everyone had known that since their cradle. No question was raised about the status of Yugoslavia as a "non-aligned" power punctilious in its avoidance of bias toward either of the "super-powers"; and, certainly never willing to help lubricate the track of Soviet policy in the Middle East.

But then, even that most eminent of journals, *Strategic Survey* of London, could find no occasion to comment on the item dated 27 October 1978, in its own "Chronology" of events in Europe: "Yugoslavia reported servicing Soviet submarines; first instance of non-Warsaw Pact country overhauling Soviet warships."[81]

Aside from the fact that a Soviet submarine and a submarine tender were repaired at the Yugoslavian port of Kotor after the passage of the Yugoslav law permitting foreign warship repairs in Yugoslavian ports in April 1974, and the subsequent repair of other Soviet warships in Yugoslav ports, *Strategic Survey,* belying its title, did not see fit to comment on what to ordinary minds might seem a matter of some strategic significance.[82]

So perhaps one could hardly criticize the State Department for being ignorant of the comings and goings of Soviet submarines from Yugoslav ports. Thus, William H. Luers, Deputy Assistant Secretary of State for European Affairs in a report to the House International Relations Committee on 7 September 1978, omitted any discussion of Yugoslavia. His report entitled "Eastern Europe: An Overview," stated:

> This discussion does not cover Yugoslavia or Albania. Both are Communist, but neither is a member of the Warsaw Pact. Yugoslavia is non-aligned, and our relations with it are qualitatively very different from those of [sic] the Warsaw Pact member states.[83]

The Under Secretary did say, however, that: "We deal with each country as a sovereign nation while taking into account the political and geographical realities of the area." So presumably, Soviet naval forces based on the Adriatic ports of Yugoslavia enter into neither the political nor geographical realities of the area.

The manner in which Yugoslavia has been brought to be either tool or consort in the development of Soviet policy in the Mediterranean can only be

81. *Strategic Survey, 1978* (London: The International Institute for Strategic Studies, 1979), p. 27.

82. Axel Horhager, *op. cit., International Defense Review,* Vol. 9, No. 5 (October 1976); and, "Tito Tightens the Screws," *Los Angeles Times,* 24 March 1975, p. 6, Pt. X. *The Christian Science Monitor,* for example, reported in 23 November 1976, that "for the past two years only Soviet units, usually diesel submarines and submarine tenders have used them [the Yugoslav ports]." See "Soviet-Yugoslav port deal casts shadow over Albania," 23 November 1976, p. 3.

83. *Eastern Europe: An Overview,* Department of State Publication 8953, European and British Commonwealth Series 82, October 1978.

surmised. *The Economist* proposed as one possibility, in 1974, that the Soviet Union had threatened Tito with a *coup d'état,* perhaps to gain access for the Soviet fleet to Yugoslav ports on the Adriatic or to get Yugoslavia to attend the international communist conference then being organized.[84] Certainly such a threat could have been lent credibility by student uprisings in Zagreb in 1971, the apparently open involvement of Soviet, Czech, and Hungarian diplomats in the activities of pro-Soviet elements amongst Communist Parties in Croatia, the Voivodina, Montenegro and the Kosavo region, and an *Ustashi* raid carried out from Austrian territory.[85]

Whatever the manner in which Soviet-Yugoslav cooperation was brought about, it seems more than mere chance that Premier Alexei Kosygin should have spent a week in Yugoslavia on a visit that ended only six days before the outbreak of the 1973 Middle East war. Kosygin's tour of the country and conferences with Tito and the Chairman of the Yugoslav Federal Council must have coincided with the conclusion of arrangements for the employment of those Soviet forces in Yugoslavia who would support the Syrian-Egyptian attack on Israel. The evidence suggests that while Israel and the United States were caught by surprise when the Eygptians launched their attack across the Suez Canal, the Soviet Union was not. A notable increase in Soviet ships and aircraft moving supplies to Egypt and Syria began up to ten days before the outbreak of war on the 6th of October. Weeks before, Soviet transports had moved a Moroccan contingent from Algerian ports to Syria in anticipation of the outbreak of war. On the 2nd of October, the Soviets launched a set of spy satellites into orbit over the Middle East, four days before the Egyptians stormed across the Suez Canal.[86]

The communique issued by the two countries on the conclusion of Kosygin's visit spoke of many things; amongst which:

84. "Yugoslavia and Russia: Another 1948," *The Economist* (London), 21 September 1974, p. 38.

85. "Croatian Charges Nationalists Hoped for Foreign Intervention," *New York Times,* 18 December 1971, p. 6; "Clash with Croatians Reported Gravely Damaging Yugoslavia," *ibid.*, 20 December 1971, p. 8; and, "New Croatian Hostel Raid—352 Held," *San Francisco Chronicle,* 22 December 1971, p. 10. All of these deal with the student uprising in Zagreb. See then, "Yugoslavs Said to Quash Pro-Moscow Movement," *The Washington Post,* 10 September 1974, p. A 17; "Soviet Aid Alleged for Anti-Tito Group," *ibid.*, 19 September 1974, p. A 25; "High Soviet Diplomat Linked to Anti-Tito Group," 25 September 1974, p. A 14; and "A Pro-Soviet Plot in Yugoslavia," *The World Today* (London), Vol. 30, No. 11, November 1974, pp. 45-48. The *Ustashi* involvement—the *Ustashi* is a Croatian terrorist movement, pro-Nazi during the war, but now presumed to be run by the KGB—is noted in "Croatian Exiles Blamed for Yugoslav Jet Crash," *Los Angeles Times,* 28 January 1972, p. 19; "Can Tito Avoid Defeat?" *To The Point* (Johannesburg) Vol. 1, No. 2, 29 January 1972, pp. 11-14; the Ustashi raid from Austria in part in "Aided Rebels, Five Yugoslavs found guilty of aiding two guerilla infiltrators . . .," *The South China Morning Post* (Hong Kong), 12 March 1975, p. 5; and "*Kommunist* Scores Vienna Trial of Ustasha Terrorists," Belgrade TANJUG in English 0933 GMT 28 April 75, in *FBIS,* Vol. II *Eastern Europe,* 29 April 1975, p. I 1 ; and, "Discovery of Ustasha Training Ground Near Salzburg," Belgrade TANJUG in English 1610 GMT 3 July 73, in *FBIS,* Vol. VI, *Western Europe,* 5 July 1973, p. R 1.

86. "Kosygin ends week-long visit in Belgrade, Yugoslav-Soviet talks hint detente likely," *The Christian Science Monitor,* 2 October 1973, p. 2; "Links seen to Soviet Arms, Arab Attack," *Los Angeles Times,* 6 November 1973, p. 5; "Russ Shipping to Arab Nations Seen Easing: Sources in Istanbul Say Air Transport Flights Over Turkey Also Have Decreased," *ibid.;* reference to Moroccan Contigent is in *The Report on World Affairs,* July to December 1973, Vol. 54, Nos. 3 and 4, p. 30, as well as elsewhere.

> the resolute support [by the two powers] for the peoples of Indochina in their struggle for complete independence and the right freely and without impediment to decide their own destiny . . . ;
>
> comprehensive support to the Provisional Revolutionary Government of the Republic of South Vietnam [the Viet Cong];
>
> complete support for the liberation struggle of the peoples of Cambodia;
>
> The liberation of all Arab territories seized by Israel in 1967.
>
> The heads of government believe that all conditions and prerequisites exist for the comprehensive expansion of Soviet-Yugoslav cooperation.[87]

Whether through pervasive optimism or selective ignorance, the Department of State permits itself the view that Yugoslavia is "unaligned." Yugoslav-Soviet cooperation provides advanced bases for Soviet operations in the Mediterranean and Africa. Inevitably U.S. military policy reflects the nonalignment and not the cooperation. It is hardly likely that the many-sided cooperation between the Soviet Union and Yugoslavia escaped the notice of allied intelligence if a casual observer could find out about it from the open press. If an Austrian newspaper could report the presence of Soviet paratroopers in Yugoslavia and the passage of Soviet military aircraft through the country, it is difficult to imagine that things of that nature would have remained unnoticed by the defense attachés of the powers whose strategic interests are at stake. Neither the Soviet nor Yugoslav government has troubled to conceal these things. Even *Gramma,* the official organ of the Central Committee of the Communist Party of Cuba, could take notice of the relationship between the Soviet Union and Yugoslavia. On the occasion of the visit to Cuba of the federal secretary of defense of the Socialist Federative Republic of Yugoslavia, the Havana newspaper also reported on those who had attended "Shield 76," the Warsaw pact maneuvers held in Poland; they included the Cuban minister of defense, as well as delegations from East Germany, Hungary, the Soviet Union, Romania, Czechoslovakia, Bulgaria, Mongolia, Vietnam, and Yugoslavia.[88]

The use by the Soviet fleet of Yugoslav ports for repair and servicing, while not at all secret, since even the Yugoslav radio reported "visits" of Soviet naval vessels, seemingly aroused no more concern for the security of the southern flank of NATO than does the use of Cuban ports by the Soviet Fleet arouse concern about the security of the American gulf coast.[89]

87. "Kosygin's Visit to Yugoslavia: In the Interests of Cooperation," *Pravda,* 26 September 1973, p. 3; and, "Joint Soviet-Yugoslav Communique," *Pravda,* 3 October 1973, pp. 11-12, 31.

88. "Division Commander Raul Castro is Guest at Shield 76 Maneuvers by Warsaw Treaty Troops," and, "Army General Nikola Ljubicic Leaves Cuba After Friendly Visit," *Gramma* (Havana), 19 September 1976, p. 1.

89. "Soviet Navy Detachment Arrives in Split," Zagreb Domestic Service in Serbo-Croatian 8829 GMT 3 Oct 74 *FBIS,* Vol. II, *Eastern Europe,* 3 October 1974, p. I 14; "Soviet Warships Begin Visit to

Yet the Soviet Union has been to considerable pains and expense in its relations with Tito's government. Save for the risk of arousing Western anxieties, which may have seemed great in the beginning but in retrospect could be seen as no risk at all, the Yugoslav project can hardly have been less expensive than the development of Cuba as a Soviet base. Soviet purposes in the matter present therefore an intriguing question.

If the Soviet Union had simply smashed Tito's government, everyone of any note would have understood instantly that it was simply another Czechoslovakia: a matter of bruised Soviet pride, fear that the Socialist Commonwealth would go downhill if Tito were not eventually disciplined, or some other reason having nothing to do with the fate of the Western Allies. But the Yugoslav affair has been handled with a Florentine skill: judicious development of economic and commercial relationships that profit Yugoslavia surely as much as they do the Soviet Union; careful attention to the equipment of the Yugoslav armed forces; some rather nice demonstrations of the Soviet capability to cause Tito trouble, through the *Ustashi* raid and by exploitation of the "cominformists"; Bulgarian reminders of disputed claims to Yugoslav Macedonia; and, withal, a seeming liberality in respect to Tito and his government that leaves them free as the air, to outward appearances at least. Of course it may all have been inadvertent or anomalous policies much like those, one is encouraged to believe, that ended with Soviet missiles in Cuba. After all, what do the Soviets know of Borgian craft or Byzantine subtlety. It would be frightening indeed if the facts were to suggest that the Soviet Union actually set out to achieve naval and air supremacy in the Central Mediterranean and that Soviet policy toward Yugoslavia was dictated with that purpose in mind. It might lead one to ask why in this age of universal peace, East-West *détente,* and "essential equivalence," the Soviet Union would require to be supreme anywhere outside their own territory and outside that of the nations over whom they claim the right to rule.

Izvestia, the Soviet government's newspaper, answered the question over a decade ago, at least in respect to the Mediterranean. Urging that the United States withdraw from the Mediterranean entirely, because the Mediterranean should be turned "into a sea of peace":

Split," Belgrade TANJUG Domestic Service in Serbo-Croatian 0924 GMT 12 May 75, *ibid.,* 12 May 1975, p. I 9; "Soviet Warships Arrive in Cruz Harbor for Visit," Belgrade TANJUG Domestic Service in Serbo-Croatian 0233 GMT 30 Oct 75, *ibid.,* 3 November 1975, p. I 8; then see report of Soviet naval units at Tivat in the Bay of Kotor in "Soviet-Yugoslav port deal casts shadow over Albania," *The Christian Science Monitor,* 23 November 1976, p. 4; and, in "Chronologies: Europe" report of servicing Soviet submarines, 27 October 1978, in *Strategic Survey 1978*, p. 129.

> The Soviet Union is a Black Sea power and as such a Mediterranean power too. . . . The Soviet Fleet is a factor which contributes toward consolidation of security of the whole Mediterranean area.[90]

Vice Admiral N. I. Smirnov, who, by 1974, was First Deputy Commander-in-Chief of the Soviet Navy, wrote in 1968, that:

> The Soviet Fleet, unlike that of the NATO countries, is not a demonstration of military power. . . . Our ships are envoys of peace and friendship, and are always well received at the various ports of call. The Soviet Fleet represents a threat only to the lovers of military adventures and to nobody else. . . . Our state is, as is well known, a Black Sea and therefore a Mediterranean power. . . .[91]

While neither *Izvestia* nor Admiral Smirnov drew the analogy between the Soviet Fleet in the Mediterranean and the Soviet Army in places like East Germany, Hungary and Czechoslovakia, the roles of the two forces in the preservation and, as in the Mediterranean, the expansion of the *Pax Sovietica,* seem to parallel one another. Beyond that, Admiral Smirnov's view that: "Nobody can be allowed to turn the Mediterranean into a hot-bed of war which could plunge humanity into the abyss of a world nuclear catastrophe," and that: "The presence of Soviet ships in the Mediterranean Sea is subordinate to this lofty aim," reveals a crucial strategic reality: the Soviet Fleet in the Mediterranean is intended to deny NATO the option to defend its southern flank.

90. Cited in "Izvestia Suggests U.S. Leave Mediterranean," *Los Angeles Times,* 12 November 1968, p. 15, pt. II.

91. Vice Admiral N. I. Smirnov, "Soviet Navy in the Mediterranean," *Red Star,* 12 November 1968, as cited in *Survival* (London), Vol. XI, No. 2 (February 1969), pp. 65-66.

VII. Grand Strategy—Securing the Mediterranean

THE SOVIET PRESENCE IN YUGOSLAVIA CANNOT BY ITSELF GRANT THE SOVIET UNION THE CAPABILITY FOR ESTABLISHING NAVAL SUPREMACY IN THE CENTRAL MEDITERRANEAN. Yugoslavia, however, is one part of the strategic axis—the rest of which extends north into Hungary, Austria and Czechoslovakia and south across the Mediterranean into Libya.

Austria

Two months before Kosygin's visit to Yugoslavia in September 1973, Janos Kadar, leader of the Hungarian Socialist Workers party, met with Tito in Yugoslavia for talks that were characterized as "warmer and less encumbered by political suspicion, or economic rigidity than the relations of either country with any other member of the Warsaw Pact. . . ."[1]

Amongst those things discussed at this, and earlier meetings between Hungarian and Yugoslav officials, were the developing economic ties between the two countries. These were to be fostered by the creation of a joint-banking consortium, a joint governmental commission for economic relations and agreements for "joint appearances on third markets." Most significant, consideration was given to the construction of the Adria oil pipeline for the transportation of Middle East crude oil to Yugoslavia, Hungary and Czechoslovakia. Czechoslovakia was a party to the agreement and the oil for the pipeline would come from Libya.

In 1972, the Soviet Union signed an agreement with the Libyan government to develop, with Soviet help, that country's oil resources. Yugoslavia for its part was to construct a tanker port in the North Adriatic to receive the oil and 500 miles of pipeline reaching to ports on the Sava and Danube and connecting to branch lines for delivery of oil to the Hungarian refinery at Szazhalombatta and the Czech refinery at Bratislava.[2]

1. "Hungary and Yugoslavia: A Unique Relationship?" *Radio Free Europe Research, East Europe, Hungary*/12, 10 August 1973.

2. "Libya oil pact signed with Russ," *Palo Alto Times,* 6 March 1972, p. 6; and, "East-bloc trio will share oil pipeline," *The Christian Science Monitor,* 14 February 1974, p. 4.

While Yugoslavia was responsible for construction of the new oil-handling port up the Adriatic, it also assisted in the development of facilities at the southern end of the oil route in Libya. From April 1973 onward, the Belgrade construction company, Ivan Milutinovic, undertook development of ports along the Libyan coast from Tunisia to the Egyptian wire, carrying out a major development of the port of Misurata, 130 miles east of Tripoli.[3]

The meeting between Kadar and Tito followed the removal from party posts and government office of the most prominent members of the Hungarian national minority in the Vojvoidina, where a half million Hungarians live within the Yugoslav Republic. The purges of Hungarians from party and state posts began in October, the year before, and apparently were not yet over by the time of the Tito-Kadar meetings. One might have supposed that such treatment of the leaders of the Hungarian national minority in Yugoslavia would have been a source of friction between Hungary and Yugoslavia, since those who were purged were associated with the preservation of Magyar culture in the Vojvoidina.[4]

Such an obvious suppression of minority sentiment and culture is most often a cause of friction between the suppressor-nation and that country from which a national minority claims origin. The purge amongst Hungarians in Yugoslavia, however, appeared not to arouse the Hungarian government. Indeed, the communiqué concluding the Kadar-Tito talks spoke of the understanding and good-neighborliness that the Hungarian minority so *helped* to promote. Such a view lends the impression that the Hungarian-Yugoslav connection was so needful of strengthening that it overrode Hungarian concerns about the fate of brethren in the Vojvoidina—concerns which the Hungarian government had not felt constrained to express when Hungarian minorities were abused in Czechoslovakia or Romania. And, as though to lend further evidence of the warm relations, the Minister of National Defense of the People's Republic of Hungary paid a five-day "official visit" to Yugoslavia in March 1974, inspecting units of the Yugoslav's People's Army.[5]

The visit of the Hungarian Defense Minister took place only 20 days after the revelations on Austrian television of a Warsaw Pact contingency plan for invasion of Yugoslavia through Austria using Czech and Hungarian troops in support of the Red Army. Whether the visit of the Hungarian Defense

3. "Libyan Port Construction," Belgrade, TANJUG, in English 0910 GMT 7 Oct 75, in *FBIS*, Vol. II, *Eastern Europe*, 9 October 1975, p. I 10. See also, "Libya," in *Report on World Affairs, July to December 1973*, Vol. 54, Nos. 3 and 4, pp. 16-17.

4. "Thoughts Behind Purges in Vojvoidina," *Radio Free Europe Research: Yugoslavia: Party*, 16 July 1973.

5. "Hungarian Defense Minister in Skopje with Petrovski," Belgrade, TANJUG, in English, 1315 GMT 12 March 1974, in *FBIS*, Vol. II, *Eastern Europe*, 13 March 1974, p. I 4.

Minister was at all connected with the Austrian broadcast cannot be easily discerned. There seems little doubt, however, that the visit came with the blessings of the Soviet Union. Hungary was not in a position to act independently in such matters so long as Soviet troops were garrisoned in its land. In fact it was only a few months later that the Soviet garrison was reported to have been increased by 60,000 Warsaw Pact troops, bringing foreign troops in Hungary up to 130,000 men.[6]

Yugoslav-Hungarian relations have been strikingly similar to those between the Soviet Union and Yugoslavia. In respect to industrial and commercial intercourse they seem to continue so to this day. It seems reasonable, therefore, to assume that Hungarian policy toward Yugoslavia does not depart far from the lines laid down in Moscow. For while it is said that the Soviet Southern Army Group is stationed "temporarily" in Hungary, it is in fact stationed there.[7]

After the events of August 1968—the Warsaw Pact invasion of Czechoslovakia—it hardly seems necessary to describe the close relationship between Czech policy and Soviet desires. If there is doubt, however, the fact that Czechoslovakia, along with Poland, has been entrusted with the manufacture of the new Soviet tank, the T-72, ought to suggest that Czech-Soviet relations are not the conventional ones to be expected between one sovereign power and another. The fact that Romania is also to produce T-72 tanks, as soon as the factory for them is completed, may suggest, despite the claims of conventional wisdom, the nature of that country's relationship with the Soviet Union.[8]

The Austro-Soviet Connection

The Austrian connection to the Soviet Union and its willing and unwilling allies, does not derive from any shared love of Marxist-Leninism or hopes for a socialist commonwealth. The Republic of Austria is a constitutional and parliamentary democracy. It was established by mandate of the electorate in 25 November 1945, and according to the provisions of the constitution of 1920 as amended in 1929. In the recognition accorded the new government of Austria by the Allied Council in Austria—in the Four-Power Agreement for establishing Machinery of Control in Austria, concluded on 28 June 1946, and finally in the 1955 State Treaty with Austria—

6. Agence France-Presse report: "Paper Says Troops Mass in Hungary," *Washington Post,* 18 September 1974, p. A 17.

7. "Soviet Armed Forces Day. A Wreath-laying ceremony. . . . On behalf of the Soviet Southern Army Group temporarily stationed in Hungary. Its commanding officer Colonel-General F. Krivda laid a wreath." (Photo Caption), *Neuste Nachrichten* (Budapest), 24-25 February 1979, p. 2.

8. "T-72 production outside the U.S.S.R.," *International Defense Review,* Vol. 12, No. 4 (1979), p. 481.

the United States, the United Kingdom, the Soviet Union and the French Republic all adhered to the provision that Austria be a democratic State.[9]

The State Treaty granted Austria its independence from the Allied Council in Austria and the Western powers withdrew civilian administrators who had overseen Austrian affairs for the Western powers. For its part, the Soviet Union withdrew the army of occupation that had governed the Soviet Zone of Austria. The Western powers considered Austria to have been forcibly seized by Nazi Germany in 1939 and therefore a territory liberated from Nazi domination. The Soviet Union, having recognized the incorporation of Austria into the Third Reich at the time of the Nazi-Soviet treaty in 1939, considered Austria to have become an occupied enemy territory when Allied armies entered the country in April 1945. Therefore, the Soviet Union felt justified in demanding a high price for the withdrawal of the Red Army from eastern Austria. In an Austrian-Soviet agreement separate from the State Treaty, the Soviet Union required Austria to pay 150 million dollars to reclaim former German property in the country and 2 million dollars for the assets of the Danube Shipping Company. In order to receive possession of the oilfields and refineries in eastern Austria, the Austrian government promised to deliver 10 million tons of crude oil per year to the Soviet Union for a period of ten years.[10]

At the time that the Austrian State Treaty came into force, the Austrian government declared the country's "perpetual neutrality" and pledged, "Austria will never join a military alliance or allow the establishment of military bases of foreign states on its territory."[11]

Unlike the other European countries occupied by Soviet forces at the end of the Second World War, therefore, Austria became a democracy whose outlook was pro-Western. Austrian neutrality was meant to reassure the Soviet Union. To some observers in the West, the willingness of the Soviet Union to end its occupation of Austrian territory was an indication of Soviet determination to end the Cold War.[12]

Such an optimistic view of Soviet policy toward Austria, notwithstanding, the Austrian government seems to have entertained no illusion about

9. "Recognition of Austrian Government, January 7, 1946"; "Control Machinery in Austria" in *A Decade of American Foreign Policy: Basic Documents, 1941-49,* 81st Congress, 1st Session, Senate, Document No. 123 (Washington, D.C.: U.S.G.P.O., 1950), pp. 614-20; Article I of the 1955 State Treaty reads: "The Allied and Associated Powers recognize that Austria is re-established as a sovereign, independent and democratic State." See Hans Kelsen, *Principles of International Law,* Second Edition (New York: Holt, Rinehart and Winston, Inc., 1966), p. 385n.

10. The order of events in Austria is given in *Political Handbook of the World, Parliaments and Press as of January 1, 1951* (New York: Harper & Brothers, 1951), p. 8; provisions of the Soviet-Austrian Agreement ending Soviet Occupation, are in *1956 Britannica Book of the Year* under "Austria," pp. 74-75.

11. *1956 Britannica Book of the Year,* "Austria," p. 74.

12. "Talks on Austria: Soviet Premier on low-key visit," *Palo Alto Times,* 30 June 1973, p. 7.

Austria's status in respect to the Soviet Union. When Alexei Kosygin visited Austria in July 1973, the communiqué issued by the Soviet Premier and the Austrian Chancellor "emphasized the significance of the Austrian State Treaty and Austria's constitutionally established permanent neutrality, which strengthens not only Austria's independence but its international standing." Beyond that, it was said, "permanent neutrality pursued by Austria has made a substantial contribution to the further deepening of good neighbor relations between Austria and the U.S.S.R."[13]

The phrases "Austria's independence" and "good neighbor relations between Austria and the U.S.S.R." had an interesting interpretation placed upon them at the end of September, two months after Kosygin's visit to Vienna. Two heavily-armed Arab terrorists crossed into Austria from Czechoslovakia, seized three Soviet Jews who were on their way to Israel and an Austrian customs officer, and demanded that Austria close the Jewish transit camp at Schoenau Castle. The Austrian government closed the camp and the Arab terrorists released their hostages and fled by plane to Libya. Chancellor Kreisky of Austria replied to criticism of his government's action from the United States and other powers by pointing out that the terrorists had crossed the Czech border without difficulty, although they were heavily armed. The Czech border with Austria one of the most closely controlled borders of any in the Communist world. If Czechoslovakia had permitted the crossing by the terrorists in a Czech train, it must have been because the Soviet government had desired it. Czechoslovakia could not permit itself any liberties where Soviet policy was concerned. The Austrian foreign minister in explaining his country's refusal to yield to American requests to reopen the transit camp, said that Austria could not reopen the camp for fear of Soviet demands to close it again: "Today it is President Nixon, but tomorrow the first secretary of the Soviet Communist Party might not be pleased."[14]

Whether Kosygin had explained the political realities to the Austrian Chancellor during the Russian's visit in July, or the Austrian Chancellor had grasped them beforehand, the definition of Austrian "independence" and Soviet "friendship" could hardly have been more explicit. As if to emphasize yet further the position in which Austria was to consider itself in respect to the Soviet Union, President Podgorny of the Soviet Union, the following year, scolded the Austrian Chancellor for anti-Soviet material appearing in

13. "Soviet-Austrian Communique," *Pravda,* 6 July 1973, pp. 1 and 4, in *The Current Digest of the Soviet Press,* Vol. XXV, No. 27, 1 August 1973, p. 5.

14. "Rejected Nixon's Pleas Because of Soviet Factor, Austria Says," *Los Angeles Times,* 5 October 1973, p. 1; "Kreisky Forcefully Rejects Nixon Pleas to Keep Camp Open," *ibid.*, 4 October 1973, p. 1; and, "U.S. Disagreement on Austria Decision Told," *ibid.*, 2 October 1973, p. 12, and in the same place, "Keep Promise Terrorist Unit Warns Austria."

Austrian newspapers. At that time, during a visit to Moscow the Chancellor was encouraged to place Austria in the same relation to the Soviet Union as that enjoyed by Finland. The Chancellor refused such a formal status for Austria.[15] If the principle of "Finlandization" was declined, the fact of it was already well on the way to realization.

Realization was rooted in a simple political truth: Austria, like Finland, remains independent at the pleasure and convenience of the Soviet Union. Should the Soviet Union move, one day, to bring Austria into the Socialist Commonwealth, by whatever means, it may expect to do so without hindrance. Any rush by others to defend Austria's independence would without doubt be on a scale matched only by that evoked by the threat to Czech independence in October 1938, March 1939, February 1948 and August 1968. Austrians, whatever their political preferences, must know that well.

Commerce

The incorporation of Austria into the Soviet strategic axis stretching on down into Africa has, of course, remained unremarked. Soviet partners in the enterprise have been, among others, Poland and Hungary, with Czechoslovakia furnishing an occasional menacing counterpoint to the commercial harmony offered by the rest.

In September 1971, Austria and Poland signed a five-year trade agreement under which all mutual payments would be made in freely-convertible currencies.[16] That system of payments was then extended throughout the membership of COMECON at the ministerial meetings of that body held in Katowice in April 1973.[17]

At the same Moscow meetings where Austria was offered a chance to become another Finland, a ten-year trade agreement was concluded between the two powers. One of the provisions provided for Austrian firms to construct a variety of industrial facilities in the Soviet Union. The facilities included those having to do with the steel, paper, wood, and shipbuilding industries.[18]

September 1973 was a bad month for Czech-Austrian relations. Czech authorities had permitted armed hijackers to cross into Austria and the Czech air force had forced down Austrian aircraft on two occasions (causing the

15. "Soviet Chill Apparent on Kreisky Trip: Nixon's Reception Expected to Show Contrast to Austrian," *Los Angeles Times*, 26 June 1974, p. 8.

16. "Austria," in *The Report on World Affairs: A Summary of World Events in June, July, September* 1972 (London), pp. 302-3.

17. "COMECO: La creation d'une monnaie commune convertible," *Le Monde Diplomatique* (Paris), May 1973, p. 30.

18. "Austria," in *The Report on World Affairs July to December* 1973, (London), Vol. 54, Nos. 3 and 4, pp. 57-58.

deaths of the pilots). Austrian relations with Hungary however improved measurably. Hungarian officials expressed the desire to have relations with Austria to be "a model of cooperation between countries of differing social systems." Measures were taken at that time to loosen the restrictions on traffic between the two countries[19] reducing them to the merest formalities, while Austrian banks had agreed to advance loans for the construction of tourist hotels inside Hungary.[20]

Agreements were already in existence for visa-free travel between Austria and two other Warsaw Pact powers, Poland and Romania. In February 1976 Chancellor Kreisky visited Czechoslovakia, apparently ending the hostility of that country toward Austria—it was the first visit of an Austrian government leader in forty years. The following year, in November, the Czech Prime Minister, Comrade Lubomir Strougal returned the visit, the first such visit by a Czech head of government to Austria since the founding of the Czech republic in 1918.[21]

Such interstate formalities provided only a surface indication of other matters of more substantial consequence. In 1975, agreements were reached between the two governments that the *Pressburgerbahn* which had for years stopped at Wolfsthal in Austria, be once again extended to Bratislava in Czechoslovakia; and, the one-kilometer section of the Vienna-Brno rail line, at the Austrian-Czech border, be electrified like the rest of line on both sides of the border. Negotiations were undertaken at the same time for the continuation, on Austrian territory, of the Prague-Linz superhighway to be followed by the opening of other highways linking the two countries.[22]

In October 1975, the Austrian-state steel concern Voest-Alpine concluded an agreement with Polish state foreign trade agencies for the exchange of 11 billion schillings worth of goods. In exchange for Austrian steel products, Poland was to deliver coal, coking coal and other Polish products. Meanwhile the Austrian motor company, Steyr-Daimler-Puch and the Polish state motor concern, Polmot, negotiated agreements covering the sale of 16-ton heavy Austrian motor lorries to Poland, and the erection of a truck plant and the transfer of technology for truck manufacturing in Poland.[23]

19. "Another Iron Curtain Gap: Hungary and Austria take first steps toward creating an 'open border,'" *The Christian Science Monitor,* 15 November 1973, p. 4. Austrian-Czech relations are reviewed in "Czechoslovak Hostility Toward Austria Grows," *Los Angeles Times,* 16 December 1973, p. 7, p. II.

20. "Austria, Hungary drop barriers for travellers across the border," *The Christian Science Monitor,* 4 January 1979, p. 5.

21. *Report on World Affairs January to March 1976* (London), 1976/1, p. 50; and, "Czech visit to Vienna an 'icebreaker,'" *The Christian Science Monitor,* 23 November 1977, p. 9.

22. "Austrian-CSSR Transportation Links," *Vienna VOLKSSTIMME* in German, 8 June 1975, p. 3, in *FBIS,* Vol. VII, *Western Europe,* 10 July 1975, p. E 2.

23. "Austria," in *Report on World Affairs January to March 1976* (London), 1976/1, p. 50.

Arms

It is evident that the reopening of uninterrupted motor and rail travel with Czechoslovakia facilitated trade between Austria and Poland, as well as that between Czechoslovakia and Austria. There have apparently been other advantages as well to the thawing of relations between Austria and Czechoslovakia.

For example, there was the case of the 4,000 Austrian Steyr sub-machine guns. It is commonly known that Czechoslovakia and East Germany are the purveyors of small arms and light infantry weapons for those revolutionary, guerrilla or terrorists groups in the world whose operations, in the view of the Soviet Union, contribute to Socialist progress. Czechoslovakia produces absolutely first-rate weapons itself. Yet, in August 1975, the Czechoslovak foreign trade agency, Mercuria, contracted for the purchase of 4,000 Steyr sub-machine guns for delivery to Czechoslovakia. The deal had been approved by the Ministries of Interior, Foreign Affairs, and Defense in Vienna under the condition that the arms be moved by air freight to Prague so that they could not be rerouted to some other place. Austrian policy eschews delivery of arms to any place where a crisis exists. The arms were loaded on an aircraft at Vienna-Schwechat under documentation showing that they were "machines" going to Prague. The aircraft, a U.S. built Boeing transport, had been sold by an American airline to an East European airline. When the plane came into Vienna, the markings of the East European airline had been painted out, and the plane had come from Lisbon not from Prague. Because the aircraft was not properly licensed to carry passengers or freight in Austria, Austrian authorities held up the shipment and the plane took off for Prague. It appeared to the Austrian government that the arms, procured by Czechoslovakia, were intended for one of the political factions in Portugal which was then in the midst of political turmoil.[24]

Austria is neutral, unwarlike, and not at all inclined to be implicated in anyone else's civil disturbances. Still, a purchase order from Prague for 4,000 small arms could hardly be refused without offending Czechoslovakia or Moscow. Soviet-Czech carelessness in failing to obtain proper clearance for the cargo flight to take place may have been less contempt for Austrian law than haste engendered by the pressure of events in Portugal. One can understand the procurement of Steyr weapons by Czechoslovakia if one considers that Austrian sub-machine guns in the hands of some fractious group in

24. "Foreign Office Examines Arms Deal: Three Ministries Previously Approved the Export of the 4,000 Submachine guns," *Kurier* (Vienna), 26 August 1975, p. 9, as cited in *FBIS*, Vol. VII, *Western Europe*, 29 August 1975, p. E 1; "The 'Machines for Prague' Were Submachine Guns from Steyr: 4,000 Arms—for Whom?" *Kurier* (Vienna), 27 August 1975, p. 5, as cited in *ibid.*, 27 August 1975 p. E 1. See, as well, "Portugal: The Battle for the barracks," in *Foreign Report* (London), No. 1410, 8 October 1975, p. 1. More recently see, "Vienna is Talking about Contraband Weapons," *San Francisco Chronicle*, 25 June 1979, p. 14

Portugal would have excited little comment about the group's ultimate allegiance. Soviet, Czech, or East German weapons would have been a dead giveaway. Use of an aircraft easily identifiable as of U.S. origin was a master stroke. If the weapons were intercepted short of the intended users, then the CIA would have been inferred to be the culprit, and thereby could demonstrate how the iniquitous Americans were interfering in Portugal's domestic affairs.

In a similar incident in December 1976, 600 rifles with telescopic sights and 400,000 rounds of ammunition, all intended for Syria, were seized at the Vienna airport. While the matter was being investigated, the arms and ammunition disappeared, reappearing eventually, according to reports, in Syria, having come via a Yugoslav port.[25]

The Austrian Dilemma: The Entanglement of Neutrality

The position of Austria in all of this is not enviable. Austria had pledged to be neutral and never to "join a military alliance or allow . . . military bases of foreign states on its territory." This pledge was welcomed by the Soviet Union for its "substantial contribution . . . to good neighbor relations between Austria and the U.S.S.R." In China, *Peking Review* took note of the unfortunate circumstances in which Austria found itself with "the Soviet Army showing its strength in a place less than two hours drive from Vienna."[26]

In 1973, for example, "good neighbor relations" meant that Austria would permit the training of Warsaw Pact troops *on its territory,* in spite of its constitutionally-sanctioned neutrality.[27] When the Austrian Defense Minister proposed in January 1977, a revision of the Austrian peace treaty to permit Austrian forces to equip themselves with "defensive" rockets, the Chancellor "rejected the proposal, saying it would lead to confrontation with the Soviet Union."[28]

An equally interesting aspect of "good neighbor relations" with the Soviet Union concerns Vneshtorgbank, the Foreign Trade Bank of the Soviet Union. Through its correspondent banks in Austria, and they appear to include all of the principal Austrian banks, Vneshtorgbank finances trade

25. "Austria," in *Report on World Affairs January to March 1977,* 1977/1, pp. 49-50.

26. "Report From Vienna: *Apprehension Along the Danube,*" *Peking Review,* No. 14, 4 April 1975, pp. 26 and 31.

27. "Austria: Pact Troops Trained," *Military Review,* March 1973, p. 98: "The Austrian military command in Salzburg has confirmed reports that army alpine guides of neutral Austria are beginning to train Warsaw Pact troops. Twenty-three officers and NCOs of the Hungarian armed forces have received mountain training at Saalfelden, the light infantry school near Salzburg. At the same time, three Romanian helicopter pilots learned how to fly into narrow alpine valleys and land in rugged alpine terrain."

28. "Austria," *Report on World Affairs January to March 1977,* 1977/1, pp. 49-50.

between Austrian firms and Soviet foreign trade enterprises. As the director of the Soviet bank expressed it, "by financing trade between Austria and the Soviet Union, the banks contribute toward the expansion and strengthening of the trade relations between our two countries." Typical of the transactions was that providing for the supply of pipes, equipment and materials for the Soviet gas industry. In an agreement concluded on 1 June 1968, the Austrian banks raised 110 million dollars to lend to Vneshtorgbank to finance purchases from Austrian firms. A second agreement in November 1974 provided for a loan to Russia of 2.5 billion schillings (132.5 million dollars). In return for the favor the Soviet Union proposed to supply up to 2 billion cubic meters of natural gas per year to Austria until the year 2000. Thus, as the Comrade Director put it: "Austria obtains a reliable energy source for a long time to come, while the Soviet Union strengthens its gas industry and obtains an additional foreign currency source for the purchase of products that are necessary for the development of its national economy."[29]

Here is the Soviet Union that could, so to speak, buy Austria outright from Kremlin petty cash—the Soviet Union's Gross National Product was reported as 300 billion dollars in 1973—borrowing money from a country whose Gross National Product was barely a tenth that of the Soviet Union.

An agreement for the annual delivery of an additional 500 million cubic meters of Soviet natural gas was concluded by the Soviet Deputy Foreign Trade Minister and the Director General of the Austrian Oil Administration in August 1975, the deliveries to take place from 1 January 1978 to the end of the year 2000. In return, it was agreed, that the Austrian Voest Steel Company would deliver a further 300,000 tons of steel pipe, bringing the total to be delivered to the Soviet Union to a million tons of pipe. To finance payment for the pipe, the Austrian Control bank granted the Soviet Foreign Trade Bank a loan of 2.8 billion schillings or 148.4 million dollars.[30]

The typical market price then for export natural gas, Canadian natural gas imported into the United States, for example, was one dollar per 28 cubic meters. Therefore Austria obtained the promise of delivery of an additional 17 million dollars worth of gas, in return for which Austrian banks would raise a loan of 148.4 million dollars for the use of the Soviet Foreign Trade Bank. Altogether, between May and September 1975, Austrian banks undertook to supply to the Soviet Union in connection with Austrian gas purchases almost 300 million dollars. On 27 November 1975, the Austrian government announced that it was raising a 300 million dollar loan on the

29. Yu. A. Ivanov, chairman of the U.S.S.R. Foreign Trade Bank, "Trail Blazers of Soviet Trade," *Die Presse* (Vienna), 6 May 1975, p. 9, as cited in *FBIS*, Vol. VII, *Western Europe*, 7 May 1975, p. E 1.

30. "AUSTRIA CONCLUDES NEW GAS AGREEMENT WITH USSR," *Wiener Zeitung*, 22 August 1975, p. 7, as cited in *FBIS*, Vol. VII, *Western Europe*, 29 August 1975, p. E 1.

Euromarket, a loan in which all the principal Austrian banks were involved.[31] In January of the following year, the Soviet Union agreed to the delivery of an additional 900 million cubic meters of natural gas.[32]

The Soviet Union gained a number of attendant advantages. Austria and other West European customers for Soviet natural gas financed the expansion of the Soviet gas industry, and supplied the pipes for the pipelines and the equipment for pumping and handling of the gas in the Soviet Union as well as within their own countries. Austria provided western credits to the Soviet Foreign Trade bank through loans raised by Austrian banks in the European money market, loans for whose repayment Austria assumed the burden. The Soviet Union redeems the loans, presumably, under the terms of agreement arrived at between Austria and COMECON in which East European monies were considered to be freely convertible when spent within the confines of COMECON. More important, however, in respect to Austria's relationship to the Warsaw Pact powers, Austria has come to depend on the Soviet Union to supply 51 percent of its natural gas. Natural gas supplied an estimated nineteen percent of Austria's energy requirements in 1976.[33] The balance of Austria's energy requirements in 1976 were met by coal (including coke and lignite), about 19 percent; hydroelectric power, about 10 percent; and petroleum, over 50 percent. In 1975, the East European countries supplied over 46 percent of Austria's requirements for fuel.[34] Austrian attempts to become less dependent on foreign energy were frustrated in November 1978 when a referendum was held to decide whether the newly-constructed nuclear power plant at Zwentendorf would be permitted to begin operations. Austrian voters turned down nuclear power. In place of the nuclear plant, now being dismantled, will be constructed a coal-fired power plant, the coal for which will come from Poland.[35]

But it does not stop there. Seventy percent of Austria's coal and coke must come from abroad. As one might guess, the principal suppliers of those commodities to Austria are Poland, Czechoslovakia and the Soviet Union. Eighty percent of the petroleum Austria consumed in 1976 had to be imported. That commodity comes from the Soviet Union and various Middle Western and African counries. One of the oil-supplying countries is Libya. Consequently, the Austro-Libyan agreement of April 1975 is seen to be more than a casual trade agreement, insofar as Austria was concerned. Concluded

31. "Austria," in *Report on World Affairs October to December 1975*, Vol. 56, No. 4, pp. 46-47.

32. "Austria," *Report on World Affairs January to March 1976*, 1976/1, p. 50.

33. Statistics given in "Domestic Production and Consumption of Primary Energy," in *Austrian Information: Special Issue on the Austrian Economy*, The Austrian Information Service, Vol. 30, No. 3, 1977, p. 7.

34. "Sources of Imported Energy," *ibid.*

35. "Austria's Nuclear 'White Elephant,'" *The Christian Science Monitor*, 7 November 1978, p. 9; and, "Caloric Power Instead of Nuclear Plant," *Austrian Information*, Vol. 32, No. 4/5 (1979), p. 12.

during a visit to Vienna by the Libyan Prime Minister and taking effect in October 1975, the agreement provided for the formation of a Libyan-Austrian government commission. That commission implements cooperation in the fields of construction, industry, agriculture, cultivation of virgin territory, electrical power, transfer of technology and *oil.* One Austrian company already has begun building 14 grain silos of 20,000 tons capacity each; a second Austrian firm along with a Bulgarian partner had begun installing air-conditioning in nearly a score of clinics in Libya. The Voest-Alpine Steel Corporation was subcontracting on the construction of the Marsa Brega Chemical Works.[36]

Austria finds itself therefore at the center of a great web of commercial activity stretching north into Poland, south through Yugoslavia into Libya and east into Hungary and beyond into Russian Siberia. Along the highways and rail lines linking Austria with Czechoslovakia and Poland move Czech and Polish goods to Rijeka and other Yugoslav Adriatic ports. Over a million and a half tons of Czech goods would move through the ports of Rijeka in 1975.[37] At the nearby island of Krk, there starts the great oil pipeline, financed chiefly by Yugoslavia, Hungary, Czechoslovakia, Libya and Kuwait, to carry Libyan and other oil north to Czechoslovakia, east through Yugoslavia to Hungary, and doubtless to Austria as well.[38]

Entangled as it is in the trade of the Eastern Bloc of nations, it is no wonder that a Member of the Austrian parliament could charge the Austrian government with "orienting toward the Eastern Bloc, primarily the Soviet Union."[39] Almost every country with which Austria must trade in order to obtain the greater part of the fuel to maintain itself and the prosperity of its citizens, resides within the political control of Moscow or is so much under Moscow influence as to be considered a client.

Libya

Terrorism

The southern end of the strategic axis extends, for the moment at least, to Libya. The Libyan regime was initially and naively characterized as not

36. "Austrian-Libyan Cooperation," *Weiner Zeitung,* 27 November 1975, p. 7, as cited in *FBIS,* Vol. VII, *Western Europe,* 11 December 1975, p. E 2.

37. "Czechoslovak Goods Transit," *Vjesnik* (Zagreb), 2 October 1975, p. 6, as cited in *FBIS,* Vol. II, *Eastern Europe,* 22 October 1975, p. I 15.

38. "Petroleum Pipeline Construction," TANJUG (Belgrade) in English 117 GMT 16 October 75, as cited in *FBIS,* Vol. II, *Eastern Europe,* 22 October 75, p. I 15; "Yugoslavia, Hungary, Czechoslovakia Agree on Pipeline," Peking *Nona* in English, 2041 GMT, 4 July 74, as cited in *FBIS,* Vol. I, *China,* 9 July 1974, pp. A 22-A 23.

39. "Peking-Oriented Foreign Policy Urged in Parliament," Vienna Domestic Service in German 1118 GMT 10 Dec 1975, as cited in *FBIS,* Vol. VII, *Western Europe,* 11 December 1975, p. E 2.

being able to last unless its leader Colonel Qaddafi and his henchmen could learn the facts of world affairs. The Colonel and his fellows unfortunately have learned them well.[40] Part *condottiers*, part *Mahdi*, Colonel Qaddafi seeds Libya as a kind of Bedouin Prussia to the movement for Arab unity.[41] Yet, he holds the principal bridgehead for Soviet influence in North Africa. Like the Old Man of the Mountain, he sends forth terrorists throughout the world to wield the Libyan sword of Islam. The "sword" most frequently is a Czech, Soviet, or East German AK, grenade, or rocket launcher. Libya has been, at once training camp, treasury and arsenal for terrorists around the world. An attempted *coup d'état* in Morocco in 1971 found Libya ready to support the ringleaders of the *coup*.[42]

The Black September, killers of the Israeli team at the Munich Olympics in 1972, were led by a Libyan and equipped with Soviet arms. Their fellows who murdered the U.S. envoy to the Sudan and his assistant, in 1973, when the release of Sirhan Sirhan from prison was refused, were Black Septemberists. Libya was amongst the first to send troops to help keep Idi Amin in power in Uganda when that worthy's position was threatened in 1973. Libya was also amongst the last to support the doomed dictator when his African neighbors drove him from office.[43]

Libya has supplied East European arms to the IRA terrorists in Northern Ireland and Qaddafi has openly supported that movement while boasting of his support for guerrilla organizations *within* the United States.[44]

The charities to which the Colonel from Libya subscribes are those with which the Soviet Union materially sympathizes. The Popular Front for the Liberation of Palestine remains a favorite of both and the parent of the PRLP, the Palestine Liberation Organization, takes pride in the connection. As Zehdi Terzi, the Palestine Liberation Organization's chief representative at the United Nations expressed it: "The Soviet Union has supported us morally, politically and materially. I think our national council has made it

40. "12 Enigmatic Young Men Rule Libya," *Los Angeles Times*, 6 May 1970, p. 7, pt. VII.

41. Anthony McDermott, "Qaddafi and Libya," *The World Today*, Vol. 29, No. 9, September 1973, pp. 398-408.

42. "Libya," in *The Report on World Affairs June, July, September 1971*, Vol. 52, No. 3, October 1971, pp. 250-51.

43. "Libya," in *Britannica Book of the Year 1973*, pp. 414-15, and "Uganda, Now for the Future," *To the Point* (Johannesburg), 20 April 1979, p. 39, and see, "3 Arab Guerillas charged with murder of Israeli—Bonn Gets Ultimatum from Black September," *Asahr Evening News* (Tokyo), 8 September 1972, p. 1.

44. On Arms to the IRA see *Britannica Book of the Year 1973*, p. 414; "Libya," *The Report on World Affairs April to June 1973*, Vol. 54, No. 2, p. 16, and, for the delivery of Soviet-made weapons from Libya, see *Times* (London), 29 March 1973, p. 1; for Colonel Qaddafi's support of terrorists in the United States see *Britannica Book of the Year 1973*, p. 414; and, for details of Libyan support for terrorists in the United States, see Ehud Yonay, "The PLO Underground in California," and, "The American Targets of Palestinian Terrorism," both in *New West*, Northern California edition, Vol. 4, No. 5, 26 February 1979, pp. 22-31.

very clear that we are proud of our relations with the Socialist countries, especially the Soviet Union."[45]

Although Libya is a nation of less than 3 million people and its iniquitous acts against neighbor and stranger alike are legend, *no* Western apprehension or dissent is voiced.[46]

The Western World had taken comfort in the Libyan dictator's protestations of anti-Soviet sentiments, for how could a fanatic Moslem ever come to an arrangement of any kind with the atheistic Soviet Union. But in May 1974, the Prime Minister of Libya visited Moscow where he and the leaders of the Soviet Union concluded a trade agreement. The Iraqi News Agency reported that an arms agreement had been concluded at the same time.[47] The month before Colonel Qaddafi had said: "We have always looked on the Soviet Union as a friend and our relations are now better than they were."[48]

In May 1975, Alexei Kosygin paid an official visit to Libya. The Libyan Prime Minister, Abdul Salam Jallud, expressed the Libyan government's position in respect to the Soviet Union and the future of Libyan-Soviet relations:

> We highly appreciate the position of the socialist countries, headed by the Soviet Union, with respect to the Arab nation and the revolutionary forces that are waging a struggle for the elimination of imperialism. . . .
>
> I would like once again to give a high appraisal of the assistance, economic and military, that the Soviet Union is giving to the revolutionary and progressive forces. But I would like to say that there are possibilities for the further development of this assistance so that, relying on it, we would be able to defeat Zionism and imperialism, in the same way that the defeats in Vietnam and Cambodia took place. . . .[49]

Of Arms and Strategic Reversals

The Egyptian newspaper *Al Ahram* claimed that the meetings had concluded with an agreement by the Soviet Union to deliver 100 million dollars worth of arms to Libya in exchange for installation of Soviet naval and air bases. While everyone denied the possibility of such an arrangement, a flotilla of Soviet ships from the Mediterranean Fleet called in at Tripoli. Soviet instructors were assigned to the former U.S. air base at Wheelus.[50]

45. "Interview (with Thalif Dean of *Asiaweek*) 'We're Part of Liberation Movements,'" *Asiaweek* (Hong Kong), Vol. 5, No. 25, 29 June 1979, p. 34.

46. "Libya sees Opening in Chad impasse; French want Out," *The Christian Science Monitor,* 27 April 1979, p. 10; Sudan discussed briefly in *Foreign Report,* No. 1555, 11 October 1978.

47. "Libya," in *The Report on World Affairs 1 January to 30 June 1974,* Vol. 55, Nos. 1 & 2, p. 8.

48. "Libya: Turn-around in Tripoli," *To The Point International* (Antwerp), Vol. 2, No. 13, 28 June 1975, pp. 24-25.

49. "Kosygin Visits Libya and Tunisia: Talks with Jallud in Tripoli; In a Friendly Atmosphere," *Pravda,* 14 May 1975, pp. 1 and 4, in *The Current Digest of the Soviet Press,* Vol. XXVII, No. 20, 11 June 1975, pp. 10-13.

50. "Libya: Turn-around in Tripoli," *To The Point International* (Antwerp), Vol. 2, No. 13, 28 June 1975, pp. 24-25.

In May of the following year, the *Washington Post* noted that Libya was receiving arms and equipment from the Soviet Union and Eastern Europe "in quantities that far exceed the Libyan armed forces' capacity to use them." The *Post* observed that as many as 600 Russians were stationed in Libya and that "hundreds of young Libyans" had been reported "to be receiving military training in the Soviet Union," but found "no evidence to confirm reports published outside Libya that the Soviets have established bases here [in Libya] or that they exert any substantial influence on Libyan policy." Instead, "there are plenty of signs that the Libyans," to whom communism is anathema, "are more nervous about the Russians than they ever were about the United States." The *Post* found it incomprehensible that the 32,000 man Libyan army could find use for, let alone operate, 2,000 Soviet tanks, two squadrons of MiG-23s, numbers of TU-22 bombers, arrays of anti-tank guns, surface-to-air missiles and helicopters delivered by the Soviet Union.[51]

Such metropolitan condescension seemed to imply that this erstwhile band of desert-dwellers could hardly be expected to master anything more sophisticated than a camel. Therefore no strategic significance should be attached to Soviet arms in Libya.

Quite unremembered were the feats of a similar folk, also armed and equipped by the Soviet Union, who, not yet three years since, had crossed the Suez Canal and effected the liberation of the Sinai: a strategic outcome of some consequence.

In December 1976, Colonel Qaddafi made his own pilgrimage to Moscow, during which the Soviet Union promised to build Libya's first nuclear power station and to install a natural gas pipeline to serve the new steel plant at Misurata.[52]

Hardly a month after the *Post*'s story, the *Christian Science Monitor* reported Libyan preparations for reception of the first submarine to be delivered by the Soviet Union. By September 1978, Libya had received three Soviet *Foxtrot*-class submarines with three more to come.[53] The *Foxtrot*-class submarine is diesel-electric, cruises at 18 knots surface and 16 knots submerged. It can stay at sea for seventy days and carries either 22 torpedoes or 44 mines.[54] These six *Foxtrot* submarines would require a total of 480 officers and men for their operation; the Libyan navy has 3,000 men, although it had

51. "Libya Seen Deluged With Soviet Arms," *Washington Post,* 25 May 1976, p. A 10; and, "Flow of Russ Arms Into Libya Growing," *Los Angeles Times,* 6 June 1976, p. 32.

52. *Report on World Affairs October to December 1976,* 1976/4, p. 8. For an additional report of a Soviet nuclear reactor for Libya, see "October 4—Western Press reports from Paris disclosed that the Soviet Union had agreed to construct a 300-Megawatt nuclear reactor in Libya," in *Chronologies of Major Developments in Selected Areas of International Relations,* Cumulative Edition 1978, International Relations Committee, House of Representatives, p. 23.

53. "Libya to receive first Soviet subs," *The Christian Science Monitor,* 1 July 1976, p. 2.

54. *The Military Balance, 1978-1979* (September 1978), p. 40.

only 1,200 men when the first submarine was in process of transfer from the Soviet Union.[55]

By September 1978, the Soviets had delivered to Libya, besides submarines, 5 *Osa II*-class, Soviet fast patrol boats armed with the *Styx*, guided missiles, and a Soviet *Polnocny*-class amphibious ship. The Libyan Air Force had received by that time a squadron of 12 Soviet TU-22 bombers, 2 interceptor squadrons with 24 MiG-23s and some MiG-23 aircraft for pilot training.[56] Radio Tripoli reported on September 1978 that .the Libyan Air Force had been equipped with MiG-25 aircraft in April. Colonel Qaddafi boasted that these advanced aircraft were not yet even in the inventories of any of the Soviet Union's European allies.[57]

There were some who thought the flow of Soviet arms into the Mediterranean areas might have sinister purposes. Vice Admiral James D. Watkins, Commander U.S. Sixth Fleet, after September 1978, suggested that some thought might be given to the possibility that the strategic balance in the Mediterranean was shifting in favor of the Soviet Union.[58] His rather restrained words reflected, one supposes, more the delicacy of his position than uncertainty about what actually has been transpiring. One cannot expect a flag officer to speak bluntly about sinister Soviet purposes while his civilian superiors who have the constitutional obligation to ensure the safety of the nation are at great pains to dispel any suspicions of Soviet motives. It is not a question of moral courage for the flag officer. It is the choice between remaining a flag officer where he might help in the defense of the nation, or being placed on half-pay ashore where his professional skill will be lost to the country.

In May 1979, Colonel Qaddafi said, "hostile policy of the United States may force us to permit the fleets of the Soviet Union to be supplied from Libyan ports."[59] The "hostile policy" to which the Libyan dictator referred was the Egyptian-Israeli peace treaty.

Barely ten years ago U.S. and British warships could use the harbors at Benghazi, Tripoli and Tobruk. British and American fighter-bombers could stage in and out of Libyan air bases. Allied military power easily could reach countries friendly to the West, like Tunisia, Morocco, Ethiopia, Chad, and Israel. Libyan oil flowed to Western Europe and the United States.

Now Soviet aircraft operate from the old Allied bases, Soviet warships call in at Libyan ports, Soviet and Cuban forces stage through Libyan air-

55. Strengths are given in *The Military Balance, 1977-1978*, and for the earlier date, 1976, in *Combat Fleets of the World, 1976/77: Their Ships, Aircraft and Armament*. Characteristics of the *Foxtrot*-class appear in the latter work as well as in *Weyers Flottentaschen buch*.

56. *The Military Balance, 1978-1979*, p. 40.

57. "Libya Claims to have MiG-25s," *Kayhan International Edition* (Tehran), 2 September 1978, p. 1.

58. "Flood of Soviet Arms to Mediterranean Area Cited," *Los Angeles Times*, 12 January 1979, p. 16.

59. "Libya May Let Soviet Warships Use Its Ports," *Los Angeles Times*, 25 May 1979, p. 4.

fields. Libya has become a military power in its own right, an arsenal for Soviet arms in Africa, and, one more center for the training and support of terrorists. Beyond that, Libya now supplies oil to Eastern Europe. Allied warships must take care to avoid minefields laid in Libyan coastal waters. In any crisis in the Mediterranean, Allied aircraft carriers cannot safely operate within range of Libyan air or submarine bases. One would suppose that in the scale according to which such things are measured, it could be said that a marked change has occurred in the Western position in the Mediterranean.

The Libyan-Yugoslav Connection

If that were not enough there is the Libyan-Yugoslav connection. The Libyan navy follows Libyan oil north to the Adriatic ports of Yugoslavia;[60] Libyan money goes to help develop the oil pipeline through Yugoslavia to Hungary and Czechoslovakia, while Libya and Yugoslavia coordinate strategy in respect to the "non-aligned" nations.[61] Libya acquired two squadrons of Yugoslavian *Galeb* aircraft for counter-insurgency operations, and another seventeen to be used as trainers. Yugoslavia, for its part will, it is said, build an arms plant in Libya to manufacture ammunition and spare parts for the Soviet weapons in the Libyan arsenals and gun parks, while establishing training camps for the Palestinian terrorists inside Yugoslavia, but near the Bulgarian border.[62]

The Libyan-Yugoslav connection seems to have been given substantial fibre in November 1973, when Colonel Qaddafi visited Belgrade. At that time, it was said that Yugoslavia would build tankers with which to carry Libyan oil and it was confirmed that Yugoslavia would receive Libyan oil. Whether coincidental or directly as a consequence, the Soviet Union was already deploying forces into and through Yugoslavia in connection with Soviet support for its Arab allies in the Middle East War.[63]

While Yugoslavia is the northern approach for Soviet arms and influence via the Adriatic to North Africa, Libya also is the bridgehead, south across the Mediterranean. Both Libya and Yugoslavia profess to be fiercely "non-aligned"; each appears jealous of its independence of foreign influence. Yet both serve as purveyors for Soviet policy and strategy. No doubt, Yugoslavia does so out of Marxist sentimentality and because its internal circumstances render it too vulnerable to do otherwise. Libya acts out of Moslem romanticism and desire to gain the imperial rewards due an acting, pro-consul of the

60. "Libyan Warships Arrive—Split—" Belgrade TANJUG Domestic Service in Serbo-Croatian 0815 GMT 31 July 75, cited in *FBIS*, Vol. II, *Eastern Europe*, 5 August 1975, p. I 10.

61. "LIBYAN FOREIGN MINISTRY DELEGATION HOLDS TALKS," Belgrade TANJUG in English 1757 GMT 11 April 75: "The Libyan delegation is led by . . . head of the Libyan bureau for non-alignment." Cited in *FBIS*, Vol. II, *Eastern Europe*, 16 April 1975, p. I 5.

62. *Foreign Report* (London) No. 1543, 19 July 1978; No. 1555, 11 October 1978.

63. *The Report on World Affairs July to December 1973*, Vol. 54, Nos. 3 and 4, pp. 16-17.

"Third Rome." Just as Cuba's Castro looks to become head of a socialist federation of the Gulf and Caribbean, Le Duan of Vietnam looks to become head of a socialist federation of Indo-China, so must Qaddafi think ahead to the day when he can lead a socialist federation of Arab states.

Malta

Libyan oil, Warsaw Pact weapons and Soviet strategy link eastern Europe to North Africa, and the central tier of the strategic axis is Malta, that tiny island sixty miles south of Sicily and 200 miles north of Tripolitania.

Malta was that "unsinkable aircraft carrier" in the Mediterranean during the Second World War, whose people earned for themselves the George Cross for courage and endurance under persistent Axis air attack and blockade. Malta gained independence in 1964; declared itself to be a republic in December 1974; and in August 1976, the Maltese government declared it would be neutral after the termination of the base agreement with Great Britain in 1979.[64]

At least as early as 1969, the Soviet Union began dealing for the use of Malta as a Mediterranean port-of-call for its shipping. This came at a time, following the Egyptian defeat in the 1967 Middle East War, when the Soviet Union was at pains to establish itself finally as a Mediterranean naval power.[65] At about the same time the Soviet Union began supplying arms to Libya in sufficient quantities to be noticed in the West.[66] As though to confirm the Soviet military interest in the area, *The Soviet Military Review* began publishing an edition in Arabic in September 1970.[67]

64. "Chronology: Europe," *Strategic Survey, 1976*, p. 123.

65. "Moscow Seeks Malta for Mediterranean Port," *The Christian Science Monitor*, 11 August 1969, p. 2. See as well, "Israel: Broken Link in Chain of Bases," *Los Angeles Times*, 27 October 1968, p. 3, section G; "How the Bear Learned to Swim," *The Economist*, Vol. 237, No. 6635, 24 October 1970, pp. 16-17; "Watch on the Med: Expanded Soviet Naval Activity in Mediterranean Seen as Attempt to Bolster Morale of Arab Nations," *The Christian Science Monitor*, 30 August 1969, p. 1; "Deep Water Port: Russians Build Navy Base in Egypt" (Mersa Matruh), *San Francisco Chronicle*, 14 November 1970, p. 15; "Russians Reported Dealing to Use Spanish Ports," *Chicago Tribune*, 22 January 1969, p. 17; "Russ Warships Using Mediterranean Isle," *Chicago Daily News*, 17 November 1969, p. 19; and, see photographs of Soviet naval vessels using Suda Bay, Crete, as an anchorage, in *Issues*, No. 2: "NATO and the Defense of Europe," Department of State Publication 8476 (Washington: U.S.G.P.O., 1969), p. 25.

66. "Russ Send Libya Tanks, Other Arms," *Los Angeles Times*, 23 July 1970, p. 1; "Soviet Tanks Delivered to Libya," *San Francisco Chronicle*, 23 July 1970, p. 1; and, "Major Identified Arms Agreements, July 1969-June 1970," *The Military Balance 1970-1971* (London: Institute of Strategic Studies, 1970), p. 116.

67. "For the Attention of Our Readers: As from September 1970, *Soviet Military Review* now appearing in English and French will also be published in Arabic." *Soviet Military Review* (Moscow) No. 8 (68), August 1970, p. 62. See articles in subsequent issues on the requirements for desert warfare, for example: Colonels A. Sidorchuk and M. Gordienko, "Combat Operations in a Desert," and Colonel A. Rodin, "Fire and Maneuver Support: Operations of an Artillery Battalion in A Desert," *ibid.*, No. 12 (72), December 1970, pp. 18-30.

Mr. Mintoff, the Premier of Malta, was on record quite early as stating that he would not allow a Soviet base in Malta.[68] Soviet merchant ships however were welcomed for the port fees and repair bills incurred when using Maltese yards,[69] some of the facilities of which had been paid for by the People's Republic of China. In June 1978, the Soviet Union posted a delegation to Malta, not the first of its kind to visit Malta since the island's independence. This delegation came to entertain Mr. Mintoff's requests for Soviet economic assistance and because two months before, Mr. Mintoff had forbidden Soviet shipping the use of Malta's harbors. That contretemps resulted from the Maltese discovery that Soviet vessels were undercutting Sea Malta, the Maltese shipping line, on the north Europe to Malta route.[70] The Maltese Premier discovered what has been a commonplace for sometime: Soviet and East European merchant ships offer reduced rates for the more attractive cargoes, leaving less rewarding ones to Western shipping lines.[71] The Soviet Union conceded to Malta, however, a raise in Soviet shipping rates in the ports served by Sea Malta, so Maltese shipping would suffer less of a disadvantage. As a further concession, the Soviet Union initiated a weekly service to Malta by Aeroflot in order to encourage tourism for the island. The value of the latter to Malta's tourist industry may seem nominal in light of the fact that Air Malta operates twenty-two flights a week to Western European cities and is served by fifteen flights a week by various West European airlines.[72] It is difficult to picture scores of Soviet citizens lining up at an Aeroflot ticket office in downtown Moscow to make reservations for flights to Malta. Like Aeroflot's service to Havana, Pyongyang, Hanoi, Tripoli, and Spitsbergen, service to Malta may not be for your conventional tourist.[73]

The inauguration of air service from Moscow to Malta coincided with the opening of a Soviet trade office in Valetta, Malta, in order to improve trade between the two countries. It is understood that the next step is to be the

68. *Report on World Affairs: A Summary of World Events in June, July, September* 1971, Vol. 52, No. 3, October 1971, p. 314.

69. "U.S.S.R. Ambassador Meets with the Prime Minister of Malta," *Pravda,* 21 August 1971, p. 5: "The Ambassador informed the Maltese government that the appropriate Soviet departments have been instructed to dry-dock Soviet ships in Malta for repairs." In *The Current Digest of the Soviet Press,* Vol. XXIII, No. 34, 21 September 1971, p. 19; and, see "Malta's Political Switch Hints a Mediterranean 'Cuba,'" *Christian Science Monitor,* 28 June 1971, p. 1.

70. "Malta: Prospects of Aid from Soviets No Brighter," *To the Point,* 16 June 1978, p. 16.

71. See Verband Deutscher Reeder newsletter cited in "More Red Sails," *To The Point International* (Antwerp), Vol. 2, No. 19, 20 September 1975, pp. 33-34.

72. Air services to and from Malta are described in *Traveller's Guide to the Middle East* (London: IC Magazines Limited, 1978), p. 216.

73. The opening of scheduled air service to Spitsbergen by Aeroflot is remarked in "Kremlin Sees Norse Isle as Vital: Russ Begin Spitsbergen Air Service," *Los Angeles Times,* 10 September 1975, p. 5; for Peking's view of the Spitsbergen service see "Penetrating Every Nook and Corner," *Peking Review,* No. 15, 9 April 1976, pp. 17-18: "It is obvious that the Soviet Union wants to turn Spitsbergen Islands into a forward base for establishing a sea passage for its fleet and menacing Europe from the northern flank."

upgrading of the Soviet diplomatic mission in the Maltese capital.[74] On 1 April 1979, H.M.S. *London* departed the Grand Harbor, Valetta, carrying the last British Flag Officer to serve as officer commanding, Royal Naval Forces, Malta. This departure ended British ties to the island and severed the island's indirect links with NATO. One of those present for the celebration was Colonel Qaddafi of Libya.[75]

As a prelude to the withdrawal of British forces from Malta, Mr. Mintoff had demanded that France, Italy, Algeria, and Libya enter an alliance to guarantee Malta's future after the British departure. Libya and Algeria agreed "readily, unstintingly and unreservedly." France and Italy did *not*.[76]

A New Strategic Axis

Yugoslavia and Libya are both "neutral" and "non-aligned." Within the framework of their professed neutrality and non-alignment they permit the Soviet Union the use of their territory for military purposes. Libya, for example, permits Soviet naval aviation to operate from Libyan airfields and to operate radar and electronic monitoring stations within Libyan territory but for support of Soviet naval and air operations in the Mediterranean. During the Ethiopian war against Somalia and against the Eritrean liberation movement, Libyan airfields were used by Soviet transport aircraft en route to the battle zone with Soviet and East German arms and personnel.[77] In July 1977, during the brief fighting between Libya and Egypt, Soviet MiG-25s conducted reconnaissance over Egypt from Libyan bases.[78]

In November 1977, the Soviet Union tested its capability to airlift three divisions into Africa or the Middle East "within ten hours . . . and occupy by surprise and without major difficulty several countries of those regions." One of the routes used was via Tripoli, Libya.[79]

Yugoslavia permits its ports to service Soviet warships and its airfields, which have presumably been enlarged for the purpose, to stage Soviet military airlifts through to Africa.[80]

74. "Sowjets drangen starker ins Mittelmeeer: Russiches 'Handelsburo' auf Malta," *Soldat und Technik*, February 1979, p. 96.

75. "Malta severs military links with Britain," *South China Morning Post* (Hong Kong), 1 April 1979, p. 5.

76. "Malta: Mintoff gets Bashy over aid Alliance," *To the Point*, Vol. 7, No. 43, 27 October 1978, p. 19.

77. For the East German role in Africa, see "Moscow's Next target in Africa," *London Sunday Telegraph*, 20 February 1977, carried as a "paid advertisement" in *The Washington Post*, 15 March 1977, p. A 7; and, "East Germany's Menacing New 'Africa Korps,'" *South China Morning Post*, 30 July 1978, p. 2.

78. "Soviet Navy Bears down on NATO," *The Christian Science Monitor*, 2 August 1977, p. 4.

79. Report from *Le Figaro* (Paris) cited in "Soviet Airlift Test Reported," *San Francisco Chronicle*, 23 June 1978, p. 17; operations described in greater detail in "Russia's Airlift Warning to the West," *Foreign Report*, No. 1517, 21 December 1977, pp. 1-3.

80. Work on Yugoslav air fields reported in "Dubrovnik Airport Runway to be Reconstructed,"

The ease with which the "non-aligned" nations fit into Soviet strategic deployments, and the apparent willingness with which such nations accommodate over-flights, transit stops, and support operations contrast with the difficulty the United States had in getting twelve F-15s to Saudi Arabia at the height of the Iran crisis. The Secretary of State had to intervene personally in order to gain permission for some of the aircraft to land in Spain, an ally of the United States, on their return journey. And, it is said that those that landed at Lisbon were required to do so at dusk "to avoid notice." Portugal is also an ally of the United States.[81]

Colonel Qaddafi's presence in Malta to celebrate the departure of the Royal Navy after so many years, was not simply a *pro forma* welcome of one more country to the ranks of the "non-aligned" and "neutral." From the time that Mr. Mintoff first became Premier of Malta, he and Colonel Qaddafi have exchanged frequent visits. During a visit to Malta in December 1974, the Colonel told the Maltese that since the ancestors of the Maltese had been Phoenicians, and while the Phoenicians had been Arab, Libyans and Maltese had common ancestors and therefore a common destiny.[82]

While such a notion might have run against the grain of the predominantly Roman Catholic population of Malta, Malta has become almost a dependent of Libya. As might be expected, it is Libyan oil that the Maltese government sells to the Maltese people. Eight months before the Royal Navy left Malta, Libyan air force personnel flew five military helicopters into the old Royal Air Force base at Hal Far, Malta, and began its conversion to a helicopter base.[83] It hardly seems necessary to add, that following a five-day visit to Moscow in May 1979, Tito stopped off in Malta on his way home from visiting Algeria and Libya. He said, in Valletta, that the closure of foreign military bases on Malta represented an important victory for the "Non-Aligned Movement."[84]

If Libya and Yugoslavia find it useful or necessary to serve Soviet strategic purposes in the Mediterranean, the Middle East and Africa, it seems unlikely that tiny Malta will be permitted to find otherwise. That is especially so

---

POLITIKA (Belgrade), 7 January 1975, p. 6, cited in *FBIS*, Vol. II, *Eastern Europe*, 14 January 1975, p. I 10; "Zagreb Airport Reopens," Belgrade TANJUG in English 1322 GMT, 22 August 1974, cited in *ibid.*, 26 August 1974, p. I 3; and see concerning Soviet-built airfield at Petrovac near Skopje and the airfield at Zabljak, built to accommodate the Soviet Antonov transport (An-22), in Axel Hornhager, "Yugoslavia's Defense: The Logic of Politics," *International Defense Review* (Geneva).

81. U.S. to Display Air Muscle in Saudi Arabia: Plans 'Fly-in' of F-15s at Arabs' Request to Show Concern on Iran," *Los Angeles Times*, 11 January 1979, p. 1; and, "42 Planes Were Involved Getting DOD's F-15s to Saudi Arabia," *Armed Forces Journal International*, March 1979, p. 12.

82. "Libya," in *The Report on World Affairs July to December 1974*, Vol. 55, Nos. 3 and 4, p. 8; and, "Libya-Malta: Qaddafi a-wooing," *To The Point International*, Vol. 3, No. 14, 12 July 1976, pp. 21-22.

83. "Chronology: Europe," *Strategic Survey 1978*, p. 129; and, "Malta: Mintoff gets Bashy over aid alliance," *To The Point*, Vol. 7, No. 43, 27 October 1978, p. 19.

84. "Tito to Visit Libya and Malta," *The Christian Science Monitor*, 25 May 1979, p. 2; "Tito Praises Maltese Move," *San Francisco Chronicle*, 6 June 1979, p. 50; but see also, "Yugoslavia: Assurance for Tito by non-aligned states," *To The Point*, Vol. 8, No. 28, 15 June 1979, p. 14.

when both Libya and Yugoslavia serve as the procurers of Maltese favors for the men of the Kremlin. The West may well pretend or even believe that nothing has really changed save that Malta has become both "neutral" and "non-aligned."[85] Just as one hears that there are no Soviet bases in Cuba, Vietnam, Libya, or Yugoslavia, one shall hear soon of none in Malta, as well.

Perhaps only Albania in the Mediterranean is prepared to face the new situation with candor. The regime in Albania, unreconstructedly Stalinist without apology, began to draw away from Yugoslavia when Soviet naval vessels started using the Yugoslav port of Tivat, a port whose facilities Albania had occasionally used. *Zeri i Popullit,* the party newspaper warned, in January 1977, that the Soviet Union was attempting to recapture the sphere of influence in the Balkans once held by Tsarist Russia. This was being attempted through the use of military threats and offers of economic aid. "They intend," the newspaper said, "to get their hands on Greece in order to extend their railways onto its territory and thus link their Mediterranean fleet to their capital."[86]

In 1978 when Albania turned away from China, its ally for sixteen years, it may be that Enver Hoxha, the Albanian dictator, was merely recognizing the new reality in the Mediterranean: the Warsaw Pact has advanced its strategic perimeter westward into the Central Mediterranean along an axis extending from northern Europe into Africa. In the words of Alexei Kosygin, spoken in Libya in 1975: "This has become possible thanks to the fact that the overall balances of forces in the world has changed in favor of socialism and of all progressive, peace-loving forces."[87] It should be noted that one of the changes in "the overall balance of forces" mentioned by Comrade Kosygin, at the time, was effected by the "wonderful victories" of North Vietnam, that country so exemplary of "all progressive and peace-loving forces."

Africa and European Defense

It is not inconsequential for the peoples of Africa and the West that the Soviet Union, with its Cuban and East European allies, has become the paramount power on the African continent. If the "liberation" of Africa is not yet complete, it is not because the West has placed any notable obstacles in the pathways of the "liberators." What is of greater and more immediate

85. "Malta Announces Neutrality After 1979 termination of base agreement with Britain," in "Chronology," 31 August 1976, *Strategic Survey 1976*, p. 123.

86. *Zeri i Popullit* (Tirana), 4 January 1977, as cited in "Albania Warns of Soviet Meddling in Balkans," *The Japan Times* (Tokyo), 6 January 1977, p. 4; and, see "Soviet-Yugoslav port deal casts shadow over Albania," *The Christian Science Monitor*, 23 November 1976, p. 4.

87. "Kosygin Visits Libya and Tunisia: Talks with Jallud in Tripoli: In a Friendly Atmosphere," *Pravda*, 14 May 1975, pp. 1 and 4, in *The Current Digest of the Soviet Press*, Vol. XXVII, No. 20, 11 June 1975, pp. 10-14.

consequence for the Free World as well as Africa, is the damage that has been inflicted on the capabilities of the Western Democracies to defend Europe. To the extent that the Western Democracies have permitted the "overall balance of forces" to be altered against them, the damage has been self-inflicted. The United States need not have betrayed its allies at Suez in 1956, in order to purchase the goodwill of the Soviet Union. The worth of that goodwill was revealed in Cuba in 1962. Canada, Japan, and the countries of Western Europe, need not to have considered the defense of Cambodía, Laos, and South Vietnam to be no more than the perverseness of some American presidents. The defeat of the United States and its Australian, New Zealand, Philippine and South Korean allies, did nothing to strengthen the Free World, to promote international stability, or to benefit the peoples of Indo-China. Rather, the fall of Indo-China to the Communists gave every reason to suppose that the West had grown weary of the effort to defend itself and that the next time its defense would be even weaker. The success of the Soviet campaign in Africa has done nothing to dispel such a notion. As Adolph Hitler said:

> The wise victor will, if possible, always impose his claim on the defeated people stage by stage, dealing with the people that has grown defeated, and this is every people which has voluntarily submitted to force.
>
> He may then rely on the fact that in not one of these further acts of oppression will it seem sufficient reason to take up arms again.[88]

It is not just that the new strategic axis constructed by the Soviet Union through Austria to Libya would make it easier for the Soviet Union to conquer Western Europe in a war. The new strategic axis opens further options for strategic progress in the Mediterranean while reducing those of the Western Alliance for the defense of Europe's southern flank. Recall once again the circumstances of the Middle East War of 1973. The Soviet Union decided the outcome of that war because it threatened intervention on the side of Egypt if the Israeli forces would not desist from destruction of the Egyptian Army. The United States was unwilling to risk conflict in an area where it enjoyed no strategic advantage. Soviet aircraft could dominate the Eastern Mediterranean to such an extent that U.S. aircraft carriers could not have survived to provide air cover for U.S. forces or for the defense of Israel. The peace that followed Israel's defeat not only deprived Israel of the Sinai and left Egyptian forces across the Suez Canal, it reopened the canal to grant

88. Cited in "Eden Quotes *Mein Kampf* to Enlighten Commons," *New York Times*, 16 March 1939, p. 16. Eden's speech in Commons was made on the occasion of the German occupation of Czechoslovakia on 15 March 1939 in violation of Hitler's solemn promise of October 1939, that he had no further territorial demands to make in Europe.

strategic mobility to the Soviet fleets from the Mediterranean and Black Sea. Not only is Israel less capable now, than it was before the 1973 war, to defend its own territory until help comes, but also Egypt is now isolated from its Arab allies, while Soviet, Cuban and Ethiopian forces are poised at the borders of the Sudan where Libyan trained guerrillas cross at will to support civil insurrection against the Sudanese government. Libya sits with its Soviet ally on Egypt's western border seeking the overthrow of Anwar Sadat without whom the so-painfully drawn treaty between Israel and Egypt cannot endure. Is the United States now more capable of intervention on behalf of Israel, and now Egypt too, than it was capable of intervening on behalf of Israel in 1973? The United States has fewer aircraft carriers to risk now than it had in 1973. The U.S. armed forces are smaller by 300,000 than they were in 1973; the navy has fewer surface ships and submarines than it had in 1973; Warsaw Pact forces have increased since 1973, and the balance of strategic nuclear forces now favors the Soviet Union. Iran was an ally in 1973, now it is not. The basing of Soviet ships in the Adriatic, Libya and eventually Malta, covered by Soviet aircraft based in Yugoslavia, Libya, and Malta will have done nothing but reduce the capability of the United States to intervene in the Eastern Mediterranean. Can all of these things have failed to impress themselves on NATO members in that region?

Turkey

In 1968, the Turkish Labor Party opposed Turkey's membership in NATO:

> We [Turkey] must disassociate ourselves from NATO right now while the climate of opinion throughout the world is quite favorable for such action. . . . NATO offers Turkey no safeguards. . . . Why then did we come to believe that NATO—or in reality the United States—would safeguard and defend us? We just took America's word for it. . . .[89]

These sentiments were voiced before the British and Americans pulled out of Libya to be replaced by the Russians; before Ethiopia joined the Soviet camp; before the Americans pulled out of Morocco; before the U.S. embargo on arms to Turkey; before the American defeat in Vietnam; before the regime change in Afghanistan; and before the revolution in Iran. Turkey has been exploring more friendly relations with the Soviet Union, and accepting economic assistance from that country. Is it a wonder that the Turkish government feels compelled to consult the Soviet Union before granting permission to the United States to use Turkish bases for U-2 aircraft with which to monitor Soviet compliance with SALT?

89. Behice Boran, in *MILLIYET* (Istanbul), cited in *Atlas*, July 1968, p. 34.

It cannot have helped Turkish sensibilities to have had the United States spend enormous efforts in personalized diplomacy to attain a peace treaty between Egypt and Israel while declining to expend similar efforts to settle the acute conflict between two supposedly valuable allies, Greece and Turkey

Greece, for its part, has begun to exchange naval visits with the Soviet Union and contemplates whether to continue its connection with NATO.[90]

How much more difficult it is now for Turks to believe in NATO, than it was in 1968 when the Turkish Labor Party argued for withdrawal of Turkey from NATO; and, how much more susceptible must Turkey now be to the kinds of economic blandishments and military threats which the Soviet Union seems so successfully to have used to co-opt Yugoslavia.

The strategic axis from Rijeka down the Adriatic, across the Ionian Sea to Malta and on to Libya passes just eastward of Sicily. In Sicily a separatist movement presses for independence from Italy: the national Sicilian Front. It is not incredible to suppose that Libya, Malta, and the Soviet Union would assist such a movement when the island of Sicily is so close to their strategic axis. Similar movements exist in Sardinia and on the French island of Corsica. It is not even improbable that the Soviet Union would miss the chance to create more "neutral" and "non-aligned" island-states in the Mediterranean. If the Soviet Union would support separatist elements in Yugoslavia, a fellow communist state, one hardly imagines the Soviet Union would hesitate doing the same within Italian or French territory. It is, perhaps, easy to forget, that the Soviet Union sent volunteers all the way to Spain during that country's civil war. That was well before the Soviet Union could lay claim to being a Mediterranean power.[91]

Italy

The advance of the Soviet perimeter in the Mediterranean makes political events in Italy crucial to Allied fortunes in the Western Mediterranean. A coalition government in Italy that permits the Italian Communists to move Italy away from NATO would be decisive. While one knows that Italian Communists are not really Communists like other Communists, it is not certain that the Italian Communists know it. While the West waits for them to find out, the Soviet Union will have gained a strategic advantage of incomparable value.

The strategic change for Italy need not be accompanied by the raising of the Hammer and Sickle over the Vatican or the declaration of a People's Republic of Italy. The change can come in a dozen other ways. Perhaps there

90. "Greece's Soviet connection," *The Christian Science Monitor,* September 14, 1978, p. 4.

91. "5 Italian Separatist Groups Gain Strength: Sicily, Sardinia Pressing for Eventual Independence from Rome," *Los Angeles Times,* 8 July 1979, p. 10, p. 1-A.

would be a guerrilla operation in southern Italy while the Red Brigade paralyzes the northern cities amidst general strikes, slowdowns, and interruptions in vital services. The Red Brigade and guerrillas are supported by arms landed across the beaches on the Adriatic coast, with the Soviet Mediterranean Fleet standing off-shore. Or arms are flown in from Yugoslavia, up from Malta, or across from Libya. Left-wing groups fight right-wing groups in the streets and all fight the police and army who are caught between. Astute investigative reporting reveals long-standing ties between the CIA and the Italian government to the shock and amazement of all decent-thinking peoples. The Italian police and the army are discovered to be doing to the terrorists and guerrillas what the terrorists have been doing all along to their innocent victims. The U.S. Ambassador to the United Nations points out how many political prisoners there are in Italian jails, many of whom are innocent of any wrong-doing save perhaps the bombing of a railroad station, destruction of a pipeline, or the kidnapping of a public servant or industrialist. Full-page advertisements appear in the *New York Times, Washington Post,* and other distinguished newspapers, with the names of prominent American thinkers, humanists, and just plain folks, deploring police repression in Italy while reminding those who may have forgotten that Mussolini was a fascist and an Italian. The State Department joins the World Council of Churches and other charitable organizations in condemning the carelessness of human rights being displayed by the Italian government in putting down the insurrection. The Soviet government and the "non-aligned" nations express their deep sympathy for the plight of the Italian people and warn that any foreign interference in Italy's internal affairs will constitute a grave provocation to all peace-loving peoples throughout the world.

Libya places an embargo on oil to Italy until the Italian government changes its ways. The government reads the handwriting on the wall and resigns in favor of a government of national reconciliation made up of moderate revolutionaries, some socialists, and a communist or two just to be fair. The price of national reconciliation is withdrawal of Italy from NATO and a declaration of Italian neutrality and non-alignment.

Circumstances, both fortuitous and contrived, have thus turned Italy away from the West. The contrived circumstances are fostered by the proximity of the Soviet strategic axis, the willing help of those within Italy who serve the Soviet cause, and the unwary assistance of those who think any change an improvement. However such a change might come about, the proximity of Soviet power and influence in the central Mediterranean would discourage any substantial response by NATO, as would the reluctance of the Western powers to interfere in the internal affairs of a fellow democracy.

That may seem a fanciful scenario which could never be played out in Italy. After all Italy is not Ethiopia, Iran, South Vietnam, or Nicaragua. It is hardly optimistic to suggest that what has happened in one country can happen in another, even if it can. But there may well be a kind of cascade effect about such things. The creation of the Libyan Socialist Republic in 1969, did nothing to stabilize matters elsewhere in the world, rather it has made uneasy the rulers of the un-converted countries that border Libya. The "Socialist Revolution" in Algeria and Libya threatens the regimes in Tunisia[92] and Morocco; Chad and the Sudan are granted no time in which to get their affairs in order, before they are subject to the attentions of their radical neighbors.

It would be far more difficult than it is, to bring Italy away from NATO if Libya and Yugoslavia were firmly anti-Soviet and pro-Western; if Italy did not get much of its oil from Libya; if the Soviet Mediterranean Fleet could not base in the Adriatic and use Algerian and Libyan ports; and, if the Royal Navy had not left Malta.

The changes that have occurred in the Mediterranean have been chiefly *political* although their effects have been *strategic*. Nowhere has the Soviet Union had to wage war to change the strategic circumstances in its favor, although wars in the area have frequently opened opportunities for new strategic gains. Every change favorable to the Soviet Union has reduced NATO's capability to defend Western Europe. But *none* of these changes—strategic gains for the Soviet Union—has been paid for by a price anywhere near commensurate with its value.[93]

The Situation: Past and Present

One may see the strategic role of the Mediterranean for the defense of Western Europe from what occurred there during the second World War. In September 1939, the Allies dominated the Mediterranean from Syria to Gibraltar, despite the fact that Italy, though as yet not at war, was pro-German and therefore hostile to the Allied cause. When Italy entered the war as France fell in June 1940, the strategic situation drastically shifted against Britain in the Mediterranean. The superb Italian fleet now entered the war, while the French Mediterranean Fleet was no longer on the British side; the Italian army in Libya threatened Egypt and the Italian Air Force kept Malta

92. See for example, "Tunisian Reports Libyan Death Plot," *Los Angeles Times*, 23 March 1976, p. 10.

93. An illustration of the cost-to-value relationship in strategy might be the Japanese attack on the Philippines in December 1941. Acquisition of the Philippines provided positions from which to cover the flank of Japanese lines of communications to Indo-China, Malaya and the Netherlands East Indies, denied the allies the use of the islands for an advanced base for the attack on the Japanese Home Islands, and, furnished a central position from which to reinforce the Japanese Mandated Islands. The Philippines in Japanese hands then were a strategic asset. The fact that the Philippine and American forces held out until May 1942, tied down Japanese sea, air and ground units that would otherwise have been used to seize territory in Australia before the Allies were prepared to defend that country. The cost to the Japanese lay in the men, ships and planes lost to take the Philippines and in the delay to the development of their strategic operations, a delay that permitted the Allies to meet and stop the Japanese at Guadalcanal.

under bombing attack. British Imperial and Commonwealth troops held the Middle East and defeated the Italian army in Libya, while the Mediterranean Fleet based on Alexandria and Force "H" based on Gibraltar kept the Italian Fleet in check.

The situation altered dramatically again in 1941 when Germany seized Yugoslavia, Greece, and the Greek Island of Crete. The loss of troops, aircraft, and ships in the futile attempt to defend Greece and Sicily and North Africa shifted the balance of air strength against Britain in the Mediterranean.

British naval forces and convoys could move east from Gibraltar only at great cost by fighting their way through under constant air attack from Italian bases on the mainland and Sicily, and from German air bases in Greece and Libya. Yet the Axis did not control the Mediterranean. Egypt could be reinforced from around the Cape of Good Hope and through the Suez Canal, and air reinforcements could come across country from Takoradi on the Gold Coast via the Sudan to Egypt. The British and Maltese defied Axis attacks of unparalleled ferocity on the island, so that Malta remained throughout the critical period an incomparable asset. The 10th Submarine Flotilla operated from Malta against the German and Italian supply corridor to Tunisia and Libya.[94] Those operations helped to prevnt Rommel from accumulating sufficient strength and supplies to defeat the Eight Army in the Western Desert.[95]

The tenuous British hold on the Mediterranean, which denied ultimate control to the Axis, was made possible by the use of Gibraltar for Force "H", the incredible tenacity of the Malta defense, and the British hold on Alexandria, the Delta, and the Suez Canal. The British held Gibraltar because the Spanish Dictator, Francisco Franco, resisted German pressures to join the Axis and refused to permit German forces passage across Spain to attack it;[96] and, because French Morocco, although under Vichy administration, never entered the war until it was liberated by American forces in 1942. The failure of the Axis powers to secure the Mediterranean and North Africa before the United States entered the war permitted an Allied build-up in Egypt, Morocco and Algeria that led to expulsion of the Axis forces from North Africa.

94. An account of 10th Flotilla operations against Axis supply lines is given in Rear Admiral G. W. G. Simpson, *Periscope View: A Professional Autobiography* (London: Macmillan, 1972); and, in Alastair Mars, *British Submarines at War, 1939-1945* (Annapolis: U.S. Naval Institute, 1971). Some other operations of the Royal Navy based on Malta are in Peter C. Smith and Edwin Walker, *The Battles of the Malta Striking Forces* (Annapolis: U.S. Naval Institute, 1974).

95. See for example, 2 November 1942, the Panzer Army's supply situation: "That day we had fired off 450 tons of ammunition; only 190 tons had arrived brought by three destroyers to Tobruk." *The Rommel Papers* (New York: Harcourt, Brace and Company, 1953), p. 318.

96. See in particular Letter: Hitler to Franco, 6 February 1941, and Letter: General Franco to Hitler, El Pardo, 26 February 1941, in *The Spanish Government and the Axis: Official German Documents, Dept. of State Publication* 2483, European Series, 8 March 1946, pp. 28-35.

The purpose of Allied landings in North Africa in November 1942 and of the British offensive from Egypt after the second battle of El Alamein, at the end of October, was expressed in the Directive to the Commander-in-Chief, of the Allied Expeditionary Force:

> The President and the Prime Minister have agreed that combined military operations be directed against Africa . . . with a view to gaining, in conjunction with Allied Forces in the Middle East, complete control of North Africa from the Atlantic to the Red Sea.

The landings at Oran, Algiers, Tunis, and Casablanca were to be made "in order that appropriate bases for continued and intensified air, ground, and sea operations will be readily available."[97] The objectives underlying that directive were elaborated by Major General L. H. Brereton, U.S. Army Middle East Air Forces commander. In his strategic estimate of the Middle Eastern war, issued on 5 August 1942, before the Anglo-American landings in Northwest Africa, he indicated three major objectives for the Allied air forces:

> Assist in the destruction of Rommel's *Afrika Korps;*
>
> Secure sea and air communications on and over the Mediterranean;
>
> Carry out a sustained air offensive against Italy, the oil installations at Ploesti and in the Caucasus if the latter should fall under Axis control.[98]

In the process of "cleansing the North African shore," in Winston Churchill's words, the Mediterranean was to be freed of the Axis "releasing large armies and air forces for new enterprises" while eliminating one of the Axis partners, Italy, from the war.[99]

Even as the Axis was being cleared from North Africa, the Allied air offensive was launched from North African airfields against Italy and targets in Greece and the Balkans. North Africa became the staging area for the invasion of Sicily in July and of Italy itself in September, the invasion of southern France, following the Allied landings in Normandy was staged from North Africa and Italy, supported by air operations from Italy.

As should be evident, North Africa and the Mediterranean bear a strategic relationship to the defense of Western Europe. Failure of the Axis powers completely to dominate the Mediterranean hastened Axis defeat. Allied suc-

97. Directive for CinC, Allied Expeditionary Force, as approved at 36th mtg Combined Chiefs of Staff, 13 August 42, Tab 26a, Item 1, Exec 5, cited in Maurice Matloff and Edwin M. Snell, *Strategic Planning for Coalition Warfare, 1941-1942,* in Sub-series: *The War Department* in Series: *United States Army in World War II* (Washington, D.C.: Department of the Army, 1953), p. 291.

98. Cited in entry for 5 August 1942, in *The Army Air Forces in World War II: Combat Chronology, 1941-45* (Washington, D.C.: U.S.G.P.O., 1973), p. 31.

99. Denis Richards and Hilary St. George Saunders, *Royal Air Force, 1939-1945,* Volume II: *The Fight Avails* (London: H.M.S.O., 1954), p. 274.

cess in regaining dominance in the Mediterranean exposed all of Southern Europe to Allied operations from bases themselves secure from Axis attack. Despite the strategic setbacks suffered by Britain in the Mediterranean, she managed to hold Trans-Jordan, Iraq, Cyprus, Egypt, and above all the Suez Canal, in the east. Both Malta and Gibraltar remained British. Even so it required three years of fighting, first by Britain alone, and then by Britain with the United States, to cleanse the Mediterranean of Axis military power.

The Mediterranean today is no longer a British protectorate. Of the countries that border the Mediterranean none is, by itself, capable of denying the Soviet Union the use of the Mediterranean as an area of military operations. The United States Fleet remains in the Mediterranean on sufferance, the sufferance of the Soviet Union and its vassals. According to the words of a Congressional report, the great convenience of the Sixth Fleet, "as a suitable alternative to a permanent land base," lies in the fact that it "is mobile and can be withdrawn expeditiously." That is what the Sixth Fleet can do! What it cannot do, according to the same report, is "sustain extended military operations, [and] support certain logistical operations such as the military resupply of Israel. . . ." Beyond that the Fleet is tied to home ports for maintenance and re-supply, home ports in the United States that is. The report goes on to suggest: "While a land base may infer [*sic*] permanence and stability, the Sixth Fleet may represent, quite literally, a floating symbol in a region of the world where symbols and gestures may mean more than immutable realities."[100]

Well, there you are. The Sixth Fleet is a symbol of United States interests in the Mediterranean and of the strength and determination of the Free World to defend itself—so long are there is not any trouble, in which case the Fleet can be expeditiously withdrawn, to serve, no doubt, somewhere else, where there is not any trouble, and where symbolism can pass for reality.

While the strategic reach of NATO into the eastern Mediterranean becomes less and less believable, that of the Soviet Union becomes more and more visible. This situation cannot help but affect the outlook of both Greece and Turkey who, like Israel and Egypt, become more and more isolated from the West and therefore more susceptible to Soviet influence in whatever form. It will not have escaped the notice of these countries that in the next great crisis in the eastern Mediterranean, American aircraft carriers will confront much resistance in getting past Malta in either direction, whether to intervene eastward or to escape westward. With American strategic assets

100. *United States Foreign Policy Objectives and Overseas Military Installations*, prepared for the Committee on Foreign Relations, United States Senate, by the Congressional Research Service, Library of Congress, April 1979, p. 83.

having grown so slender, it becomes difficult to believe that the United States would expend any of them just to save an ally in the eastern Mediterranean.

If Israel is attacked again as it was in 1973, its survival will depend, as it did in 1973, on the equipment and munitions it can get from the United States. There is no way of getting the equipment and munitions to Israel without passing through air and sea space subject to Soviet control. There is certainly no reason to suppose that the United States would risk war with the Soviet Union just for the survival of Israel. Egypt can fall under Soviet influence, once again, as easily as Anwar Sadat can be assassinated. In any NATO-Soviet war, it is almost certain that NATO will lack the capability to reinforce either Turkey or Greece. And, both countries, aware of the fact, will incline toward making the best accommodation possible with the Soviet Union. The lines at any American service station tell one how things stand for NATO elsewhere in the Middle East.

Soviet air and naval power will control the eastern Mediterranean and reach beyond to the west of Malta. Allied air fields in Italy will, if Italy remains in NATO, fall within easy range of Soviet land-based missiles, Soviet aircraft flying from Libya, Yugoslavia, and Bulgaria, and the ships of the Soviet Mediterranean Fleet, based from Latakia westward to the Sicilian Channel and beyond.[101]

Where, during the Second World War, the African hinterland remained beyond Axis control, that hinterland is today beyond Allied control. Those African countries that have not already succumbed to "Liberation" are so fragile of constitution as to make their submission little more than a matter of time.

In 1941, the assault on and capture of Crete cost the German *Wehrmacht* at least 5,000 and perhaps as many as 17,000 casualties along with the loss of 200 combat aircraft. The time lost and the casualties suffered to seize Crete weakened the German effort to secure Syria and Iraq, and delayed the attack on Russia so that the German army reached the outskirts of Moscow too late to capture the city before winter set in.[102]

Places as strategically important as Crete was in 1941, or more so, have fallen to Soviet control or beneath Soviet influence without resistance from the West and virtually without cost to the Soviet Union. What the Axis had to expend in men, ships, and aircraft, to seize in the Mediterranean during World War II, have fallen to the Soviet Union or its hirelings virtually

101. "Seven Mediterranean Ports Open to Russian Fleet: 6 Other Anchorages Also in Use, Study Shows, Power Balance Called 'Precarious,'" *Los Angeles Times,* 28 February 1979, p. 4.

102. The relation of Crete to the defense of Moscow is described in *A Sailor's Odyssey: The Autobiography of Admiral of the Fleet Viscount Cunningham of Hyndhope* (London: Hutchinson & Co., Ltd., 1951), p. 392; German losses in the capture of Crete are given in S. W. C. Pack, *The Battle for Crete* (Annapolis: U.S. Naval Institute, 1973).

unnoticed and through default. Should war come to Europe, Soviet resources need not be expended to secure the Mediterranean but can be invested elsewhere to secure even greater strategic advantages.

VIII. Defending Europe

THE SOVIET UNION HAS MANAGED THE CONSTRUCTION OF A STRATEGIC AXIS STRETCHING SOUTHWARD THROUGH AUSTRIA AND YUGOSLAVIA INTO NORTH AFRICA. The northern portion of that axis is of no less interest than that which now rests on Libya.

Austria and West German Defense

The forward edge of the Warsaw Pact battle area rests on the Rhineland and on the Dutch and Belgium frontiers with Germany, while the line of departure for Warsaw Pact forces on the Central front of NATO rests on that twelve foot high fence that stretches from Lubeck Bay in the north to the Plockenstein (Plechy), in the South, where the West German, Austrian and Czech borders meet, northeast of Passau.[1]

The Austrian border with West Germany extends southwestward toward a common border with Switzerland at the Bodensee north of Bregenz, 300 kilometers or about 200 miles away. At its nearest point, the border is less than forty miles from the heart of Munich. That nearest point is the crossing at the Achenpass, about fifty miles by good highway from Munich. Just east of the Achenpass, about 25 miles, is the major highway crossing by the Inn River at Kiefersfelden. This highway, "E 86," connects Innsbruck (via "E 17") to the Munich-Salzburg autobahn, thirty-six miles by highway from Munich and perhaps twelve miles from the Austrian border. There are a number of other crossing points into Germany between the Czech border and Salzburg and beyond, from minor regional roads to major highways, but almost all of which enter the great highway network of which Munich is the hub. Major and lesser highways radiate from Munich in all directions making Munich a central tactical objective in any military campaign fought south-to-north or east-to-west in Bavaria.

1. *Freytag-Berndt Touristen Wanderkarte,* 1:100,000, No. 26: Muhlviertel und Bohmerwald (Vienna) 461-66; and, *Munchen,* 1:500,000, Ausgabe 3-DMG, Serie M 444, Sheet 33, Militargeographischer Amt, 1966.

A glance at the map with that fact in mind illuminates the strategic importance of Austria to the defense of southern Germany and the Upper Rhineland. Recall here that under the provisions of the Austrian State Treaty and the Austrian Constitution, Austria is neutral.[2] To defend that neutrality, Austria maintains an army of 33,000 men of which 18,000 are conscripts who serve for six months each. The Czech frontier, with Austria which stretches from Bratislava (Pressburg), 40 miles east of Vienna around to where the West German border begins with Austria, is 230 miles. The Hungarian border with Austria, which begins just south of Bratislava, extends for 144 miles. Presuming the entire Austrian army to be present for duty on any particular day, it would appear roughly as follows: 3 tank battalions, 6 mechanized infantry battalions, and 17 infantry battalions supported by nine artillery battalions.

The Austrian army has a total tank inventory of 150 M-47 tanks and 120 M-60 medium tanks. The Austrian tank forces fall into some kind of perspective if one considers that a single Soviet motorized rifle division has 266 tanks.[3] Evidently, the 23 infantry battalions and three tank battalions would have some difficulty covering a frontier 374 miles long.

A U.S. Army mechanized battalion, for example, is expected to have the capability to defend a front of up to 7,500 meters in width, when the battalion is operating as part of a brigade of a division, with tanks attached and artillery firing in direct and general support from division and higher echelons, and with tactical air support.[4]

Clearly the Austrian Army would be hard-pressed to defend even a stretch of the Austrian frontiers with Hungary and Czechoslovakia against Warsaw Pact Forces; should the 120 mile long frontier with Yugoslavia require defending as well, the task would be out of the question. The Soviet Southern Group of Armies keeps about two motorized rifle and two tank divisions in Hungary, while the Hungarian Army deploys, in peacetime, one tank and five motorized rifle divisions. By itself, the Hungarian Army is nearly three times as large as the Austrian Army. In Czechoslovakia, a Soviet Army, presumably the Seventh, holds three motorized rifle and two tank divisions, while the Czech Army deploys five tank and five motorized rifle divisions. Under such circumstances, the Austrian army with its 270 tanks might expect to face 6,140 Warsaw Pact medium tanks.

When it is suggested here that Austria remains independent at the pleasure of the Soviet Union, it is not merely a political aphorism, but a tactical and strategic reality. One comes to understand, however, why the Soviet

2. Dr. Axel Horshager, "Theory and Practice of Austrian Neutrality."
3. *The Military Balance, 1978-1979,* p. 29.
4. *Brigade and Division Operations* (Armor/Mechanized), FM 71-100 (Draft, March 1977), pp. 3-6.

Union finally accepted the Austrian State Treaty in 1955, and withdrew its forces from Austrian territory. As a neutral country, in the sense that Belgium was in 1914 and 1940, and Switzerland and Sweden are today, Austria may not belong to an alliance and is therefore not a member of the North Atlantic Treaty Organization. If Austria were to be occupied by forces of the Warsaw Pact, NATO has *no* commitment to come to Austria's defense, as it has to any of its members who might be attacked.

It is unlikely that the United States and its allies would be any more willing to risk war today to save Austria than France and Britain were in 1938 when Germany occupied Austria in violation of the Treaties of Versailles and St. Germain. Occupation of Austria by the German Army in 1938 gives an excellent example of how quickly that small country can be seized.

At 1600 hours (4 P.M.) on the 10th of March the warning order was given to the commander who would lead the movement of troops into Austria. These troops included the 2nd Panzer Division and the Waffen-SS Division, SS-*Leibstandarte* "Adolph Hitler"; the former located at Wurzburg, 250 miles from Passau on the Austrian border, while the SS Division was at Berlin, 428 miles from Passau. Thc two divisions moved across the border into Austria, an hour late, at 9 o'clock on the morning of the 12th of March. The advanced guard of two battalions passed through Linz 58 miles from Passau by noon with the main body arriving shortly thereafter. While the advanced guard continued on to St. Polten, 36 miles from Vienna, the 2nd Panzer and the SS Division were held up to greet Hitler's arrival at Linz. They did not leave that place until 9 o'clock in the evening, to arrive in Vienna at 1 o'clock on the morning of the 13th of March. The total elapsed time from the warning order to the panzer divisions, at their home stations, until the arrival in Vienna was forty-eight hours. The 2nd Panzer Division moved 420 miles and the Waffen-SS Division moved 598 miles during the forty-eight hours. There was no Austrian resistance to delay the German advance. There was, however, a thirteen-hour halt at the frontier while the various units were assembled and supplies of gasoline collected for the march. The main body of troops was held up in Linz, the highway to Vienna was torn up for repairs, and there was a snowstorm. Of the forty-eight hours then, marching time from the frontier to Vienna was only seven hours.[5]

In May 1945, divisions of the XIIth and XXth Corps of General Patton's Third Army invested Austria via crossings of the Inn River at Passau and

5. Details of the investment of Austria are in General Heinz Guderian, *Panzer Leader* (New York: E. P. Dutton, 1952), pp. 49-53; mileages, where not given in Guderian's book are taken from Map: *Deutschland, Osterreich Benelux,* 1; 1,000,000 Michelin No. 987, 3d Edition, 1977 which has both the old roads Passau-Linz-Vienna and the newer motor highways.

Branau. Against scattered resistance which held up the advance and which required the artillery to deploy in support of the armor and tanks, the advance took less than a day.[6]

The relative ease with which armies may march into Austria from Germany are some indication of the vulnerability of the Austro-German frontier to invasion by mobile forces moving in either direction. At the same time, however, it should be noted that while German panzer units had to drive 170 miles to reach Vienna from Passau at the German frontier, the Czech Frontier at Bratislava, east of Vienna, is only forty miles from that city; the border at Angern is 24 miles from Vienna; the highway from Brno in Czechoslovakia, crosses into Austria at Mikulov, 78 miles from Vienna. The border between Austria and Hungary at Hegyeshalom is forty miles from Vienna; and, the crossing at Sopron, Hungary is also forty miles from the city.

The invasion of Czechoslovakia in 1968, gives some indication of the time required to seize a small country according to today's standards of military operations. During the night of the 20th of August, a Soviet airborne division flew out of Leningrad to seize the main airport at Prague while Warsaw Pact ground troops entered the city itself by 3:30 on the morning of the 21st. By the evening of the 21st, some 400,000 Soviet, Polish, East German, Hungarian and Bulgarian troops had occupied the entire country, moving across the Czech frontier from Poland, East Germany, Hungary, and the Soviet Union.[7]

Here is the case of a modern, industrial nation, equipped with an army five times the size of present-day Austria, with ten times as many tanks and combat aircraft, with an area half again as large, and with twice the population of Austria, falling to an invading enemy in a few hours. It does not seem probable that Austria could be expected to take longer to occupy than did Czechoslovakia.

Austria, therefore, in its present state, constitutes a valuable strategic asset for the Warsaw Pact and an even greater strategic deficit for NATO. It is a greater strategic deficit for NATO than it is a strategic asset for the Soviet Union for a number of reasons.

6. Some details of that movement are in Charles B. MacDonald, *The Last Offensive* in sub-series: *The European Theater of Operations* Series: *United States Army in World War II* (Washington, D.C.: Office of the Chief of Military History, 1973). On this occasion author was present in 608 Field Artillery Battalion, 71st Infantry Division, XX Corps, *Third Army*.

7. Soviet 1st Army from East Germany: 4 Soviet and one East German division; Soviet 20th Army from East Germany and Poland: 4 Soviet and one East German division (armored); Polish Army: three or four divisions from Poland; Five Soviet Divisions from Southern Poland and the U.S.S.R.; two Hungarian Divisions with elements of four Soviet divisions; 24th Soviet Air Army from East Germany; and, Soviet airborne division from Leningrad. Some details are given in "Lessons from the Czech Invasion," *International Defense Review* (Geneva), 1/1969, pp. 27-29; General James H. Polk, "Reflections on the Czechoslovakian Invasion, 1969," *Strategic Review*, Vol. V, No. 1, Winter 1977, pp. 30-37; and *Strategic Survey 1968* (London: The Institute for Strategic Studies, 1969), pp. 20-21.

The Problems of Neutrality

Recall here how democratic governments behave when they are faced with the problem of violating neutral territory in the course of a war. Britain and France would not violate Dutch or Belgium neutrality in 1940. Therefore it was not until after the Netherlands and Belgium were invaded by German forces that Allied armies were permitted to enter Dutch and Belgian territory. German forces began the seizure of Belgium and Holland at 5:35 A.M. the morning of 10 May 1940. The French Army and the British Expeditionary Force crossed the Belgian frontier at 1:00 P.M. the afternoon of the same day. The six and a half hour delay led to a meeting and an engagement with German forces that the Allies lost, and which eventuated in an Allied retreat that ended at Dunkirk.[8] British forces in Malaya were not permitted to violate Siam's neutrality in 1941. A British advance into southern Siam to seize Singora and Patani would have denied Japanese forces the use of the Singora-Kota Bharu rail line down the east coast, the Singora-Alor Star road, and the Patani-Kroh road that linked with the road system on the West Coast, leading to Singapore. In the event, neither operation was possible by the time the Japanese had landed on 8 December 1941. Failure to defend either Singora or Patani—they fell to the Japanese in the early hours of the 8th of December—lost the British northern Malaya and unleashed the costly British retreat that led eventually to the loss of Singapore.[9]

One need but recall the explosive reaction to the U.S. and South Vietnamese invasion of neutral Cambodia in 1970, to appreciate how democratic peoples react when their governments violate another country's neutrality. The reaction then was despite the fact that North Vietnamese regulars had already violated Cambodia's neutrality by deploying 40,000 troops into Cambodian territory; a fact so well known that even the *New York Times* and *Washington Post* had reported it at length.[10]

8. L. F. Ellis, *The War in France and Flanders, 1939-1940* in *History of the Second World War: United Kingdom Series* (London: H.M.S.O., 1953), pp. 35f.

9. S. Woodburn Kirby, *The War Against Japan,* Volume I; *The Loss of Singapore* in *History of the Second World War United Kingdom Series* (London: H.M.S.O., 1957), pp. 76-77, 173, 174-75, 180-82; and, by the same author, *Singapore: The Chain of Disasters* (London: Cassell, 1971); see also, Colonel Masenobn Tsuji, *Singapore: The Japanese Version* (New York: St. Martins Press, 1960), p. 61.

10. See "Cambodia," in *Britannica Book of the Year, 1970*, covering the year 1969, in which Prince Sihanouk is reported as commenting on "the involvement of North Vietnamese and Viet Cong troops in Cambodia," and on the infiltration of North Vietnamese units of "up to regiment size," pp. 182-83. See also, *Strategic Survey, 1969,* p. 46: "No pretense was maintained during 1969 that the 'Vietnam' war did not also extend into Cambodia and Laos. Prince Sihanouk complained bitterly about the support given by North Vietnam and the Viet Cong to local 'Red Khmer' insurgents as well as the virtual Communist annexation of Cambodian territory in the Svay Rieng salient and the north-eastern provinces along the Ho Chi-minh Trail." See as well, *Strategic Survey, 1970*, pp. 39-40; and, *The Report on World Affairs* (April, May, June 1970), Vol. 51, No. 2, July 1970, pp. 197-198, and subsequent issues as well.

If those who claimed membership in the American intellectual community were aware that the Viet Cong and North Vietnamese were using Cambodia as a sanctuary from which to kill Americans and South Vietnamese in South Vietnam, and yet were outraged at U.S. and South Vietnamese "violation" of Cambodia's neutrality, think what a NATO violation of Austrian neutrality would bring.[11] One scarcely dares contemplate the outpourings of rage and consternation from editorial pages and television commentaries. Just as in 1970, we should see academic life disrupted as professor and undergraduate alike fled classroom and library seeking the solace of ski slope, surfboard, or coffee house, to lighten the burden of remorse at the violation of tiny Austria's neutrality.

No. The pre-emptive occupation of Austria by NATO to deny it to the Warsaw Pact is not a serious possibility. And that is one aspect of Austria's strategic importance to the Soviet Union. The Soviet Union may pre-empt Austria, the Allies may not.

Austria's occupation would not, however, be likely to occur as a prelude to war in Europe. NATO would not go to war with the Warsaw Pact if Austria were occupied. The Soviet Union need not go to war in order to occupy Austria. Rather when Austria's turn comes, it will come at the same time as the turn of Western Europe.

If the leaders of the Soviet Union feel compelled to go to war in order to secure the submission of Western Europe, the war will be so general in the world that the loss of Austria will hardly be noted. Those who will note it however—and this is the important aspect of the role to be played by Austria in Soviet strategy—will be the defenders of West Germany, particularly the defenders of the southern part of West Germany.

NATO's Central Front

The mission assigned to the forces on the Central Front of NATO is to "stop any Warsaw Pact attack with a minimum loss of NATO territory, and ensure the prompt restoration of prewar boundaries."[12]

Even the most optimistic assessments of the ratio of forces between the Warsaw Pact and NATO on the Central Front (from the Baltic Sea to the Austrian border with Germany) concedes that the ratio of strength is in favor of the Warsaw Pact. One such optimistic assessment, for example, that of the

11. For example, Mr. G. B. Trudeau, an eminent, anti-Vietnam War, comic strip artist, has one of his characters, a "Ms. Huan" say of the U.S.-South Vietnam invasion of Cambodia, "Neutrality is not like virginity. It does not disappear after the first violation." G. B. Trudeau, "Doonesbury," in "Chronicle Comics," *San Francisco Chronicle,* Sunday, 22 July 1979, p. 4, upper section, panel number 6.

12. "Forward Deployments," in *Manpower Requirements Report for FY 1979,* Department of Defense, February 1978, p. V17.

Secretary of Defense in his *Annual Report* for 1980, acknowledges that the Soviet Union has 45,000 tanks while the United States has but 10,000 tanks. The Secretary discounts such a "raw comparison" as an indication of "Soviet military superiority in Central Europe." Yet elsewhere in his report he says that amongst the future objectives for NATO Defense is to be able to double the size of U.S. ground forces in Europe within ten days after the start of a Warsaw Pact attack, while admitting that the United States presently lacks such a capability. The implication therefore persists that Warsaw Pact forces do not enjoy superiority over NATO forces on the Central Front, unless the Warsaw Pact forces attack, in which case NATO forces would be too weak to hold without doubling the forces present.[13]

The Chairman of the Joint Chiefs of Staff's *Posture Statement for Fiscal Year 1980* voices a less optimistic assessment: "Soviet ground forces confront NATO with quantitative superiority. . . . The Soviet division force combines with East European divisions to pose a strong Warsaw Pact treat to NATO."[14]

The West German *White Paper* on defense for 1975-1976, noted the large increase in tanks, artillery pieces, tactical aircraft and other equipments over the period between 1970 to 1975, with 58 Warsaw Pact divisions to only 27 NATO divisions on the Central Front. As a further note, the *White Paper* reported: "The Warsaw Pact can increase the number of its divisions in central Europe more quickly than NATO. The correlation of forces continues to be unfavorable to the Atlantic Alliance, upon introduction of the reserves of both sides."[15]

It might seem unfair to seize on the phrase, "correlation of forces . . . unfavorable to the Atlantic Alliance," and interpret it as meaning NATO forces are weaker than Warsaw Pact forces; the fact is that since the German *White Paper* was published the "correlation of forces" has grown even more unfavorable to the Atlantic Alliance. In the period 1975-1978, for example,

Number of Soviet tanks increased from 40,000 to 50,000: plus 10,000
Number of U.S. tanks increased from 10,100 to 10,500: plus 400

The number of artillery pieces in the Soviet Army increased from 17,000 to 20,000: plus 3,000
The number of artillery pieces in the U.S. Army decreased from 2,700 to 2,500: minus 200

13. *Department of Defense Annual Report Fiscal Year 1980 (Selected Excerpts),* Harold Brown, Secretary of Defense to the Congress on the FY 1980, FY 1981 Authorization Request, 25 January 1979, p. 11: "raw comparison"; and, p. 201 "double-in-place ground forces."

14. *United States Military Posture for Fiscal Year 1980: An Overview by General David C. Jones, USAF, Chairman of the Joint Chiefs of Staff,* p. 22.

15. *White Paper 1975/1976: The Security of the Federal Republic of Germany and the Development of the Federal Armed Forces,* published by the Federal Minister of Defense on behalf of the Federal Government, 20 January 1976, pp. 31-37.

On the Northern and Central Front of Europe,

Number of Soviet tanks increased from 11,500 to 13,650; plus 2,150
Total of Warsaw Pact tanks increased from 19,000 to 21,100: plus 2,100

Total of NATO tanks in 1975 (November) was 7,000
Total of NATO tanks in 1978 (November) was 7,000: plus zero.

Total of Warsaw Pact artillery pieces increased from 5,600 to 10,000: plus 4,400

Total of Warsaw Pact tactical aircraft in Northern and Central Europe decreased from 4,125 to 4,059: minus 70

Total of NATO tactical aircraft increased from 2,050 to 2,475: plus 425,

(Before taking comfort from the increase of NATO tactical aircraft and the decrease of Warsaw Pact tactical aircraft of the Northern and Central Front, one must note that in 1976, the United States had 5,000 combat aircraft in its Air Force. In 1978 it had 3,400 for a reduction of 1,600 aircraft. Navy combat aircraft numbered 1,900 in 1976 and 1,100 in 1978, or a reduction of 800 aircraft, or, a total reduction for Air Force and Navy of 2,400.)[16]

By the end of September 1979, the number of Soviet tanks will have risen by 3,000, since that is the Soviet rate of production of such vehicles. That would not include tanks produced by East Germany, Czechoslovakia, and Poland, which might add another 1,000.[17] In the same period the Soviet aircraft industry will have turned out an additional 1,000 fighter aircraft.[18] The United States will have produced an estimated 469 tanks during the same period and perhaps a third as many planes.[19]

While such "raw comparisons" may not be convincing evidence to the Secretary of Defense, of Soviet and Warsaw Pact military superiority over NATO, the most conservative assessment must certainly lead to the conclusion that the trends against NATO are anything but favorable. While one may feel compelled to discount the concern of military commanders in the field who must face odds of three or four to one against their forces, it is only

16. Comparisons are given on the basis of reports in *The Military Balance, 1975-1976* published in September 1975 and in *The Military Balance, 1978-1979* published in September 1978.

17. "Soviets Double T64s in GDR," *International Defense Review* (Geneva), Vol. 11, No. 5 (1978), p. 668; and see "T-72 Production Outside the USSR," *International Defense Review* (Geneva), Vol. 12, No. 4 (1979) p. 481.

18. *United States Military Posture for FY 1980,* The Organization of the Joint Chiefs of Staff, p. 58.

19. Estimate of U.S. Tank Production for 1979, is cited from U.S. Army sources in Kenneth H. Jacobsen and David E. Benson, *The Limits of Detente: Implications for U.S. Defense* (Menlo Park: SRI International, July 1978), p. 10, U.S. aircraft production for the same period is an optimistic estimate.

reasonable to discount the optimism of political leaders who need not face such odds in the field and who are seldom held accountable for lost battles when field commanders can be made to carry the can. One recalls for example, the quick removal and ready condemnation of the Army and Navy commanders at Pearl Harbor after the disaster of 7 December 1941. It is more difficult to recall the name of any political leader, senator, or congressman, whose career was ended with the attack on Pearl Harbor, although they were, presumably, taken as unawares as the commanders at Pearl Harbor. They bore a good deal more of the responsibility for the lack of U.S. preparation for war.

After an examination of such figures as those that have been given here, as well as others that are no less ominous in their implications, the average high school graduate might be excused for concluding that the Warsaw Pact is stronger than NATO and more fully prepared for war. In the same way, since NATO has fewer of almost everything with which to wage war than does the Soviet Union one might assume that NATO is at some disadvantage when confronting the Warsaw Pact. That being the case, the role of Austria in NATO's defense of Europe on the Central Front is easily apparent.

Austria is vulnerable to swift occupation by the forces of the Warsaw Pact located close to Austria's borders. Austria lacks the military strength to offer more than nominal resistance to such an occupation. NATO forces may not enter Austria without violating that country's neutrality.

The mission assigned to the forces on the Central Front of NATO is to "stop any Warsaw Pact attack with a minimum loss of NATO territory, and ensure the prompt restoration of prewar boundaries."[20]

NATO Liabilities

Given what appear to be grossly unfavorable ratios of forces between NATO and its adversary on the Central Front, the most optimistic assessment of NATO's chances would seem to fall within the following characterization: if the forces of the Warsaw Pact make all possible mistakes they could sensibly be expected to make; if the forces of NATO respond perfectly to the situation presented by the attack and do not make any mistakes, then, NATO will have its work cut out for itself just to hold Warsaw Pact forces somewhere before they reach the Rhine.

One of the mistakes the Soviet Union will not make when the forces of the Warsaw Pact move into West Germany is to fail to occupy Austria within the very first hours of the invasion of West Germany.

20. "Forward Deployments," in *Manpower Requirements Report* for FY 1979, Department of Defense, February 1978, p. V 17.

Austria can be expected to fall to the Warsaw Pact forces that will have crossed the Hungarian and Czech borders to seize Vienna and Linz, while others will have moved from Czechoslovakia across the German frontier, southeast between Philippsreut and Haidmuhlle, along Highway 12 and other roads, to secure the crossing from Austria into Germany at Passau. This would cover the advance of the units at Linz as they move northwest toward Passau and west to Scharding, Branau, and Salzburg. Forces reaching Salzburg will be 82 miles from Munich via Highway 304 and 78 miles via expressway E 11. Operations toward Munich from Austria and Czechoslovakia would place Warsaw Pact forces south and southwest of Regensburg; that is, to the rear of the West German 4th Panzer Grenadier Division, reported to be at Regensberg. The 4th is disposed so as to cover the Czech frontier in the area where the Pilsen to Regensburg road crosses into West Germany at Cham.[21]

A Warsaw Pact attack through Austria toward Munich and NATO's rear areas, is limited only by the density of forces that could be handled rapidly on the Austrian road-net. There are more than sufficient divisions available in the region around Austria without weakening any Warsaw Pact attack further north on the NATO front. The number of divisions available *before* mobilization includes: *Hungary:* 5 Hungarian and 4 Soviet Motorized rifle divisions; 1 Hungarian tank and 2 Soviet tank divisions; *Czechoslovakia:* 5 Czech and 3 Soviet Motorized rifle divisions; 5 Czech and 2 or 3 Soviet tank divisions; *Carpathian Military District of the Soviet Union* (adjacent to Czechoslovakia and Hungary) 10 Soviet divisions.[22]

NATO forces, now barely adequate to cover the frontier from Lubeck south to the Austrian frontier, will find themselves, on the day the Warsaw Pact moves against Western Europe, required to defend an additional 200 miles of frontier as Austria is overrun. The additional 200 miles of front will not be an extension of the present NATO front to the south, but will stretch instead along the southern flank of those NATO forces that must face east toward Czechoslovakia and northeast toward East Germany. Within at most, 24 hours, NATO forces will be facing a threat to Munich from the south, if that city has not already been invested by airborne troops.[23]

21. Location of 4th Panzer Grenadier Division at Regensburg was reported in Map: "Standorte der Landstreitkrafte im Geteilten Deutschland," in Ferdinand Otto Miksche, "Bundeswehre ohne atomaren Feureschutz," *Wehr and Wirtschaft* (Munich), January 1974, pp. 18-45.

22. *The Military Balance, 1978-1979* reports only five Soviet divisions in Czechoslovakia; Jacquelyn K. Davis and Robert L. Pfaltzgraff, Jr., "Soviet Theater Strategy: Implications for NATO," USSI Report 78-1, United States Strategic Institute, 1978, report the Central Group (Czechoslovakia) to have in its Western Group, 10th and 13th Tank Divisions, and 16th Guards Motorized Rifle Division; the Eastern Group to have 51st Tank, and the 55th and 66th Motorized Rifle Divisions, or six divisions.

23. As mentioned previously, Allied intelligence agents spoke to Soviet parachute troops, part of the Soviet airborne division that had seized the Prague airport in August 1968, who thought they were going to be used to seize the *Munich* airport, rather than the airport at Prague. See General James A.

It would not be possible to switch NATO forces defending the north-south front to cover the Austrian border, since it is likely they will have all they can handle defending against the Warsaw Pact forces coming from East Germany and Czechoslovakia. As it is, considerable time would be required to move NATO forces forward to where they might block the attack from the east. For example, the Royal Netherlands Army is supposed to contribute a full corps of ten brigades (about 45,000 men) plus supporting elements to the forward defense of NATO in West Germany while guarding the lines of communication from Holland to the Central Front. In peacetime, the 1st Netherland Corps in West Germany (Seedorf) has one brigade with some divisional troops. The problem of bringing up the rest of the Corps from the Netherlands is described as follow:

> To complete the Corps, nine more brigades [five of which are active, four reserve], two divisional headquarters, corps troops, communications units, helicoper units . . . have to be added. Although the five active brigades can be moved into the FRG the most quickly, overall reaction time clearly depends on how long it takes to call up the four reserve brigades, bring them into barracks from their homes, issue them with weapons, equipment and stores, embark them in their vehicles and then to drive into Germany and deploy, recognizing that road movement may well be difficult in conditions at the time.

General de Jager, the Chief of Staff of the Royal Netherlands Army, said: "Movement [of the brigades] to their deployment positions is by road rather than air, since the distance is only 300-400 kilometers and there are no water barriers." It is unlikely, however, that even the five active brigades can be in position within forty-eight hours.[24] While nine-tenths of the Netherlands corps has to move up to 240 miles to reach its battle station, the Soviet 9th Motorized Rifle Division and the 8th East German Motorized Rifle Division (both kept at war-strength in peacetime) need move but 80 miles from the vicinity of Schwerin to reach Hamburg in West Germany.

The Difficulties of Defense: Hof

The NATO front from Lubeck south to the Austrian frontier is only 400 miles long measured in a straight line. The actual length of the border between East and West from Lubeck south is nearer 730 miles. The border wends east and west as well as meandering southward, and, sometimes even

---

Polk, *op. cit.*, p. 37. Soviet Army Order of Battle includes 8 airborne divisions; Czech Army Order of Battle includes 1 airborne regiment; *The Military Balance*, 1978-1979, pp. 9 and 13.

24. R. D. M. Furlong, "Dutch Defense Policy for the 80's: Less Nuclear More Conventional," and "Army Faces Key Deployment Problem," *International Defense Review*, Vol. 12, No. 3 (1979), pp. 319-22.

Map A

NATO GROUND FORCES IN WEST GERMANY
GROUP OF SOVIET ARMIES IN GERMANY

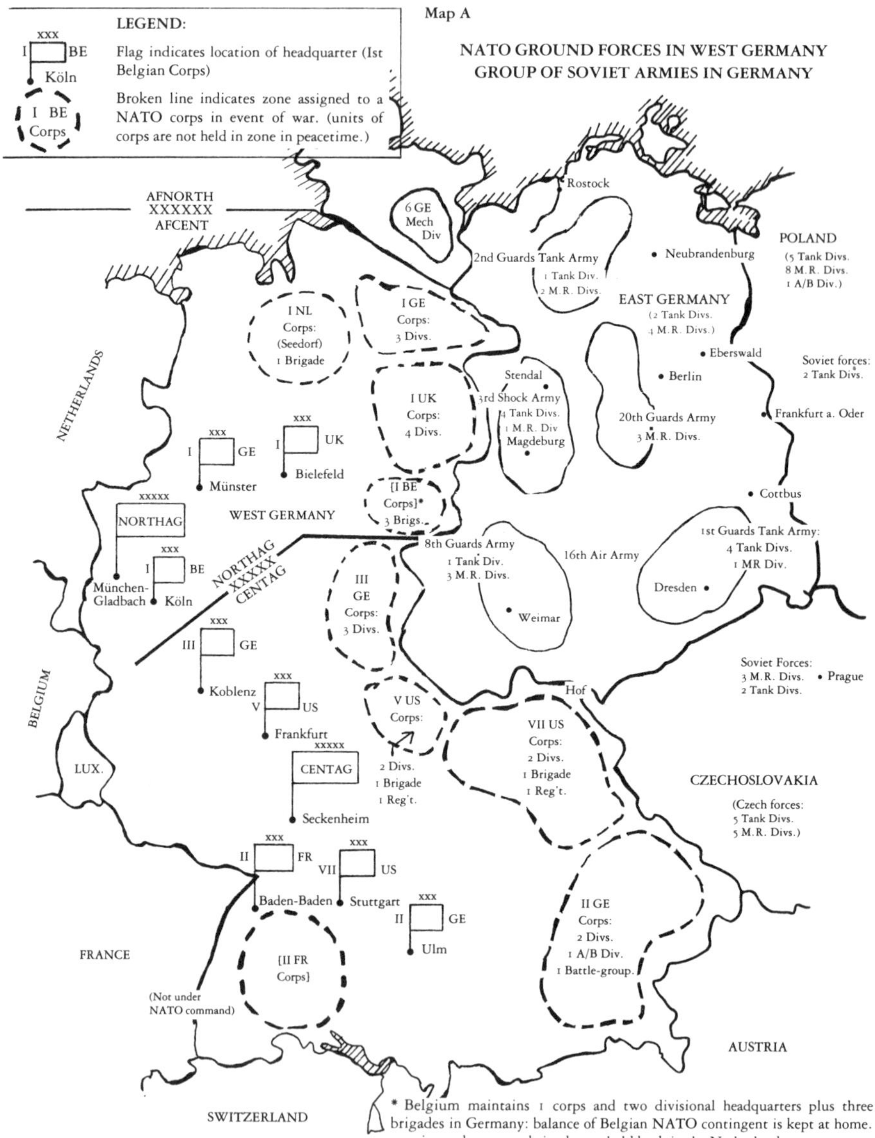

* Belgium maintains 1 corps and two divisional headquarters plus three brigades in Germany: balance of Belgian NATO contingent is kept at home. 5 active and 4 reserve brigades are held back in the Netherlands.

Map B

CENTRAL ARMY GROUP (CENTAG) FRONT: Deployment of US and West German divisions and of Warsaw Pact divisions capable of intervening against CENTAG. (See Table I, following, for details of deployment.)

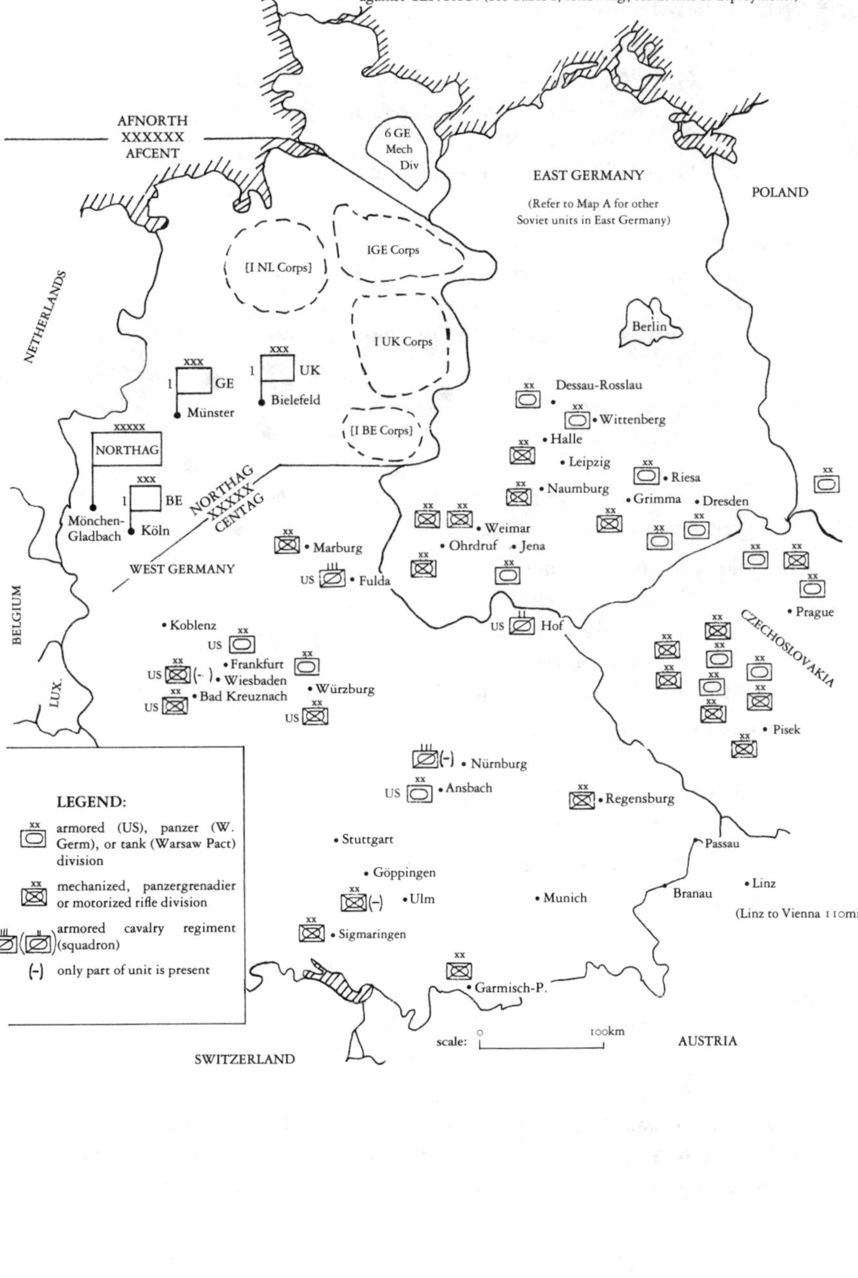

Table I.
Details of NATO and Warsaw Pact Deployment

Group of Soviet Forces, Germany (GSFG)—Headquarters, Zossen-Wunsdorf

34th Artillery Division—Potsdam

1st Guards Tank Army—Dresden
- 6th Guards Tank Division—Lutherstadt-Wittenberg
- 7th Guards Tank Division—Dessau-Rosslau
- 9th Tank Division—Riesa
- 11th Guards Tank Division—Dresden
- 27th Guards Motorized Rifle Division—Halle

2d Guards Army—Fürstenberg
- 9th Guards Tank Division—Neustrelitz
- 32nd Motorized Rifle Division—Perleberg
- 94th Guards Motorized Rifle Division—Schwerin

3rd Shock Army—Magdeberg
- 10th Guards Tank Division—Krampnitz
- 12th Guards Tank Division—Neuruppin
- 47th Guards Tank Division—Hillersleben
- 207th Guards Motorized Rifle Division—Stendal
- 25th Tank Division—Vogelsang

8th Guards Army—Weimar
- 20th Guards Tank Division—Jena
- 20th Guards Motorized Rifle Division—Grimma
- 39th Guards Motorized Rifle Division—Ohrdruf
- 57th Guards Motorized Rifle Division—Naumburg

20th Guards Army—Eberswalde
- 6th Guards Motorized Rifle Division—Bernau
- 14th Guards Motorized Rifle Division—Jüterbog
- 35th Guards Motorized Division—Döberitz

16th Tactical Air Army—Zossen-Wunsdorf

Approximate Totals: 375,000 men
7,605 tanks
2,000 artillery pieces (exclusive of mortars, rocket launchers, missiles, and air defense artillery)
1,400 aircraft in Tactical Air Army 40,000 men

(SOURCE: Order of Battle and location given in "Fünf Sowjet-Armee in Mitteldeutschland," *Soldat und Technik,* March 1978, p. 155; strengths derived from *The Military Balance, 1978-1979* [London: IISS, 1978], pp. 102-103. Personnel totals given in Friederich Wiener, *The Armies of the Warsaw Pact Nations,* Second Edition [Vienna: Carl Ueberreuter Publishers, 1978], p. 25.)

East German Army (NVA—Nationale Volksarmee)

7th Tank Division—Dresden
11th Motorized Rifle Division—Halle
8t Motorized Rifle Division—Schwerin
1st Motorized Rifle Division—Potsdam
u/i Tank Division—Eggesin
4th Motorized Rifle Division—Erfurt

Totals: East German Army 107,000 men
2,620 tanks
627 artillery pieces
335 combat aircraft, 36,000 men in Air Force

(SOURCE: Location given in "Funf Sowjet-Armee in Mitteldeutschland," *Soldat und Technic,* March 1978, p. 155; "Dreissig Jahr deutsche Streitkrafte unter Sowjetkommando: Das Militarwesen der DDR," *Ibid.,* October 1978, pp. 517-20; and, "Mot Schutzentruppe der NVA (Nationale Volsarmee)," *Ibid.,* March 1979, pp. 126-27. Strengths given in *The Military Balance, 1979-1980* [London: IISS, 1979], pp. 14-15.)

Southwest Front of the Warsaw Pact—Headquarters, Tábor, Czechoslovakia

Soviet Central Group of Forces (CGF)—Czechoslovakia

u/i Tank Division—northwest of Mlada Boleslav
u/i Motorized Rifle Division—Turnov
u/i Tank Division—south of Milovice
Approximate Strength: 75,000 men, 1,600 tanks
u/i Motorized Rifle Division—Budejovice
u/i Motorized Rifle Division—Zvolen

Czechoslovak Army

(vicinity Pribram)
u/i Tank Division
u/i Motorized Rifle Division
u/i Motorized Rifle Division
u/i Motorized Rifle Division

(vicinity Pisek)
u/i Tank Division
u/i Tank Division
u/i Motorized Rifle Division
u/i Motorized Rifle Division

Approximate stengths; Czech Army 140,000 men
3,400 tanks
920 artillery pieces
462 combat aircraft

(SOURCE: Friederich Wiener, *The Armies of the Warsaw Pact Nations,* Second Edition, pp. 30, 31, and 64. Czech Army strength in *The Military Balance, 1979-1980,* p. 14. [*u/i means unidentified.*]

NATO Forces on the Central Army Group (CENTAG) Front

Central Army Group—Headquarter, Seckenheim

III German Corps—Koblenz
- 2nd Panzergrenadier Division—Marburg
- 12th Panzer Division—Veitshochheim

V U.S. Corps—Frankfurt am Main
- 8th Infantry Division (Mechanized)—Bad Kreuznach
- 3rd Armored Division—Frankfurt-Darmstadt
- A brigade of the 4th Infantry Division (Mechanized)—Wiesbaden (4th Division is kept back in the United States)
- 11th Armored Cavalry Regiment—Fulda

VII U.S. Corps—Stuttgart-Möhringen
- 3rd Infantry Division (Mechanized)-Würzburg
- 1st Armored Division—Ansbach
- A brigade of the 1st Infantry Division (Mechanized)—Göppingen (1st Division is kept back in the United States)
- 2nd Armored Cavalry Regiment—Nürnberg

II German Corps—Ulm
- u/i Panzergrenadier Division—Garmisch-Partenkirchen
- 4th Panzergrenadier Division—Regensburg
- 10th Panzergrenadier Division—Sigmaringen

Approximated Totals of West German and U.S. Forces in CENTAG:	184,444	men and women
	2,774	tanks
	194	tactical fighter aircraft
Total U.S. Army Forces in West Germany:	193,000	men and women
	3000	tanks including those in storage for strategic reserves.

Table II
Data on the "Hof" Problem

Highway Distances

Hof to Nürnberg	80 miles
Dresden to Hof	108 miles
Leipzig to Hof	75 miles
Weimar to Naila	65 miles
Hof to Wurzburg	94 miles

At Dresden or in vicinity: Soviet First Guards Tank Army with
6th Guards Tank Division at Wittenberg
7th Guards Tank Division at Dessau-Rosslau
9th Tank Division at Riesa
11th Guards Tank Division at Dresden
27th Guards Motorized Division at Halle
7th Tank Division (East German) at Dresden
11th Motorized Rifle Division (East German) at Halle

At Weimar or in vicinity: Soviet Eighth Guards Army with
20th Guards Tank Division at Jena
20th Guards Motorized Rifle Division at Grimma
39th Guards Motorized Rifle Division at Ohrdruf
57th Guards Motorized Rifle Division at Naumburg

(Order of Battle Data in "Funf Sowjet-Armeen in Mitteldeutschland," *Soldat und Technik*, 3/1978, March 1978, p. 155.)

Soviet Tank Division: 11,000 men, 415 tanks
Soviet Motorized Rifle Division: 13,000 men, 296 tanks

(Soviet divisions in the Group of Soviet Forces in Germany are kept at war-strength; data in *The Military Balance, 1978-1979,* pp. 102-3.)

At Nürnberg and Hof: U.S. 2nd Armored Cavalry Regiment

A Wurzburg and Veitschochheim: U.S. 3rd Infantry Division (Mechanized)
W. German 12th Panzer Division (Tank)

U.S. Armored Cavalry Regiment: 3,297 men, 51 tanks
U.S. Mechanized Divisions: 17,800 men, 216 tanks
West German Panzer Division: 15,000 men, 231 tanks

cuts back north for a short distance. The configuration of the border creates, in some places, areas that are almost indefensible because of their location, but areas which nonetheless must be defended. Thus the border begins to turn eastward, 24 miles northeast of Fulda; it does not turn southward finally until it reaches a point seven miles north of Hof. Although the border covers a distance of 160 miles here, the straightline distance is only 96 miles. Hof, a West German city, is thus situated with a corner of the East German frontier that is barely a mile away to the east of the city, and only seven miles away to the north.

The city of Hof furnishes an excellent example of the difficulties inherent in defending a border that nowhere conforms to sound tactical arrangements. In the town itself are located elements of a U.S. armored cavalry regiment, presumably a squadron of the 2d, whose headquarters is in Nürnberg, about 100 miles south. The function of the armored cavalry is to help watch the so-called Hof Gap. Northeast of the Hof Gap in East Germany are located the headquarters of the Soviet First Guards Tank Army of four tank divisions and one motorized rifle division and the East German 1st Motorized Rifle Division. Dresden is about 108 miles from Hof, and most of the divisions assigned to the 1st Guards Tank Army are located within that distance from the border at Hof.

Seventy miles north and a bit west of Hof is located the East German city of Weimar, the headquarters of the Soviet 8th Guards Army of one tank and three motorized rifle divisions, plus the nearby East German 11th Motorized Rifle Division.[25] One route of advance for the Soviet First Guards Army would be along the axis of the highway system that converges from Leipzig, Dresden, and Halle, to a point just west of Hof, and then branches westward toward Bamberg and Frankfurt, and southward to Bayreuth and Nürnberg. The axis of advance of the 8th Guards Army would probably be southwestward toward Frankfurt. While the directions of such advances are speculative, it is clear from the tactical circumstances that Hof would be east of both Soviet armies as they advanced south and west into West Germany.

The presumed squadron of the 2d U.S. Armored Cavalry Regiment in Hof would have the task of covering the border north and east of Hof to delay the advance of the Warsaw Pact forces until the U.S. and West German units 120 miles and more distant can be brought up to counter-attack the invaders. The armored cavalry squadron would have to oversee about 21 obvious cross-

25. Order of Battle of Group of Soviet Forces in Germany, including identification and location is in "Funf Sowjet-Armeen in Mittledeutschland," *Soldat und Technik,* March 1978, p. 155. Order of Battle of East German Army (NVA) is in "Mot Schutzentruppe der NVA (Nationale Voksarmae)," *Soldat und Technik,* March 1979, pp. 126-27.

ing-points along about 42 miles of front stretching from northwest of Hof around to the east of the town.[26]

The squadron consists of three troops, each with three platoons; one tank company with 17 main battle tanks; and, a howitzer battery with six self-propelled 155-mm. howitzers. A total of about 63 armored personnel carriers, 27 light tanks, 9 mortars, and six 155-mm. howitzers, supported by regimental air cavalry if available, will cover 42 miles of border and watch over the likely crossings.[27]

If the squadron is fortunate in having covered the right crossings and can succeed in delaying the enemy's advance, they might expect to face a force the size of a division before they have finished and begun their withdrawal, if withdrawal is possible and permitted.

That Soviet division will have 266 tanks, 375 armored personnel carriers, and 110 artillery pieces plus 18 122-mm. multiple rocket launchers, and 54 120 mm. mortars. If the Soviet division does not merely by-pass or brush aside our armored cavalry squadron, it might send against it one or two of its 9 motorized Rifle battalions; each of those has available about 45 armored personnel carriers, thirteen medium tanks, 6 122-mm. guns, and 6 120-mm. mortars.[28] In addition the Soviet battalion or battalions may call upon reinforcement from the regiments of which they are a part, and artillery fires from regimental, divisional artillery, and army artillery, plus long-range rockets, tactical air, attack helicopters, and whatever else seems worthwhile to invest in what will be a minor engagement for Soviet forces.

Our armored cavalry squadron will have enjoyed the leisure to reconnoiter the defensive positions it will occupy. The Soviet force will have the advantage of choosing the manner and route by which it will advance; and it will employ the advantage of surprise and overwhelming strength.[29]

The Benefits of Surprise

Surprise will be attained strategically by concealment of the preparations for war or by their dissimulation as the ordinary operations of Warsaw Pact

26. Crossing points are shown on Map, 1:50,000, HOF, Ostl. Frankenwald Norl. Fichtelgebirge, Fritsch Wanderkarte No. 64 (Hof: Landkartenverlag, n.d.).

27. Organization, equipment, operations and capabilities of armed cavalry are given in *How To Fight Manual: Cavalry,* FM 17-95, United States Army Armored School, Fort Knox, Kentucky, April 1976, pars. 3-7 to 3-18, and Section VIII: "Delay."

28. Soviet motorized rifle division table of organization and equipment is in *The Military Balance, 1978-1979,* pp. 102-13.

29. The organization and manner for the advance of a Soviet motorized rifle battalion as the advanced element of a Soviet division is given in C. N. Donnelly, "The 'March' in Soviet Tactical Doctrine," *RUSI: Journal of the Royal United Services Institution for Defense Studies,* Vol. 119, No. 3, September 1974, pp. 77-80; see also, "Defeat of a Defending Enemy and Exploitation of Success: 1. Overcoming a Zone of Security (or Cover)," Chapter V. in A. A. Sidorenko, *The Offensive* (Moscow 1970), published under that title by U.S.G.P.O.

forces at peace. For example, every spring and autumn, Aeroflot passenger aircraft are commandeered to move 100,000 to 120,000 troops into the Group of Soviet Troops in Eastern Europe to replace an equal number who are flown out.[30]

While such a massive movement of troops into eastern Europe would certainly be a prelude to an attack on the West, that kind of movement has become so routine by now as no longer to constitute a warning of impending attack. Warsaw Pact troops seem to be constantly on maneuvers or performing command post and other exercises, so that any genuine warnings of war are lost in the general noise provided by the routine operations of the Eastern Armies. In July 1968, for example, before the Czech invasion, the Soviet Union held a Rear Services Exercise presumed at the time to be a test of the logistics system. The exercise was widely publicized in the Soviet press, thousands of reservists were called up, civilian transport was mobilized, for what appeared as logistical exercises from the Baltic to the Black Sea. All seemed perfectly routine. In fact, the exercises covered the filling out of Soviet combat units to war strength, and were part of the preparations for the Czech invasion. U.S. Air Force radar picked up the flights of transports leaving Leningrad, but since they were going toward Czechoslovakia, it was not considered significant for U.S. forces.[31]

The frequency and regularity of military exercises and similar warlike moves tend to render all such moves ambiguous in intent. The reluctance of Western political leaders to interpret any Soviet action as hostile combines with the Soviet competence in deception to render a surprise attack feasible. The very notion that the Soviet Union might launch a surprise attack is virtually anathema amongst defense "experts," although those who may have to meet such an attack are less persuaded that such a thing is impossible. The Chinese have been amongst those who see a Soviet surprise attack as extremely likely:

> The Kremlin's strategy against Western Europe is clearly oriented to an offensive and a surprise attack so as to seize the initiative in war. To ensure its success and gain superiority over the West, the Soviet revisionists have put their military buildup in high gear in the 70s when their lip service to "peace" was as its loudest. They have leaned more and more heavily in their military dispositions in Europe on adding to both their nuclear capabilities and conventional forces in the forward areas facing West European countries.[32]

30. Peter Borgart, "USSR develops new IL-86 variants," *International Defense Review,* Vol. 11, No. 7, 1978, pp. 1015-16.

31. General James H. Polk, U.S. Army (Ret.), "Reflections on the Czechoslovak Invasion, 1968," pp. 30-37.

32. "New Tsars Hold Western Europe In Deadly Bear-Hug," *Peking Review,* No. 49, 3 December 1976, p. 16; and, see also "Chou Sharply Criticizes Russia, Warns Against Surprise Attack," *Los Angeles Times,* 1 September 1973, p. 1.

The French, who have had some painful experiences with surprise in war, have suggested that Warsaw Pact forces could launch a surprise attack with as little as 48 hours preparations; be at the Rhine in another 48 hours; and attacking British ports within a week. The French consider that "the element of surprise regarding the location, time, size and type of attack to be used is a basic principle of Soviet military doctrine."[33] That notion seems borne out in Soviet military writings concerning the importance of surprise in winning battles and wars:

> *VNEZAPNOST* [surprise]—One of the principles of military art, ensuring success in battle and in operations. Surprise makes it possible to inflict heavy losses upon the enemy in short periods of time, to paralyze his will, and to deprive him of the possibility of offering organized resistance. Surprise is achieved in the following ways: by using various types and methods of combat, by misleading the enemy as to one's own intentions, by safeguarding the security of operational plans; by decisive action and skillful maneuver, by unexpected use of nuclear weapons; and by using means and methods with which the enemy is unfamiliar. Surprise may be tactical, operational or strategic.[34]

The Belgians, who have been caught in surprise attacks in two world wars, entertain the notion that "utilizing the maximum of surprise and the lack of preparation of the West, the Soviets could launch an attack and be on the Rhine in 48 hours."[35]

A report by a General in NATO concluded that 20 Soviet and 6 East German divisions could, within three hours, move from their peacetime locations to the West German frontier ready to continue on into Western Europe. Participation in a surprise attack by some of the 16,000 Soviet secret agents, reported to be in West Germany, would include destruction of communications and warning systems to enhance surprise and confuse the defense of NATO.[36]

It is generally routine for large bodies of troops about to enter a zone of major operations to be preceded by reconnaissance forces that obtain information about the enemy and the terrain along the route of advance of the main body of the force. Reconnaissance forces will be highly mobile, with considerable firepower and excellent communications. Both ground units and helicopters will be used in order to cover as much area as possible ahead of the

33. "French Report says Soviets have surprise attack capability," *The Christian Science Monitor,* 15 January 1979, p. 10.

34. *Dictionary of Basic Military Terms: A Soviet View,* Translation by the DGIS Multilingual Section, Translation Bureau, Secretary of State Department, Ottawa, Canada (Washington, D.C.: U.S.G.P.O., 1976), p. 35. See also, V. Ye. Savkin, *The Basic Principles of Operational Art and Tactics* (Moscow, 1972), published under that title by U.S.G.P.O., Washington, D.C., 1974, pp. 230-40.

35. "Russ Could Drive to Rhine in 2 Days, Belgian Declares," *Los Angeles Times,* 11 January 1977, p. 11.

36. "Successful Red Attack in Europe Seen," *Los Angeles Times,* 16 March 1976, p. 14.

advance. Ground reconnaissance forces will collect information about trafficability of bridges and roads for heavy vehicles, the state of the terrain for cross-country movement, the location and strength of enemy defenses, and the siting and nature of obstacles that might be used to delay or divert the advance. Helicopter reconnaissance units will be used to detect enemy movements into the prospective battle area, to locate artillery and anti-tank emplacements, and similar enemy deployments that can impede the advance.

Such reconnaissance forces may operate as far ahead of the main body of troops as thirty miles, and therefore, detection of such operations will constitute a warning to the defenders of an enemy advance. In order to preserve surprise, Soviet tactical doctrine for commencing a war in a place like Western Europe, is to avoid use of reconnaissance forces in the initial phase of the opening attack, but to move instead immediately into the area to be overrun with forces from the main body, forces that will be of sufficient strength quickly to overwhelm any defense. Therefore, preliminary reconnaissance will be conducted by means other than those customarily employed.[37]

Some of the requirements for reconnaissance will be met by satellite coverage and some very high altitude aerial reconnaissance which the Soviet Union routinely conducts. Soviet and other East European agents operate on the ground to obtain information about NATO order of battle, operational plans, location of communications centers, supply depots, and special weapons installations. Soviet signal reconnaissance monitors all electronic eminations, including strategic and tactical communications. But all of those things are simply routine and to be expected. It is the reconnaissance of the West European highway network that is the most interesting and uncoventional.

In March 1974, *Pravda* reported the formation of *Sovtransavto* (Soviet Motor Transport Company) to organize the shipment of freight and passengers between the Soviet Union and other countries. In any 24-hour period, *Pravda* reported, there are more than 1,000 Soviet trucks on the highways of Europe. They pull semi-trailers of up to 25 tons, delivering, as it is said, from door-to-door, with "tens of thousands of foreign firms and 30 U.S.S.R. ministries and departments among its clients."[38] In 1975, the Soviet Union joined the International Road Transport Union whose members may send trucks across international borders along international highways without being subjected to inspection at frontiers. Thus a cargo may be transported by truck from within East Europe to the Port of Rotterdam, for example, loaded aboard ship and leave for overseas without ever having been

37. P. H. Vigor, "Soviet Reconnaissance: Part I," *RUSI: Journal of the Royal United Services Institution for Defense Studies,* Vol. 120, No. 4, December 1975, pp. 41-43; and, Chris Donnelly, "Soviet Reconnaissance-II," *ibid.*, Vol. 121, No. 1, March 1976, pp. 68-75.

38. "Europe on All Sides," *Pravda,* 30 March 1974, p. 6, in *The Current Digest of the Soviet Press,* Vol. XXVI, No. 13, 24 April 1974, pp. 18-19.

charged duty or subjected to inspection. While the Dutch police have suspected that East European trucks are used to supply arms to terrorists, NATO intelligence has reason to suspect that drivers of the trucks are intelligence agents and that some of them are commanders of Soviet tank units learning the roads of Western Europe.[39]

The fact that the borders between Hungary and Austria and Austria and Czechoslovakia have been gradually opened to increased traffic and tourism clearly makes the investment of Austria easier than it otherwise would be. Similar actions elsewhere along the borders between East and West in Europe may appear as the outcome of the "easing of tensions" between the two sides. Easing of tensions, avoidance of the appearance of crisis, and relaxation of defense may indicate the growth of friendly relations and the expansion of international cooperation. It is unfortunately true, that the appearance of such things also may prepare the way for a surprise attack that will catch one entirely off-guard.

The Strategic Logic: Europe

It has been suggested here that the Soviet strategic axis extends northward into Europe as well as southward into Africa. Austria's place in that Axis seems to be evident. But how could Yugoslavia, Malta, and Libya be used to effect the outcome of battles taking place in West Germany?

Looking from North to South in Europe, it is evident that strategic logic would lead the Soviet Union to occupy Finland, seize northern Norway, occupy Spitsbergen to hold the North Cape route open for the Soviet Northern Fleet and to advance the Soviet air patrol and air defense line into the North Atlantic. Seizure of the entrances to the Baltic in the manner of the German attack on Norway and Denmark in April 1940, would securely close the Baltic to NATO and threaten the German ports on the North Sea through which Allied supplies and reinforcements from the sea would otherwise move. This would transpire while Warsaw Pact armies are driving across the North German plain to secure the highway system connecting the Dutch and Belgian ports to the NATO Central Front. By securing the highway network, Warsaw Pact forces may hasten their own advance while preventing resupply and reinforcement by ground transport of the U.S. and West German forces defending southern Germany. Reinforcement and resupply of the defenders of southern Germany would therefore have to be by air, if that is possible.

39. "Soviet Trucking Operation May Supply Espionage Net," *The Washington Post,* 17 April 1976, p. 7.

During the early years of United States participation in World War II, ground combat troops were taught how to defend themselves with small arms fire against enemy air attack. In the later stages of the war, such training came to be less and less emphasized because the Allies acquired sufficient aircraft to establish and maintain air superiority over the battlefield, in Europe, at least. The number of troops being trained for anti-aircraft work were reduced by the summer of 1943, while some of those already trained were transferred to the infantry and other branches of service where they were needed more.

By the end of the war, it had become conventional to expect that the United States would invariably enjoy air superiority over the battlefield. In fact, it was considered almost mandatory that U.S. forces operating against an enemy would be furnished with virtually an impenetrable air cover. Infantry therefore no longer needed to be prepared to deal with more than the occasional intrusion by enemy aircraft that had somehow evaded the superb air cover.

By 1975, the situation in the air had changed so radically *vis à vis* the United States and its principal enemy, the Soviet Union, that once again the infantry was being taught how to defend itself, using infantry weapons, against air attack. A manual published in 1975, summarized the problem:

> In the past, the US Army fought on the battlefield with little worry about enemy aircraft. And in furture conflicts, the Air Force and air defenders will keep many of the enemy aircraft off our backs. But the basic fact is that potential enemy air forces have more aircraft than we do. It is likely we will not enjoy air superiority in future conflicts.[40]

Thus, when one speaks of air resupply and reinforcement, it must be considered that such operations will have to be carried on under circumstances where the enemy is capable of dominating air routes into the rear of the battle area.

If that is true, air resupply will be virtually impossible while close air support by Allied air forces over the battle area will be difficult if possible at all. With that in mind, one can look at the role of the southern end of the Soviet strategic axis.

The Sixth Fleet in the Mediterranean has two aircraft carriers capable of launching as many as 90 aircraft each. Fighter aircraft like the F-14 Tomcat, F-4 Phantom, interceptors like the F-8 Crusader and various attack aircraft and attack versions of the named aircraft can operate from 300 to 500 miles

40. *Small Arms Defense Against Air Attack,* TC 23-44, U.S. Army Air Defense School (Washington, D.C., U.S.G.P.O., 1975), pp. 1 and 24; see also, *The Rifle Squads (Mechanicized and Light Infantry),* TC 7-1 (Washington, D.C.: U.S.G.P.O., 1976), pp. 336-37.

from the aircraft carriers to provide air cover and close support to troops on the ground. All of Austria and southern Bavaria, at least as far as Munich, is within range of such aircraft operating from carriers located at the nothernmost edge of the 50 meter depth curve in the upper Adriatic. Aircraft like the F-4 Phantom, configured as fighter-bombers, for example, can carry up to 16,000 pounds of bombs, missiles, or nuclear weapons out to a range of 520 miles. The advance of Warsaw Pact forces into Austria and their attack northward to Munich could, through carrier air attack, be disrupted, delayed or even halted.[41]

If Soviet naval forces operate in the Adriatic, and Soviet air forces operate from Yugoslav airfields, U.S. carriers may not expect to intervene in the land battle in Central Europe. If the Soviet Union is successful in maintaining its strategic axis into Africa up to the time that the European land battle starts, they need not worry about Allied intervention from the Mediterranean.

It has not been intended to give more than a faint glimpse of what war for Western Europe would be like. Nothing here does more than suggest the scale and intensity of combat operations of which the Soviet Union and its allies are capable. It is not proposed that Warsaw Pact forces will make no errors in judgment or tactics. But it is sheer illusion to suppose that NATO forces in their present state would be able to exploit such errors. In order to exploit an enemy's errors one requires the freedom of action and the material resources to do so. NATO defenders will have neither if the defense remains in its present state or achieves the faint improvements that have been recommended for it.[42] A study completed early in 1977, for example, recommended that the number of artillery pieces in the U.S. divisions in Europe be increased by 80 percent to help offset Warsaw Pact superiority in artillery pieces.[43] The NATO ministers concluded in their meetings held in May 1977, that there should be "a crash program to quickly increase [*sic*] the alliance's conventional firepower."[44] Suiting action to words, eight months later, the United States Army *began planning* to send several additional artillery battalions, or around 54 artillery pieces, to Europe during 1978.[45] Fifty-four artillery pieces is six more than half the number in a single Soviet division.

41. Operational characteristics of U.S. carrier based aircraft is given in *Combat Fleets of the World, 1976/1977*, pp. 465-66.

42. "NATO: A Special Report on Western Defense and a look at the summit conference in Washington next week: Priority is to maintain momentum," *The Times* (London), 26 May 1978, pp. 21-25.

43. "Study suggests doubling U.S. Army Firepower: Artillery deficiency a primary concern," *The Christian Science Monitor*, 18 February 1977, p. 24.

44. "NATO orders crash program to counter Soviet buildup," *The Christian Science Monitor*, 19 May 1977, p. 3.

45. "The U.S. Army plans. . . ," in "News in Brief," *Los Angeles Times*, 13 January 1978.

When Soviet military craftsmen detect a weakness or vulnerability in their forces, they seem to take every possible opportunity to correct it. If correction is not possible, then the vulnerability or weakness is compensated for elsewhere in such a fashion as to render it unimportant. If an important objective must be gained, the Soviet Union is rarely satisfied to set in hand only one measure for its accomplishment when three or four different measures will render accomplishment more certain.

Not satisfied with bridging operations that can lay a river crossing at the rate of five meters per minute,[46] the Soviets have amphibious tanks and armored personnel carriers to cross barriers of water as well as medium tanks that can cross on the bottom of rivers, underneath the water. If that will not entirely suffice to speed the advance, the Soviets are prepared to use troop-carrying helicopters, to drop parachutists and heavy equipment from transport aircraft, or to land them if air heads have already been seized.

In addition to some 4,600 tactical aircraft with which to support ground forces in the advance, the Soviets have 491 medium range bombers with which to attack targets in NATO. If that does not suffice, there are some 500 intermediate range and medium range ballistic missiles to deal with targets throughout Western Europe as well as elsewhere. One hundred of the ballistic missiles are the new, mobile SS-20s that carry three independently-targetable war heads of 150 kilotons yield to a range of 4,000 miles. It is expected that 300 to 400 such missiles will be deployed which can then hit up to twelve hundred targets in Western Europe.[47]

If Soviet tactical aircraft, medium bombers, IRBM and MRBM forces are not quite appropriate for the task in hand, there is the *Scaleboard* missile that is organic to the Soviet Front Army. It is a mobile missile with a range of 400 miles carrying a one megaton war head. If that will not do, then there is the new *Frog* missile, with a 540 mile range, of which 150 have been reported to be deployed with the Group of Soviet Forces in Germany, it probably has only a one kiloton war head.[48] All of that besides the full complement of short-range rockets, heavy, medium and light artillery and mortars.

If the Soviets wish a target to be neutralized without demolishing it, they are prepared to use rockets or other means to deliver chemical or biological agents that will merely kill personnel without bending the target out of

46. See description of Soviet PMP pontoon-laying trucks in "Israelis Display Captured Russian Material," *International Defense Review*, June 1975, pp. 318-19. Egyptian troops laid ten bridges across the Suez Canal, under fire and air attack, when they were expected by the Israelis to lay not more than one in 24 hours.

47. "Soviet Union Deploys SS-20," *International Defense Review*, Vol. 11, No. 2 (1978), p. 145; see also, Joseph D. Douglas, Jr., "Soviet Nuclear Strategy in Europe: A Selective Targeting Doctrine," *Strategic Review*, Vol. V, No. 4, Fall 1977, pp. 19-32.

48. "Sowjet-Atom-Raketen fur Entfernungen bis 800 km.," *Soldat und Technik*, No. 11, November 1978, p. 594.

shape.[49] Needless to say Warsaw Pact troops are equipped to protect themselves from nuclear, chemical and biological agents. Tanks, armored personnel carriers and other vehicles are equipped with air filters, and pressurized air systems to protect troops against air contaminated by nuclear fallout, chemical and biological agents.[50]

The ground and air armies of the Soviet Union and its allies are equipped and positioned to wage highly mobile warfare, around the clock, across battlefields dominated by Soviet missiles, tactical air and artillery, and where nuclear, biological and chemical weapons have been employed.

Are all of those superb capabilities intended for nothing more than a fighting retreat on Moscow when that fabled day arrives that the twenty or so NATO divisions fling themselves across East Germany to liberate the Poles? Or are the Soviet exertions aimed at gaining one more increment of strategic advantage toward accomplishment of strategic superiority? In short, are they preparations for war?

49. Even East German forces are being prepared for nuclear biological and chemical warfare. Each East German division is being equipped with NBC combat battalions. They will use the Russian BM 21 rocket launcher. Two batteries of six launchers each can fire 500 to 600 rockets in less than a minute, to a range of 15,000 meters. See, "Chemical Warheads for East German Army," *International Defense Review,* Vol. 11, No. 8 (1978), p. 1207. "Russ Missiles Reported Armed with Toxic Gas," *Los Angeles Times,* 10 November 1976, p. 16.

50. For example, see Lt. Colonel-Engineer V. Strelkov, "Self-Propelled Antiaircraft Gun (ZSU-23-4)," *Znamenosets,* No. 7, July 1975, pp. 16-17 translated in *Soviet Press: Selected Translations* (Bolling Air Force Base, D.C.) No. 786, pp. 188-92: "It is outfitted with antinuclear protection. . . . Radioactive dust is removed from the air entering the vehicle . . . a higher pressure inside the vehicle, which prevents contaminated outside air from entering . . ."; see also, for mechanized unit decontamination equipment, "Entstrahlung, Entigiftung, und Entseuchung mit Turbo-Triebwerken," *Soldat und Technik,* March 1973, p. 250; "Die AC-Abwehrtruppe der Warshau Pakt-Heere," *ibid.,* September 1976, p. 479; "Tschechoslowakei ABC-Dekontaminierungsgerat," and, "NVA: Entigiftungsanlage: TZ-74," in "Erkennungsblatter," *ibid.,* September 1978, following page 235; "Biological Warfare: Suspicions of Soviet Activity," *Science,* Vol. 192, No. 4234, 2 April 1976, pp. 38f; and, for description of Soviet operations under conditions of nuclear, biological and chemical contamination, see, C. N. Donnelly, "Soviet Techniques for Combat in Built Up Areas," *International Defense Review,* Vol. 10, No. 2, April 1977, pp. 239-42; and see, "Soviets Violating U.S. biological War Pact?," *The Christian Science Monitor,* 16 June 1976, p. 2.

IX. The Platitudes of Peace—The Vocabulary of War

THE STRATEGIC CONDITIONS UNDER WHICH THE SOVIET UNION MAY CONDUCT ITS MILITARY CAMPAIGN FOR THE CONQUEST OF WESTERN EUROPE have been altered, over a period of years, by Soviet Strategy toward Czechoslovakia, Cuba, Yugoslavia and the rest. In the West, little has been done to counter or cancel the strategic advantage so patiently accumulated by the Soviet Union. One may not cancel what one does not see.

Of Action and Inaction

It became evident, for example, that the Soviet Seventh Army would be left behind in Czechoslovakia, in 1968, after the Polish, East German, Hungarian and Bulgarian troops were withdrawn.[1] None asked why such a garrisoning of Czechoslovakia should be necessary when, as the Warsaw Pact had just demonstrated, it was possible to take the country over in four to ten hours. The Czech Army and Secret Police remained loyal to the Soviet Union. The Czech Army had remained decently quiet in its barracks during the invasion and the Czech Secret Police helped the KGB round up suspects for the purges that would follow.

Because of these events the Soviet Union was able to increase by 25 percent the strength of its ground forces facing the Central Front of NATO, while lengthening the front that NATO forces would have to guard against a possible Soviet surprise attack. Surely that was a strategic change of some local magnitude. It was not as though Czechoslovakia had been garrisoned by Soviet military police units or KGB troops which would have reflected a Soviet concern about internal security in Czechoslovakia. This was a "Soviet Army," comprising three motorized rifle divisions and two tank divisions, capable of operating as a mobile force, as part of a Warsaw Pact Front Army.

The Supreme Allied Commander in Europe said, at the time: "'The military balance in Central Europe has been very significantly altered to the

1. "Czech Army Unit Evacuates A Base for Russians: Division is Being Relocated from Military Reservation in Vicinity of Prague," *New York Times*, 1 October 1968, p. 10.

disadvantage of the West.' Soviet troops are much farther west than at any time in recent years . . . and an extensive mobilization of men, communications and transport equipment has been achieved to support forward units."[2]

The U.S. Secretary of Defense, on the other hand, concluded that the new Soviet Army facing NATO from Czechoslovakia, "will not require increased U.S. troop strength in Europe."[3] There were 300,000 U.S. military personnel in Europe at the time.

Indeed, so little impression was left by the Soviet move into Czechoslovakia, that U.S. forces in NATO were actually *reduced* by 27,000. In the the years after Czechoslovakia, NATO forces on the Central Front fell by about 50,000; Soviet Forces on the Central Front increased 50,000 in 1968. The number of Canadian troops in Germany fell from 10,000 to 2,800; the Soviet Premier, Alexei Kosygin, congratulated the Canadian government on the wisdom of its decision.[4] The Royal Danish Army dropped from 28,000 down to 21,000.[5] The Royal Netherlands Army decreased from 83,550 to 75,000. The Belgian Army was reduced by 14,600 troops, leaving a total of 63,400.[6]

Having raised no alarm amongst the members of NATO by its increase of 50,000 combat troops on NATO's central front, the Soviet Union added a further 76,500 troops by increasing the size of each of its divisions in East Germany and Czechoslovakia. At the same time they increased the number of their tanks, armored personnel carriers, and artillery pieces. Further, increase in the Polish, Czech, East German and Hungarian armed forces accounted for an expansion of at least 200,000 personnel in Warsaw Pact forces on the Central Front.

If the West regretted the suppression of Czechoslovakia for the third time in thirty years, policy toward the Soviet Union after 1968 failed to reflect such regret. If the West drew any strategic implications about the defense of West Germany from the forward positioning of another Soviet Army in Central Europe, no implications could be discerned in the military policies of the democracies.

In retrospect, the Soviet march into Czechoslovakia in 1968 might appear to have been a genuine gamble, were it viewed *in isolation.* It was not a gamble at all. Considering what had happened in Cuba from 1959 onwards, there remained no legitimate reason to suppose that the Western Allies

2. "Power Balance Found Disrupted: Lemnitzer Evaluates Soviet Czechoslovak Action," *Baltimore Sun,* 29 October 1968, p. 1.

3. "Clifford Sees No Need for European Buildup," *Los Angeles Times,* 11 September 1968, p. 12.

4. Canadian decision reported in *Strategic Survey, 1969,* p. 93; Soviet premier's congratulations reported in "Kosygin Lauds Canada NATO Force Pullout," *Los Angeles Times,* 15 May 1971, p. 9.

5. Danish Army strength in *Military Balance, 1968-1969* and *Military Balance, 1979-1979;* and, see "Denmark: Force Reduction," *Military Review,* Vol. LII, No. 2, February 1972, p. 103.

6. The *Military Balance* for the years covered shows the troop reductions.

would treat the Soviet move into Czechoslovakia as anything other than a local matter of no concern to the West. In 1959, the regime of Fulgencio Batista was overthrown by Fidel Castro. Batista's "repressive" regime—it tolerated six different opposition parties and 23 independent newspapers—was replaced by a regime that tolerated no opposition parties and permitted no newspapers save its own to be published.[7]

Castro's attitude towards freedom of the press and political opposition did not seem to be taken as a warning about the nature of the regime any more than the arming of Cuba by the Soviet Union was taken as a warning of a change for the worst in the West's strategic situation. James Reston of the *New York Times* had thought that Cuba could become a real military threat to the United States. But the Under-Secretary of State pointed out that tanks, guns, fighter aircraft, air defense weapons and anti-shipping missiles supplied by the Soviet Union to Cuba, were purely defensive in purpose. Even if all the missiles were put together, they could not reach Florida, the Under-Secretary assured Congress. As the *The Observer* (London) succintly observed:

> To the Russians Cuba is militarily as much a liability as West Berlin is to the Western Powers. . . . The Communist base in Cuba does not really add anything to the military power of Russia.
>
> If, of course, Castro were to use his armed forces . . . to attack a neighboring country . . . that would be a different matter.[8]

Of course, it is only fair to say that the *The Observer* did not know of the "missile crisis" that would erupt within nine days; nor could one expect the Department of State to be conversant with such strategical matters. However, eight years later, despite the "missile crisis," no measures had as yet been taken to counter the strategic advantage gained by the Soviet Union through its Cuban policy.

By 1970, the Soviet Union could irrefutably be said to be using Cuban harbors for the use of their fleet. The then Assistant Secretary of Defense reported confidently on Cuba: "We do not perceive a direct threat to the U.S. mainland *at this time.*" He allowed, however, that Soviet assistance had given Cuba the best-equipped armed forces in Latin America, although they lacked either sea or airlift for operations outside of Cuba. "We can expect," he said, "that Soviet naval vessels and reconnaissance aircraft will continue to visit Cuba."[9]

7. Lists of newspapers published and opposition parties operating in Cuba before 1959 are in *Political Handbook of the World* for the period. See also "Cuba" in *1959 Britannica Book of the Year.*

8. "Dialogue on Cuba," *The Observer* (London), 14 October 1962, p. 10. Mr. Reston's views and the statement of the Under-Secretary of State, George Ball, are cited in the same place.

9. "Caribbean Soviet Naval Presence Expected to Continue," *Aviation Week and Space Technology,* Vol. 93, No. 9, 31 August 1970, p. 22. Italics added.

While lacking the sea or airlift to threaten the continental United States, Cuba did manage, somehow, to get its soldiers to Africa for the Angolan campaign in 1975; to use its ships to drop KGB agents in far-away Hong Kong; and, ultimately, to deploy into Africa and the Middle East between 50 and 60 thousand troops.[10]

The marriage of Cuban and Soviet policies in Africa and the Middle East was consummated in combat upon African battlefields; and the regular deployment into Cuba of Soviet air, ground and naval units could be taken as significant changes in the strategic reach of the two allies. But in April 1979, Congress was reassured, once again; there was no need for the United States to take any measures to compensate for what might seem to be an improvement in Soviet strategic mobility, and a worsening of the American strategic position in the Caribbean:

> Given the absence of a significant outside threat or a substantial military presence in the region, the United States had not seen the need for countervailing military power. It has not dedicated specific U.S. forces of any magnitude for the defense of its southern flank and has not undertaken major forward defense deployments in the region . . . the United States has judged military bases to be essentially irrelevant, and most likely inimical to U.S. security interests in Latin America.[11]

One of the "non-major forward defense deployments in the region" is the Fleet Marine Ground Defense Force at Guantanamo, Cuba, 500 miles from Miami, Florida. The mission of the 432 U.S. Marines that comprise the force, is to defend the U.S. naval installations located there by right of the treaty with Cuba of 1934. If in the performance of their mission the marines were to find that the 3,000 Cuban Border Guards, the 10,000 Cuban State Security troops, or elements of the Cuban and Soviet armed forces, located on the island, were more than they could handle, help could be sought from the other "non-major defense deployment" in the area: the 173 U.S. marines and 344 U.S. soldiers who look after the defense of Puerto Rico, 600 miles from Guantanamo.

One has been firmly assured, however, that a recent increase in the Soviet military presence in Cuba has been a "very modest" one; the 12,000 Russian folks in Cuba are required to be there, it is said, to show the Cubans how to use and maintain the weapons and equipment the Soviet Union has sent to the island over the last 20 years.[12]

10. *Strategic Survey, 1975:* "Angola," pp. 27-38; "Russian Agents Pass as Seamen: Cuban Vessels Land KGB Spies," *South China Morning Post* (Hong Kong), 4 April 1976, p. 1; and *Military Balance, 1978-1979,* gives Cuban troop-strength abroad, see p. 74.

11. *United States Foreign Policy Objectives and Overseas Installations,* Report to the Committee on Foreign Relations, United States Senate, 96th Congress, 1st Session, April 1979, p. 198.

12. "A 'Modest Increase' of Russians in Cuba," *San Francisco Chronicle,* 8 August 1979, p. 13.

After the press reported, in February 1978, that Soviet pilots were assisting in Cuba's air defense, the Secretary of State acknowledged the presence of "a few more" Soviet air units in Cuba than in the past. He did not find it worrisome since there was no particular pattern in it. The Secretary of Defense suggested the Soviet units were "involved in training fights." "This sort of thing," he said, "has been going on for years. It doesn't change anything."[13]

Reports that the Soviets were "establishing a high-ranking command structure within its [*sic*] military contingent in Cuba," were shrugged off by the State Department in July 1979: "There is no evidence of any substantial increase in the Soviet military presence in Cuba over the past several years or of the presence of a Soviet military base. Apart from the military group which has been advising Cuban troops for 15 years, our intelligence warrants no conclusion that there are any other significant Soviet forces in Cuba."[14]

In August, the Chairman of the Senate Foreign Relations Committee announced that there were Soviet combat troops in Cuba. The State Department's spokesman admitted that there were 2,000 to 3,000 Soviet combat troops "newly discovered" in Cuba. There were, he said, armored, artillery and infantry elements, but it "poses no threat to the United States and violates no understanding banning offensive weapons in Cuba."[15]

There were cynics amongst those who gossip about such things. They suggested that the Chairman of the Senate Committee was in trouble in his coming re-election campaign and he was just trying to establish his standing as a real "Hawk" with the folks back home—it might help to counter the bad press he had received for voting for the Panama Canal treaty. Other cynics suggested it was a ploy on the part of the Department of State so we could return Guantanamo to Cuba in return for withdrawal of the Soviet "combat unit." Obviously the latter did little justice to the State Department's point of view, for they said: "This is no Cuban Missile crisis." And, further, discussions with the Soviet Union will continue. They obviously were not at all perturbed.

All of this was only an anomoly *if* one considered that whatever the Soviets might be doing in Cuba, it had no impact on the strategic disposition of the United States anyway.

13. "More Soviet Pilots Than Usual in Cuba, Vance Says," *Los Angeles Times,* 15 February 1978, p. 9.

14. "News in Brief": "There is no evidence . . .," *Los Angeles Times,* 22 July 1979, p. 2. Cited statement (by Secretary Vance) is however in "Soviet Union Deploying combat troops in Cuba," *The Peninsula Times Tribune,* 31 August 1979, p. A-1.

15. "Soviet Combat Unit In Cuba Is Confirmed," *San Francisco Chronicle,* 1 September 1979, p. 1.

War and Politics

Should one dismiss Cuba and Czechoslovakia as two quite discrete enterprises undertaken for no common purpose and motivated by nothing more than some obscure Socialist anxiety? Why should the great and powerful Soviet Motherland, which we are assured has internal problems that would vex a saint, rush across 6,000 miles of ocean to save a Cuban eccentric just because he claims to be a communist? Why should that same great and powerful nation fling 25 combat divisions onto a small country it already holds captive just because some college students are reading poetry aloud in its streets? The first would seem quixotic and the second just plain dumb. Yet those are two adjectives the least likely to spring to mind when characterizing the figures who conduct the affairs of the Soviet Union. What if the Soviet advance into Cuba and into Czechoslovakia was neither quixotic nor dumb? What if each was a deliberate and calculated act of high Soviet policy, of which the common character was military and the common purpose strategic?

One can demonstrate quite easily that Soviet actions in each place resulted in the enhancement of Soviet capabilities to wage a successful land war for Western Europe while consequently reducing Western capabilities to do so. It is not therefore extravagant to suppose that the strategic conception that ties Cuba to Czechoslovakia applies in other places where Soviet policy is at work.

It would not be very important that the Soviet Union embraces the theoretical statement that war is politics in a violent form, if there were no material means through which the statement could be translated into action. However much one might wish to suppose that Soviet military preparations and strategic *demarches* are unconnected to Soviet policy, those things cannot be considered as occuring in a vacuum. No evidence suggests that a separation exists in the Soviet regime between those who conduct the affairs of the Soviet Union at home and abroad and those who formulate strategic and military policy. Soviet foreign policy in no way reflects the kind of division in view that exists in the West between those who conduct foreign relations and those who practice military science.

It is this misunderstanding of the Communist view of the relationship among politics, strategy and war that blinds the democracies to the significance of Soviet actions in Cuba and elsewhere. This difference in view lies at the very heart of the conflict between democracy and totalitarianism. The failure of the democracies to prevail in the conflict would signal the ending of the democratic view of politics as the foundation of government anywhere in the Western World. For, as it is said: "a new world war will be a decisive armed clash between the opposed world social systems."[16]

A Dangerous Optimism

A persistent optimism pervades American policy toward the Soviet Union. It is bolstered by unshakeable convictions about Soviet weaknesses, American strength, the impossibility of nuclear war, and an overall belief in the ultimate goodwill of the communists. There is a kind of sentimental attachment to communism that is fostered by the belief that all communists would be democrats if only given just half a chance. One writer expressed such sentiments in May 1939, three months before the Hitler-Stalin Pact cleared the way for the Soviet-German division of Poland:

> With all their faults the Communists perform necessary functions in the confused struggle of our time. They have helped to build up and to run a string of organizations—known as "fronts" by their opponents—which clearly serve the cause not of "totalitarian doctrine" but of a more workable democracy. And the value of those organizations lies largely in the energy and discipline and zeal of their Communist members.
>
> . . . I am inclined to believe that the Communists have developed a sort of double mental bookkeeping by means of which they are able to account for their love of Stalin and their adherence to the New Deal. At any rate, the effect of their conversion, sincere or strategical, is to postpone serious revolutionary objectives to some post-next-war millenium and to leave them free for democratic endeavor in this world.[17]

Others at the time, distinguished men and women in the United States, like Vincent Sheean, I. J. Stone, S. J. Perelman, and James Thurber, pleaded that the Soviet Union ought not to be considered in the same category as Hitler's Germany. In an appeal "To All Active Supporters of Democracy and Peace," written two weeks before the Hitler-Stalin Pact was concluded, they outlined the good points of the Soviet Union:

> The Soviet Union continues as always to be a bulwark against war and aggression, and works unceasingly for a peaceful international order.
>
> It has eliminated racial and national prejudices within its borders . . . and made the expression of anti-Semitism or any racial animosity a criminal offense.
>
> It has built the trade unions, in which almost 24,000,000 workers are organized into the fabric of society.

16. Sokolovsky, *op. cit.*, p. 208.

17. Freda Kirchwey, "'Red Totalitarianism,'" *The Nation,* Vol. 148, No. 22, 27 May 1939, pp. 605-6.

> The Soviet Union considers political dictatorship a transitional form and has shown a steadily expanding democracy in every sphere.
>
> Soviet aims and achievements make it clear that there exists a sound and permanent basis in mutual ideals for cooperation between the U.S.A. and the U.S.S.R. in behalf of world peace and the security and freedom of all nations.[18]

Such ingenuousness may have been excusable in 1939. How could humorists, political commentators, and other publicists know Soviet trade-unions were company-unions with the company being the State and Party; that the Soviet Union was about to divide the spoils of eastern Europe with Adolph Hitler; that amongst the Soviet efforts for peace and against aggression would be an attack on Finland; and, that far from becoming more democratic, the regime could match, and indeed had, the brutality of the Nazis. One of the signers of the letter of appeal was to be the author of a widely used college textbook on the Soviet Union; he apparently did not know about the extent of the slaughter of the Kulaks that took place during the "Liquidate the Kulaks" campaign (1929-32), soon enough to include it in his 1947 edition. He says of the results of the campaign to collectivize agriculture: "Opposition and doubt gave way to confidence and energetic participation in the new agriculture, which had demonstrated its superiority over the old ways."[19]

Such outlooks as those expressed in 1939 by some otherwise, intelligent Americans, have their progeny in the world of American foreign policy and strategy. They fuel the pervasive optimism about the nature and objectives of Soviet policy while lending a peculiar wistfulness to the view the United States government adopts toward Soviet actions in the world.

The optimistic theme takes a variety of forms. Drew Pearson wrote in 1967:

> Khrushchev had his own problems with the Red Army and Russian Defense industries. The latter are just as demanding as Boeing, General Dynamics and the big defense plants in the U.S.
>
> Now that Russia has narrowed the missile gap down to about three to one favoring the United States, there are definite signs that the Soviet military budget is being whittled down.

18. "To All Active Supporters of Democracy and Peace," letter dated, 10 August 1939, New York, in "Letters to the Editor," *The Nation,* Vol. 149, No. 9, 26 August 1939, p. 228.

19. "Lurid accounts, mostly fictional, appeared in the Nazi press in Germany and in the Hearst press in the United States. . . ." See Frederick L. Schuman, *Soviet Politics at Home and Abroad,* first published in February 1946, Fourth Printing (New York: Alfred Knopf, 1947), pp. 216-19.

> American reports from Moscow indicate that the recent public announcement of a military increase was issued chiefly for political effect. . . . Now that Brezhnev is more secure . . . [he] is strong enough to meet the United States halfway on arms stabilization.[20]

Joseph Kraft wrote in 1968, five weeks before the Czech invasion:

> But precisely because they [the Russians] have forces to work with inside Czechoslovakia, the Russians are not as obliged to be as crude as they once were. They have a margin of safety in Eastern Europe which combines with many other factors to make it easier for Moscow to work towards detente with Washington.[21]

The desire to see moderation in Soviet policy toward the West leads to all sorts of arguments why the Soviet Union will not or cannot do that which in fact it is doing to advance its interests at the expense of the West. Even when the Soviet government makes no pretense about its policies, they are interpreted as harmless by the West; inconsequential; or, even helpful.

In 1966, when the Soviet Union announced a substantial increase in military expenditures, the *New York Times* reassured its readers that a study of the new Soviet economic plan suggested only a marginal shift in resources toward military preparedness.[22] That view of the Soviet military budget simply followed logically from the U.S. government's optimistic view of Soviet policy: ". . . Moscow is thought to be more free, now, to develop the spirit of Tashkent and to work openly for a more stable and less perilous world."[23]

The idea that the Soviet economy just barely creaks along has been a persistent one. In 1971, it was remarked how burdensome it was to the Soviet economy to furnish all that military equipment to North Vietnam, Cuba, and Egypt and to support the members of the Warsaw Pact:

> One of the most important things the Russians will have to take into account . . . is the growing strain their foreign policy is imposing on their economy. Propping up their clients abroad is proving a costly business.
>
> It is a whopping burden for an economy that is in pretty feeble condition already. Small wonder if the Russians are looking around for ways of reducing it.[24]

20. Drew Pearson, "U.S. Russia Drawing Much Closer Together," 2 January 1967.
21. Joseph Kraft, "Russia's Using the Velvet Glove on Her Satellites," *Los Angeles Times,* 11 July 1968, p. 5, pt. II.
22. "Soviet Planning Guns and Butter: Increases are Scheduled for spending on Military and Consumer Goods," *New York Times,* 25 December 1966, p. 1.
23. "U.S. Anticipates Soviet Moderation," *The Christian Science Monitor,* 10 June 1966, p. 1.
24. "Economy is Creaking: Russia Finds Friends Are Costly," *San Francisco Chronicle,* 22 March 1971, p. 1.

However creaking the Soviet economy may have been in 1971, that was, notwithstanding, the year that Soviet steel production *exceeded* that of the United States by 12.8 million tons.[25]

But the outlook was optimistic:

> The present Soviet leadership under Communist Party Chief Leonid I. Brezhnev appears wholly committed to the new consumer-oriented style of five-year planning. This should result in more wariness in the Kremlin itself against anything smacking of ruthlessness in world affairs.[26]

The Secretary of Defense had already assessed the economic difficulties of the Soviet Union and concluded:

> The pressure on Soviet decision-makers makes us reasonably confident that their expressed interest in strategic arms talks is genuine. For the Soviet Union even to attempt to keep pace in a strategic arms race of large proportions would be enormously costly for them in financial terms, and it would divert badly needed resources from the civilian sector of the economy.[27]

In the previous five years the Soviet Union had deployed 800 ICBMs and would deploy another 600 in the next five years. Yet, as though to confirm and fullfill Western hopes for a slowing of the Soviet armaments program, the International Institute for Strategic Studies in London, reported that the Soviet Union had slowed down in its deployment of ICBMs. A notable event, since by the time of the report the Soviet ICBM force was only 1,510, as compared to the U.S. ICBM force of 1054.[28]

When in 1970, it was discovered that the Soviet Union seemed to have paused for nine months before installing one set of heavy missiles, the SS-9, for which silos had been prepared, it was immediately concluded that it had been a shy attempt on the part of the Russians to signal deliberate restraint on installation of multi-warhead missiles. It was only when the United States ignored the pause, it was said, that the Russians decided to go ahead with the deployment.[29] It was not clear why it should have been inevitable that the Soviet Union was "signalling restraint" by holding back the SS-9s. It had proceeded with the development of other more modern missiles during the

25. "Soviet Steel mills outproduce U.S.," *Palo Alto Times,* 27 January 1972, p. 8.

26. "Russ Shift Economy Towards Goods, Food: 5-year Plan to Satisfy Consumers Could Have Wide Impact on Communists, West," *Los Angeles Times,* 18 July 1971, p. 5, sec. C.

27. *The 1970 Defense Budget and Defense Program for Fiscal Years 1970-74: A Statement by Secretary of Defense Clark Clifford* in *Naval Review 1970, U.S. Naval Institute Proceedings,* Vol. 96, No. 5 (807), May 1970.

28. "Analysts Find Deployment Of Soviet Missiles Slowed," *New York Times,* 3 September 1971, p. 2.

29. "Work on New Soviet Missile Sites Resumes: Nine-month Pause Ends, Following intense Russian Tests of Multiheaded Payloads," *Los Angeles Times,* 11 July 1970, p. 3.

same period, and ended the year with 199 more missiles than it had started with. The possibility that the deployment might have been delayed, if it was at all, by technical difficulties was not even suggested. Yet elsewhere one was being assured that the Soviet Union was absolutely eons behind the United States in technology. For this reason, the United States had little to fear from the Soviet advantage in numbers of missiles and size of warheads.[30] It was explained, at the time, that the United States only used small very accurate warheads, leaving the inference to be drawn that the 20 to 25 megaton warheads on the Soviet SS-9s were the unavoidable consequence of Soviet technological backwardness.

Like the pre-war myth of the near-sighted Japanese pilots who could not see far enough to hit a target, the new myth persisted that Soviet strategic rockets had to be gigantic as well as more numerous to make up for a want of accuracy.

Such ideas would hardly be notable were it not that they would come to dominate American policy and strategy. In explaining the first SALT agreement to the nation, President Nixon said:

> The Soviet Union competes best in the matter of sheer numbers and this competition has been reduced by the SALT agreement, while competition in technology has been preserved, and because that is the U.S. strong point, the United States enjoys a significant advantage because of technological superiority.[31]

But the President had already decided that strategic superiority was no longer needed to defend the United States. Something called "strategic sufficiency" became the characterization of the U.S. military posture in the world. It had been concluded that the only purpose of armed forces was *political* not military: "the overriding purpose of our strategic posture is *political* and defensive; to deny other countries the ability to impose their will on the United States and its allies under the weight of strategic military superiority."[32]

Two Views of Politics

It is *not* a commonly held view in democratic societies that war and politics are the same thing, that war is simply the continuation of politics by violent means. Such a view of war is incompatible with the notion that politics comprises discourse, argument, negotiation, compromise and ac-

30. "Federation of Scientists Says Ads Alleging Soviet Nuclear Lead are in Error and Use 'Scare Tactics,'" *New York Times*, 27 October 1970, p. 13.

31. *United States Foreign Policy for the 1970's: Shaping A Durable Peace*, A Report by President Richard Nixon to the Congress, 3 May 1973, pp. 194-95.

32. "U.S. No Longer Relies on Nuclear Superiority: Nixon Message to Congress Limits Power at Sufficiency to Overcome Alien Threats," *Los Angeles Times*, 19 February 1970, p. 17. Italics added.

commodation. Politics in the democratic society is neither ubiquitous nor paramount. The principal realm of human activity in the democratic regime is a private one from which politics is and ought to be excluded. The goal of politics is to render the private realm secure from intrusion, to preserve it as the arena within which citizens may seek fulfillment without themselves having to resort to coercion or violence against others. Politics is to use the instruments of government to promote that atmosphere and those conditions under which citizens seem most likely to be able to develop and prosper, if that is what they seek, while leaving untrammelled as far as possible, those who do not so choose to seek.

The totalitarian regime, assuming that it enjoys a monopoly of truth about "the political destiny" of mankind, asserts the principle that all things are subject to politics. The only reason a private realm continues to exist at all is because the regime has yet to find the administrative means to regulate it; ultimately it will be regulated. Regulation is essential to the fulfillment of the goals of the society as they are defined by the state and the party.[33]

During the Moscow International Book Fair, in September 1979, the Chairman of the State Publishing Committee ordered seized scores of books before they could be exhibited. The observer from the American Association of Book Publishers found the confiscation "an incredible process." The Soviet Chief Censor who was chairman of the organizing committee for the Book Fair, explained that the seized books could not be exhibited "because they do not serve the purpose of detente, they do not serve the spiritual exchange of mutual understanding between peoples but encourage hostility." Freedom of the press was not to be applied to "freedom of fascist propaganda." The official view of the Soviet Government was expressed as follows: "The Second international book fair in Moscow offers fresh evidence of the consistent implementation in the Soviet Union of the Helsinki Accords concerning book exchanges and the Soviet Union's constant efforts to deepen cultural intercourse and mutual understanding."[34]

Here is the evident contrast between the democratic regime and the totalitarian one: the democratic regime flourishes on the often disorderly propagation of ideas, views, opinions and prejudices, however unpopular with the government or the public; the totalitarian regime flourishes only under the controlled dissemination of that which is accepted as the truth by those who operate the regime.

33. There is a helpful discussion of these things in Herman Finer, *Theory and Practice of Modern Government* (New York: Henry Holt and Company, 1949), "The Democratic and the Dictatorial State," pp. 951-54. See also, A. D. Lindsay, *The Modern Democratic State* (New York: Oxford University Press, 1947).

34. "Censors seize books at Moscow fair," *The News and Observer* (Raleigh, North Carolina), 4 September 1979, p. 3.

Because war is coercion and violence, it is seen within democratic regimes to be inimical to democracy and may even be considered unnatural. Thus George Kennan, to repeat, objects to "people who talk about war as though it were perfectly natural that if you could go to war you would." In speaking of his advocacy of a policy to contain communism, expressed in "The Sources of Soviet Conduct," written in 1947, he explains that he meant "not containment by military means of a military threat, but the *political containment of a political threat.*" Such containment was to be accomplished by demonstrating to the world that the United States "knows what it wants . . . is coping successfully with the problems of its internal life and the responsibilities of a world power, and which has a spiritual vitality capable of holding its own among the major ideological currents of the time. . . ."[35] As can be seen here, the containment of communism really depended on a kind of dedication to moral reform within the United States; an activity having very little bearing on the nature and physical power of the external threat. That is quite similar to the view taken of Czechoslovakia a year and half after the Nazi occupation of the country:

> Irresponsible Czechs . . . find it easy to dream of dramatic liberation and revenge. But the more realistic and responsible leaders are sincere in their efforts to combat this line of thought.
>
> Their task is a difficult one. They have to contend not only with German harshness and stupidity. They also have to contend with the psychological short-comings of their own people: the nationalistic and linguistic prejudices, the narrow horizon, the social uncertainty, the lack of realism, and the tendency to romanticism in political thought.

According to this view, the Czech condition under German occupation was a function of Czech shortcomings, not German military power. But: "The cornerstone of any long-term Czech policy must be a modus vivendi with the Germans . . . they [the Czechs] can hope for some measure of success only if they are able to disarm German distrust."[36]

In this view, the moral quality of Czech society was more important than the fact that Adolph Hitler used war as an extension of German politics. The Czech defeat must therefore be seen in its true light as chiefly a failure of the Czech peoples to demonstrate their moral superiority over the Nazis. And of course, the Nazis would have argued that the defeat of Czechoslovakia stemmed from the moral inferiority of the Czechs because, as democrats, they

35. Marilyn Berger, "An Appeal for Thought," *New York Times Magazine*, 7 May 1978, pp. 42f. Italics added.

36. "Despatch of July 17, 1939, from Consul General Linnell to the Department of State, on the Situation in the Protectorate," in George F. Kennan, *From Prague After Munich: Diplomatic Papers 1938-1940* (Princeton: Princeton University Press, 1968), pp. 226-40.

could not be expected to see the relationship between politics and war in the way that the Nazis did.

When Henry Kissinger expressed his bewilderment about the motives behind Soviet actions in Cuba in 1962, his frame of reference was characteristically democratic:

> What tempted the Soviets into so rash, so foolhardy an adventure as establishing missile bases on an island only ninety miles from our shores?
>
> Given the vulnerability of those bases, it is difficult to understand to what military problem they were addressed.
>
> The chief benefit the Soviets would have obtained from these bases was *political,* not military.[37]

If the West's leading thinker on strategic matters found himself bemused by Soviet policy in Cuba, it is small wonder that others less astute than he should miss the strategic significance of Soviet policy in Austria, Yugoslavia, Libya and elsewhere. The distinction drawn between *military* and *political,* as though the two words described enterprises different in nature and intent, illuminates the difficulty the leaders of the West have in coming to grips with Soviet policy throughout the world.

If in Western eyes, politics and war are distinct from one another, then it becomes increasingly clear how the United States could seek a *political* solution in Vietnam as though it were an alternative to a *military* resolution of the war. The North Vietnamese and their allies, embracing the notion that war and politics differ in method but not nature, pursued a straightforward military victory, at the conference table as well as on the battlefield. At the latter day when American military power and tactical competence altered the conditions of war to favor the United States, the North Vietnamese came to the conference table to prevent defeat on the battlefield. The United States negotiated to reach a settlement, the North Vietnamese to preserve their armed forces, to retain strategic positions in South Vietnam. Thus they set the stage for their eventual victory in the war. An essential requirement for that victory was the removal of U.S. forces from South Vietnam.

In December 1963, the Central Committee of the Vietnam Workers Party, the ruling Communist Party in North Vietnam, issued a resolution outlining the war aims of North Vietnam. It read, in part:

> Now that we are stronger than the enemy politically we must continue to strengthen our political forces. However we are still weaker than the enemy militarily. Therefore the key point at the present time is to make

37. Henry A. Kissinger, "Reflections on Cuba," *The Reporter,* 22 November 1962, pp. 21-24. Italics added.

> outstanding efforts to rapidly strengthen our military forces in order to create a basic change in the balance of forces between the enemy and us in South Vietnam. We are using our political and moral strength with our military and material weakness to oppose an enemy who is weak politically and morally but strong militarily and materially. We should understand the protracted war guideline, but on the other hand we must also seize opportunites to win victories. . . .[38]

The United States used the bombing of North Vietnam to get the North Vietnamese to negotiate a "political" settlement of the war. The price the North Vietnamese demanded for beginning negotiations was a halt to the bombing of the North; the price for a "political" settlement of the war was the withdrawal of all U.S. forces from Vietnam.[39]

In exchange for a lessening of the allied military effort against North Vietnam, North Vietnam would agree to a "political" settlement, which to the North Vietnamese meant the establishment of those conditions that would guarantee military victory.

For North Vietnam, the conference table was an extension of the battlefield, one more arena for protracted warfare. For Americans, the conference table was an alternative to the battlefield, a place for negotiations—politics, not war.[40]

The United States negotiated to achieve an accommodation that would stop the violence. Such a view proves perfectly consistent with the democratic notion that violence ought not to rule politics. The North Vietnamese negotiated to gain a strategic advantage on the battlefield—to win the war. That was perfectly consistent with the notion that "war is the tool of politics," and that "politics creates favorable conditions for military strategy."[41]

The President of the United States announced the conclusion of negotiation for peace in Vietnam in an address to the Nation on 23 January 1973:

38. "Resolution" cited in "Secret Papers Reveal Hanoi Escalation Plan," *Los Angeles Times*, 30 June 1971, p. 16.

39. See in "Hanoi Held Insisting on Warsaw Site," *Los Angeles Times*, 27 April 1968, p. 11; and see ". . . Hanoi is indeed prepared to hold talks with the United States—though on its own terms," point 3, in the terms, "Unconditional end to bombing of North Vietnam." In "Document May Indicate Hanoi Is Ready to Talk: Insistence on Own Terms Implied in Seized Paper of Army's Political Staff," *Los Angeles Times*, 30 April 1968, p. 1.

40. Robert Kennedy, for example, argued that extending the Christmas Truce of 1965 might open the avenue to lead the Vietnamese war to the conference table—"The conflict can be brought from the battlefield to conference table." In "Kennedy Favors Truce Extension: Would Continue if Vietcong 'Substantially Honors' It," *New York Times*, 25 December 1965, p. 2; and, see "A Hanoi Response to Pause in Raids is Sought by U.S.: It Waits for North Vietnam to Indicate a Willingness to Negotiate a Peace Accord," *ibid.*, 28 December 1965, p. 1.

41. "In determining the essence of war, Marxism-Leninism uses as its point of departure the position that war is not an aim in itself, but only a tool of politics. The acceptance of war as a tool of politics also determines the interrelation of military strategy and politics, which is based on the principle if the full dependence of the former on the latter." Marshall of the Soviet Union V. D. Sokolovsky, *Soviet Military Strategy*, pp. 14-15.

> We today have concluded an agreement to end the war and bring peace with honor in Vietnam and Southeast Asia. . . .
>
> Now that we have achieved an honorable agreement, let us be proud that America did not settle for a peace that would have betrayed our allies, that would have abandoned our prisoners of war, and that would have ended the war for us but would have continued the war for 50 million people of Indo China.
>
> The people of South Vietnam have been guaranteed the right to determine their own future, without outside interference.[42]

The "Agreement on Ending the War and Restoring Peace in Vietnam" was signed in Paris on 27 January 1973. The Agreement contained some 23 articles; the protocols to the Agreement a further 49 articles. In December, not two years later, the North Vietnamese Army began a methodical campaign to reduce the defenses of South Vietnam. Two years, almost to the day, after all U.S. combat forces had been withdrawn from Indo-China, Saigon fell to the North Vietnamese Army. Thus did the United States negotiate for peace and the independence of South Vietnam. It achieved neither. Thus did North Vietnam negotiate for a strategic advantage and victory. It achieved both. Politics had cleared the way for strategy to bring military victory.

Le Duc Tho, who declined his share of the Nobel Prize for making "peace" in Vietnam, demonstrated the perspective of those who would win the victory on the battlefield: "The enemy has 5 divisions against our 15. Thus we cannot fail to win victory. At present, all official U.S. statements have ruled out the possibilities of renewing U.S. intervention. The situation is very favorable, and our capabilities are great. We must firmly grasp the opportunity and quickly and firmly do our job."[43]

The victories denied the Communists on the battlefields of South Vietnam were recouped strategically through a campaign waged within the West. Campuses, editorial offices, film and television studios became the strategic arena. It did not matter that Americans and Europeans who opposed the war, did so out of decent motives and with high moral purposes. The motives and purposes were the strategic weapons, which lacking any other, the communists used to achieve a favorable "balance of forces" within Indo-China itself.

42. "Documentation of Vietnam Agreement," News Release, Department of State, Office of Media Services, 24 January 1973.

43. In an address to the North Vietnamese Corps Commanders on the occasion of their briefing for the final campaign to seize Saigon. See "Continuation of article 'Great Spring Victory' by Sen Gen Van Tien Dung as related to NHAN DAN Correspondent . . .)," part of "Lightening Speed," sub-titled, "The Campaign Bearing Uncle Ho's Name." Hanoi in Vietnamese to Vietnam 2330 GMT 3 May 76, as cited in *FBIS,* Vol. IV: *Asia and Pacific,* 5 May 1976, pp. K 8-K 10. But see prior and subsequent issues as well.

Decent men and women, who mobilized for what they thought to be good ends would be mockingly thanked by the leaders of North Vietnam for what was, after all, an indecent victory. The politics of peace in the West was the politics of war for the communist conquest of Indo-China.

Preparations?

There is a notion abroad, amongst both well-educated and well-meaning people, that it does not really matter what the Soviet Union does militarily or strategically, since the possibility of the Soviet Union ever attacking anyone, least of all us, is so improbable as to seem absurd. In this view, the real burden rests on the United States to show good faith, restraint and patience. After all, it is said, Soviet strategic superiority—whatever that means—does not allow the Soviet Union to do anything anyway. What good is strategic superiority if there is not to be a war? Soviet armaments and military preparations certainly do not threaten world peace, they are an eccentricity that must be indulged in the interest of international amity. But U.S. strategic superiority is entirely different. There is just no telling what mischief those folks who work in the bowels of the Pentagon will get up to if they think the United States is stronger than the Soviet Union. That is: decent regimes, if strong, will act indecently; and, indecent regimes, if strong, will act decently.

When President Kennedy called for the preparations of fall-out shelters in July 1961, during the Berlin Crisis of that year, a lively discussion followed. The gist of the arguments of those who opposed such a departure was that protection of the civil population of the United States was intolerable. Why?

> Under the spell of this false sense of security the American people may become more willing to support an adventurist military policy, rather than more fervent in demanding disarmament negotiations, just as our leaders may become less hesitant about pushing their terrible buttons.
>
> But in addition to this, civil defense tends to provoke war precisely because it improves our political deterrence.[44]

A group of social scientists, meeting under the auspices of the National Institute of Mental Health and the American Psychological Association, concluded that nothing but harm could come to America from a civil defense program. Aside from the fact that a civil defense program would bring out the worst in Americans, it would limit the freedom of action of the

44. Erich Fromm and Michael Maccoby, "A Debate on the Question of Civil Defense," *Survival*, Vol. 4, No. 2, March-April 1962, pp. 50-66.

government to negotiate for disarmament and peace. One professor even said, that he had found in talking to Russians that "many Russians, plain citizens as well as officials, see in the U.S. civil defense program a threat of war." Indeed, The President's call for a civil defense program, "was seen in both the U.S. and U.S.S.R. as a signal that war was near. . . ."[45]

And, the Soviet view of civil defense was quite as the professor had said. The Soviet Union called the West German program to have every householder equip his house with gas masks, food rations, drinking water, and blackout equipment, "a plan for the creation of a large-scale army and for mobilization of all the country's economic resources for a new—and by no means defensive—war."[46]

Fortunately for those concerned with not provoking the Russians to war, the Civil Defense program in the United States died a most quiet death.[47] Protection of the general population in the United States from nuclear attack was just too expensive.

The massive bomb shelters built to protect Congressmen and other Federal officials from nuclear attack, alone had cost a billion dollars to build and 42 million dollars a year to maintain.[48] A Congressional committee looking into the matter of providing the population of the United States with protection from nuclear attack found that to do so would be foolish.[49] But of perhaps more importance to the committee's conclusion was the view that: "Some defense experts believe civil defense is a de-stabilizing influence in the nuclear power balance," because it made it look like the United States might be getting ready for war.[50]

Convinced that any measures taken to protect the general population of the United States from nuclear attack were certain to be taken as indications of American preparations for war, that they were de-stabilizers of the strategic nuclear balance, and a general provocation to the Soviet Union, such measures have not been put in hand.

One was appalled therefore, when it became apparent that the Soviet Union was undertaking an elaborate civil defense program. It included blast shelters around Moscow, the burying of food stocks, rehearsal for the evacuation of cities, relocation of heavy industry away from metropolitan areas,

45. Arthur L. Waskow, "The Shelter-Centered Society," *Scientific American,* Vol. 206, No. 5, May 1962, pp. 46-50.

46. "Militarization Continues—New Bonn 'Emergency Laws,'" *Pravda,* 4 July 1965, p. 5, in *The Current Digest of the Soviet Press,* Vol. XVII, No. 27, 28 July 1965, pp. 25-26.

47. "He's Falling Behind: Lone Inspector Tries to Keep Track of L.A. Fallout Shelters," *Los Angeles Times,* 24 September 1972, p. B.

48. "$1 Billion Spent So Far: Nuclear Hideaway for U.S. Leaders Questioned," *Los Angeles Times,* 5 December 1978, p. 1.

49. "More U.S. Civil Defense Called Foolish," *Los Angeles Times,* 17 May 1977, p. 4.

50. "Panel Says U.S. Is Unprepared for Attack, Disaster," *Los Angeles Times,* 9 May 1977, p. 1.

instruction of the general population in protection against nuclear, chemical and biological attack, and the creation of a separate service of the Soviet Armed Forces to organize protection for the civilian population. In ten years, it was said that the Soviet Union had spent 65 billion dollars to provide civil defense, in addition to the value of volunteer measures contributed by the citizenry at large.[51]

Surely here was an alarming development. The Soviet civil defense program would upset the strategic balance, free the hands of those people in the Kremlin to press their terrible buttons; and, all told it could be seen as evidence of the Soviet intention to go to war. No. Not at all. As one professor from MIT explained it:

> it seems that the Soviets' civil defense program is one aspect of their natural defensiveness—the same sort of defensiveness that compels them to maintain an ABM [anti-ballistic missile] site in Moscow even though they must know it to be ineffective against any deliberate attack.
>
> . . . the patterns of Soviet history, the nature of the Soviet political system, and the historically-rooted fear of invasion among Soviet leaders suggest that the Soviet civil defense system (to the extent that one exists) has been and is seen by Soviet leaders as a hedge, as a defensive system. There is little historic evidence from which to infer any other conclusion.[52]

The real problem, as our professor was quick to point out, was not that the leaders of the Soviet Union, doubtlessly caught up in a frightening world, had authorized an elaborate civil defense program to instill "a faith that the Communist Party watches over and protects its people"; the real

51. Evidence of the Soviet civil defense preparations may be seen in the following: "Die Zivilverteidigung in der Sowjetunion," *Soldat und Technik* (Frankfurt am Main), February 1978, pp. 92-97; C. N. Donnelly, "Civil Defense in the Soviet Union," *International Defense Review* (Geneva), Vol. 10, No. 4, August 1977, pp. 635-44; "Soviets Stress Civil Defense," *Atlanta Constitution*, 30 November 1966, p. 1; "Military Training in the Factories: The Plant Training Center," *Krasnaya zvezda*, 12 January 1972, p. 1, in *The Current Digest of the Soviet Press*, Vol. XXIII, No. 2, p. 12; "An Authoritative Review of Civil Defense Preparedness: Important Aspect of Instruction," *Uchitelskaya*, 24 August 1974, p. 1, *ibid.*, Vol. XXVII, No. 5, p. 18; "Civil Defense: Concern of Entire Collective," *Krasnaya zvezda*, 19 August 1977, p. 1, *ibid.*, Vol. XXIX, No. 33, pp. 18-19; "Mass destruction weapons: Protective Measures in the Soviet Union," *International Civil Defence* (Geneva), No. 195, September 1971, p. 3; "Demonstration exercises by Plant Civil Defence in the Soviet Union," *ibid.*, No. 209, November 1972, p. 6; General-Colonel Aleksandr Terentyevich Altunin, Deputy Minister of Defense and Chief of the Soviet Civil Defense Organization, "The Main Direction," *Voyennyye znaniya*, October 1976, in *Strategic Review*, Summer 1977, pp. 101-5; "Evacuation Plan Printed in Soviet: Tadzhikstan, Near China, Calls for Vigilance," *New York Times*, 1 November 1971, p. 2; N. Kalinina, Murmansk Oblast Civil Defense Headquarters, "Take Care of the Shelters," *Soviet Press, Selected Translations*, No. 77-1, January 1977, pp. 21-23: P. T. Yegorov, *et al*, *Civil Defense* in *Soviet Military Thought Series*, U.S.G.P.P. No. 008-070-00382-1; "New Hard Evidence on Soviet Civil Defense," *Air Force Magazine*, April 1977, p. 23; "Soviet Civil Defense," Special Report No. 47, Department of State, September 1978; and, *United States and Soviet City Defense: Considerations for Congress*, Senate, 94th Congress, 2d Session, 30 September 1976.

52. Fred M. Kaplan, "The Soviet Civil Defense Myth: Part 2," *Bulletin of the Atomic Scientists*, April 1978, pp. 41-48, and see Part 1 in *ibid.*, March 1978, pp. 15-20.

problem was that there were people in the United States that noticed it. And we all know what that means: "the new emphasis on civil defense [in the United States] is the entering wedge of a campaign which will result by slow steps in major shelter programs for the future. . . ." And, what was even worse, "demand for active defenses as well."[53]

Another equally eminent scholar, in the field of particle physics, said that, "even if the Soviet Union were conducting an effective civil defense program, this is in itself no reason why we should imitate such a move." He went on to point out the real culprits in all this "to do" about civil defense: "The very fact that proponents of increased defense expenditures and a harder political line are arguing that a Soviet shelter program indicates aggressive intent on their part bears witness to the fact that increased civil defense induces a military response and is thus an integral part of the arms race."[54]

While that statement may lack the logical elegance of Newton's propositions, it certainly left no doubt about what American priorities ought to be: avoid an arms race at all costs. The real possibility that the strategic balance might have been upset by a Soviet civil defense program was irrelevant, if not downright exaggeration.

The President, responding to the concerns of those who saw the danger in Soviet civil defense, proposed doubling the annual budget for U.S. civil defense. Shortly afterwards, responding to those who thought Soviet civil defense a mere sham, he cut the proposed budget for civil defense and transferred the program out of the Defense Department.[55]

So once again, misplaced good nature and strategic ignorance permitted the Soviet Union another modest strategic advantage. If the Soviet civil defense program proved to be as extensive as some experts seemed to think, then in a nuclear war, 98 per cent of the Soviet population would survive and Soviet industry would recover from nuclear attack in two to four years. The United States, without a civil defense program, would lose up to half its population and it would take 12 years for industry to recover.[56]

Apparently unperturbed by the prospect of offending the Soviet Union, the Peoples Republic of China sought to provide underground shelters to protect the population of its cities.[57] U.S. Congressmen touring Dairen in

53. "Weapons-analyst" Richard Garvin as cited in *ibid.*

54. Testimony before Joint Committee on Defense Production by Dr. Wolfgang Panofsky as cited in "Views Diverge on Strong Civil Defense," *Aviation Week and Space Technology*, 3 May 1976, p. 17.

55. "Defense: A Boost for Civil Safety," *San Francisco Sunday Examiner and Chronicle, This World*, 25 June 1978, p. 7; "Carter Puts Severe Limit on Spending for Civil Defense," *San Francisco Chronicle*, 28 December 1978, p. 8. Budget for Civil Defense was 86 million in 1976; it rose to 97 million in FY 1979, *Department of Defense Annual Report, Fiscal Year 1979*, p. 370.

56. "Soviet Civil Defense: Insiders Argue Whether Strategic Balance is Shaken," *Science*, 10 December 1976, p. 1141.

57. "What to do if Holocaust Comes: Chinese Learn Nuclear Defense," *The Christian Science Monitor*, 11 December 1974, p. 4.

1976, reported seeing a shelter that would hold 60,000 people and that was equipped to provide uncontaminated water and air for those being sheltered.[58] Sweden has installed industry underground, provided hard-rock shelter for naval vessels, aircraft and military installations, and shelters for the population, as well as having an elaborate civil defense organization.[59] The Finns, who have some notion of what Russian "defensiveness" can be like,[60] had provided shelters for almost half the population by 1977, and intend to be able to shelter the entire population by 1980.[61] Switzerland which has not been at war with anyone since their own civil war, has been preparing blast shelters for its entire population, as well as underground military installations for its defense. Its program is to be completed by 1990.[62] Yugoslavia holds air-raid drills for its population and has required its civilians to provide themselves with "the minimum obligatory means for personal radiological, biological, and chemical protection." It is reported that: "The final deadline for the purchase of this equipment is in 1983."[63]

Such measures being undertaken by presumably sensible people may be an indication of what can be expected over the next few years. In any case, those countries mentioned above are not alone in their efforts to provide protection from acts of war for their populations. Countries on both sides of the Iron Curtain are doing that which is within their power and resources to do to defend their civil populations. How odd it is that those who govern in the United States would think it extravagant to do the same.

The West Bemused

So the Soviet Union continues to accumulate military capability and strategic positions from which to use that capability against the West. The West looks on bemused at the growth of Soviet military power, wondering at

58. "Congressmen Report on China's Underground Shelters," *Los Angeles Times*, n.d. But also, concerning shelters in Wuhan, see "Tea Inside a Chinese Mountain," *The Christian Science Monitor*, 20 April 1979, p. 13.

59. *The Total Defense of Sweden*, Press Department of the Swedish Defense Staff, 1963; "New Form of Civil Defense in Sweden," *International Civil Defence* (Geneva), No. 272, February 1978, p. 7.

60. "Bombs Ravage Helsinki: The Horror of Madrid, Barcelona and Warsaw Begin Again," "A Progressive, peace-loving People Wantonly attacked in Flagrant Violation of a Non-Aggression Pact and Lenin's Words." In *The Illustrated London News*, Vol. 105, No. 2747, 16 December 1939, p. 891.

61. "Finn Defense Relies on 'Guerrilla' Army," *Los Angeles Times*, 29 May 1977, p. 4; "Schutzrumbau ist in Finnland Pflicht: Ab 1980 ist die gesamte Bevolkerung gesichert," *Soldat und Technik*, April 1978, p. 193.

62. "Ready in 1990: Civil Defense: Swiss Build for Everyone," *Los Angeles Times*, 16 March 1977, p. 1; and, "Switzerland: Neutral but Prepared for War," *To the Point*, 18 May 1979, p. 15.

63. "Belgrade Residents Must Purchase CBR Protection Equipment: From the Belgrade City Secretariat for National Defense: By 1983 CBR Protection in Every Household," *Borba* (Belgrade), 6 November 1977, p. 7 as cited in *FBIS*, Vol. II, *Eastern Europe*, n.d.; then see "Air Defense Exercise in Yugoslavia Reported," Peking NCNA Broadcast in English, 1501 GMT, 28 Oct 74, cited in *FBIS*, Vol. I, *Peoples Republic of China*, 29 October 1974, p. A 12.

the purpose of a Soviet military capability that seems "far out of proportion to any rational calculation of their defense needs."[64] Fearful of re-opening the "Cold War," paralyzed at the thought of perpetuating the "Arms Race," the West seeks explanations for the Soviet race for arms when no one else seems to be racing. "Bureaucratic inertia," or the "strength of the military-industrial establishment in the Soviet political structure,"[65] are offered as explanations, as though the Soviet leaders were incapable of discerning the meaning and purpose of military power; as though Soviet leaders were victims of a "sense of helplessness and inevitability in the way great powers allow their arms arsenals and arms budgets constantly to escalate."[66] It just has to be that Soviet leaders are not masters in their own house. If they were, they would never buy all those weapons.

The feeling persists that it really must be something the West is doing wrong; that the United States in particular has failed to do those things that would reassure the Soviet Union about its safety. The United States simply has not considered the extraordinary sensibilities of the Soviet Union. It has been argued, for example, that, if it but would: "The United States can be a generous partner in the strategic relationship between the United States and the Soviet Union. Washington can let Soviet power catch up and use U.S. restraint as an indication of good faith."[67]

The depiction of the Soviet Union as pathetically desirous of nothing more than a decent parity in arms with the United States, fitted well with Leonid Brezhnev's statement of U.S.-Soviet mutual responsibilities and of the obsolescence of the Cold War. At San Clemente, California, in June 1973, Brezhnev said:

> The general atmosphere in the world depends to no small extent on the climate prevailing in relations between our two countries. Neither economic nor military might nor international prestige gives our two countries any special privileges but they do invest them with special responsibility for the destinies of universal peace and for preventing war.[68]

Brezhnev's speech seemed quite different from the idea of struggle "between the two world systems" that *Pravda* had spoken of sometime earlier: "The developing countries that are freeing themselves of colonial

64. *United States Military Posture for FY 1980,* p. iv.

65. *Department of Defense Annual Report Fiscal Year 1980,* pp. 4-5.

66. Charles W. Yost, "Up the Arms Escalator," *The Christian Science Monitor,* 10 January 1974, p. 24.

67. Lawrence T. Caldwell, "U.S. Can Afford 'Generosity' of Arms Parity," *Los Angeles Times,* 28 July 1974, p. 5, pt. V.

68. Address by Leonid I. Brezhnev following conversations with President Nixon at San Clemente, California: "Brezhnev's Speech to U.S.—Cold War is 'Outgrown,'" *San Francisco Chronicle,* 25 June 1973, p. 1.

oppression . . . form an inseparable part of the anti-imperialist front. This proves that there are no real neutrals in the struggle for the two world systems. All classes, parties and states manifest a relationship toward that struggle."[69]

But then the sentiments expressed at San Clemente carry no hint of the picture Brezhnev had drawn of the Soviet position and world outlook for the East German Communists, only six weeks before the San Clemente talk:

> The leaders of the Communist Party of the Soviet Union and the Socialist Unity Party of Germany emphasized that the positive changes in international life are to a decisive extent connected with the coordinated purposeful actions of the Socialist states. In today's conditions, new opportunities are opening up for the cohesion of the socialist countries, the world Communist movement and all progressive forces in the struggle for the people's interests . . . the influence of socialism has grown and the positions of the revolutionary forces have gained strength.[70]

The image of Soviet leaders painfully scratching to attain "strategic parity" with the United States certainly did not conform to Soviet strategic and military projections:

> When speaking of the building of the Armed Forces as a whole and of each branch separately, it must be taken into account that the most important principle of Soviet military science—victory in war by the combined forces of all branches of the Armed Forces and of all means of conflict with maximum utilization of all their combat capabilities—remains in force at the present time. Therefore, the requirement of the need for developing and improving all branches of the Armed Forces, their armaments, equipment, organization and training must serve as the foundation for building the Armed Forces. However, the main emphasis must be placed on those forces and weapons which will be used for solving the chief problems and achieving the main aims of war, i. e., to develop primarily those forces and weapons which will play the most active role in the war.
>
> In the building of armed forces, it is also necessary to consider all the trends of their development by the enemy in order that there be a counter-measure for each new weapon developed by the enemy. The main thing here is to have continual superiority over the enemy in the basic branches of the armed forces, and in the basic means and methods of warfare.[71]

69. "Ideological Struggles: Proletarian Internationalism and Defense of the Achievements of Socialism," *Pravda,* 30 April 1969, p. 1, in *The Current Digest of the Soviet Press,* Vol. XXI, No. 15, 25 May 1969, p. 10.

70. "L. I. Brezhnev's Friendly Visit to the German Democratic Republic," *Pravda,* 14 May 1973, p. 1, in *The Current Digest of the Soviet Press,* Vol. XXV, No. 19, June 6, 1973, pp. 5-7.

71. V. D. Sokolovskiy (ed.), *Military Strategy* (Trans.), Military Technology Divisions, Air Force Systems Command, pp. 360-61. Published in Russian in 1962.

Three years after those words appeared in print in the Soviet Union, the U.S. Secretary of Defense was proclaiming the perpetual superiority of U.S. strategic forces: "the Soviets have decided that they have lost the quantitative race, and they are not seeking to engage us in that contest. It means that there is no indication that the Soviets are seeking to develop a strategic force as large as ours."[72]

That was the year when the United States had 854 ICBMs while the Soviet Union had about 270. At the end of 1966, the Secretary of Defense reflecting on the discovery that the Soviet Union was deploying ICBMs at a faster rate than had been thought possible, assured the country: "That the United States has as many ICBMs today as the latest national intelligence estimate gives the Soviet Union several years hence." Two other points were made as well, the United States need take no steps to meet the new threat beyond those that had already been programmed; and, a comparative count of ICBMs had no real *military* significance only a *political* one.[73] The "programmed" strength of the U.S. ICBM force was to be 1054, a figure reached by 1967.[74]

In January 1967, a month after the discovery that the Soviet Union's rate of increase in ICBMs was greater than expected, the Secretary of Defense assured Congress that the United States had a 3 to 1 superiority in strategic nuclear weapons over the Soviet Union. Although the number of U.S. strategic bombers was to be reduced, "United States deterrent power will remain overwhelmingly superior."[75]

Within thirteen months, the Defense Department would report that 1,000 sites for ICBMs had been prepared in the Soviet Union. While the United States had reached its "programmed" level of ICBM deployment, 1054, the Soviet Union was in process of deploying only fifty-four fewer missiles than the United States had deployed.[76] The Secretary of Defense reported to Congress, however, that the U.S. enjoyed a superiority of four-to-one over the Soviet Union. He joined with "most of the nation's planners and analysts" in the belief that Moscow would probably be content to level off at 1,000 ICBMs. In any case U.S. nuclear superiority would be preserved. It would be preserved by replacing some of its older ICBMs with new ones over a period of five or six years. The new ones would carry three warheads

72. "Is Russia Slowing Down in Arms Race: Interview with Robert McNamara, Secretary of Defense," *U.S. News and World Report,* 13 April 1965, as cited in William R. Van Cleave, "Implications of Success or Failure of Salt," unpublished ms., 1970.

73. "Russia Rushes ICBMs, U.S. Studies Own Pace," *Washington Star,* 7 December 1966, p. 1.

74. "Russian Missiles Estimated at 400: But Capital Sources Assert U.S. Strength is 1,480," *New York Times,* 9 June 1966, p. 10. Note that of the "1,480" missiles mentioned in the article, 576 were *Polaris*-type missiles which could be considered intercontinental only in the sense that submarines would carry them to a point within range of Soviet targets.

75. "Nuclear Edge Over Russia Placed at 3-1," *Baltimore Sun,* 27 January 1967, p. 1.

76. "U.S. Sees Soviet Closing Gap on Strategic Missiles," *New York Times,* 18 February 1968, p. 1.

instead of one; although the total nuclear explosive yield of each new missile would be half that of the older missile.[77] But the U.S. strategic bomber force was to be reduced further.

The Soviet Union had begun testing multi-warhead missiles at least two-and-half years before the United States reached the decision to install missiles with MIRV, as it is called.[78]

It was the possession of 41 Polaris submarines, each with 16 missiles that lent the United States confidence in its "nuclear superiority" over the Soviet Union; that, and the conviction that the Soviet Union "lagged two years behind the United States in missile war-head technology."[79] Of course the Soviet Union did have around 700 intermediate and medium range ballistic missiles which the United States did not consider to be relevant to the issue of U.S. superiority. Since the Soviet missiles in this category could not reach beyond Paris and London; and since the United States did not possess any such missiles, the Soviet medium and inter-mediate range missiles simply were not counted. Nor were 700 Soviet medium bombers (4,000 mile range) entered in the calculations of the strategic balance, since the United States had none of those either.[80]

The strategic advantage, at least in numerical terms, lent by the U.S. Polaris submarine force (41 boats, 16 missiles per boat) suddenly disappeared when, in 1971, it was recognized finally that the Soviet Union was in the process of deploying its 42nd Polaris-type submarine and was producing further such submarines at a rate of between five and ten per year.[81] The Soviet Union had been deploying submarines with ballistic missiles for eight years by this time, but the number of missiles on the earlier boats was small, and many of the boats were diesel-powered rather than nuclear-powered. There were also, by 1970, some 33 nuclear and 16 diesel-powered submarines that carried cruise missiles with ranges up to 300 miles and kiloton yield nuclear warheads. These latter were not considered in the strategic nuclear balance, although strictly speaking they were strategic weapons since the submarines carrying them had the cruising range to operate easily off the coasts of the United States. They could in fact deliver nuclear warheads against Strategic Air Command bomber bases within continental United States.

77. "Up Goes MIRV (Multiple Independently Targetable Re-entry Vehicle) XXX: The Americans have got a way to preserve their nuclear lead over the Russians—," *The Economist* (London), 31 August 1968, p. 115.

78. "Russian Plan for Improving ICBMs Hinted: Tell Multiple Warhead Missile Program," *Chicago Tribune*, 14 December 1966, p. 5, sec. 1-A.

79. Statement on Soviet warhead technology in "Russia Testing MIRV System," *San Francisco Chronicle*, 9 June 1972, p. 24.

80. Soviet Medium bomber and IRBM, MRBM forces are reported in the *Military Balance* for successive years.

81. "Missile Sub Lead Given to Russians," *Los Angeles Times*, 22 November 1971, p. 9.

In April 1965, the Secretary of Defense had confidently reported that the Soviet Union gave no indication of attempting to match U.S. strategic nuclear forces. The U.S. standing in strategic weapons that year was as follows:

854 ICBMs
496 Polaris submarine launched missiles
630 strategic bombers

The Soviet Union then had deployed:

270 ICBMs
120 submarine launched ballistic missiles
190 strategic bombers

On 30 December 1970, five years later, the standings were:

(United States)	1,054	ICBMs
	656	Polaris
	517	Bombers
(Soviet Union)	1,440	ICBMs
	350	Polaris type missiles
	195	strategic bombers[82]

Much comfort has been taken in recent years from words and phrases like "sufficiency," "virtual parity" and "strategic stability." A whole new glossary of terms has grown up to reassure that all is well with the safety of the United States. Each new disclosure of an addition to the Soviet arsenal has called forth from "strategic" thinkers or defense "experts" in the United States, a new assessment of the American situation. Each new assessment produces another set of words or phrases that would, in the mind, at least off-set the new Soviet advance. Every new accretion to Soviet strategic capabilities has been met by a new definition of what constitutes a true "strategic balance"; a definition that by coincidence would demonstrate that there had been no real change of any consequence to the safety of the West. The simple folk might think that many and bigger clubs in the hands of determined men are more than a match for fewer and smaller ones in the hands of the uncertain.

82. "Table 2: Strategic Force Strengths," *Defense Report on President Nixon's Strategy for Peace: Statement of Secretary of Defense Melvin R. Laird* . . . 19 March 1971.

SALT: A "Solemn Farce"?

During the very time when the Soviet Union was extending itself to overmatch the United States in nuclear forces, there were those in the United States, who, viewing the whole matter with Olympian objectivity, admonished the government of the United States to recognize the new realities in international relations. The Soviet Union was really seeking the same things as the United States:

> . . . both the Soviet Union and the United States are capable of recognizing a mutual interest in an increase in international stability, a decrease in the prospect of the use of force, especially where either of them are involved, and a relief from the economic burdens of rising military budgets.
>
> Both sides have already begun to make this recognition and to guide their policies by it.[83]

It was clear to others who viewed the world objectively, that the United States was really laggard in doing the right sort of thing to uncover those hidden but higher motives of the Soviet Union, revelation of which would promote peace in the world: "So little time and effort are devoted to establishing areas of mutual agreement, mutual interest, and potential new and future areas of cooperative effort with the Soviets and other communist powers. . . ."[84]

Others saw the Soviet Union as the innocent victim of the "arms race," reluctantly acquiring strategic missiles at the behest of Soviet "public opinion."

> The Soviets would like to see a scaling down of the missile forces and an approach to some form of parity. . . . They seem to be willing to accept smaller numbers of missiles as an adequate deterrent, and they appear, quite sincerely, to believe that the fewer missiles on both sides, the better. However, a considerable transformation in political attitudes will have to take place before much reduction in our present missile forces can be envisioned.[85]

Doubtless mindful of such admonitions, the United States embarked on lengthy preparations and negotiations to arrive at some agreement with the Soviet Union to limit strategic nuclear weapons. Known as the SALT talks (Strategic Arms Limitation Talks) the United States intended them: "To

83. Carl Kaysen, "American Military Policy," *Survival*, Vol. XI, No. 2, February 1969, pp. 51-56.

84. Sydney J. Slomich, "Arms Control and Disarmament: The Great Evasion," *Bulletin of the Atomic Scientists*, June 1968.

85. Leonard S. Rodberg, "AMB—Some Arms Control Issues," *Bulletin of the Atomic Scientists*, June 1967.

enhance international security by maintaining a stable U.S.-Soviet strategic relationship through limitations on the development of strategic armaments."[86]

It was assumed that the Soviet Union was as interested in something called "strategic stability" as the United States. Presumably "strategic stability" was a state of being in which neither country would be able to take advantage of the other through the use of strategic nuclear weapons. The difficulty is that one had strategic stability, in a manner of speaking, at the close of Word War II, after both Germany and Japan had been rendered incapable of waging war. The United States was the *only* possessor of nuclear weapons. A monopoly of military power permits a high degree of strategic stability. The kind of strategic stability envisaged by the United States in SALT, however was based on some notion of parity in strategic nuclear forces. It was based also on the assumption that conflict between the United States and the Soviet Union was chiefly *political* and not *military.* It was also tied up with the belief on the part of the American government that both the Soviet Union and the United States had a common interest in preserving a peaceful and stable world order.

The strategic stability that was intended to emerge from SALT and its successors, was to be rooted in a common renunciation of attempts to gain strategic and military preeminence in the world. While it had for some time been the conclusion in the United States that numbers of nuclear weapons were not the crucial factor in the strategic balance—a conclusion arrived at about the time that it was discovered that the Soviet Union had greater numbers of ICBMs and ballistic missile submarines—it was invevitable that negotiations would turn on numbers of weapons rather than on anything else. The United States wished to do no more than retain what was called a "credible deterrence." A "credible deterrence" supposedly would convince the other side that the United States could absorb an all out nuclear attack and still retain sufficient strategic nuclear forces to inflict "unacceptable damage" on its attacker. That, of course, depended on the prospective attacker's belief in the capability of the United States to mount a nuclear attack after having suffered one itself; and, on a common definition of "unacceptable damage." That would come to be known as "mutual assured destruction." Any measures taken by either side to protect populations or industry from nuclear attack would constitute a violation of the principle of "mutual assured destruction." The safety of the United States then ultimately was to rest on the conviction amongst Soviet leaders that they could not win a nuclear war without losing more Russians than they cared to lose.

86. "Strategic Arms Limitation Talks," Address by Secretary of State Rodgers, in *The Department of State Bulletin,* Vol. LXI, No. 1588, 1 December 1969, pp. 465-68.

American leaders, in negotiating SALT, saw a kind of mirror image of themselves in the Kremlin. Russian leaders were, it was believed, pursuing a policy of no war—only *political* competition with the West—and a strategy of no win, if one may be permitted the use of that self-contradictory phrase. Some would see the inherent fallacy in such a view of the world: "Strength figures that reflect U.S. superiority, parity or inferiority vis-à-vis the Soviet Union with regard to nuclear delivery systems, total numbers of warheads and megatonnage are meaningless unless related to the strategy they support."[87]

In short, if the Soviet Union was merely worried that the United States was about to spring upon it when the Soviet back was turned, a slight margin of superiority in Soviet strategic forces would help to allay Soviet anxiety. If on the other hand, the Soviet Union was developing the capability to wage a successful war, it would attempt to equip itself with as great a variety and number of nuclear weapons as the traffic would bear; and it would agree to whatever limitations in arms the United States would impose on itself.

It seems cruel to call SALT I a "solemn farce," as Winston Churchill had characterized that other great disarmament effort before the Second World War. Yet what else was it?

The United States, not ten years before, had enjoyed unequivocal strategic nuclear superiority with which to defend itself and its allies. It had then foresworn that superiority for something called "strategic sufficiency." With that act of misplaced, strategic goodwill, it then engaged in negotiations with the Soviet Union to dissuade that nation from assuming the position of nuclear superiority so recently vacated by the United States.

It was considered a diplomatic coup that the SALT agreement limited the Soviet Union to no more than 1,618 ICBMs and 950 submarine-launched ballistic missiles on 62 Polaris-type submarines. The United States was permitted to keep 1,054 ICBMs and to increase its Polaris submarine force by 3 boats for a total of 44, carrying altogether 707 ballistic missiles. The nature of the coup was that otherwise the Soviet Union would continue to build 250 ICBMs a year and launch ten Polaris-type submarines a year. The reason the Soviet Union gained no advantage in all of this was because the United States had more strategic bombers than the Soviet Union and a lead in "qualitative factors—including weapon dependability and general weapon sophistication"; as well as in the number of warheads.[88]

The U.S. strategic bomber force, which had contributed so much to maintaining the balance against the Soviet advantage in submarines and

87. John M. Collins, *The Impact of SALT I on US Nuclear Deterrence: A Military Assessment*, Library of Congress, Congressional Research Service, 26 July 1972, p. CRS-i.

88. *Peace, National Security, and the SALT Agreements*, News Release, Department of State, 1 August 1972.

ICBMs, as it was said, contained 522 strategic bombers at the time of the SALT I agreement. That force has now been reduced to 376 aircraft.[89] The three additional Polaris-type submarines permitted the United States by the SALT agreement were never produced. The new *Trident* submarines will not begin to enter service until 1981.

SALT I had permitted both countries to have two anti-ballistic missile sites. At the time, the Soviet Union had one already erected around Moscow. The United States was to have erected one around Washington, D.C. and a second to defend the ICBM fields in North Dakota. At the Moscow Summit of July 1970, the United States gave up the right to build the site to protect Washington, D.C.; in exchange, the Soviet Union agreed not to add a second such site. When the ABM site in North Dakota was completed, it was shut down and the missiles for it dispersed into storage.[90]

In the Soviet Union, after SALT I, matters proceeded as they had before. In the United States, there was much foot-shuffling and throat-clearing when various defense malcontents suggested that the Soviet Union was cheating on the SALT agreements.[91] State Department and Arms Control and Disarmament Agency spokesmen were quick to respond to such outrageous charges. It had been reported in 1975, for example, that U.S. spy satellites were being blinded over the Soviet Union. Such satellites were, according to the SALT agreement, one of the principal means for each country to check the other's compliance. The Secretary of State cast doubt on the charges, indicating that such incidents as had been reported were really the result of a series of large natural gas fires caused by numerous breaks in Soviet natural gas pipelines.[92]

89. *Department of Defense Annual Report, Fiscal Year 1980,* p. 66.

90. "Antimissile base construction halted," *Palo Alto Times,* 27 May 1972, p. 1; "Bill to Scrap Missile Site Defense Given OK," *Los Angeles Times,* 27 November 1973, p. 19.

91. On Soviet cheating see the following: on violations of the Moscow treaty on underground weapons tests, see "Russia May Have Broken A-Test Vow," *Los Angeles Times,* 6 August 1976, p. 7; "Soviets Set Off Bigger Atom Blasts Than Allowed, White House Believes," *Washington Post,* 13 October 1976, p. A 2; and "Underground nuclear blast 'a violation By Soviet Union,'" *The Peninsula Times Tribune* (Palo Alto), 28 June 1979, p. F-6. On SALT violations, see "U.S. Asks Meeting On SALT Violations," *Washington Post,* 16 November 1974, p. A 2; "White House Accused of Suppressing Charges of Soviet Arms Pact Violations," *Los Angeles Times,* 14 November 1975, p. 4; Colin S. Grey, "SALT I Aftermath: Have the Soviets Been Cheating?," *Air Force Magazine,* November 1975, pp. 28-33; "Soviets Admit Violation of SALT Accord," *Washington Post,* 26 May 1976, p. 2; "Another Salt Violation Spotted: Deployment of SS-20 missiles to Kamchatka held counter to agreement because of doubled range estimate," *Aviation Week & Space Technology,* 31 May 1976, pp. 12-14; "Will Arms Cheating be Swept Under the Rug?" *Los Angeles Times,* 30 May 1977, p. 5; and, Mark M. Lowenthal, *SALT Verification,* Library of Congress, 78-142-F, 10 July 1978; "Vance Denies Soviet Cheating on SALT," *The Christian Science Monitor,* 1 March 1978, p. 1; "Russians Block U.S. Satellites," *San Francisco Chronicle,* 10 July 1978, p. 38; "Soviet Encoding of Data Said to Threaten SALT-2," *International Herald Tribune* (Paris), 12 March 1979, p. 1; "Critic Says Soviets Can Foil Arms Pact," *Los Angeles Times,* 28 December 1978, p. 4; "'Verification'—Slippery Key to SALT," *San Francisco Chronicle,* 16 June 1979, p. 8.

92. *SALT ONE: Compliance/SALT TWO: Verification,* Department of State, Selected Documents No. 7, February 1978, pp. 9-10.

One can speculate on that contention. The intensity of light generated by natural gas burning in the atmosphere is, in part, a function of the incomplete combustion of the fuel, as solid particles of soot are formed through thermal fractionation. These particles, heated to incandescence, rushing out into the atmosphere emit the familiar light of the gas fire. The intensity of the light is not increased by greater quantities of burning gas; only the volume of space illuminated is greater. It is the difference between lighting a baseball diamond with one floodlight and with a hundred floodlights, of the same intensity as the one. The light is no more intense, it is only greater in terms of the area illuminated. How burning gas from broken pipelines could blind a satellite capable of absorbing the light energy from ignition of an ICBM rocket motor, without harm, is indeed interesting. Nearly as interesting as the occurence of "several large fires caused by breaks along natural gas pipelines in the Soviet Union."

One occurence that some thought to be Soviet cheating was the reported deployment of SS-20 missiles in silos on Kamchatka in the North Pacific. The missile was of intermediate range and therefore not counted as an ICBM under the SALT agreement. As deployed it had a two-stage motor, giving it range of about 3,000 miles. But the two stages were really part of another missile, the SS-X-16, which had three stages and was therefore your standard ICBM. As the SS-20, the missile carries three independently-targetable warheads.[93] The Secretary of State took a reasoned view of the occurence, pointing out that as an SS-20, the missile could not reach the "contiguous 48 states," just the Aleutians and Western Alaska. He did not mention whether the SS-20 could reach the Alaska pipeline, the Prudhoe oilfields or the tanker terminal at Valdez. He did say, however, that the United States would detect any testing of the SS-20, were it tried as an ICBM.[94] It was to be hoped that the SS-20 would not become an ICBM without its being tested as such first. In the government's view, the SS-20 might be perturbating for Alaskans, but no real problem for the United States.

Soviet testing of killer-satellites, designed to knock out reconnaissance, surveillance, and communications satellites in space were begun as early as 1968. The development of a Soviet capability to destroy U.S. satellites in space posed a threat to United States ability to collect data for early-warning to maintain communications with its forces abroad and to collect information on the deployment of Soviet forces.[95]

93. "Another SALT Violation Spotted," *Aviation Week and Space Technology,* 31 May 1976, pp. 12-14; "Soviet Union Deploys SS-20," in *International Defense Review,* Vol. 11, No. 2, 1978, p. 145.

94. *SALT ONE: Compliance/SALT TWO: Verification,* p. 10.

95. "Soviet Buildup Threatens U.S. Power Balance," *Los Angeles Times,* 28 October 1971, p. 6, pt. II; "Killer Satellites: U.S Faces Up to Soviet Lead: Reds Near Potential That Could Deny Use of Space Without Firing a Missile," *ibid.,* 15 October 1972, p. 1.

The testing of anti-satellite weapons was suspended by the Soviet Union between 1972 and 1976, then testing was resumed. Nine satellite interceptions were attempted between 1976 and 1978, using Soviet satellites as targets. A particulary ominous test in December 1977, demonstrated the Soviet capability to maneuver a satellite in such a fashion as to destroy another satellite by high explosives.[96]

In his report to the Senate International Relations Committee, the Secretary of State indicated that testing killer-satellites was not a violation of the SALT I agreements; only the actual use of such a weapon against a U.S. satellite would be a violation.[97]

The Secretary of Defense reported to Congress in his posture statement issued in January 1979: "Our studies of the threat and the potential means to counter it will continue this year." The Secretary planned to spend 80.5 million dollars during the fiscal year of 1980 on such studies.[98]

If there was real cheating on SALT by the Soviet Union the Soviets were too clever to admit it, and American officials were not particulary eager to see it revealed. It is clear that the Soviet Union has taken every opportunity to exploit the loopholes in SALT to their own advantage. The Americans thought there was a "spirit of SALT" which would prevent that. But like the "spirit of Tashkent," the "spirit of Geneva," the "spirit of Glassboro," and the "spirit of Camp David," the "spirit of SALT" originated in the minds of American diplomats and policymakers, and extended to the limit of the U.S. coastline. The Americans hoped to build confidence in "strategic stability" through SALT. The Soviet Union is not interested in strategic stability save that which will emerge when they have strategic superiority. Soviet leaders did not need to take measures to build American confidence in any case. The United States was doing nothing to threaten the emergence of Soviet strategic advantages, and the SALT agreement merely confirmed that fact.

As one American congressman summarized the problem of Soviet cheating: they "would gain little by cheating on nuclear arms limitation . . . and it would be fairly easy to catch them if they did." "Even if the Soviets cheat in every single way that might evade detection, they will add little to their strategic power and may actually reduce their military strength elsewhere."[99]

96. Details of Soviet satellite interceptions are in "Pentagon Worried By Satellite Dependence: Three times Soviet hunter-killers passed close to U.S. satellite," *Los Angeles Times*, 19 March 1978, p. 2. Other reports include, "Russia Tests Space Killer of Satellites: Latest Interception Is Apparent Failure," *International Herald Tribune* (Paris), 1 June 1977, p. 4; "Soviet Test of Killer Satellite Seen as Success," *Los Angeles Times*, 28 June 1977, p. 12; "Soviets Test Satellite-Killer," *ibid.*, 5 June 1978, p. 2; and, "Soviet test of killer satellite reported on eve of U.S. talks," *The Christian Science Monitor*, 5 June 1978, p. 16.

97. "U.S. Report Defends SALT Compliance," *Washington Post*, 1 March 1978, p. A 2.

98. *Department of Defense Annual Report, Fiscal Year 1980*, pp. 129-32.

99. "Aspin Says SALT Cheating Would Gain Soviets Little," *The Washington Post*, 27 March 1978, p. A 10.

With such a strong commitment to arms control on the part of the United States, the problem is not whether the Soviet Union would cheat, or whether the cheating would be detected; the problem is what the United States would do about it.

SALT I with its codicils, memoranda of understanding, interim agreements, definitions agreed upon and not agreed upon, did not halt the "Arms Race." It merely confirmed the withdrawal of one of the participants—the United States. Official American confidence in SALT as a measure promoting strategic stability, could stem only from self-deception or wishful thinking. There was nothing in Soviet military policy that would stand as evidence of Soviet strategic restraint.

With a speed unanticipated by the United States, the Soviet Union deployed three new types of ICBMs, in 1975; all apparently capable of carrying more than one warhead. The SS-18, for example, was said to be able to carry either one 18 megaton warhead or eight 1 megaton warheads. Later assessments would suggest that eight or ten warheads of only 600 kilotons was the payload of the SS-18. The SS-19 deployed at the same time, could carry no more than six warheads of 550 kilotons yield each.[100]

The first SALT agreements designed to "slow the arms race," were passed for ratification by the Senate of the United States, 3 August 1972, and entered into force in October. By 1975, the Soviet Union was spending three times more on ICBMs than it had in 1972.[101]

It was about 1974 that the rosy optimism coloring U.S. estimates of Soviet military expenditures began to fade. Although there had always been those who were skeptical of the U.S. estimates of Soviet military spending, one especially persistent skeptic, William T. Lee, managed to overcome, to some extent, institutional and political reluctance to correlate what the Soviet Union was actually doing with what they must have been spending to do it.[102]

Despite the apparent vigor of the Soviet strategic weapons programs, the Secretary of Defense would "believe" that the Soviet Union and the United States "had become more or less equal" in strategic nuclear weapons.[103] This

100. "Russ Missile Speedup Told by Rumsfeld," *San Francisco Chronicle,* 28 September 1976, p. 17; see also, "Four New ICBM's—three of them MIRVs: Soviet Arms gains Surprise Washington," *The Christian Science Monitor,* 15 March 1974, p. 5F; for later data see "Soviet Missiles—not quite so potent," *ibid.,* 1 June 1979, p. 12.

101. "Soviet Defense Funds Estimate Doubled," *Aviation Week and Space Technology,* 24 May 1976, pp. 18-20.

102. William T. Lee, *Understanding the Soviet Military Threat: How CIA Estimates Went Astray,* Agenda Paper No. 6 (New York: National Strategy Information Center, 1977), also published as a chapter in William Schneider, Jr., and Francis P. Hoeber, eds., *Arms, Men and Military Budgets, Issues for Fiscal Year 1977* (New York: Crane, Russak, 1976). See also, William T. Lee, *Soviet Defense Expenditures, 1955-1975, An Unconventional Approach* (New York: Praeger, 1977).

103. "U.S.-Russia near equals on arms, Sec. Brown says," *Palo Alto Times,* 24 March 1977, p. 3.

article of faith reached the press at the same time that it was revealed that the Soviet Union now had deployed on submarines about 300 of their new SS-N-8 missiles, whose range was such as to permit Soviet submarines to fire missiles against the United States *without leaving Russian ports.* That meant that Soviet missile submarines leaving port for patrol stations at sea could no longer be depended on as an indicator of an attack.[104] U.S. missile submarines capable of that were not yet constructed and the first of such submarines would not be completed before November 1980. As though to confirm the Secretary of Defense's optimistic view of strategic matters, the CIA asserted that the United States was "well ahead" of the Soviet Union in military technology.[105]

Barely six months later, in January 1978, the Secretary of Defense expressed the government's surprise that the Soviet Union was installing new missiles with more warheads and improving accuracy "more rapidly than we had expected a year ago." He said, the Russians had added about 1,000 strategic nuclear warheads in 1977—twice the increase that had been forecast in 1976. The Secretary reassured Congress: "But SALT will mean greater stability and predictability in the strategic challenge we face."[106]

In 1978, it was reported by the Secretary of Defense that a new long-range bomber was under development to replace the Tu-95 *Bear.* It is scheduled for operational use by 1983.[107]

Under SALT I and the ABM agreement, it was said, "the Soviets pushed the interpretation of the provisions to the limit."[108] It might be supposed that the Soviets would do the same thing under SALT II.

The one new land-based ICBM being planned by the United States, the MX, which the President was said to be "close to approving," would not be deployed until 1986, *if* then. The MX would require 4,600 shelters to be constructed and 15,000 miles of roads, probably in southern Utah and Nevada. Aside from the development of the missile, itself time-consuming, there remains the sticky problem of acquiring land and water rights for construction of the hideaways, and of satisfying the requirements of environmental impact statements, as well as environmentalists who do not much care for nuclear weapons anyway.[109] The prospects for a new strategic bomber

104. "Missiles on Soviet subs can reach U.S. from port," *ibid.*, p. 2; see also, "Russians Fire Multiple Warhead Missile from Sub for First Time," *Los Angeles Times,* 24 November 1976, p. 6.

105. "CIA Chief's View: Soviet Military Lag Claimed," *San Francisco Chronicle,* 16 August 1977, p. 8.

106. "Despite SALT, Reds massing bigger, better war machine," *Palo Alto Times,* 25 January 1978, p. 5.

107. "Russ Developing New Bomber, Brown Reports," *Los Angeles Times,* 3 February 1978, p. 1.

108. *The Strategic Arms Limitations Talks,* Reports No. 46, p. 2.

109. "MX missile faces legal snags," *San Francisco Sunday Examiner and Chronicle,* 19 August 1979, p. 2.

to replace the elderly B-52s is dim, the one candidate for the office, the B-1, having been cancelled.

Upon such auspicious foundations have the hopes for SALT II been erected. SALT I, defying the laws of nature, had performed a miracle. Starting with two more nuclear launchers than the United States in 1972, the Soviet Union spent money like water, bought more and better rockets by the score, launched submarines by the bunch, improved older rockets and warheads at a marvelous rate, ending in 1978 with 400 launchers more than in 1972. The United States, starting with two less launchers in 1972, adding nothing but reducing the number of its launchers by 23 long-range bombers, managed, somehow, to remain abreast of the Soviet Union.[110] So that, in the words of the State Department, "SALT II will allow us to *maintain* nuclear parity." According to that authority: "Under SALT I, the Soviet Union was allowed over 2,300 missiles, the United States just over 1,700. SALT I thus created a "perception" of Soviet superiority, even though the superiority was not real." In this instance, the State Department was excluding count of long-range (strategic) bombers. But, SALT II will be concluded with the United States having "slightly over 2,000 delivery vehicles, the Soviet Union will have 2,250." (The figure 2,000 in this statement, counts the U.S. strategic bomber force). Through this miracle of mathematics, it becomes evident, to all save the most unrefined, that if you enjoyed parity when your adversary had 600 missiles more than you, surely you will enjoy parity when he has only 250 more than you. If acceptance of such miracles is difficult, the words of the State Department ought to remove any difficulty: "Arms control is, in its essence, a confidence building exercise." Accepting 2,000 as the same thing as 2,250, is, therefore: "Part of our growing up and learning to live with this situation."[111]

The vice-premier of the People's Republic of China, still child-like in his attitude toward numbers, warned that "it would be a mistake to count on the new strategic arms limitation agreement to check the military threat of the Soviet Union." "Not this agreement or any other," he said, "will restrain the expansionism of the Soviet Union."[112]

Clearly the Chinese vice-premier did not understand that SALT II is "designed to slow strategic competition."[113] He may think strategic competition is like war, surely an old-fashioned point of view. But then the Chinese tend to think of politics and war as closely related phenomena.[114]

110. Comparative numbers of launchers—ICBMs, submarine launched ballistic missiles, and long-range bombers—are given in *The Military Balance, 1978-1979,* pp. 82-83. Italics added.

111. Speech by Leslie H. Gelb, Director of the Bureau of Politics-Military Affairs, before the San Diego World Affairs Council, 30 January 1979, "The Facts of SALT II," *Current Policy,* No. 65, April 1979.

112. "Deng Cautions U.S. on SALT Accord," *Los Angeles Times,* 11 May 1979, p. 9.

113. Leslie Gelb, "The Facts of SALT II," p. 1.

114. "Political power grows out the barrel of a gun." In Mao Tse-tung, "Problems of War and

If arms control is a "confidence building exercise" as the man from State said, the conclusion of SALT II will be a true test of confidence. Curiosities and anomolies abound in the treaty and related documents. One memorandum, intended to establish the "data base on the number of strategic offensive arms" attested to by the President of the United States and by General Secretary Brezhnev gives a count of strategic bombers on both sides. The United States reported 574 heavy bombers—B-52s. The Soviet Union reported 156. The U.S. figure included presumably the 349 B-52s which are operational and the 187 in "inactive storage."[115] The total of those two figures in only 536; the Secretary of Defense's *Annual Report for FY 1980* listed only 316 B-52s which agrees with the number of B-52s given in *The Military Balance, 1978-1979;* that source also notes an additional 50 B-52s used for training. The differences between the figures in the "Memorandum" and those reported by the Defense Department range from nominal to 38 bombers.

In any case, the United States reported bombers in storage, used for training and bombers operational as part of the strategic forces. The Soviet Union's report, apparently did not include any that might be in storage nor did it include the additional 44 strategic bombers used as tankers or the 70 strategic bombers deployed with Soviet Naval Forces.[116] So while the United States reported *larger* than existing strategic bomber strength to the Soviet Union, the Soviet Union reported a *smaller* than existing strategic bomber strength to the United States.[117]

Because the Tu-22M *Backfire* bomber seemed to some Americans to be a strategic bomber, although the Soviet Union called it a "medium-range bomber," General Secretary Brezhnev handed a statement to President Carter to add to the SALT II agreement. The "Soviet Backfire Statement" included the following undertakings:

> The Soviet side . . . does not intend to give this airplane the capability of operating at inter-continental distances;
>
> . . . that it will not increase the radius of action of this airplane in such a way as to enable it to strike targets on the territory of the USA. Nor does it intend to give it such a capability in any other manner, including by in-flight refueling.

Strategy," *Selected Works* Vol. II, as cited in Lin Piao, *Long Live the Victory of the People's War* (Peking: Foreign Language Press, 1965), p. 44.

115. *United States Military Posture for FY 1980,* p. 67.

116. Soviet strategic bombers include the Tu-95 *Bear* and the Miya-4 *Bison*; in the Long Range Air Force, 100 *Bears,* 35 *Bison;* 44 Mya-4 *Bisons* as tankers; Soviet Navy has 70 Tu-95 *Bears.* From *The Military Balance, 1978-1979,* pp. 8-10.

117. Memorandum of Understanding between the United States of America and the Union of Soviet Socialist Republics Regarding the Establishment of a Data Base on the Numbers of Strategic Offensive Arms, in *SALT II Agreement,* Vienna, 18 June 1979, Selected Documents No. 12A, Department of State, p. 49.

> . . . it will not increase the production rate of this aircraft as compared to the present time.
>
> . . . Soviet Backfire production rate would not exceed 30 per year.[118]

The *Backfire* was not counted as a strategic launcher in arriving at the total number of strategic offensive arms, even though, according to the State Department: "The Backfire can reach a signficant number of targets in the United States on one-way, high-altitude unrefueled missions."[119]

The *Backfire* has been observed in "bombing runs" that lasted more than ten hours. Since its maximum speed is Mach 2.5, or over 1500 miles per hour, that would give it intercontinental range and then some.[120]

The *Backfire* has been observed firing long-range cruise missiles out to a distance of 700 miles.[121] Aircraft capable of firing missiles to a range of 600 kilometers were, according to the Secretary of Defense, supposed to be counted as heavy bombers.

The *Backfire* had been observed with refueling probes until the time for signing the SALT II agreement approached when such probes were removed.[122]

The *Backfire* bomber was being produced at a rate of 36 a year, in August 1978, with a likely increase to 40 a year by 1979.[123] And, a new version of the *Backfire* with extended range is being developed.[124]

Only about 300 or 400 *Backfire* bombers are now expected to be produced for the Soviet Long Range Air Force. The evident capability of the aircraft to hit the United States from the Soviet Union, even if only on one-way mission, can hardly be discounted as inconsiderable in the event of war. There is little reason to suppose that such one-way missions would not be flown if they would gain some military advantage during war-time. The aircraft could fly in, deliver its bombs or cruise missiles against U.S. targets and then fly on to Cuba, or some other "neutral" country, where plane and crew might be used again for other missions against the United States. Or, the crew might simply parachute to earth in the United States to be treated, according

118. "Soviet Backfire Statement," written statement handed President Carter by President Brezhnev, 16 June 1979, in *SALT II Agreement*, p. 50.

119. *The Strategic Arms Limitation Talks*, Department of State Special Report 46 (revised), May 1979, p. 11.

120. "Arms Expert's View on SALT: 'Brezhnev Lied About Backfire,'" *San Francisco Chronicle*, 17 July 1979, p. 8.

121. "Russ Arms Test That May Hamper SALT Reported: Cruise Long-Range Missile was Fired from Backfire Bomber, Administration Sources Say," *Los Angeles Times*, 2 February 1979, p. 1.

122. "Soviets Developing Two Bombers: USSR moves raise questions in Administration of SALT ceilings covering strategic delivery vehicle, MIRVs," *Aviation Week & Space Technology*, 19 February 1979, pp. 14-18.

123. "Soviets Gradually increase Backfire bomber production," *Palo Alto Times*, 10 August 1978, p. 20.

124. *Aviation Week & Space Technology*, 19 February 1979, *loc. cit.*

to law, as prisoners of war. The precedent in war for such one-way missions is not difficult to find. General Doolittle's B-25 raid against Tokyo flown from the U.S.S. *Hornet* was a one-way mission with the flyers ending in China, if they were lucky, or before a military court in Japan when they were not.

But *Backfire* represents the confusion of purpose that has characterized the SALT negotiations from their very start. The altogether fragile assurances elicited from the Soviet government that *Backfire* would not be employed intercontinentally, were elicited because otherwise *Backfire* might prevent Senate ratification of the SALT II agreement. It was not elicited because *Backfire* might be one more strategic threat to the United States. In short, it was interference with SALT ratification that was the principal issue not whether the Soviet Union would use *Backfire* in a war against the United States. And what does the United States do if, after SALT II is ratified, *Backfire* appears once again with refueling probes, armed with cruise missiles with a range of 700 miles, or otherwise configured to hit the United States? Shall we then renounce SALT II and embark on a rearmament program, or simply approach the Soviet Union and ask if they really were serious about the "Backfire Statement"? If the Soviets begin producing the bomber at a greater rate than that indicated in the statement, when do we blow the whistle? When the rate reaches 33, 42, or 50, a year?

One can almost hear the dialogue as some American official makes discreet enquiries of the Russian in charge of Soviet compliance with arms control agreement: Excuse upon excuse is offered. The Russian fully allows for the beneficial possibility of any ingenuous rationalization. Finally, the discreet American interlocutor is presented with a *fait accompli*.

If that seems too comic for such a serious topic, then one must consider the views attributed to the Arms Control and Disarmament Agency on the topic of *Backfire*:

> While we believe it unlikely that the Soviets would violate these assurances during peacetime, there are no assurances that will ensure that Backfire would not be used against the continental United States in wartime.[125]

One Western writer draws an interesting picture of the Soviet outlook toward SALT negotations:

> In the end, they [the Soviets] seem to adopt very simple, basic, uncomplicated positions and attitudes on SALT. They negotiate for two simple and straightforward purposes. The first is to try and gain some strategic or military advantage out of the negotiations. The second is to

125. Cited as "a paper prepared for the Senate in February 1978," in Seymour Weiss, a former director of the Bureau of Politico-Military Affairs, Department of State, "As It Now Stands, There Is No Safety in SALT," *Los Angeles Times*, 26 August 1979, p. 3, pt. V.

> try to stop you from gaining or increasing what they perceive to be an advantage.
>
> They operate from the very elemental military doctrine of whether you've got superiority or not, and if you haven't got it, then it might be worth negotiating to get it. But you certainly don't give up an advantage for the sake of an agreement.[126]

The Soviet negotiators seem interested in who is going to be able to win the war; as though war were perfectly natural, and to be expected. That would be consistent with the instruction given to those "Soviet officers, generals and admirals studying Marxist-Leninist teachings on war and the armed forces in general":

> *"War as a Special State of Society."*
>
> War is a many-faceted and complex socio-political phenomenon. . . . The essence of war is the continuation of politics by means of armed force. This is the main characteristic of war. Therefore, this definition of the essence of war does not include many of the important ways that are used to secure victory in the war, notably economic, diplomatic and other forms of struggle. The definition of the content of war and that of the forms holding and expressing this content are much more all embracing. These definitions include a wide range of processes that are attending the armed struggle, are connected with it and serve to achieve the political aims of the war, the aim of gaining victory.[127]

That seems to mean that even in the course of disarmament talks, the Soviet Union might attempt to win some advantage that would contribute toward achieving eventual victory in war. Can it really be true that Soviet negotiations for the Strategic Arms Limitation Treaties are nothing more than part of the preparations for war? That would place Soviet leaders in no better odor than Adolph Hitler, who said:

> The prevailing circumstances have obliged me to speak, for a decade or more, of almost nothing but peace. Only, in fact, by continuously declaring the German desire for peace and Germany's peaceful intentions was I able, step by step, to secure freedom for the German people and to provide Germany with the armaments which have, time and time again, always been the essential preconditions for any further move.[128]

126. Dr. Christian Bertram, Director of the International Institute for Strategic Studies as quoted in "Arms Control Debate Polarized the Experts: Warnke, Nitze Personify Rival Camps Arguing Politics, Strategy, Technology," *Los Angeles Times*, 8 January 1978, p. 1.

127. *Marxism-Leninism on War and Army* (Moscow: Progress Publishers, 1972) p. 10; published in the United States by the U.S.G.P.O., 1976.

128. "Hitler's Secret Address to Representatives of the German Press, Munich, 10 November 1938," Appendix B in Z. A. B. Zeman, *Nazi Propaganda*, pp. 212-25.

That certainly would not fit the expectations of those who see Soviet armament as the expression of the "enormous propensity in the Soviet Union to accumulate military power in all of its forms"[129]; as the consequence of bureaucratic incompetence—they do not know how to turn-off the factories that make weapons; or, simply a "traditional emphasis on 'bigness' as a symbol of 'goodness.'"[130]

129. Helmut Sonnenfeldt, as cited in "Keeping Our Cool Over Russia: Former Kissinger Brain Truster Says Soviet Union has Real Weaknesses," *Los Angeles Times,* 5 April 1978, p. 5.

130. Dennis Ross, "Rethinking Soviet Strategic Policy: Inputs and Implications," ACIS Working Paper No. 5, Center for Arms Control and International Security, University of California at Los Angeles, June 1977, p. 3.

Conclusion: The Perilous Sums of Strategy

CHANGES IN THE STRATEGIC ENVIRONMENT ALTER THE CONDITIONS UNDER WHICH WAR WILL BE WAGED. The accumulation of strategic advantages on one side and of disadvantages on the other help define who can win and who most likely will lose a war. These advantages also set the cost for avoiding defeat or securing victory.

One may not easily weigh the particular value of one small advantage over another similar advantage. But the accumulated effect of many such small advantages may so strongly enhance military capability—the capability to wage war successfully—that victory in war may approach a foregone conclusion.

* * * * *

Germany—after the first World War—provides a useful illustration. The foundation of German military capabilities for the next war consisted of the preservation of German military organization, the expansion of German heavy industry, and the efforts put into what has here been called "secret" rearmament. The rapid acceleration of German rearmament after the Nazis came to power was only possible because the groundwork for it had been laid over the previous fifteen years. When Hitler re-militarized the Rhineland in 1936, Germany was still much weaker in military capability than the allies. The movement of the German Army into the Rhineland together with the plebiscite that returned the Saar to Germany advanced Germany's military frontier so that it now rested on the eastern borders of Belgium and Luxembourg. This may seem only a modest strategic advance for Germany, yet, it was an important first step for the further development of German military power. Having accepted without protest the German advance, the Allies, had they now wished to wage war, must advance their armies across France to Germany's southern border. They could not pass through Belgium, Holland or Luxembourg since those countries were neutral and the Allies respected that neutrality.

From the German point of view, the strategic environment had substantially changed:

1. Advancing the military frontier to the eastern borders of Belgium and Luxembourg, permitted Belgian and Luxembourg neutrality to block, in effect, the short route between France and Berlin while the German Army could now protect the great concentration of industry in the Ruhr and Rhineland. It should be recalled that French occupation of the industrial area had earlier forced the German government to accede to Allied demands.

2. The return of the Saar to Germany advanced the German military frontier southward so that, with the re-militarization of the Rhineland Palitinate, the German Army could be placed so as to cover the approaches to the German industrial areas from the south at the same time that the German Army would be on the left flank of any Allied attempt to invade southern Germany through the Vosges.

3. So long as there was no substantial German Army, of course, the allies need but walk into Germany to do their pleasure. But the advance of the military frontiers plus the emergence of a fair-sized German Army could not alone have prevented a German defeat had the allies been determined. But because of the Army and the strategic terrain that had been recovered, the allies would have had to wage a serious war. Reluctance to do that permitted Germany, then, to proceed with rearmament at a faster pace. The construction of the Siegfried Line of fortifications along the German border with France meant that the German Army could be used for offensive operations elsewhere since the fortifications would take the place of those German army divisions that would otherwise have had to deploy along the frontier with France. That is why, for example, the Germans could send all of their Army except about eleven divisions against Poland even after France and England were at war with Germany. Despite allied superiority in numbers of troops over Germany, the Allies could not attack across Holland, Belgium and Luxembourg because they were neutral, and the allies could not bring themselves to attack across the French border with Germany because they feared the cost in casualties of having to assault prepared fortifications.

Every step Germany took after the re-militarization of the Rhineland merely increased its strategic advantages while the German air force, army and submarine fleet were being expanded. *Anschluss* with Austria added manpower and industry while advancing Germany's military frontier up to Hungary and outflanking, in the south, the Czech fortifications. Czechoslovakia provided further industry, the advance of the military frontier eastward, and a position from which to outflank Poland from the south.

The first act of the strategic drama posed the greatest risk for Germany and would have been the cheapest for the allies to cancel. Once Germany took that risk and won the strategic advantage, each succeeding action was less risky for Germany, because as each new occasion presented itself, effective allied would become *more* costly. If the allies would not act when the cost of preventing a German success was slight, would they act when the cost became ever more high? So the Germans reasoned.

The German movement into the Rhineland would have been unimportant if Germany had merely been reasserting sovereignty over territory belonging to it. It was easy for France and England to see the German action in such a light and therefore difficult for them to respond adequately to the action as though it were strategically important. But the fact—however hard it may have been to discern—was that holding the Rhineland contributed to German preparations for war.

The real test of German military capability came in France and Flanders in 1940. Having secured its eastern and southern frontiers, and destroyed the Polish armed forces, Germany was free to attack the West. German military power could not have been considered equal to Western military power at the time. The combined armies, air forces, and navies of Denmark, Norway, Holland, Belgium, France and England easily outnumbered those of Germany. Since military coordination existed only between France and England, the preponderance of Western military power could not be brought to bear. Divided at the outset, unprepared for coalition war, all save England were removed as effective enemies by German military power. At that point Germany together with its ally Italy enjoyed military mastery in Western Europe. This strategic superiority as it might be called, initially was accumulated through "political" means, then, threats of force, and finally through war.

In twenty years a defeated and powerless nation had become the world's paramount military power and the master of Western Europe. The stages in the German metamorphosis from vanquished to victor were carried out before the very eyes of those who, through enormous exertion, had barely prevented Germany's attaining mastery of Europe in its first attempt.

Every step Germany took marked a shift in the strategic circumstances for the allies. In the beginning the steps were too ambiguous or too unimportant to require their reversal. When the steps became more important and less ambiguous, then the price of their reversal seemed too high for people who would not disrupt the peace and who would not therefore prepare for war. So long as the allies believed Germany would not make war, they could not bring themselves to act. When Germany made war anyway, despite all allied beliefs, strategic circumstances marginally favored the allies. What almost irretrievably tipped the scale against the allies was their lack of miliary preparation and the strength of German determination. If the military odds are anywhere near to being equal, an indecisive uncoordinated defense is no match for a determined and competent attack.

* * * * *

Today it is Czechoslovakia, Cuba and all those other places and events that add to a formidable strategic total favoring the cause of the Soviet Union. Not the least are items reckoned in the sum which cast serious doubt on the ability of the West to think clearly enough to defend itself, let alone to win a war:

> the disaster of allied policy at Suez in 1956, not the least cause of which was a greater American concern for Soviet interests in Hungary than for the vital interests of France and England in the Middle East;
>
> the failure of the United States to deny the Soviet Union the use of Cuba as a naval, military and air base in the Gulf of Mexico, a failure compounded by a set of mind that still refuses admission to the fact of the existence of such a base;[1]
>
> the unalloyed sense of triumph of many who claim membership in the Western intellectual, academic and artistic communities, at the American defeat in Vietnam, as though the Communist victory would bring political democracy and an end to repression of human freedom; although a Communist victory never has before;
>
> the illusion in the West that the Soviet Union would be willing to negotiate away its strategic superiority just because the United States had already dones so; and
>
> the Western submission to the Arab oil embargo to purchase the goodwill of regimes no better than that in Nicaragua whose overthrow brought such joy.

The kind of military measures put in hand by the Soviet Union and its allies over the past decade seem like preparations for war. Taking a more optimistic view of the matter, the Secretary of Defense speculated in May 1977, that the increase in the number of tanks, artillery pieces, and tactical aircraft in Eastern Europe might be "because the Soviet Union needs to keep its labor force turning out weapons. The U.S.S.R. is a bureaucracy and doesn't find it easy to change direction."[2] Such optimism seemed totally unwarranted at the time, and is even less so now. But that is the same Secretary of Defense who in January 1979, could say with apparent equanimity:

> I am, of course aware that we estimate the Soviets as having more than 45,000 tanks, while the United States has only 10,000. But while we recognize the Soviet armor threat, that raw comparison does not con-

1. "'It would seem that the presence of Russian troops in Cuba poses a much more serious threat to Mr. Castro's self-described status of non-alignment than it does to the security of the United States,' said a senior White House official." *The Durham Sun,* 5 September 1979, p. 1.

2. Secretary of Defense Harold Brown, at a National Press Club question-and-answer session, May 1977, as cited in *National Defense,* Vol. LXII, No. 343, July-August 1977, p. 7.

> vince me of Soviet military superiority in Central Europe . . . our allies happen to have tanks as well; and anti-tank launchers—of which we and our allies have acquired more than 17,000.[3]

NATO does indeed have on the Central Front some 7,000 tanks—the Warsaw Pact has 21,000 there. As to anti-tank launchers which the Secretary finds to be such a comfort, the Soviet Union could, in 1978, muster scarcely 27,000. While the Secretary thought it unlikely that the Soviet Union could possibly deploy all of its 45,000 plus tanks against NATO's 7,000, neither does it seem possible that NATO will be able to deploy all of its 17,000 anti-tank launchers against the 21,000 tanks the Warsaw Pact would deploy against NATO on the Central Front.

Every strategic, technical or tactical advantage gained by the Soviet Union, if not nullified or compensated for by the West, reduces the freedom of action of the West to wage effective war, while increasing the Soviet capability to do so. The more the balance tilts toward the Soviet Union, the less likely it is that the West can take advantage of whatever weaknesses or vulnerabilities the Russians may have.

When the sum of assets on one side outweighs that on the other, the defects and mistakes of the weaker side are compounded while those on the stronger side lose strategic significance. It may be, for example, that plane for plane and pilot for pilot, Warsaw Pact air forces are inferior to those of the West—at least, it has been customary to assure ourselves that such is the case.[4] It really does not matter about the superiority of Allied aircraft and pilots, if all the NATO airfields have been taken out by Soviet nuclear missiles, seized by Warsaw Pact airborne troops, sabotaged by terrorists, rendered uninhabitable by biological and chemical agents, or overrun by Soviet armor. It does not really count for our side that Soviet tanks may be vulnerable to NATO anti-tank guided missiles, if most of the guided missiles are still back in the NATO depots when the Soviet tanks overrun NATO's forward positions.

It will not prove overly salutary for the allied cause that the U.S. 1st Infantry Division at New Ulm in West Germany, can hold off two or three Warsaw Pact divisions if two brigades of the division are still back in Fort Riley, Kansas, when the Warsaw Pact armies go past New Ulm.[5] If the division could actually hold up two or three Warsaw Pact divisions, when it is at full strength, it certainly would not be able to do so: if Soviet tactical or

3. *Department of Defense Annual Report Fiscal Year 1980,* p. 11.

4. See for example, Alain C. Enthoven, "Arms and Men: The Military Balance in Europe," in *United States Relations with Europe in the Decade of the 1970's,* Hearings before the Representatives, 91st Congress, 2d Session, February-April 1970, pp. 203-7.

5. "Forward Deployment: End FY 1979 Tactical/Mobility Forces," *Manpower Requirements Report for FY 1979,* Department of Defense, February 1978, pp. V-17 and V-20.

long-range air forces attack the transports bringing the two brigades from the United States; if the Warsaw Pact does overrun the 1st Division within the 24 to 38 hours it would take to get the two additional brigades to Germany; if there are no airfields upon which the transports can land with the brigades from Kansas; if the airfields that are in operation are not within walking distance of the vehicles and equipment stockpiled for the brigades coming from the United States; if the depots where the equipment is stockpiled have been destroyed, occupied by Warsaw pact forces, or rendered uninhabitable by nuclear, biological or chemical agents; if the flow of refugees fleeing the Soviet armies does interfere with the movement of reinforcements to where the fighting is going on; if Soviet air and missile attacks do hold up the movement of the brigades to the battle area; if, in the confusion, anyone knows where the 1st U.S. Infrantry Division is fighting.

And, of course, all of the foregoing is irrelevant if the airfields in the United States from which reinforcements have to move to Europe have been taken out by Soviet strategic weapons.

That is quite a number of "ifs" upon which to pin the favorable outcome of a battle for West Germany. There are others of equal importance that bear on the outcome of the land battle for Germany. It may very well be, for example, that Soviet aircraft and pilots are the equal of their Allied counterparts, that one Soviet motorized rifle division is the equivalent of one U.S. mechanized division. When one is warned not to make "the Russians Seem Ten Feet Tall," should one then suppose that we of the West are "ten-feet tall."[6]

The structuring and equipment of NATO and particularly of U.S. forces to fit some preferred gambit by the Soviet Union, preferred because the Allies have the forces with which to cope with that gambit, is a product of the belief that war is not possible, that the Soviet Union would never contemplate the defeat of the West. Such an optimistic view permits contemplation of and planning for *only* the most modest efforts on the part of the Soviet Union to gain its objectives. To contemplate the worst case possible in a war with the Soviet Union is to glance into the abyss. Perhaps, this explains why the West seems only able to anticipate the best cases—never the worst.

* * * * *

Misperception of the nature of strategic competition has made otherwise intelligent beings pin their hopes on SALT. Strategic competition between the United States and the Soviet Union is not like a conflict over fishing

6. Fred Warner Neal, "Making the Russians Seem Ten Feet Tall," *The Washington Star,* 4 September 1977, p. F-4.

rights or tariff policy. It is a struggle for supremacy. It is not a polite diplomatic difference that can be resolved by compromise and conciliation. "Building confidence" in the Soviet Union by eschewing strategic superiority only hastens the time when the Soviet Union will enjoy not merely strategic superiority but *strategic monopoly.* To argue as some have, that American resistance to the Soviet drive for supremacy will strengthen the power of the "Hawks" in the Soviet government deludes one into seeing sheep amongst the lions when only lions are present.[7] Presumably the Hawks or hardliners in the Soviet regime are those who would go all out and smash the West at whatever cost. The moderates are those who would wait until the West is powerless and then do it.[8]

When Baron Marschall von Biebestein took up his position as ambassador to the Court of St. James's shortly after the Agadir Crisis, he remarked to Sir Edward Grey, the British Foreign Secretary, that: "It is not hard to tell the truth, the difficulty is to get it believed." This recalled to the mind of the Foreign Secretary the remarks attributed to Count Bismarck, that the most certain way in diplomacy to deceive people is to tell them the truth. This suggested to Sir Edward the notion that in Foreign Affairs, generally more mischief and loss has been incurred owing to incredulity than credulity.[9]

In a country like England or the United States where the newspapers and other agencies for disseminating news enjoy protection from government and public control, the observations of the Foreign Secretary and the Ambassador can well be augmented. A fashionable truth or an article of faith will enjoy greater currency than grimmer facts however objective the latter may be. For example, a recent *New York Times* dispatch was a front-page story in a client newspaper with the headline, "Optimism on U.S.-Soviet Power Balance." And the story included the assertion that "the Carter experts see future trends as more favorable and less ominous for the U.S. than the Ford Administration had thought." The "comprehensive study" had found the "United States and the Soviet Union to be in rough strategic parity"; "it eases," the

7. "Tough Statements by our Secretary of Defense or others . . . pull the rug out from under the more moderate and strengthen the arguments of the military and other hardliners." Averell Harriman, 15 August 1974, cited in *The Defense Monitor,* Vol. 3, No. 8, October 1974, p. 2; "SALT will, I believe, strengthen the more reasonable group [in the Kremlin] . . . the Hawks would be strengthened . . . by a failure to ratify," in, "Harriman Testifies for the Arms Pact," *San Francisco Chronicle,* 20 July 1979, p. 6.; Roy Medvedev, a Soviet "dissident" writing from Moscow, "Senate Rejection of SALT II Would strengthen Soviet Hawks," *Los Angeles Times,* 12 August 1979, p. 3, pt. V.

8. For another definition of a Soviet "moderate," see George F. Kennan, "The Time has Come to Exorcise the Ghost of Stalin: 'Today's Soviet Regime is Headed by a Moderate, Regarded by All Who Know Him as a Man of Peace,'" *Los Angeles Times,* 13 December 1977, p. 3, pt. 1-C. Let's see now, who knows Brezhnev? There is Andropov, head of the KGB! But then see James Reston, "A Poignant Figure at the SALT Talks," (the figure: Brezhnev) *San Francisco Sunday Examiner and Chronicle,* 24 June 1979, p. 3.

9. Viscount Grey of Fallodon, *Twenty-Five Years, 1892-1916,* Vol. I (New York: Frederick A. Stokes, 1925), pp. 237-39.

story continued, "the pressures for such a rapid increase in military spending and could help Carter achieve an overall balanced budget by fiscal year 1981."[10]

All the magic or "buzz" words to authenticate the optimistic view appeared in the story: "comprehensive study," "strategic equivalence," "senior White House planner," and "rough strategic balance." And the results of the study were further authenticated in the story by associating it with the name of a great eastern University and a distinguished "strategic analyst."

By contrast to the Carter study's findings that future trends are more favorable and less ominous to the United States "than the Ford Administration had thought" is the assertion that: "On the basis of fundamental changes in the *balance of forces* in the world, a profound restructuring of the entire system of international relations is taking place." This Soviet assessment of the power balance appeared in the Resolution of the Communist Party of the Soviet Union Central Committee on 31 January 1977.[11]

In a warning to the Red Army, it was said: "Detente among governments intensifies rather than weakens ideological combat. Peaceful coexistence does not signify an acknowledgement that the capitalist system, with all its social vices, is eternal; nor does it constitute peaceful cohabitation of socialism and capitalism; *rather it creates fresh possibilities* for stepping up the struggle against imperialism." And, "the struggle today centers around detente. Certain circles in the capitalist world *have been obliged* to take some steps toward detente as a result of the *great shift in the balances of world power in favor of socialism*."[12]

It is certainly not academically respectable, intellectually fashionable or politically expedient to speak or write as though there were some genuine possibility of war. As the late Senator Humphrey put it so well: "Usually around budget time every year, we discover that the Russians are doing everything we feared they might do and even more."[13]

Jerome B. Weisner, a noted expert on defense and related matters, observed that much of the scare talk about the Russians derived from writers who "are dependent upon officers and civilians in the Department of Defense and upon Congressmen sitting on the committees dealing with defense matters for most of their information." But he points out that we are saved

10. "Carter Study: Optimism on U.S.-Soviet Power Balance," *San Francisco Chronicle,* 8 July 1977, p. 1.

11. "On the 60th Anniversary of the Great October Revolution," *Pravda,* 1 February 1977, p. 1, in *The Current Digest of the Soviet Press,* Vol. XXIX, No. 5, 2 March 1977, p. 10f.

12. "Detente Brings Subversion, Military Warned: The Ideological Struggle in Conditions of Detente," by Major General D. Volkonogov in *Kommunist vooruzhennykh sil,* No. 3, February 1977, pp. 9-23. *The Current Digest of the Soviet Press,* Vol. XXIX, No. 5, pp. 5-7. (italics added)

13. Hubert H. Humphrey, "An End to Nuclear Gamesmanship," *Science and Public Affairs: The Bulletin of the Atomic Scientists,* Vol. XXVIII, No. 3 (March 1972), pp. 12-15.

from the consequences of this defense conspiracy because not "all journalists reporting the Washington scene reflect the viewpoint of the weapons advocates." "Most journalists," he says, "have sufficient initiative and independence to dig in deeply."[14]

Branding those who would expand "defense capabilities" as the "Arms Zealots," one professor, puts them nicely in their place as the "Arms Coalition" or "AC" and demonstrates that they are "overselling Soviet capabilities" and "underselling" those of the United States.[15] By doing so those who argue for greater preparedness "may be doing a great disservice to American interests . . . may add fuel to the arms race and can even forestall meaningful arms control at a crucial moment." The professor allows that some of those who see danger in Soviet military capabilities speak from deep conviction, but generally it is the cynical *(sic)* self-interest of those whose "meal-ticket" is involved in future development of weaponry that see a "Soviet threat."

Other professional defense experts are even more forthright in their criticism of those who bombard the American people with silly fears that the United States might be falling behind the Soviet Union in military capability. And as it turns out, these experts see the United States to be superior to the Soviet Union in nearly every important category of military capability and those who argue otherwise to be merely stimulating the Soviet Union to buy even more weapons which in turn will be an excuse for these wretched alarmists to argue for even greater U.S. defense expenditure.[16]

In general, these experts agree with those who write about such matters in the Soviet Union, that the United States is invariably guilty of "fuelling the arms race," recreating the "cold war," and pandering to the unholy appetites of the Defense Department, or the Pentagon as it is called. None however seem to agree with the Soviet Union or the People's Republic of China that there is going to be a war. Indeed, it is said that in a recent book George Kennan wrote that: "A war regarded as inevitable or even probable, and therefore much prepared for, has a very good chance of being fought."[17] It is supposed that Mr. Kennan was referring chiefly to Americans who predict war and not to those predictions of war made by the Soviet Union and the People's Republic of China.

The notion that war is unthinkable, or ought not to be thought about, is reinforced by the belief that nuclear war would destroy both the United

14. Jerome B. Weisner, "The Cold War is Dead, But the Arms Race Rumbles On," *Bulletin of the Atomic Scientists,* (June 1967), pp. 6-9.

15. Daniel Yergin, "The Arms Zealots," *Harper's,* June 1977, pp. 64-76.

16. "The Artificial Crisis of American Security," *The Defense Monitor,* Center for Defense Information, Washington, D.C., Vol. V, No. 3, May 1976.

17. "George Kennan's Message," *The Christian Science Monitor,* 22 July 1977, p. 31.

States and the Soviet Union with the implication that the United States need not prepare for war and that whatever the Soviet Union may be doing in the way of increasing its armaments, it certainly cannot be thought to be preparing for war.[18]

This view is based on the theory that war between nuclear powers would be so destructive as to leave no winners and therefore resort to arms has ceased to represent a rational policy for nuclear powers in dealing with one another. As Richard Pipes, another professor, has pointed out in suggesting that the Soviet Union might well believe it could win a nuclear war: Clausewitz's dictum that war is politics pursued by other means "is widely believed in the United States to have lost its validity after Hiroshima and Nagasaki."[19]

While Professor Pipes must be judged guilty of breaching the academic fashion of disbelieving in war, he does raise an interesting point. Does the Soviet Union think it could emerge victorous and relatively unscathed from a nuclear war? If it does not, but only indulges in dramatic rhetoric to frighten the West, then there is nothing to worry about. But if the Soviet preparations are indeed based on the assumption that war is to come, then the United States is entertaining a fatal delusion.

The notion that the dreadful destruction of war provides by that very fact its own deterrent is not a new one. General C. P. Summerall, one time Chief of Staff of the Army, wrote that one major compensation of modern war was derived from "the knowledge that the cost of modern war to both victor and vanguished, is so great as to exercise a welcome deterrent effect upon those who would make war."[20]

Inventions of terrible weapons often have been thought to render war impossible. One writer tells of how a New York newspaper reported in 1880 the words of Dr. J. H. McLean who had just invented a breech-loading, repeating cannon: "The art of war will be no more in a few years. Terrible perfection shall make war impossible. . . . War is a thing of the past."[21]

The same writer has pointed out that Theodore Herzl a 19th Century prophet of Zionism, predicted that one day science would bring the possibility of slaughtering whole peoples within man's reach and that then, once

18. "Nuclear War Would Destroy U.S., Russia, Panel Concludes," *Palo Alto Times,* 17 May 1977, p. 5 which reports the conclusion of a Congressional Committee on the value of Soviet Civil Defense and the lack of necessity for such a defense on the part of the United States. The same sentiment was expressed in an address to U.S. troops in Germany by the Secretary of Defense: "U.S., Russia near Equals on Arms, Sec. Brown Says," *Palo Alto Times,* 24 March 1977, p. 9.

19. Richard Pipes, "Why the Soviet Union Thinks It Could Fight and Win a Nuclear War," *Commentary,* Vol. 64, No. 1, July 1977.

20. *The R.O.T.C. Manual: Infantry, First Year Basic,* Vol. I, 19th Edition (Harrisburg: Military Service Publishing Company, 1937), pp. 1-37.

21. Cited in William H. Honan, "The Peaceful Use of Terror," *The New Republic,* 27 April 1963, pp. 19-21.

and for all, man would recoil in horror from the crime of genocide. "A man who would discover a terrible explosive would do more for peace than a thousand of its mild apostles." When asked if he thought another world war possible, Thomas A. Edison averred that the appalling destruction of another such war would act as a restraining force upon all nations of earth. Albert Einstein stated that "the atom 'may intimidate the human race into bringing order into its international affairs, which, without the pressure of fear it would not do.'"[22]

Many reasons have been found to support the belief that some future war, which in the event did occur, would not occur. During discussions at the White House on revision of the Neutrality Act in July 1939, when it was hoped that such a revision would give Hitler some pause, Senator Borah said: "No one can foretell what may happen. But my feeling and belief is that we are not going to have a war. Germany isn't ready for it." When Secretary of State Cordell Hull protested that diplomatic correspondence from Europe indicated the imminence of war, Senator Borah discounted such indications stating that he had his own sources of information that indicated there would not be war.[23]

But even as astute a man as Cordell Hull would state in 1933, that the United States "have no substantial interest, or motive whatever to enter upon a naval race with Japan. There is nothing that need take us to the Orient much less to induce us to prepare for naval conflict on account of any oriental considerations."[24]

As late as the week before the attack on Pearl Harbor, *Newsweek* magazine (dated 8 December 1941) would report the words of Herbert Hoover that there was no danger of war with Japan because they were too preoccupied in China, they were threatened by Russia, and they were a Capitalist nation whose economy would be disruped by a major war.

Norman Angell wrote in 1910, in his book *The Great Illusion,* of a new era in the Twentieh Century in which the principles and axioms of bygone days would no longer be valid because the civilized powers of the world are so bound together by trade and commerce as to render war not only suicidal but virtually impossible. "Power, in short, is no longer the medium of exchange in international politics." Germany, in particular, he said, could not possibly gain anything by going to war and therefore would not.

On 16 March 1939, the day after Germany occupied that part of Czechoslovakia that remained to the Czechs after the Munich Agreement, a *New*

22. Honan, *op. cit.*

23. *The Memoirs of Cordell Hull,* Vol. 1 (New York: The Macmillan Company, 1948), pp. 648-70 and, William L. Langer and S. Everett Gleason, *The Challenge to Isolation, 1937-1940* (New York: Harper and Brothers, 1952), pp. 144-45.

24. *The Memoirs of Cordell Hull,* Vol. 1, pp. 287-88.

York Times editorial stated that Germany faced economic collapse. A later editorial suggested that now Hitler would be unable to get the foreign exchange he so desperately needed. And later still, the newspaper suggested that Germany was too poor for a prolonged war.

Victor Zorza writing in the *Washington Post* in October 1972 announced the coming of a new generation of peace: "Cold assessment of the facts of international life form a judgement that the self-interest of the great powers imposes on them patterns of cooperation that none can evade." And, the Chairman of the Joint Committee on Defense Production said on 16 May 1977: "No rational Soviet leader would risk starting a nuclear war because that war would inevitably destroy the Soviet Union as a great power."[25]

It is difficult not to be cheered by such authoritative predictions of peace. And it is authoritative when a distinguished American like George Kennan tells us of all the compelling reasons why the Soviet Union would not dream of attacking anyone, let alone the United States. It is a comfort to be assured by *The Christian Science Monitor* that the Iron Curtain is rusting away.[26] Of course, the *Monitor* did not mean the actual barrier, which in recent years has been strenghened where it runs from Schlutup in the North to Prex in the South, by land mines, mantraps, radar and blockhouses.[27] The *Monitor* meant to find some basis for optimism in the relationship between the Communist powers of Europe and the liberal democracies of the West. That same tone emerged from reports of a meeting of famous scholars and statesmen held in California in 1977, where it was decided that since the West was anachronistic there was no need for its defense.[28]

A U.S. Senator visits Israel and finds that circumstances there "will help us along the road to peace."[29] That was the day before a complaint was lodged with the United Nations that Egypt had stationed men and missiles along the Suez Canal in violation of the agreement not to do so.[30]

A Senator from one of the Atlantic Coast states returned from his visit to the Middle East to report that there is a common desire to settle the 30 year old state of war in the region.[31] That was only a week after the Egyptian

25. "Congressional Study: Soviet Civil Defense Efforts Discounted," *San Francisco Chronicle*, 17 May 1977, p. 8.

26. "The Iron Curtain is Rusting Away," *The Christian Science Monitor*, 5 July 1977, p. 39.

27. See "E. Germans Streamline Border Crossing: Heavy Flow of Visitors Speeded; new Barriers Thwart Escape," *Los Angeles Times*, 23 June 1977, p. 20; "East Germans are Still Prepared to Pay a High Price for Their Freedom: Breaching the Wall—Deadly Game Goes On," *The South China Morning Post*, 15 June 1975, p. 13; and, "Mine System Installed Along German Border," *Palo Alto Times*, 11 August 1977, p. 4.

28. "Scholars gather to Peer at the Future, Emerge Optimistic on World's Prospects," *Los Angeles Times*, 28 March 1977, p. 17.

29. "Senator Stone 'happy' After Talks with Begin," and "Stone Encouraged After Talks on Peace with Leaders Here," *The Jerusalem Post*, International Edition, 7 June 1977, pp. 5 and 1.

30. "Israel Charges Egypt with Suez Violations," *International Herald Triburne*, 9 June 1977, p. 1.

31. "Javits Lauds U.S. Mideast Policy," *San Francisco Chronicle*, 23 July 1977, p. 10.

Army and Air Force launched a series of apparently devastating attacks on Soviet and Libyan installations in Cyrenaica and Tripolitania,[32] and amidst a civil war in Lebanon that continues.

None of this is meant to ridicule the desire of civilized men and women for peace. It is only natural that those who seek justice and who prefer liberty to totalitariansm will wish for peace rather than war. It is the fundamental merit of liberal democracy to be hopeful about improving the condition of mankind and wherever possible to seek accommodation rather than conflict. But liberty has not yet been preserved by refusing to believe that bad things can happen. It is only a charming conceit to suppose that fearful things cannot happen if one refuses to believe that they will.

One should easily be able to recognize that politics is the organization and application of power for the achievement of some purpose. Power is the capacity to destroy but where human beings are concerned it is the ability to inflict pain that accomplishes the purposes of policy. The intellectual community, if such there is in the United States, may persuade itself that power is not intrinsic to politics. It is difficult to understand how they can have forgotten that the revolution of 1789 in Europe spread its enlightenment by fire and sword; that the progress of Marxian socialism has littered the soil of the old Russian Empire, China and Indo-China with the graves of those who dissented; and that the National Socialist Revolution was extinguished not through economic assistance and "people-to-people" diplomacy but by the force of arms. Indeed, in our own country a half-million Americans gave their lives in the struggle to secure the Federal Constitution and to eliminate slavery; and, that school in Little Rock was not integrated by kindly admonitions from some distant putting green, but by the fixed bayonets of an airborne battle group of the United States Army. South Vietnam was not united to the North by free elections but by a force of 15 North Vietnamese divisions seizing Saigon and destroying the South Vietnamese government and armed forces.

All that violence may seem quite irrational to those who live in secure surroundings insulated from the circumstances of the world in which most ordinary folks do have to live. Being rational does not necessarily exclude the possibility that the same facts looked at by different observers may lead to conflicting conclusions. One sees that every day in national politics and in the courtrooms of the land. When the *New York Times* concluded, after the German seizure of the rump state of Czechoslovakia in March 1939, that Germany was bankrupt, they were right. Their conclusion that such bankruptcy made war unlikely was wrong. On 22 August 1939, in an address to

32. Details of the attack are given in "Egypt's War with Libya: Why Now?" *Foreign Report* (London), No. 1497, 27 July 1977.

the German Commanders-in-Chief, Adolph Hitler outlined the reasons for going to war at that particular time: "It is easy for us to make decisions. We have nothing to lose, we have everything to gain. Because of our restrictions, our economic situation is such that we can only hold out for a few more years. Goering can confirm this. We have no other choice, we must act."[33]

* * * * *

It may be that while rational people in the United States conclude that war is rendered impossible by the prospect of mutual destruction, rational people elsewhere may believe that war would be a fruitful means for accomplishing such a monumental and historical purpose as to make the risks worth the taking.

Only by accepting the possibility of war, however distasteful it might be, can one understand the otherwise inexplicable actions of the Soviet Union in places like Czechoslovakia and Cuba. One must then consider both the nature and possible consequences of a Soviet war.

This work has concentrated on the defense of Western Europe because its loss to the Soviet Union would face the United States with decisions harder and more deadly than any ever before in its history. A Soviet Union already formidable in military power would enjoy the fruits of Europe in the very process of making it part of the Socialist Commonwealth of nations. The addition to Soviet industrial and military capability would permit the Soviet Union literally to dominate the world, even if the United States emerged from a war for Europe largely unscathed. There is, however, no reason to suppose that the United States *would* emerge unscathed.

The United States would have to decide, after the loss of Europe, whether it would be possible to liberate Europe from the Russians. Such an enterprise would be exceedingly more formidable than the liberation of Europe from the Nazis. It would take the same kind of blind and stubborn determination that the British displayed in resisting Nazism after the Fall of France, Belgium, the Netherlands, Norway and Denmark. It would require the same kind of ingenuity, ruthlessness, craftiness and skill that Britain exercised to stay in the war against Germany until Pearl Harbor was attacked. And it would take *enormous* military power.

If the United States could not bring itself to mobilize the strength to re-enter Europe and wrest it from the communists, then it would have to consider destroying Europe—its population and industry—to prevent those being used against the United States. The choices:

33. *Documents on German Foreign Policy*, Series D. Vol. VII, No. 192 as cited in *Diplomat in Berlin, 1933-1939: Papers and Memoirs of Jozef Lipski*, Waclaw Jedrzejewicz, Editor (New York: Columbia University Press, 1968), pp. 588-89.

> Liberate Europe and defeat the Soviet Union at immense cost in blood and treasure;
>
> Destroy Europe as an industrial community capable of supporting a Soviet invasion of the Western Hemisphere;
>
> Make peace with the Soviet Union and wait America's turn to become an extension of the Socialist Commonwealth of nations.

If that seems too ridiculous for thought then consider: could one have sat in one of those cafes that grace the Place Marechal Foch in the city of Arras in Artois, in June 1939, and imagine that a year later the city would be in German hands? And not just Arras, but all of France, and, indeed all of Western Europe from the North Cape to the Spanish frontier would have been conquered?

But there is no reason why a Soviet attack on NATO Europe would be the only problem with which the United States would have to deal. Japan, although its defense is guaranteed by the United States, remains independent at the pleasure of the Soviet Union. Soviet forces in the Far East are sufficient to seize the islands. Japan can expect, according to Japanese views, to be able to defend against a Soviet invasion of Hokkaido for one month during which time it would be hoped the United States would be able to send help with which to defeat the invasion.[34] The United States now has no U.S. Army ground combat troops in Japan.[35]

The Japanese evidently see that in a war under present circumstances, the U.S. Pacific Fleet could barely cope with the Soviet Far Eastern Fleet and Air Forces, that the sea lanes to Japan and Korea would be cut, but that ultimately the Unites States might hold its own. But were there to be war or a threat of war in Europe, "the US will refrain from using its Navy in the Pacific in order to keep it intact for use in Europe."[36]

By 1972, the Japanese recognized that only the technological superiority of U.S. nuclear weapons made it possible for the United States to be considered in a position of nuclear parity with the Soviet Union.[37] Now it is considered unlikely that the United States could successfully fight a Pacific War were there to be war in Europe, at the same time: "it must be said that

34. "Top Secret Plan for Defense Action in Time of Emergency; Full Text Obtained: Hypothesizes One-Month War of Resistance. If Hokkaido is Invaded . . .," *Yomiuri* (Tokyo), 10 July 1979, p. 1; "Full Text of JDA Views on Emergency to cope with Surprise Attacks," *Sankei*, 22 September 1978, p. 2.

35. "Doubts Entertained about US-Japan Maneuvers on the Ground Too," *Yomiuri*, 2 June 1979, p. 5.

36. "Military Situation in Asia; Soviet Military Bases on Kunashiri and Etorofu have Big Political Significance . . .," *Nihon Keizai* (Tokyo), 14 February 1979, p. 2.

37. "The Liberal Democratic Party's Basic Policy on Security," Security Research Council Policy Board, Liberal Democratic Party, 28 June 1972, p. 14.

the US today is no longer strong enough to halt the expansion of the Soviet Union."[38]

The events that have led to such a conclusion comprise a list of changes in the strategic environment as disquieting as those that have taken place in Europe:

> The continuing increase in Soviet naval and air forces in the Far East; the addition of aircraft carriers to the Soviet Far Eastern Fleet.[39]
>
> The reduction of U.S. forces in the Far East.[40]
>
> The Soviet use of bases in Vietnam with the threat it poses to Japanese trade routes, particularly Japan's oil traffic from the Middle East.[41]
>
> The deployment of Soviet *Backfire* bombers and SS-20 nuclear missiles to the Far East.[42]

38. "USSR Will Soon Secure Predominance . . .," *Yomiuri,* 19 March 1979, p. 2; see also, "Many Questions Involved in CARTER Diplomacy; How to Eliminate Distrust toward U.S.," *Sankei* (Tokyo), 19 March 1979, p. 4; "Defense of Japan—White Paper on Defense (Summary)," in *Defense Bulletin,* Japan Defense Agency, Vol. II, No. 2, October 1978; and, "Remarkable Increase in Soviet Forces; Far East . . .," *Tokyo Shimbun,* 27 March 1979, p. 2.

39. "Soviets Build huge port on Pacific," *The Christian Science Monitor,* 21 November 1975, p. 6; "Growing Soviet Fleet Raise Pacific Alarms," *Los Angeles Times,* 9 April 1978, p. 1; "Soviet Pacific Fleet Suddenly Showing Vigorous Moves . . .," *Mainichi* (Tokyo), 29 June 1978, p. 2; "Soviets boosting size and quality of Pacific fleet," *The Christian Science Monitor,* 6 June 1978, p. 14; "Tokyo sees Soviet Threat," *South China Morning Post,* 30 July 1978, p. 3; "JDA Direc or General Yamashita to Visit US . . . To Search for Response to Soviet Far East Forces . . .," *Yomiuri,* 11 March 1979, p. 2; "Remarkable Increase in Soviet Forces; Far East . . ." *Tokyo Shimbun,* 27 March 1979, p. 2; "Japan Military eyes growing Soviet might," *The Christian Science Monitor,* 29 August 1979, p. 1; "Japanese Cite Soviet Threat in West Pacific," *Los Angeles Times,* 8 August 1979, p. 7; "USSR to Deploy Aircraft Carrier in the Far East . . . U.S. Requests Japan to Secure Sea Lanes for Shipping," *Nihon Keizai,* 3 July 1978, p. 2; "Soviet Union to Deploy Kiev-Model Aircraft Carrier to the Pacific . . . Second Vessel Already Commissioned and in Training," *Yomiuri,* 18 July 1978, p. 2; and, "US Defense Department "Complains" about Huge Floating Dock Exported to Soviet Union . . .," *Tokyo Shimbun,* 11 November 1978, pp. 8-9; "Soviets Send Carrier to Far East," *Los Angeles Times,* 21 June 1979, p. 18.

40. "American Navy Still Dominant, Defense Secretary Says: U.S. Reports Major Increases in Soviet Far East Forces," *Los Angeles Times,* 10 November 1978, p. 1, pt. 1-B; "Navy's Capability in Pacific Questioned," *ibid.,* 14 November 1978, p. 18; "Russ Outnumber U.S. fleet in Pacific, says admiral," *Palo Alto Times,* 23 March 1979, p. B-8; "Cuts in Pacific Force Alarm U.S. Military," *Los Angeles Times,* 26 March 1979, p. 1; "Navy Looks over shoulder at fast-closing Soviets," *The Christian Science Monitor,* 21 May 1979, p. 4; "Soviet Buildup Affects Pacific Military Balance with U.S., Japan Officials Say," *Los Angeles Times,* 25 July 1979, p. 7; "US Demands Japan's Defending the Seas with Its Own Power . . . To Cope with Soviet Strengthening of Naval Power," *Yomiuri,* 2 July 1979, p. 1.

41. Y. Glazunov, "Vietnam's Road to Socialism," *International Affairs* (Moscow), No. 9, September 1978, pp. 23-30, in *Soviet Press, Selected Translations,* 79-5, May 1979; "US Requests Maritime Defense . . .," *Yomiuri,* 5 July 1978, p. 2; "Obtains Intelligence on Surface-to-Air Missiles in Cam Ranh Bay Area . . .," *Tokyo Shimbun,* 5 July 1978, p. 2; "Soviets Stun Japan with pact with Vietnam," *The Christian Science Monitor,* 6 November 1978, p. 6; "JDA Seriously Concerned over Report of Soviet Union's Starting to Use Cam Ranh Bay; Will Have Effects on Japan's Oil Shipping Route," *Sankei* (Tokyo), 18 November 1978, p. 1; "Construction of Communications Base and Aviation Control Facilities in Da Nang by USSR; Serious Effects on Security in Far East . . .," *Mainichi* (Tokyo), 26 March 1979, p. 2; "Not to Permit Construction of Foreign Military Bases; Soviet Planes' Landing at and Taking off from Vietnam . . .," *Tokyo Shimbun,* 22 April 1979, p. 2; "Soviet Listening Post Reported (Cam Ranh Bay)," *Los Angeles Times,* 17 May 1979, p. 2; and, "Will Recognize Soviet Ship Calls; Vietnam Foreign Minister's Statement," *Yomiuri,* 12 May 1979, p. 2.

42. "Deployment of Soviet Supersonic Backfire Strategic Bombers to the Far East to be Ac-

> The Development and use of an extensive military base on the islands of Etorofu and Kunashiri off the northern coast Hokkaido, in the southern Kuriles.[43]

Such measures as these indicate the Soviet capabilities to wage war in the Western Pacific. Soviet occupation of Japan would be nearly as serious a blow to the West as the occupation of Europe. Japanese industrial capacity in Soviet hands and the use of the Japanese Home Islands as a base for deploying Soviet military, naval and air power would make the Western Pacific untenable for U.S. forces. The size and location of Soviet forces presently deployed in the Far East make it almost inevitable that in a war for NATO the Soviet Union would attempt to seize Alaska and Hawaii. In addition to direct air and missile attack on the continental United States, it could be expected that Soviet submarines would operate against coastal shipping on the Pacific Coast while posing a direct threat to the West Coast itself. Those operations would not only prevent reinforcement of Japan for its defense, but would surely tie down those U.S. strategic reserves earmarked for use elsewhere.

The buildup of North Korean forces and the weakening of U.S. forces in South Korea lend no assurance that North Korea would not seize the opportunity to unify Korea by force.

All of these things are, of course, in addition to whatever devastation the strategic forces of the Soviet Union might wreak upon the population and industry of the United States itself.

* * * * *

Even if one accepts the dubious notion that the West is now almost as strong militarily as the Soviet Union and its allies, the conclusion of a Chinese-Soviet non-aggression pact or alliance would decisively change the strategic balance in favor of the Soviet Union. The Chinese harbor few illusions about Soviet intentions toward themselves. But they do not believe that the United States is now stronger than the Soviet Union.[44] Chinese

---

celerated . . . To be Based in Maritime Territory . . .," *Nihon Keizai,* 4 November 1979, p. 2. But see elsewhere as well.

43. "Soviet Military Exercises," *Asahi Evening News* (Tokyo), 10 June 1978, p. 2; "Soviet Military Activities in Vicinity of Etorofu Island Designed to Strengthen Military Bases in Far East . . .," *Nihon Keizai,* 29 June 1978, p. 1; "Large Soviet Military Base on Kunashiri; Following "Etorofu"; "Sword at Throat"; Large Increase in Ground Forces; Already Stationing 3,000 Men," *Sankei,* 17 September 1978, p. 1; "Japanese react to latest Soviet threat," *San Francisco Sunday Examiner & Chronicle,* 16 July 1978, p. 19, sec. A; "Foreign Ministry Heading Toward Lodging Strong Protest; Establishment of Military Bases on Northern Islands," *Asahi* (Tokyo), 30 January 1979, p. 1; "Strengthening of Soviet Bases on Kunashiri and Etorofu . . . Aiming at Creating "Sanctuary" for SLBM's," *ibid.,* 8 February 1979, p. 4; and, "Soviet Buildup in Islands Draws Protest from Japan," *Los Angeles Times,* 6 February 1979, p. 1.

44. "China Doubts U.S. Stronger than Russia," *Los Angeles Times,* 7 September 1977, p. 18.

warnings about the Soviet threat to the West continue to go unheeded. Can one expect China to tie its fortunes to the side which it believes will be defeated in a war? Will China not instead, prefer another version of the Hitler-Stalin pact with which to buy the time it needs to get ready?

The Soviet Union *is*, by all indications, preparing for war. The West is not.

In 1938, a British soldier protesting his own country's blindness toward its peril, wrote these words:

> Let us therefore face facts and eschew ostrich-like postures which can but serve to confuse our own people, dismay our possible allies, and incur the laughter and contempt of our possible enemies.[45]

If the West prepares for war and no war comes, we may enjoy the freedom of criticizing ourselves for our foolishness. If war comes and the West is unprepared, not merely to fight but to win, then there can be no greater folly. Our freedom will have died, killed by our blindness. Our losses will be total and irrevocable; there will be no distant armies of liberation raised to free us as we once freed Western Europe. We must be prepared to fight; if need be, for years, if necessary, alone.

The price of freedom is resolute vigilance; the cost of blindness, defeat. It is far cheaper to win an arms race than to lose a war.

45. Colonel R. H. Beadon, "Defence and Defeat," *Journal of the Royal United Services Institution*, Vol. LXXXIII, No. 259, February 1938.

Appendix

Soviet-Yugoslav Trade

In September 1974 *Tanjug* reported that Jadranbrod, a Zagreb concern had contracted to build three passenger-freight ships for Sudimport of Moscow. The three were to be built in a yard at Kraljevica near Rijeka on the Adriatic, the same yard where four other ships were under construction or on order for the Soviet Union.[1]

In December *Tanjug* reported from Leningrad that the Zagreb factory, Nikolas Tesla, "has attained another great success in transactions with the Soviet Union. . . . A telex and an interurban exchange made in the Zagreb factory have been formally put into operation today." The work had been done by "engineers and technicans from Zagreb." The Nikolas Tesla factory had already made similar exchanges for installation in Moscow, Kiev, Tallin, Kishinev, Volgorod and elsewhere and another ten such exchanges were on order for the Soviet Union.[2]

In January 1975 it was announced that a gas pipeline would be constructed from Mokrin and the Hungarian border to Belgrade as part of a gas supply network for eastern Yugoslavia and an agreement had been signed with the Soviet Union for the delivery of gas via a pipeline crossing Hungary.[3]

In April 1975, the Yugoslav and Soviet pharmaceutical industries agreed to a two year program of joint research and development on clinical applications of proeolytic enzymes.[4]

In March 1975, *Vjesnik* described the construction of an oil-fired power station, Sisak II, on the Sava River financed by credits from the Soviet Union and employing construction workers from the Soviet Union.[5]

Borba reported from Belgrade in April that a floating dock built for it at the Kherson yards in the Soviet Union was to be used on the Danube and would be financed chiefly by an 80 percent credit from Sudimport of Moscow.[6]

Later in the same month, *Tanjug* reported long-term Soviet agreement with the postal and telecommunication factory, Nikolas Tesla, for yet further installations of interurban telex and main telephone exchanges in the Soviet Union at a cost of 100 million dollars. The Soviet Deputy Minister was said to consider the Zagreb factory to be "a very worthwhile business partner."[7]

In October contracts were signed between Jugoturbina of Karlovac and Atomenergi-Export of Moscow for the delivery of 5 diesel power stations; the equipments, to be used for "Soviet atomic power plants in the period from 1976 to 1980," were acquired under a Soviet-Yugoslav intergovernmental agreement for business and technical cooperation in the construction of nuclear power plants in the Soviet Union.[8]

At the sixth session of the permanent mixed Yugoslav-Soviet commission for machine building, held in Belgrade during the last week of October 1975, it was agreed that during the period 1976-1980 mutual delivery of machines and equipment would reach a value of 5.5 billion dollars or three times what it had been during the five-year period 1970-1975.[9]

During the same month, a contract was signed between Invest-Import of Yugoslavia and the Soviet firm, Raznoeksport, for the supply of 40 million dollars worth of cable. This event marked "20 years of cooperation" between the two firms. The Yugoslav cable industry had supplied during that time 341 million dollars worth of cable to the Soviet Union, while the Soviet Union had furnished copper and aluminum to the Yugoslav company to the value of 25.7 million dollars. The new contract envisaged the delivery of 200 million dollars worth of cable over the following five years.[10]

It was a remarkable display of political tolerance on the part of both the Soviet Union and Yugoslavia that despite their supposed hostility, they could exchange over a billion and a half dollars worth of goods during the year 1976.[11] That amount was equivalent to 5% of Yugoslavia's gross national product.

1. "Ships for USSR—Belgrade, 10 Sept (TANJUG) . . .," *FBIS*, Vol. II, *Eastern Europe*, 12 September 1974, p. I 10.

2. "Equipment for USSR—Leningrad, Dec 19 (TANJUG)," *FBIS*, Vol. II, *Eastern Europe*, 26 December 1974, p. I 14.

3. "Construction of Gas Pipeline to Begin in Spring," Belgrade TANJUG Domestic Service in Serbo-Croatian 1232 GMT 10 Jan 75, in *FBIS*, Vol. II, *Eastern Europe*, 14 January 1975, p. I 7.

4. "Pharmaceutical Cooperation with USSR," Belgrade, BORBA in Serbo-Croatian 21 Apr 75, in *FBIS*, Vol. II, *Eastern Europe*, 2 May 1975, p. I 5.

5. "Sisak Power Station," *Vjesnik* (Zagreb), 6 March 1975, p. 4, in *FBIS*, Vol. II, *Eastern Europe*, 25 March 1975, p. i 18.

6. "Floating Dock," *Borba* (Belgrade), 10 April 1975, p. 7 in *FBIS*, Vol. II, *Eastern Europe*, 1 May 1975, p. I 16.

7. "Agreement with USSR—Moscow, May 27 (TANJUG)—" in *FBIS*, Vol. II, *Eastern Europe*, 5 June 1975, p. I 20.

8. "Soviet Nuclear Contract—Zagreb," October 16 (TANJUG), in *FBIS*, Vol. II, *Eastern Europe*, 22 October 1975, p. I 15.

9. "Machine Export, Import with USSR to Increase," Belgrade TANJUG Domestic Service in Serbo-Croatian 1958 GMT 27 October 1975, in *FBIS*, Vol. II, *Eastern Europe*, 3 November 1975, p. I 8.

10. "Cable Exports to Moscow," Belgrade, 3 October (TANJUG), in *FBIS*, Vol. II, *Eastern Europe*, 9 October 1975, p. I 10.

11. Based on an exchange rate of 18.74 dinars to the dollar, the total foreign trade of Yugoslavia was reported to be 205 billion 380 million dinars, of which 134 billion 510 million were imports and 70 billion 870 million were exports, of which exports to the Soviet Union were 25% and imports 10%. See "Yugoslavia," in *Britannica Book of the Year, 1977* (Chicago: Encyclopaedia Britannica, Inc., 1977), p. 738.

Index